THE POETICS OF MILITARY OCCUPATION

THE *Poetics* OF MILITARY OCCUPATION

Mzeina Allegories of Bedouin Identity Under Israeli and Egyptian Rule

Smadar Lavie

UNIVERSITY OF CALIFORNIA PRESS
BERKELEY
LOS ANGELES
OXFORD

We wish to thank the following for
photographs appearing in the book:
p.2 photo is by I.P.P.A.; p. 23 photo is by Shalom Bar-Tal;
p. 44, 88, 152, 220, 236, 339 and the front jacket photos are by
Micha Bar-Am; p. 69 photo is by Israel Sun; p. 79 photo is by
Hertzel Yossef, courtesy of Yediʿot Aharonot archive.
Maps were drawn by Tim Seymour.

University of California Press
Berkeley and Los Angeles, California

University of California Press
Oxford, England

Library of Congress Cataloging-in-Publication Data

Lavie, Smadar.
The poetics of military occupation: Mzeina allegories of Bedouin identity under Israeli and Egyptian rule / Smadar Lavie.
p. cm.
Includes bibliographical references.
ISBN 0-520-06880-7 (alk. paper)
ISBN 0-520-07552-8 (ppb.: alk. paper)
1. Bedouins—Egypt—Janūb Sīnāʿ. 2. Janūb Sīnāʿ (Egypt)—Ethnic relations. 3. Storytelling—Egypt—Janūb Sīnāʿ. 4. Storytelling—Political aspects—Egypt—Janūb Sīnāʿ. 5. Israelis—Egypt—Janūb Sīnāʿ. I. Title.
DS110.5.L2 1990 89-20336
953′.1—dc20 CIP

Printed in the United States of America

2 3 4 5 6 7 8 9

The paper used in this publication
meets the minimum requirements of
American National Standard for Information Sciences
—Permanence of Paper for
Printed Library Materials,
ANSI Z39.48-1984

A flag loses contact with reality and flies off.
A window display of beautiful women's
Dresses in blue and white. And everything
In three languages: Hebrew Arabic Death.

YEHOUDA AMIḤAI
Lamentation for Those Who Die in War

This word: "shame." No, I must write it in its original form, not in this peculiar language tainted by wrong concepts and the accumulated detritus of its owners' unrepented past, this Angrezi in which I am forced to write, and so for ever alter what is written.

SALMAN RUSHDIE
Shame

CONTENTS

NOTE ON TRANSLITERATION

The Arabic and Hebrew words in the following text are transliterated according to the Mzeina vernacular, not according to Classical Arabic. I have oriented myself more or less to the standards of the *International Journal of Middle East Studies*.

I have used the following system:

ARABIC RADICAL	ENGLISH TRANSLITERATION	ARABIC RADICAL	ENGLISH TRANSLITERATION
أ	a	ض	ḍ
ب	b	ط	ṭ
ت	t	ظ	ẓ
ث	th	ع	ᶜ
ج	j	غ	gh
ح	ḥ	ف	f
خ	kh	ق	g*
د	d	ك	k
ذ	dh	ل	l
ر	r	م	m
ز	z	ن	n
س	s	ه	h
ش	sh	و	w
ص	ṣ	ي	y

*In the Mzeina Bedouin dialect, the classical "q" becomes a "g."

Here are some suggestions for the pronunciation of the transliterated Arabic:

th	like the *th* in "thought"
ḥ	a gutteral/whispery sound, between *h* and *kh*
kh	like the *ch* in "Bach"
dh	like the *th* in "the"
sh	like the *sh* in "shark"
ṣ, ḍ, ṭ, ẓ	emphatic consonants
ᶜ	use the back of the throat
gh	like the French *r*
g	like the *g* in "good"
ā, ē, ī, ū, ō	long vowels

The remaining letters are pronounced more or less as in English.

Since Hebrew and Arabic have more or less a similar alphabet, I have chosen to transliterate the Hebrew letters using the Arabic guidelines above.

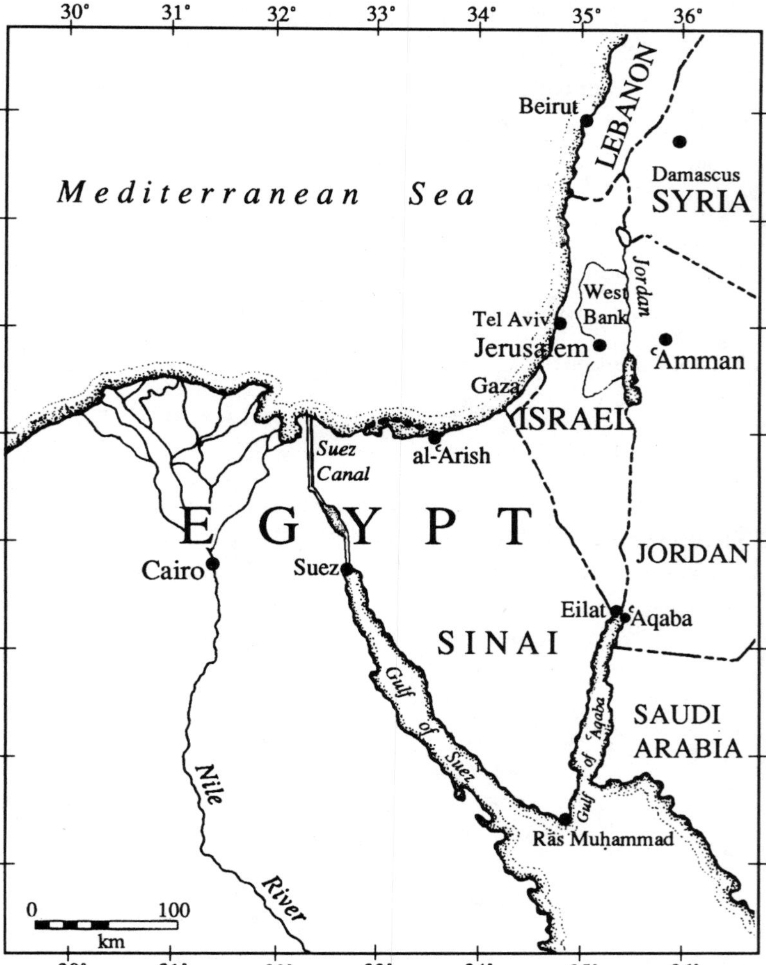

Mediterranean Sea
LEBANON
Beirut
Damascus
SYRIA
Jordan
West Bank
Tel Aviv
Jerusalem
ʿAmman
Gaza
ISRAEL
al-ʿArish
Suez Canal
EGYPT
JORDAN
Cairo
Suez
Eilat
ʿAqaba
SINAI
Gulf of Suez
Gulf of ʿAqaba
SAUDI ARABIA
Nile River
Rās Muḥammad
0
100
km
30°
31°
32°
33°
34°
35°
36°
27°
28°
29°

1
THE POETICS OF MILITARY OCCUPATION

From Experience to Text

If we no longer think of the relationship between cultures and their adherents as perfectly contiguous, totally synchronous, wholly correspondent, and if we think of cultures as permeable and, on the whole, defensive boundaries between polities, a more promising situation appears. Thus to see Others not as ontologically given but as historically constituted would be to erode the exclusivist biases we so often ascribe to cultures, our own not least. Cultures may then be represented as zones of control or of abandonment, of recollection and of forgetting, of force or of dependence, of exclusiveness or of sharing, all taking place in the global history that is our element. Exile, immigration, and the crossing of boundaries are experiences that can therefore provide us with new narrative forms or, in John Berger's phrase, with *other* ways of telling.

EDWARD SAID
"Representing the Colonized:
Anthropology's Interlocutors"

NUWĒBʿA, PASSOVER 1979. THE FIRST ISRAELI ANNUAL ROCK FESTIVAL

The Bedouin men in elegant pastel-colored terylene caftans sat in a circle on the ground, spellbound by the mimed hand gestures of a short, angular man dressed in beat-up Levis fringed at the ankles and a conspicuously short, dirty old caftan that had shrunk once upon a time in the wash. Over the caftan a brand new extra-large T-shirt, shining yellow, bore the black imprint of sun rays bursting up from behind craggy mountains that collapsed into lip-shaped sand dunes and flowed into a peaceful beach strewn with the obligatory palm trees. Above this pristine scene, a kitschy simulation of what he and his friends could see all around them, Hebrew script exhorted, "Sing a Song for Peace," and below, "Nuwēbᶜa's First Annual Rock Festival, Passover 1979." The man's face sported a week's growth of beard stubble, and his fingernails were long overdue to be cut. It was already Thursday—he had only one more day to eliminate this ritual pollution before the Friday Noon Prayer. His dingy headdress scarf, splotched with ketchup and car grease, was wrapped around not the usual white hand-knitted Muslim skullcap, but instead around a worn-out Sabra *tembel* (dunce) cap, probably forgotten by one of the tourists or settlers—it bore the Menorah emblem of the state of Israel.

Every once in a while during the silent spectacle, peals of wild laughter shook the properly attired men. Smadar, the anthropologist, armed with notebook, Nikon camera, and Sony Professional stereo tape recorder, hesitantly tiptoed into the *magᶜad rejjāl* (men's club—the men's public arena)[1] while this performance was in progress. Jumᶜa waved her over to an empty spot beside him. Smadar gestured "No, don't bother" to the men who were about to rise up and greet her by shaking her hand in counterclockwise order, as custom required. Sitting down, she immediately whispered to Jumᶜa, "What's going on?"

"Just watch," said Jumᶜa.

"I don't understand his hand gestures," she whispered back, starting to scribble in her field diary, "Apparently, South Sinai Bedouin mime differs from that of Marcel Marceau."

"I'll translate some for you. Keep writing."

The tembel-hatted man threw his hands over his head, miming frantic finger-picking of some stringed instrument. He writhed his hips, then immediately squatted on his hamstrings and ended up lying on his back kicking his legs in the air while furiously attacking the imaginary strings.

"He is playing now on the electric *sumsumīyya* (five-stringed lyre)[2] he told us about," Jumʿa whispered in her ear, as the men burst out laughing again. "For three nights we couldn't sleep because of those electric sumsumīyyas. The goats were so out of it they refused all orders from the goatherding girls, and the dogs howled back all night. Thank God it's over."

The T-shirted bony fellow had gotten up and was now jutting his chin out at his fist, an imaginary microphone, closing his eyes as if in a trance state during a pilgrimage dance. Then he made some Bedouin deaf-and-dumb sign language gestures, which most Bedouin understand.

"Sing a song for peace, cry it aloud," Jumʿa translated. "He says one of the young 'uns who knows Hebrew told him they kept singing and singing this song while they got more and more stoned, and then some of them screwed on the sand dunes while the performance was still going on."

"Hey," shouted one of the pastel-garbed men, gently tossing a few grains of sand at the mime to get his attention. "If they sing so much for peace, what are they doing on our land?"

The tembel-hatted man tilted his head up with a silly smile, formed a circle with the thumb and middle finger of his left hand, and gleefully jabbed the middle finger of his right hand in and out of it.

The group was swimming in waves of laughter. The pastel-garbed man raised his voice again, to call out: "And screwing us over while they're at it!"

Somber silence descended. The performer was wiping the sweat off his brow with the hem of his Passover 1979 T-shirt. He collapsed into an empty spot and someone served him tea.

"Now that the Feast of *Baskawīt* (biscuits) is over, the annual migration of the Jews to our beaches has at last ended," another man said. "Many people will have jobs cleaning up after them, and the goats will have lots of garbage to eat."

The Israeli anthropologist Smadar tried to smother her giggles at the irony. The South Sinai Bedouin called the Jewish Passover "The Holiday of Biscuits." For them, matzo, or the Passover unleavened bread, fell into the same category as store-bought cookies and crackers, known as "baskawīt" or biscuits.

"Who was that guy, anyway?" she whispered into Jumʿa's ear.

"Oh, don't take him seriously. He's just our local Fool."

*

Although this man was just a fool, his antic miming of the three-day rock festival raised unresolved existential dilemmas that the Mzeina Bedouin, a tribe of approximately 5,000 and the largest of the South Sinai Ṭawara intertribal alliance, had to face every day.

While the free-spirited nomadic tribes who roamed the Arabian deserts attracted turn-of-the-century European explorers in search of exotic experiences, and currently have become the nostalgic subject of ethnographic literature and films, travelers' accounts of the South Sinai tribes evoke images of less glamorous but still outlandish Bedouin. Dan Rabinowitz (1985) has recently emphasized that all nineteenth- and early twentieth-century travelers to the South Sinai, expecting to find the idealized pastoral nomads, were surprised to find instead only very few camels, sheep, and goats, and therefore concluded that the region was not prime pasture land (Rabinowitz 1985: 216). Hence, when travelers to the Eastern Deserts were still pursuing their romantic images of free and independent nomads, travelers to the South Sinai peninsula had long since been disabused of all such naivetés. The latter travelers clearly recognized that the Ṭawara Bedouin of the South Sinai were almost totally dependent on the economic centers of the colonial powers occupying their territory: the Ottoman Turks and, later, the British. By the turn of the twentieth century, Ṭawara members derived much of their income from making charcoal and also from acting as authentic travel guides for genteel pilgrims and explorers, uneasily saddled on camelback, suffering through Mount Sinai and the rest of the peninsula. Ṭawara members could sell the charcoal only in the faraway Nile Valley, four to fourteen strenuous days away by camel. Or they could share camel rides and walk fifteen to thirty days north to Jaffa, to hire themselves out as the cheapest of laborers to Palestinian orange grove owners. They also cultivated date palms in the desert's few oases, tended petite mountain gardens, hunted whatever the fragile desert ecology would yield, and fished along the ʿAqaba and Suez gulf coasts.

To this day, the basic fact is that the Mzeina have been in the hinterland of every occupier of the South Sinai, and therefore have had to depend for their survival on the occupier's center of power (Marx 1977*a*, 1980; Lavie 1989; Lavie and Young 1984). In the course of the Arab-Israeli conflict of the last fifty years, the South Sinai has been a political football tossed at least five times between Egypt and Israel. From the 1940s until 1952, the Sinai was governed by the Egyptian King Farouq but patrolled by British army units. From 1952 to 1956 it was under independent control of the Arab Republic of Egypt. Although the South Sinai has officially been an Egyptian territory since Ottoman times, the South Sinai Bedouin nonetheless still view the Egyptians as a foreign occupation force, now perhaps because the Egyptians, preoccupied by the tremendous problems in the densely populated Nile Valley, have been unable to develop much sensitivity toward the idiosyncrasies of their hinterland Bedouin population. In 1956 Israel, backed by France and Britain, staging one of the last major colonial wars over the nationalization of the Suez Canal, occupied the Sinai, but a few months later returned it to Egypt, which, by then aided by the Soviets, held on to it until 1967, when it was again occupied by Israel. Following the 1973 October War, and the politics of shuttle diplomacy and Camp David, Israel again returned the Sinai to Egypt in eight stages between January 1975 and April 1982 (see the series of maps illustrating the South Sinai international border shifts in chap. 2).

And throughout all this, the Mzeina Bedouin were nothing but pawns. The Egyptian, Israeli, British, American, and Soviet leaders never once consulted them or their leadership on issues of war, peace, occupation, or treaties.

This book attempts to show that the constant military occupation of the South Sinai precluded for the Mzeina the identity that both turn-of-the-century travelers' accounts and contemporary nostalgic literature or media accounts inscribed for the Bedouin: fierce romantic nomads on loping camels in the vast desert. On the contrary, the military occupation had penetrated Mzeini daily life so deeply and so long that it had become much more than soldiers, developers, settlers, and tourists impinging on the external political and economic relationships between the indigenous tribe and the state. The omnipresent occupations had permeated not only internal inter- and intratribal affairs, but also discourses as delicate and intimate as those between husbands and wives. Given that the Mzeina were helpless objects of external political processes, I argue that their Bedouin identity could be little more than literary allegory: tribal identity appeared as moralistic, multilayered narratives transcending the spatial and temporal boundaries of military occupation through symbolic defiance only, because for Mzeinis to openly confront any armed or unarmed occupier could mean beatings, jail, even death.

Within the tribe, only a handful of charismatic individuals had the creative capacity to allegorize the military occupation by dramatizing its humiliations and absurdities for a Bedouin audience. Yet these individuals, gifted with persuasive theatrical skills, did not perform their dramatized critiques at regular, ritual-like intervals. Only when challenged by fellow tribesmembers would a Mzeini creative individual such as the miming Fool evoke the allegory of Bedouin identity. The story would unfold during the fragile interstices of a tense, discontinuous conversation. Such precious moments, filling the otherwise awkward breaks within the flow of everyday conversation, temporarily reconstructed the image of the tribe for the listeners, even though the political situation that had generated the allegory remained unchanged.

The aim of this book is to retrace the process by which Mzeina allegories of Bedouin identity emerge from performances by various creative individuals, each of whom plays a character based on his or her own identity: the Sheikh, the Madwoman, the Ex-Smuggler, the Old Woman, the Fool, the Symbolic Battle Coordinator, and The One Who Writes Us. Embedded in these performances is the poetics of military occupation.

BEGINNINGS: FIELDWORK BY AN OCCUPIER

It might seem a bit awkward for an Israeli like myself to write an account of the resistance, even if only poetic, mounted to the Israeli occupation of the Sinai Desert. I grew up with the Zionist frontier mythology—making the desert bloom, all the while mourning the eradication of desert spaces, and museumizing Negev Bedouin culture even while expropriating Bedouin land (Lavie and Rouse 1988). As a twelve-year-old right after the 1967 war, I was instructed by my teachers, many other Israelis, and the radio to consider the Sinai "the last frontier," a phrase that in the South Sinai context of the mid-1970s had ironically altered its meaning—not simply land to conquer, but land to conquer *and* preserve. Oddly enough, aside from establishing several settlements, the Israeli government had decided purposely to leave the South Sinai barely touched, as a safari space, a nostalgic replacement for the lost Negev wilderness perhaps—an escape from the social and spatial crowdedness of a small country (now not so small) like Israel (Lavie 1988).

As one of those rugged Sabras, I spent one whole high school summer vacation climbing steep, majestic red granite mountains where lush cool springs led to small orchards of juicy pears and prolific old mulberry trees. We explored very narrow, high-walled sandstone canyons utterly barren of plant life, but thinly striped with striations of gold, purple, green, blue, red, and white. We snorkeled among the most beautiful coral reefs in the world, where golden fish, sea turtles, and poisonous cognac-and-black-striped lion fish with great fanlike spines swam among coral reefs colored lavender, peach, black, violet, orange, and ecru. And then there were the Bedouin, whom the various hiking guides introduced to us both as noble savages living in a state of nature, and as remnants of our dignified Biblical forefathers who gained their freedom from Pharoah's slavery and coalesced as a people in this very desert. I wanted to come back after my compulsory army service, despite the fact that I wholeheartedly opposed the transformation of Israel into the Israeli "Empire." I began to wonder whether there was something I was not being told about the Bedouin, such as their own response to tourists like myself, and to the whole Hollywood Ten Commandments media image of their tribes that Israel promoted to attract tourists—an image that had caused gradual Western encroachment on their encampments.

A month after my discharge from the Israeli Defense Force in 1975, I arrived at the South Sinai beach village of Dahab on a hot October afternoon (see the detailed South Sinai map in chap. 2). Innocent of formal anthropological training, but driven by curiosity about the human aspect of the supposedly dangerous Arab Other, I dropped my backpack, cassette recorder, and camera bag on the ground near a thin chicken-wire fence delineating empty sitting space in front of what looked like part of an old army barracks. Most of one side of the structure seemed to have been removed, leaving an empty wall now filled with flattened cardboard vegetable boxes bearing Hebrew, German, and English print promising red-cheeked tomatoes to thaw the European winter. On the roof a sign in English, Hebrew, and Arabic (which I learned to read only two years later) announced: Zub Mar ʿAwwād. I deduced this might be a local supermarket of sorts.[3]

Wearing my modest outfit of baggy jeans, a loose Mickey Mouse T-shirt with elbow-length sleeves, and a turquoise kerchief to cover my hair, I sank down on my big backpack to rest from the heat and was immediately swarmed by kids shouting, "A Jew! A Jew! When is she going to take off her clothes and walk into the sea?" But at that time, the only Arabic word I knew was *shukran* (thank you). Despite the fact that my grandmother's native tongue is Arabic, she had never spoken it in the family while I was growing up. All her children, as adults, had insisted she speak Hebrew with them. My mother had willfully "forgotten" her Arabic in the process of her upscale mobility to the European-Ashkenazi culture of my father, and my parents decided it would be better for me to learn French than Arabic as a second foreign language.

"Shukran," I said demurely in response to the children's greetings. They erupted in giddy laughter.

"*Eh da?*" asked one of the group, pointing at my camera bag. I took the camera out to show it to them, and they all said in unison, "*Kamara!*" I suddenly realized that this was the crucial moment of my first lesson in Mzeini Arabic, and envisioned myself, a devout young scholar, pointing at objects, exclaiming "Eh dah?", and filling my notebook with new words I would memorize at night in the glow of my flashlight.

A tall, dignified old man with gray beard stubble approached to check out the ruckus. With a wave of his hand, he scattered the kids to the four winds. He opened the structure's squeaky door, and a stuffy smell hit my nostrils. In the dim light I made out flour and rice sacks bearing Arabic script, plastic bottles of oil and cardboard boxes of waffles bearing Hebrew labels, tin cans of mackerel from Hong Kong, Bazooka chewing gum, and heavy plastic cases filled with empty Coca-Cola bottles. The old man carried my stuff in and put it under a faded postcard bearing the picture of Samīra Tawfīq, a famous Arab pop star. Yes, this Zub Mar was indeed the neighborhood supermarket.

From a nearby palm frond hut, which must have been where he lived, the old man brought out a handwoven rug, a pot of warm tea, and six glasses. He laid the rug right on the ground in the fenced-in area in front of the store. While I was wondering why he had so many glasses, men and women started arriving, and soon the six were not enough. He forbade the returning hordes of children to come inside the fence, so they clambered all over it.

How could I explain to these people, without speaking their language, that I wanted to live with them so that I could learn about their way of life?

I cleared my throat. I cleared my throat again. By then, everyone, including the kids, was totally silent.

"*Ebrāni*, *ʿIvrīt*, speak Hebrew," said one of the younger men in a mixture of Arabic and Hebrew.

And at that moment I made a decision, that as someone who might represent the current occupation even though against it, I would never speak a word of Hebrew with the Bedouin.

I cleared my throat again. I gestured with both hands at my heart, turned them to the ground, bent my head over my folded hands as if sleeping, then lifted my eyebrows up and tilted my chin, trying to convey that I was asking permission to stay overnight.

Some people smiled. "*Marḥaba!* Welcome!" said the old man. He pointed at me with his right hand, then put it on his heart. By that time it was dusk. The smudgy cliffs seemed to be falling into the sea. On the soft breeze drifted smells of fish and cumin. The men went to pray in a space cleared of big pebbles and delineated by conch shells, with the *miḥrāb*, the small protruding semicircle before which the prayer leader stood, pointing southeast, toward Mecca.

A crumpled old woman opened the flimsy plywood gate of the fence and came in, carrying on her head a large round platter loaded with fish and rice. Several men followed, returning from prayer. This, I realized, was my first chance to practice my newly acquired Arabic expression and see if it worked.

"Eh da?" I queried, pointing at the fish.

"*Ḥūt. Samak. Ḥūt, ḥūt,*" said the old man.

I left the circle of sitting people, went to the locked door of the store, and knocked nervously. The old man stared at me as if at a total loss, then hesitantly walked toward the door and opened it. I scrambled through the pocket of my backpack, grabbed the pen and notebook, and rushed back to my seat in front of the platter. Little did I know I had violated a prime rule of etiquette around the dinner table—one does not leave it just like that in the middle, without profuse apologies. Furthermore, if one leaves, one does not return. But I quickly slipped back to my seat and wrote in the notebook: "fish—ḥūt or samak." Sensing that the shocked silence probably meant I had done something wrong, I looked at the ground, hoping no one would notice how I was blushing. But then my scholarly curiosity won out. I raised my head, pointed at the rice, and exclaimed, "Eh da?"

"*Ruz. Ruz,*" said the old man.

I wrote in my notebook: "ruz—rice," unaware that everyone sitting cross-legged around the platter was waiting for the guest of honor to start eating so they could eat too.

After a long, nebulous silence, the old man grabbed my right hand

and plunged it into the sticky rice, so I grabbed some in my fist. Then he stuck my hand among the slippery white chunks of fish, so I grabbed a few of them. Then he gently maneuvered my elbow to bend my arm and get my loaded hand to my mouth. Being lefthanded, I had hardly ever been required to do anything important, other than play the piano, with my right hand, and was unable to control the sticky mass, so most of it dropped off bit by bit before it reached my mouth. By this time everyone was in an uproar of laughter, not only because of my klutziness but also because my hand had touched the food—that was the signal for the rest of them to dig their hands into the same platter and go to it.

"Oh, that's easy enough," I thought, and reached for the rice with my left hand. The moment I touched it, a stunned silence descended on the group and everyone hastily withdrew their hands. The old man patiently took my right hand back to the platter, but by this time I thought I had already made too many faux pas, whatever they might have been, and decided to give up eating for the present. I patted my tummy and waved my hands as if to say, "No more, thanks." But this also was not acceptable. So I had to keep reaching with my uncooperative right hand, just a bit at a time, so that the rest of the men and women would not stop eating. How long will this go on? Am I to sit here and eat for ever and ever? I looked around and heard some loud burps accompanied by a certain phrase, so I gathered up my courage to produce a soft burp. This time everyone beamed at me with broad smiles of approval.

"*Rabena yaḥalaf ʿaleikum*," the old man said twice, pointing at me, then repeated the phrase again. I got the idea I was supposed to say it, so I did.

"*Ṣaḥḥa waʿāfia*," everyone answered me in unison, while I scribbled both utterances down, adding, "meaning yet unknown—but important!"

By then total darkness invited a sad red moon to rise from the east out of the Saudi cliffs, and to spread its beams into the Gulf of ʿAqaba. As soon as the men left for the *ʿaṣha* (after dinner) prayer, all the women crowded around me and started patting my arms, breasts, abdomen, and legs through my clothes. They also touched my face and poked their fingers onto the kerchief around my head. I had no idea what to make of this behavior and just sat there on the ground in amazement, trying not to stiffen up. As soon as the moon rose and the men returned, the touching stopped.

Two years later one of the women told me that as of 1975, this was the closest they had ever gotten to an Israeli woman, and they just wanted to see if I was a regular human woman with flesh and bones like theirs. The head poking was to find out if I had any head lice about to lay eggs. If they had touched one, it would have popped and squirted. All the while, they feared I might slap one of them, and they were surprised that I didn't. She, and other Mzeinis, also told me they all thought that just as all those hippies had come to live in the fake Bedouin-style village built for them as a tourist trap, I had come to live in the real thing. The problem was, I never took off my clothes.

My first night in the field, I was shown a corner where I could spread my sleeping bag, but I couldn't sleep all night, wondering what the future held for me.

The first week in the field everything seemed to be going quite well. Ten to thirty children constantly formed a safety belt around me, eager to chant the name of whatever object I pointed at. My notebook rapidly filled with Arabic words, nouns, and verbs, and I was amazed to discover that, fortunately, the grammar was quite similar to that of Hebrew. I started making up baby-talk sentences that seemed to be understood.

But this idyll did not last. On my ninth day in Dahab, when I returned to the store from one of the canyons outside the settlement where I had gone to relieve myself, I was shocked to find that my backpack, sleeping bag, camera bag, and cassette recorder had disappeared. What to do? In broken Arabic I managed to inform the old man and his wife. To my surprise, they said nothing and just looked at me philosophically. Did they think it was Allah's will, or what? What was I going to do? My Arabic was not good enough to consult with them about what course of action I should take. Suddenly all those vague, ominous warnings from friends and relatives flashed through my mind: "Beware of the Arabs, young lady. You are too innocent to know anything about them yet."

But the old couple was so generous. For the first time, they invited me into their modest home. They had only one spare blanket, a thin one, so they sent a grandchild to the neighbors to fetch more. The news that all my belongings had disappeared (toilet paper excluded—how lucky I was) spread like a flash flood. In thirty-five minutes thirty-five adults, and the usual masses of children, jammed the inner yard of the couple's compound. The crowd whispered among themselves but just stared at me, saying nothing to me. I felt utterly lost. Two voices counterpointed through my mind: "What on earth are you doing here?" "Fieldwork is interesting." And soon, a young man in patched jeans and a faded Harvard T-shirt addressed me in broken Hebrew with a bittersweet, resigned smile: "You can always go to the Israeli police in Di-Zahāv. They have dogs and are very good at searching our homes."

Yes, I could have done this. But at that very moment I decided not to involve any Israeli authorities in my research, just as I had determined nine days ago never to speak Hebrew to the Mzeinis. But this moment made me understand that my fieldwork could not be objective like I thought fieldwork ought to be. How could I write "unbiased" fieldnotes about a tribe under military occupation by my own country? Anyway, if the police came in, it would be the end of my research. I would be just another Israeli.

The old man offered me a place in his own hut, and a stream of curious visitors started flowing through. In the course of a week, over fifty more people came to sympathize with me and say how sorry they were that this had happened. Though they had precious little themselves, they kept bringing me small aluminum pots of food, which I insisted we eat together. One seven-year-old boy even pressed his school notebook and pen on me, because, like the adults, he knew I was there to write.

After a week, while I was away visiting people and the hut was empty, someone left my little bag of toiletries there. I was so relieved to have my toothbrush and sunblock back. Nothing was missing. Nothing. That evening some of my blank cassettes appeared. The next morning I found my camera bag just outside the old man's hut. Then came my jeans and a couple of T-shirts. By the end of the week I had everything, including the cassette recorder and the sleeping bag. And nothing was missing. Nothing.

Had I been tested? If so, had I passed at least my first exam?

After a couple of years of hearing many arguments between old and young Mzeinis, I realized that there was a generation gap on the issue of theft from foreigners. The older generation was trying to cling to the Mzeina tradition of hospitality for everyone who arrived in the Sinai. But the younger generation protested that military officers, developers, settlers, and tourists were uninvited guests who had to be made aware that they were unwelcome. The younger Mzeinis used theft from foreigners—or as they expressed it, "taking,"—as a way to protest their presence. At times they would even "take" from foreigners things they themselves had no use for, just to make this point. Among themselves, however, Mzeinis never stole. In my thirteen years of fieldwork, despite my repeated inquiries, I heard of no thefts by Bedouin from other Bedouin.

"It is time to make you a *ṭanība* of our family," announced the old man a month later. I could understand him because my arabic had improved dramatically—there were so many people to talk to all the time.

"Ṭanība? Eh da?"

"Say a man from the Rashayda tribe in the Sudan had a blood dispute with someone, and to save his life, he ran very far away, seeking shelter (*dākhel*) with someone from the Mzeina. Let's say he is a good man struck by misfortune. We Mzeina will adopt him into our tribe. We will offer him protection. If someone harms him, it is as if he harms the whole family who adopted him. This means trouble with our *ʿurfi* (customary law), which, I want you to know, is much tougher and fairer than *your* country's law. So we will make him our *ṭanīb* (person with a fictive kinship for the purpose of protection). In the old days when we all lived in tents, this Rashayda tribesman would have run into a Mzeina family tent, held on to the center pole made of a poplar tree, and begged to become a ṭanīb."

So the next day, in the late afternoon when the goats and sheep returned from the pasture, accompanied by the goatherd, the old man's freshly divorced adolescent granddaughter, he selected one of the best kidgoats, a plump one. With the squirming kidgoat clasped tightly under his left arm, he led me with his right hand toward the southeast corner of the inner courtyard, the corner pointing toward Mecca. He made me hold on to the twenty-five by twenty-five centimeter square pole supporting that corner. It was old gray lumber, probably recycled from scaffolding at some development site.

"But didn't you say only a man can become a ṭanīb?"

"Well," mused the old man, "among the *afranj* (Westerners), aside from their bodies, it's hard to tell who's a man and who's a woman. So we can make you a ṭanība."[4]

I was still clinging to the scaffolding pole as he slaughtered the kidgoat while murmuring the opening verses of the Qur'an. He collected some of the blood into an empty cleaned-out tin can and walked over to me. He dipped his forefinger into the blood, and, murmuring more verses from the Qur'an, drew on my forehead a design like a backwards *L* followed by a straight up-and-down stroke. I later discovered that this was the *wasm* (brand) of the old man's phratry—a sign branded with hot irons onto camels' necks in case they got lost, tattooed on some women's foreheads or on the backs of the hands of those men and women who wanted it as a sign of belonging to the phratry, and also marked on hut doors for good luck and on storage boxes for identification.

While the old man was skinning the kidgoat for his wife to cook, she spontaneously lifted the thin silver medallion on a leather thong from around her neck and put it over my head. Still grasping the pole with one hand, I lifted the silver disk in the other and saw engraved on it a Bedouin man and woman whose clasped hands held the enfolded young fronds of a date palm sprout, with a star and crescent moon above. On the other side was Arabic script I was later able to decipher as mispelled Qur'anic verses.

"This will guard your way among the Bedouin," she said softly.

The miraculous grapevine (perhaps because the spectacle could be fully seen between the palm fronds that formed the hut's walls) again did its work, and neighbors started arriving to view my forehead, and to eat the meat—a rare treat reserved for religious celebrations.

Finally it was time to eat. The goat was small and the people were many. The men formed one circle around their own platter of rice dotted with a few tidbits of meat, and the women formed another around theirs. But the old woman gave me a generous plate of meat with a little rice to eat by myself.

"You expect me to eat all this meat by myself?" I exclaimed to the assembled company, throwing my hands up. Not only was I a vegetarian, a cultural concept I knew the Mzeina would not understand because they so treasured meat, but the division struck me as ridiculously unfair. So I spontaneously went over to the men's communal serving plate and carefully used my right hand to scrape half of what was on my plate onto theirs, then put the other half onto the women's serving plate.

"So, now that I am your ṭanība, where should I sit?"

After whispers within and between the circles, the old woman instructed me, "You will first eat with the men for a while, and then go eat with us women." And then she accompanied me to the men's circle and sat down with me to eat with the men.

It began to dawn on me that throughout my fieldwork, I was going to be a gender classification problem.

When I made a calculated reach toward the serving plate with my klutzy right hand, one of the men stopped me.

"Wait. Wait. Since you write and do all other clean things with your left hand, and probably do all unclean things with your right, you may eat with your left hand as long as you say *bismallah* (by the name of God)."

What a relief!

Despite all vicissitudes, fieldwork began to fall into a routine. After a year, I was fluent in the colloquial dialect of the Mzeina. After two years I could recite Bedouin poetry. By the end of the fourth year, I was even able to make up some simple verses of my own. My Yemeni grandmother was quite moved that I could converse with her in her native tongue and enjoy sharing all her proverbs and puns. Her own seven children were embarrassed to speak Arabic with her because, in the European-Ashkenazi hegemony of Israel, it is considered primitive and low class (cf. Shohat 1988).

The old man and his wife gradually became like parents to me. They first told me to call them father and mother, but after they visited my real parents in the Tel Aviv suburbs, they reconsidered. They decided that, even though my relationship with them was in terms of fictive kinship, no one could have two fathers and two mothers.

"You are her real father, so she will call you 'father,' (*abā*)" the old man declared to my father, using me as a translator. "I am her Bedouin father, and she will call me '[paternal] uncle' (*ʿam*)." For the Mzeinis, paternal uncles were almost as important as fathers.

In the course of my first four years in the field, I gradually discovered that what I had thought would be a major liability, my ambiguous gender classification, turned out to be a major asset, giving me transgender mobility. The men taught me how to fish, pollinate date trees, improvise fixing jeeps, and track camels by their individual footprints in the arcosis (those small pebblestones in the wadis). The women taught me how to herd, cook, spin, weave, play the flute, and babysit the children when they wanted some time off. I participated in rituals of weddings, births, baby uvula cutting, circumcisions of boys and girls, exorcisms of *jinn*s from people's bodies and minds, ceremonial meals in memory of the recent dead, pilgrimages, funerals, date harvest celebrations, and Muslim rituals such as the Ramaḍān fast, ʿId al-Faṭr (the holiday ending the month-long Ramaḍān), ʿId al-Aḍḥa (the sacrifice holiday ending the month of pilgrimage to Mecca), and Fadu al-Gharrā (the sacrificial meal in memory of the nocturnal journey of Muḥammad from Jerusalem to the heavens to receive the Qur'an). I was constantly weaving my way, gingerly, between the men's and women's spheres of action. I attended the exclusively male customary court hearings, but was not allowed into the exclusively male monthly meetings between the Israeli military governors and the Bedouin sheikhs they had appointed.

Therefore, throughout this book I appear in both exclusively male and exclusively female contexts, as well as in mixed-gender ones. To the Mzeinis, I was genderless. Perhaps because Mzeini men had long been accustomed to tourists, developers, soldiers, and other Westerners, both male and female, I had no trouble developing strong nonsexual friendships with them. Both men and women poked fun at how easily I moved between the genders, saying "Smadar has the body (*jism*) and soul (*nafs*) of a woman and the logical mind (*ʿagl*) of a man." They often told each other, "She can churn yogurt and play the flute, as well as gallop on camels and talk foreign currency rates." Both employed me as a go-between in romantic trysts. This would suggest that despite my trans-gender mobility, I enjoyed the trust of both men and women. In retrospect, the only person to suffer from these circumstances was myself. After my first four years in the field, four years of genderless identity, I found it a real struggle to regain a distinct sense of womanhood.[5]

To avoid preliminary categorization of my field data, I wrote it in the form of a diary rather than on cards classified by anthropological topics such as kinship, ritual, descent, and so forth. Each diary entry consisted of a description of the situation: time, duration, location, who participated, an almost verbatim record of what was said, facial expressions, hand gestures, and also my impressions about the situation. I wrote the diary in Hebrew and used Hebrew letters to transliterate the sounds of Arabic speech. After six or seven months, since I was always in some corner scribbling, I stopped being an attraction and people simply ignored me. This was how I acquired the appellation "*Dī Illi Tuktubna*" (The One Who Writes Us). People even made use of my record to verify what had been said in the heat of an argument, saying "It's even written in Smadar's notebook."

Another fieldwork strategy was to visit people's houses to chat and gossip, that is, to conduct extended open-ended interviews. After conflicts or rituals, I visited not only the event's key participants, but also the observers, to chat about what happened, that is, to document "the native point of view." I dutifully collected genealogies, descent lines, kinship and marriage networks, and the many versions of the Mzeina myth of settlement in the Sinai. Only in an oblique way did this data prove relevant to my eventual thesis about the poetics of military occupation.

To move around in the Sinai, I relied mainly on rides from Bedouin traveling from one place to another in old jeeps and pickup trucks, and later, in dilapidated Mercedes taxis. From my research grant, I also bought part ownership in a camel so I could reach most of the peninsula, still inaccessible to motorized vehicles.

In 1977 I conducted a house-to-house census in Dahab, the largest sedentarized settlement on the East Coast of the peninsula, and composed only of Mzeina. This census provided data on population size, neighborhood composition, history of structures and buildings, age distribution of residents, household composition, family assets, and marital history of individuals.

In 1978–1979 I conducted the same type of census in al-Ṭūr, the largest sedentarized Bedouin settlement on the West Coast of the peninsula, inhabited by Mzeina and all other tribes of the South Sinai Ṭawara intertribal alliance. Because I found it difficult to stay in al-Ṭūr for a long time, I completed only half the census.

To obtain information on less sedentarized populations living in encampments, I conducted population surveys in some main geographical areas of the South Sinai. In September and October 1976 I surveyed the peninsula's northeastern mountains; in January 1978 the mid-western mountains; in September 1978 the northern part of the highland plateau; and in January 1979 the southern part of the highland plateau and the southeastern and southwestern mountains.

Before each survey I collected gossip from the Mzeinis in Dahab about the encampments in the area to be surveyed. For each survey I went with two Mzeinis who were well accepted in the area. We visited two to three encampments per day. My companions from Dahab gossiped with the locals according to our prearranged plan: I gathered information about who lived in the encampment, their kinship groups, marriage and divorce patterns, the property they owned, territorial claims, sources of water and food, their occupations, migration patterns, if any, and so on.

As for official records and statistics—due to my strained relationship with the military governor, I did not even try to request these from his office. I was therefore very lucky that one day the old Mzeini trash collector at Dahab's small Israeli army base brought me a bundle of papers he had rescued from the trash, thinking it might interest me. Though unable to read either Arabic or Hebrew, he thought it had to do with Bedouin, because the pink cover page of the top document had a drawing of a man wearing a caftan and headdress, with a camel, the proverbial palm trees, and waves of the sea. This bundle turned out to be quite a treasure: unclassified military documents regarding the South Sinai Bedouin, dating from 1972 to 1977. The information concerned the military and civilian governing strategies used to control the Bedouin, which I will discuss in chapter 2, and the data that generated these policies, mainly the geographical distribution of Bedouin in the Sinai, their administrative division into tribal coalitions, tribes, phratries, and clans, and the main traditional and migrant labor occupations of the Bedouin. I also discovered 1975–1977 statistics on the number and residences of Bedouin in the eastern part of the peninsula, although I find these inaccurate according to my own census and demographic surveys.

To supplement my laboriously detailed fieldnotes, I made audio tapes of men's coffee-grinding rhythms and joke sessions, their camel-riding songs and songs to accompany dances, fishermen's musical-jocular shouts during fishing and their drunken songs and antics accompanied by the sumsumīyya, men and women reciting poetry, women's herding shouts and songs, their flute playing and wedding songs, children's songs, and various genres of speech. I was very careful to ask permission each time I wanted to make a recording, and everyone was fully aware of the presence of a cassette recorder while recording was in progress. I was interested in recording ordinary everyday conversations, to see how they were influenced by the political context of military occupation, but I found that people tended to put on a performance in front of the cassette recorder, as they were used to doing while playing their own cassette recorders. As soon as I pushed the off button, they crowded around to hear the playback of their performance. Therefore, to record the everyday dialogues—one of the main focuses of this book—I just had to write as fast as I could what people said. I blessed the fact that, once people got used to my constant scribbling, most of the time they left me alone tucked in some corner to observe the goings-on. At times they would include me in their conversation, or I would initiate my own participation.

On the whole, fieldwork was going well. I seemed to pass the occasional small loyalty tests that popped up, recognizing them as such only after the fact, because I felt more accepted.

Then in early summer of 1977, after almost two years in the field, came final exam week. I joined a fishing trip with my uncle/father, his sons, and several other men, young and old. We had to load all our gear on six camels, because no motorized vehicle could reach the shore where the red granite cliffs made their sheer drop into the sea. It was a long, five-day trip of arduous work along the scalloped coral reef that undulated in and out from the coastline ten kilometers north of

Dahab. We lived by the ebbing tides instead of the clock, fishing between tides, every five hours or so. The leader of the group was an old man with thin threads of salt sparkling in his wrinkles. As the most experienced fisherman, he knew in spite of his cataracts how to spot groups of three or four parrot fish seven meters out under water. Standing on the beach, he would consult with the other experts to decide what group of fish to attack. Then he would shield his eyes against the glaring sun and watch two seasoned fishermen, their left shoulders sagging from the lead weights of the heavy net—handwoven cotton in two layers, a white loose weave for the big fish, and a green fine weave for the small ones—walking along the edge of the shallow turquoise reef out to behind the target spot.

In back of them was a sheer drop of thirty to fifty meters into the blue-black open sea, with Saudi Arabia on the horizon. Then the old leader would do a little dance, gracefully shifting his weight from foot to foot while waving his left hand like a semaphore signal from side to side over his head. The men with the net responded by walking gingerly together, heading north to the outside edge of the reef. As soon as the leader saw that the net men were right behind the target fish, peacefully gnawing on the corals with their red, gold, and black tails just above the water line, he gracefully raised his right hand to move in a mirror image of the left. The two net men moved to either side until the net was fully open. At that moment, the youngest in the crowd, seven young men and myself, rushed into the sea, stamping and splashing and throwing stones to drive the fish into the net. With a basket on my back, its rope handles cutting into my shoulders and forehead, I ran in my plastic sneakers on the bumpy reef, praying not to fall on a poisonous stonefish—it would kill me in five minutes or less. Breathless at the net, we started killing the slippery, slithery fish by jabbing a curved forefinger from one gill-slit over to the other. Thin threads of blood diffused in the clear blue water. We hastily disentangled the dead fish from the net and flipped them over our shoulders into the baskets. We had to work very fast to get back to the beach before the sharks came after the blood.

Tired and thirsty, with blisters all over me from sun, salt, and sweat, I sighed with relief when the last day dawned.

"All I want is to load my camel and go home to pour sweet water on my aching skin," said the salty old leader, "so let's get on with the *suhūm* (the dividing of the catch)." He meted out the fish, one by one, into a circle of enough piles to give one to each fisherman. My eyes burned even more, trying to hold back tears, when I realized from the number of piles that one of them must be meant for me. One of the fishermen volunteered to be blindfolded and toss red and black stones, and white pieces of dried camel manure, one at a time, from the center out toward the piles. Before each toss, he asked who would get the pile the stone fell nearest, and someone would call out a name. It was completely random and very fair.

In the middle of all this, some of us noticed a military amphibious landing craft apparently trying to land on the coral and breaking off chunks of it. This ship was bizarrely out of place—normally such ships stayed out in the middle of the gulf. Was it a landing exercise? If so, why not in one of the deep, sandy hidden bays?

"Are the Jews getting ready for another war?" asked the salty leader.

"They might be practicing to attack Saudi Arabia from the northeast coast. They could take the Saudis by total surprise and get it all in less than six days."

"Yeah, maybe all the oil they took from Egypt in the Gulf of Suez isn't enough for them."

"No, no, no! America helps the Saudis, and it also helps Israel, so it won't let two of its children go to war with each other."

An hour passed in trading speculative political theories and also curses over the vandalizing of the very rare corals, when a small Israeli military helicopter landed just a couple of meters from our piles of fish. Out jumped an impeccably attired redheaded master sergeant, asking in broken Arabic, "Fishing licenses? IDs?" All the men scurried to their blankets and bundles to find their documents. Only I had no fishing license, because Israelis did not need one for such small amounts, and I had been so sure of myself that I had even left my ID back in the encampment.

"If you have no ID or fishing license," ordered the sergeant, "bring me your camera." He opened it, ripped the film while it was still in the camera, grabbed it out, and exposed it to the sun.

"That's what you get for taking pictures of a military landing craft," he snarled. "That's prohibited."

"But she didn't take any pictures of the ship," one Bedouin piped up. The sergeant slapped him in the face.

"Take your stuff and get in the helicopter," he commanded me. "Move it!"

By late afternoon we landed in Sharm al-Sheikh right in front of the headquarters of the South Sinai military governor, and they threw me in jail. My dramatic entrance into the dingy, stifling hot cell stunned the fourteen Bedouin men already there.

"What are *you* doing here?" some chorused in disbelief.

"We went fishing in Ras abu-Gallūm, and I didn't have my fishing license and ID."

"Welcome, welcome," one young man said. "Most of us are here for the same reason."

"Hey, Smadar, do you also have lice on your head?"

"I think so."

"If you've been in jail, and you have head lice, you are a real Bedouin."

Early in the evening the master sergeant escorted me from the cell to the office of the military governor, glowering behind his imposing desk. When I entered he murmured to the redhead, "She even smells like one."

"I hear that you are the one behind all this media coverage of the nude hippie beaches."

I realized then that the fishing license was just an excuse to get me for disclosing to a well-respected Israeli journalist this governor's extracurricular activities, selecting one-night stands from among the nude Scandinavian blondes on the beaches.

"And we here in the military government don't like journalists. And I'm sure the Bedouin don't like them either."

"Well, sir, I hope you are aware of the fact that they are Muslim, and I know that they sent you several petitions asking you to erect signs prohibiting nudity, but you gave no response."

"You know they are making money out of this too."

"But at what cost to their culture?"

"Are you on their side, or your own people's side?"

"I would rather not answer that, sir," I whispered politely, amazed that I dared to say even that much.

"Get her out of here," he barked at the redhead.

Back in the cell, I was so relieved to find my fieldnotes still in my little bundle. I asked the men if anyone had messed with them while I was gone.

"No, I don't think they care about that sort of thing," one said.

That whole night I couldn't sleep a wink, anxious about what they were going to do to me. My skin itched from salt and sweat and sunburn. I longed for a shower. Early in the morning, a burly policeman with a big mustache opened the cell and declared me free. I walked out into the brilliant sun with nothing but my bundle of sleeping bag, camera, and fieldnotes. A group of Bedouin men sweeping the streets smiled broadly when they saw me. One man, when he

THE DAILY COASTAL ISRAELI MILITARY PATROL, NUWĒBʿAT MZEINA

discovered I had no money, gave me his whole day's pay for the bus to Dahab. "Go to your father in Dahab," he said. "I hope they kept your share of the fish for you."

I arrived in Dahab at noon, and finally had a good meal and a good "shower"—cold sweet water poured from a twenty-liter jerrycan into a tin can and then over my body, along with soap and shampoo. By evening the family of my uncle/father, and the families of two of my fellow fishermen, were slaughtering goats for a feast to thank God for my return.

"I saved your share of the fish for you," said my adoptive father.

"But they are yours. You never want money from me, or anything else."

"Three months from now, we are going to go to Wadi Firān to exchange dried fish for dates. Bring this fish, and people will give you dates."

From then on, I had the full trust of all the people—every Mzeini in the South Sinai knew the story of "the night when Smadar was in jail."

In spite of the various tests of me, which were only to be expected, from the beginning of my fieldwork I had benefited from the generous tradition of Mzeini hospitality. Although the tradition was that a person was a guest for only three days, I felt that in my case this time period was unduly extended. When I protested, many said I was not a guest because I was working daily to help both the men and the women with important chores.

I wanted to compensate the old man for having me in his hut, but he refused. I tried leaving money for him in his pocket, or in the little food can used as the family kitty, or I would leave it in the place they hid the transister radio when they were not home. But whenever I left money for him, I would find it neatly folded back in my backpack, usually inside a sock.

A great opportunity to pay him back came when his prized Seiko watch stopped, and on one of my trips back to Tel Aviv, I took it for repair to the main Seiko certified service center. After this, other Mzeinis asked me to take their watches for repair, and I gladly did it. I also paid all expenses to take him and his wife, daughters, sons, and their spouses on trips to visit my family and to pray at the al-Aqṣa mosque in Jerusalem (the third-holiest site for Muslims). We also went to the movies, to the circus, and to cafes, and I bought him and his wife prescription eyeglasses. While in Jerusalem, I discovered that my old adoptive mother craved frozen chickens and chocolate cakes. Thereafter, when I traveled back to Dahab from my occasional visits to the Hebrew University in Jerusalem, I always brought her a Viennese chocolate cake from a Jerusalem bakery and picked up some frozen chickens at the local supermarket in Eilat. Also on my visits up north, I visited Mzeinis who were lonely in Israeli hospitals and really appreciated seeing me. I also bought all sorts of toys for the kids and cosmetics for the women, especially their favorite Revlon shampoo and colorful hair pins. I hoped this would reciprocate somewhat for the way the people opened their homes and hearts to me. Even after I left for Berkeley in 1979, the Mzeinis of Dahab felt free to occasionally call my grandmother and my friends in Jerusalem and invite themselves up for a couple of nights to attend Friday prayer at the al-Aqṣa mosque.

In the fall of 1978, my fourth year of fieldwork, I started applying to graduate schools to continue my studies in anthropology. Many Mzeinis were baffled.

"Why do you need to travel all the way to America to write about us?" asked the old man's eldest daughter.

"Well," her mother responded, "everything else comes from America, so the book on us will too."

In late August 1979, ten days before I left the Sinai, a cargo ship bound for Saudi Arabia made a navigational error and ended up in the Gulf of Suez, where it ran into one of the coral reefs near al-Ṭūr. To lighten their load, the hysterical Italian crew hurled overboard all sorts of esoteric gourmet delicacies: frozen Cornish game hens complete with their livers—a great Bedouin treat—neatly tucked inside in plastic pouches bearing mysterious Cyrillic script; from France, canned champignons, La Vache Qui Rit cheese, and purple sugar candies that looked like violets; huge apples, the size of cantaloupes, from the Po River Valley in Italy; commercial quantity cans of sumptuous feta cheese from Bulgaria; and plaid cans of Scottish shortbread. Like all the other Mzeinis, I rushed to grab these gifts from the sea for my extended adoptive family. I swam out to the ship with the men and later sorted the stuff with the women. For modesty's sake, I had swum in my clothes, but because they took so long to dry, I got pneumonia.

My temperature was over 40°C—hot enough to cook on, said the old man, who then, in spite of my protests, went to fetch the South African Jewish doctor, a scuba-diving accident specialist, from the nearby Israeli settlement of Di-Zahāv. The doctor ordered me to take twenty erythromycin pills per day. I lay there helpless, knowing I had to be on the other side of the world in a week, while the people kept bringing me unheard-of delicacies like lobster broth with French champignons and melted Bulgarian feta. People took turns staying with me in shifts, so I was never alone. They read from the Qur'an for my recovery and brought several traditional healers who tied amulets around my neck, flicked water on me from a holy bowl, and threw smoky blankets over me to make me cough up mucus from my lungs. Finally I had only two days to pack. I had to be in Berkeley before the beginning of the academic year.

"Those Westerners feel the urge to go to America even if they are very sick," observed the old man's second cousin.

One of my adoptive brothers insisted on accompanying me to the airport in Eilat for my flight to Tel Aviv. He hired a Mercedes taxi, and from the moment I got in, I cried and cried. At the airport I was so distraught, and my adoptive brother was so protective, that he managed to talk his way through every armed Israeli guard at all four security checkpoints, accompanying me to the very door of the propeller-driven aircraft. I was the last to climb the squeaky, rickety steel staircase to this civilian plane. Among all these suspicious military officials and security guards, watching out particularly for Arabs like my brother, he said his last words to me: "I am afraid they are going to kill you there in America. I am afraid you are going to die from all those serial rapists and murderers we keep hearing about on the radio. Will you ever get back here in one piece?" I last glimpsed him wiping his tears on the sleeve of his caftan. It was the only time I ever saw him cry.

The most precious piece of luggage I took with me to Berkeley was a large vinyl duffel bag weighing around thirty kilograms. I clung to it as Isaac Stern must have gripped his Stradivarius. Every time I changed planes, I had to have a furious argument with the airplane ground staff when I refused to check it with the luggage. I was a prime suspect—still tanned very dark olive, wearing around my neck all sorts of amulets written in Arabic that Mzeini women had given me for good luck, and destined for Berkeley.

"Open this bag," they demanded.

When everything was on the table, the security person looked at me in total shock. "What are all these notebooks, slides, negatives, and tapes about?" One even went so far as to suggest that I was trying to start a new cult.

"This is four years' worth of research materials on the 5,000 Mzeina Bedouin of the Sinai desert."

"Whaat? Who?"

"You know, those nomads with camels who live in the desert of the Middle East."

The airport officials looked at each other doubtfully. "Well, after all, she is headed for the *university* at Berkeley," came the usual shrug. So I got the benefit of the doubt, and with it permission to cling to my data.

DECIPHERING THE FIELD AND TRYING ON THEORIES

My first year as a graduate student, I did all my course work, but spent every free moment indexing my fieldnotes. I gradually noticed that, in addition to the mass of data that made perfect anthropological sense, I had a fascinating body of enigmatic data, which I could not interpret. This data consisted of verbatim transcripts of arguments that led to the sudden eruption of solo performances, not only by people in leadership positions, like the sheikhs, ex-smugglers, and the Symbolic Battle Coordinator, but also by oddball characters like old women, madwomen, and fools like the mime who opened this chapter. Although I had not started my fieldwork with a focused proposal to study any particular aspect of Mzeina culture, I had plenty of conventional data, enough for several different books. But the enigmatic sequence of collective everyday argument giving way to solo performance of a personal narrative drew me like a magnet. I read the data over and over again, each time through the optics of a different theory, but they still resisted interpretation.

Typecasting. In the spring of 1979 I read Don Handelman's (1979) article "Is Naven Ludic?: Paradox and the Communication of Identity." In that article Handelman discussed the concept of "symbolic type"—a character enacting a certain persona, at times costumed and masked, who appears during the transformation from the linear flow of regular time to the cyclical flow of ritual or play time (cf. Leach 1961), and serves as a catalyst to move the ritual or play from one act to the next (cf. Werbner 1986). Handelman based his analysis of symbolic typifications on Richard Grathoff's theory of "contextual inconsistencies, disruptions of typified patterns of social interactions" (Grathoff 1970:12) that might get resolved in play. Grathoff described sequences where the thematic, motivational, and interpretational relevance of a social situation gradually falls apart—while still seeming to make sense, it paradoxically stops making sense, because unity of context is lost (Grathoff 1970:24–33). Such situations of anomie (Durkheim 1933:192; cf. McHugh 1968) are fertile ground for the appearance of playful characters, who reduce the context to its essence and therefore enable its reorganization. Handelman describes how this can be accomplished.

The symbolic type structures the thematic field of the situation in

> congruence with its own typification—thus it reduces the relevance of other [cultural] elements to only those which are essential to its own appearance. In contrast to other analytic categorizations which appear under a multitude of terms (for example, stereotype, social type, membership category device, social role), the reality of the symbolic type is not subject to mediation or negotiation. The symbolic type is its own rationale, its own substantiation of validity. Its non-negotiable attribute permits the symbolic type to rearrange "reality" in keeping with its own image. . . . Because symbolic types are the unmediated embodiments, or the reifications of patterns of abstract ideation . . . there is a sense of absolutism about them which brooks no qualification by elements of less abstract domains of being. (Handelman 1979:185–186)[6]

Were the main actors in my enigmatic data "symbolic types" like these? When they performed their monologues, they were indeed a total embodiment of the inconsistent situation under the shifting military occupations, and therefore able to reorganize it consistently. They did not act from within a ritual frame, however. They erupted with their monologues when an ordinary discussion disintegrated and could not reach a harmonious end. They also moved loosely from being plain persons in routine situations, to being those nonnegotiable abstract total personae that constitute "symbolic types," then back again to ordinary personhood. But were they symbolic? Were they representing the tribe as a whole? Or perhaps, because the military occupation did not allow the tribe to exist as a whole, they existed only as fragments, and that was the reason there was a whole cast of them ordered in a spectrum from the dignified Symbolic Battle Coordinator, at the heart of what was left of the traditional tribe, to madwomen at the outermost margins of the tribe. But their main attribute was not in the domain of sacred action like Native American kachinas and clowns, or Sri Lankan demons (Handelman 1981; Handelman and Kapferer 1980). They were telling fantastic stories of their actual lived experience, such as the story of the Passover 1979 Rock Festival. And these people did not act according to the predetermined script of established cultural performances. Their performances were entirely improvisatory.

Renato Rosaldo has argued that "the concept of culture could barely describe, let alone analyze, flux, improvisation, and heterogeneity. . . . Culture areas . . . indeed are laced with . . . eruptions, where anthropological and other classifications fail" (Rosaldo 1988:77). He then tells us about his mentors' warnings (which he ultimately rejected): "Ambitious young anthropologists would be well advised to avoid such zones, pockets, and eruptions because they are inhabited by 'people without culture'" (1988:79). And while I was clinging to my (by now not so enigmatic) body of data, some of my mentors and colleagues kept remarking that the Mzeina were "a Bedouin tribe without a Bedouin culture"—they were not free-spirited nomads, not even historically. But was this cast of characters a temporary embodiment of the Mzeina Bedouin identity, dramatizing "simulations" (Baudrillard 1983) of what the Mzeinis believed a genuine Bedouin identity ought to be? Or were they embodying the tribe's actual identity, imposed on them by the geopolitical strife?

Going back to my fieldnotes, I discovered I had recorded many traditional stories, poems, and proverbs about heroic or foolish deeds of a pantheon of picturesque textual characters like Sheikhs, Fools, Madwomen, Symbolic Battle Coordinators, and Old Women. Did the charismatic creative individuals who attracted my scholarly curiosity have anything to do with this folkloric repository? If so, how could a person gifted with theatrical talent rise up from the heat of an argument, become such a persona and enact a performance, then become a person again, without referring to any of the traditional stories, but telling his or her own story of contemporary personal experience in the traditional form? And were these just stories? Perhaps the performers were allegorizing fragments of experience from their daily lives into oral texts that connected the tellers' here-and-now to the pantheon of traditional characters' stories reflecting the history of the tribe.

Allegorizing. Allegories are texts telling an individual story to convey a lesson for the whole group, a private story that attempts to represent the collectivity as a whole (De Man 1979:199; Jameson 1986:69).[7] Allegory, therefore, is a fragmentary form of inscription simultaneously serving two purposes—poetic expression, and didactic-political lamentation of the heroic past, now almost disappeared but to be reincarnated at some point in the eternal future (Benjamin 1977:162; Jameson 1986). It is therefore a "symbolic representation of a moral and political kind" (Benjamin 1977:168; cf. Fineman 1981:29, 31), "heal[ing] the gap between the present and the disappearing past, which without interpretation, would be otherwise irretrievable and foreclosed" (Fineman 1981:29). Allegory combines the parts to form a consistent whole (De Man 1969). It salvages the ruins of the past by using "figural language" (De Man 1979:188) to fuse them artistically into a unified story. The word allegory itself is composed of *allos*, a Greek word meaning "other," and *agoreuein*, "to speak in the *agora*," to speak openly in the marketplace or assembly. "Agoreuein" connotes public, open, declarative speech (Fletcher 1964:2). One would expect allegories to be stories that the Self tells about the Other (De Man 1979:191).

The convention in anthropology has been that the Self represents the West, importing to Third World cultures its own scientific methods of inquiry, and the Other is in the Third World and commodified into exotic text (J. Clifford 1986; Said 1989). In this book, however, I have chosen to let the voices of the colonized speak as the Self, revealing their perception of the West as the exotic Other. This presents a paradoxical reversal.

Northrop Frye (1973) has pointed out the connection between allegory and paradox, and has designed a "kind of a sliding scale" of literary forms—the allegorical is the most explicit, while the paradoxical is the most anti-explicit and elusive (Frye 1973:92, 103). How can the Mzeinis make allegories by transforming the paradoxes of their lives—yearning to be free-spirited nomads while living among daily realities like foreign military bases on their desert, police searches with dogs, encroaching foreign settlements, nude hippie tourists, and Passover rock festivals?

Stephen Greenblatt (1981) suggests that allegories are themselves paradoxical. His argument would seem quite applicable to the desperate efforts of the Mzeinis to preserve their culture in the face of continual occupation. He maintains that

> Allegory arises in periods of loss, periods in which a once powerful theological, political or familial authority is threatened with effacement. Allegory arises then from the painful absence of that which it claims to recover, and, . . . as the paradox of an order built upon its own undoing cannot be restricted to this one discursive mode, indeed, . . . the longing for an origin whose loss is the necessary condition of that longing is the character not only of all discourse but of human existence itself. (xviii)

I argue that the narratives constituting the characters' allegories entail the paradoxes both of the Mzeina and of each individual teller of such narratives. I further argue that such allegorical narratives can temporarily solve the very paradox they constitute—the paradox of being a cultural text that contains criticism of itself (cf. J. Clifford 1986:119–120). As curious as it may sound, in *being* a paradox, the allegorical narrative solves itself *as* a paradox by the very fact of the narrator's explication and redefinition of the paradox for his or her audience. (I will return to this point and amplify it in the concluding chapter, after all the characters have told their allegories.) Therefore these allegories serve as shining examples of how to live with and even exploit the Mzeini paradoxes of life under occupation, in order to relive, if only in story, their identity as Bedouin characters within the tradition of free-spirited nomadism.

RETURNINGS: FIELDWORK BY A DIASPORIC MZEINA

Between 1979 and 1985, while I was in Berkeley for graduate school, I kept in contact with my Mzeini adoptive family and many friends by mailing them cassette tapes. In these tapes I described for them the San Francisco Bay Area, the Golden Gate Bridge, the university, the American way of life, and—how could I forget?—the history of San Francisco's Haight-Ashbury district and Berkeley's People's Park. So many nude hippies floating around the South Sinai beaches traced their genealogy to the flower children of San Francisco and Berkeley that the Mzeinis were familiar with the names of these cities long before I moved there. In the tapes the Mzeinis sent me, they filled me in on all the gossip about births, marriages, divorces, celebrations, deaths, and the new political realities after the Egyptians took over Dahab in April 1982. Still fearing censorship by the Secret Police, the Mzeinis talked about the new occupier by using the same code language they had used previously to discuss the Israeli occupier. The cassettes just made me want to get back to the Sinai.

Seasoned after two years of formal graduate training in anthropology, I went back to the field in 1981 armed at last with a theoretical hypothesis to test against my already large reservoir of data about the mysterious eruptive solo performances.

"Smadar has come back from the dead!" people exclaimed. "So many Westerners who visited here went to America and were never seen again. But here you are. Thank Allah!"

Meanwhile, half of the field itself was under the rule of a different country. Egypt had recovered the western half of the Sinai from Israel under the Camp David Accord.

But everything still made sense in terms of the Grathoff-Handelman-

Kapferer hypothesis, and on both sides of the temporary border. The "symbolic types" did exist. They did impose their own "liminality" (Turner 1969:94–96) and thus ritualized the banality of everyday life when the conversational flow got stuck, and their performances symbolically protested both the occupying powers, Israel to the east and Egypt to the west. But the people performing these characters were not exactly the "symbolic types" described by Grathoff, Handelman, and Kapferer. They were telling allegories rather than acting out symbols. They were not total metaphors representing the tribe (Fernandez 1974), but rather, metonymies of it—fragments that stand for the whole. And as in the case of allegories, these people told their own personal stories to help the tribe reconstitute its Bedouin identity, fragmented by the military occupations. Their repeated efforts were only partially successful, however, because Mzeina tribal identity under occupation was "conjunctural, not essential" (J. Clifford 1988:11). So, due to all these considerations, I hypothesized that the Mzeini characters were allegorical types, rather than "symbolic types." What fully convinced me that my hypothesis was sound was the fact that the characters who were criticizing Israel on the Israeli side of the border had their counterparts across the line who were already criticizing Egypt. Although the occupier had changed, the process of allegorical emergence had not.

The new situation of the Sinai presented new fieldwork problems. After April 1982, when Israel returned the rest of the peninsula to Egypt, the Egyptian government closed the Sinai to any kind of long-term research. From 1985 on, the authorities allowed me to conduct fieldwork for only a month at a time (cf. Lavie and Rouse 1988). Although all the allegories presented here were told under Israeli occupation, I personally witnessed under Egyptian occupation other allegories of the same genre, told by the same cast of Mzeini characters. I do not include any of these here (although I do include many other details about the Egyptian occupation) because I was unable to collect enough allegories told by the various men and women enacting each character type to conflate several of them into a single narrative representative of the type. I felt the textual strategy of conflation was necessary because the personal narrative of each individual-as-type was politically vulnerable and needed the protection of disguise by others of its type. (I will describe the process of conflation in a later section of this chapter.)

In December 1985 I was excited to return to the field with my spouse, Forest Rouse, whom I had met in Berkeley. By that time the

South Sinai was under Egyptian control. I was struck by the fact that the Israeli soldiers and police had been replaced by over three times as many Egyptian police, who were busy monitoring the sparse native population and the few tourists who still came, in spite of police meddling, to lie on the beach and climb Mount Sinai to meditate on the sunrise.

"Isn't the South Sinai now a demilitarized zone?" I asked the local head of the Dahab Police Station.

"Yes," he reassured me. "We don't have any soldiers here like those Israelis did—only military-trained police."

As soon as I introduced Forest to the Mzeinis, I noticed that people started treating me with much more formality than previously. Did this have something to do with the fact that Forest was a genuine foreigner who did not know the language at all and was hesitant with the basic customs in spite of the crash course I gave him and my continued promptings? Or was it perhaps that I was now not only a married adult, though still childless, but also had entered my thirties and had a few gray hairs, a sign of maturity?

After our three guest days, all the pleasantries ended and I could start my fieldwork routine. But I found it curiously difficult to update basic information on subjects like migration and labor patterns. The moment I asked typical anthropological questions, people said, "But you already know all that. You have been here many years. Besides, now you are married." On the other hand, now that I was married, many close friends, women and men alike, were quite curious about the inner workings of my marital relationship and initiated long meandering conversations in which we compared our personal experiences of marriage.

My marriage, however, had not resolved my gender classification ambiguity. At first, out of deference to custom, I avoided the magʿad, because women of reproductive age were not permitted in the men's club. I was surprised when a boy arrived with a specific request from the older men for me to continue attending the magʿad as before, and my spouse was welcome also.

The excitement about my marriage and concern about Forest's bout of dysentery overshadowed our usual political musings and bitter criticisms of the past and current military occupations. In subsequent field trips in 1987 and 1988, the same fascination continued with the comparative analysis of personal relationships, but the Egyptians had imposed so many new development programs, rules, and regulations on the Mzeinis that they were eager to fill me in on all the changes as well as on their detailed interpretations of them.

After thirteen years of ongoing fieldwork, either in the field or through prolific correspondence by audio tape (and still continuing through direct-dial international phone calls), I had a real problem: how was I going to turn this immense mass of data into a text?

ON THE POLITICS OF WRITING CULTURE

Ethnography is a movement from "subjectively meaningful experiences emanating from our spontaneous life" (Schutz 1962:211) in the field into academic text—ranging from scribbled fieldnotes to polished, published articles and books. Culture itself can be conceived as a movement from experience, or "what has been lived through" (Bruner 1986:3) in daily life, to social text—and here I mean by "text" the most elaborate predesigned formal rituals, scriptures, and other highly stylized, rigidly followed "structural units" (1986:7). Edward Bruner has argued, however, that "there are inevitable gaps between reality, experience, and expression, and the tension among them constitutes a key problematic in anthropology" (1986:7). I argue that this tension, which governs the very movement of both culture and ethnography from experience to text, exists because the movement is both creative and political (cf. K. Dwyer 1982:xviii, 272). The political aspect of the movement tries to tame the creative, but the creative tries to evade the political.

Anthropology is characterized by two "styles of creativity" (Wagner 1981:26). Anthropologists invent not only their scholarly texts, but also the culture they study. Fieldwork itself is "a creative, productive experience" (Wagner 1981:17) in which the culture of the Other is being evoked in text "as a mirror image of our own" (1981:20; cf. Marcus and Fischer 1986:1). As Roy Wagner eloquently argues,

> Invention, then, *is* culture, and it might be helpful to think of all human beings, wherever they may be, as "fieldworkers" of a sort, controlling the culture shock of daily experience through all kinds of imagined and constructed "rules," traditions and facts. The anthropologist makes his experiences understandable (to himself as well as to his society) by perceiving them and understanding them in terms of his own familiar way of life, his Culture. He invents them as "culture." (1981:35–36)

Wagner, however, has overlooked the politics embedded in the process of creating both Culture and Ethnography. For him, "society creates itself sequentially and episodically, as a cosmological harmony" (1981:122), while Bruner argues that because "ethnography is embedded in the political process, dominant narratives are units of power as well as of meaning" (1986:19). The very origins of anthropology are related to Western colonialism, and much anthropological fieldwork is still conducted in politically volatile areas afflicted by its aftermath (Asad 1973; Berreman 1981:77; Fabian 1983; Marcus and Fischer 1986:34). Furthermore, the discourse of social science itself is part of corporate academic culture—the scholar must maneuver within an academic convention of depoliticized objectivity (K. Dwyer 1982:272; Rose 1986, 1987:24–25, 83). Therefore the nature of the anthropological project has been nostalgia, aiming to preserve "the pastoral," the way of life that was, the vanishing primitive, and save it in the text (J. Clifford 1986:112). As C. Wright Mills observed, however,

> The very enterprise of social science, as it determines fact, takes on political meaning. In a world of widely communicated nonsense, any statement of fact is of political and moral significance. All social scientists, by the fact of their existence, are involved in the struggle between enlightenment and obscurantism. In a world such as ours, to practice social science is, first of all, the politics of truth. (1959:178)

One might deduce from the above that the creative process immanent in both culture and the ethnography that invents it is leashed by the fact that both are embedded in global political processes and the academic politics of textual representation. Perhaps not only Wagner (1981) but other ethnographers who view culture from an interpretive perspective have overlooked this political embeddedness (Marcus and Fischer 1986:84) because "culture works very effectively to make invisible and even 'impossible' the actual *affiliations* that exist between the world of ideas and scholarship, on the one hand, and the world of brute politics, corporate and state power, and military force on the other" (Said 1983:8).

Ethnographic Rhetoric. How was I going to textualize my field experience? Three major problems impeded the movement of my field experience into ethnographic text. One was the fact that, because I opposed the military occupations, I found it impossible to maintain the "scientific objective gaze." Along with this, I also found that I had to impose some measure of self-censorship on the textualization process for the safety of the Mzeinis who opened their lives to me (cf. Myers 1986:140; Swedenburg 1989). The second problem was that, when one produces a rigorous text about another culture, one has to assume a structured distance between the field subject, the scholarly writing process, and the peer reading and reviewing of the final text (Strathern 1987). But I was interested in "underscor[ing] . . . the ongoingness of life and the open character of ongoing actions . . . [in experiences] arising directly out of the flow of life, with little or no explicit preparation" (Abrahams 1986:49, 63). I wished the text to maintain this feeling of immediacy, flux, open-endedness, and fragmentariness and occurred when it was still in the experiential stage.

The third problem was that I did not want to speak only in my own scholarly voice. Since I had the final authority over what went into the text, I wanted to find a way to engage my voice with the voices of Mzeini men and women, while avoiding the poetically powerful exoticizations typical of the Western multivocal depictions of Other worlds (Fischer 1988:7; Hill 1986:94). I also wanted the text to be written in such a way that it could be translated back into Arabic, its language of origin, and be read by those about whom it was written (cf. K. Dwyer 1982; Price 1983:21–26; Rose 1987:5).

The solution to the voice problem was to transcribe, whenever appropriate to my purpose, a polyphony of voices, including my own, directly out of the raw material of my diary-style fieldnotes. In all chapters except this one, the historical review, and the conclusion, I chose to transcribe very strictly, as theater-script-like polyphonic dialogues, what the women or men said to better show the interactive, conversational process leading to the emergence of the allegorical personae. When necessary, I accompanied these lines by stage directions straight from my diary, to describe the pace, tone, mood, and gestures of the participants. In the shorter vignettes, however, I simply transcribed the speakers' words in quotation marks, and set them as dialogue within conventional narrative and descriptive prose. Since "the ethnographer is a midwife, as it were, who delivers and articulates what is vernacularly expressed" (Marcus 1986:180), I felt that these textual strategies would preserve the immediacy and flux of the original lived experience. I interrupted the dialogic flow only to explain the Mzeinis' everyday assumptions that might be unfamiliar to readers.

I translated and transcribed into English many of the stormy conversations that preceded the allegorical emergences of the seven characters who are the focus of this book. But I kept my ethnographic authority by carefully selecting what lines of dialogue were to be included in the text. To protect the Mzeinis' identities, I changed the names of people and sometimes the names of places, but not times or dates, because many of these had political or religious significance, especially around the time of the Camp David Accord, or Muslim holidays. I also conflated fragments of several different dialogues on the same subject, to make it even harder to trace particular quotations to particular individuals. In addition, five of the seven characters' allegories consist of two or three conflated fragments from performances by different individuals acting the character's role at different times. In spite of these measures taken to protect the Mzeinis, every phrase spoken in the dialogue was spoken by an actual person.

In the case of one character, when I wanted to describe an organizer of the Sinai narcotics smuggling period (1952–1972), I felt quite insecure in selecting details, because I feared that some ex-smugglers might suffer retribution. So I hiked to the ex-smuggler's oasis, weighed down by a backpack full of all my indexed notes about smuggling. Together we conjured up out of my field data a fictional smuggler, an invented character who had in him many elements of a typical ex-smuggler, even though he was heavily censored by our joint effort. I include this composite as one of the seven characters to be described, interpreted, and analyzed in this book (cf. Schutz 1962:40–47).

During my 1987 visit to the South Sinai, I read large portions of the ethnographic text in progress to some of the Mzeinis who had participated in the events and asked them to criticize it and tell me if they had any reservations about it. In 1988 I read to the Mzeinis some different and nearly finished chapters of my work, but anonymously, along with other Israeli texts about their lives, in order to elicit their critique (Lavie and Rouse 1988). Comparing my work to the other ethnographies, the old man said, "All these people write *about* us, about what *they* think we are, except one—the one that just writes us, exactly as we talk, and laugh, and gesture [with our hands], just as we are." From his wily smile and a process of elimination, I deduced that the one that just wrote them was I.

In the course of the writing, I noticed that my authorial voice was gradually splitting into two antiphonal voices, speaking for two distinct parts of my Self. First was Smadar, the ordinary human woman, participating in the lived experience of the Mzeina. It was possible for Smadar to gradually merge herself into the tight-knit family and friendship networks of the Mzeinis because since infancy she had been surrounded by scores of aunts, uncles, cousins, and friends of the family on her Yemeni mother's side—an Arab social construct with fluid boundaries around people's selves. I could not conceive of my basic relationships with the Mzeina as professional "informant-researcher" relationships, because to me the Mzeinis were dear (adoptive) relatives and friends (cf. Joseph 1988:34). I refer to this Smadar throughout the text by using the personal pronoun "I." Then there was the Western-trained anthropologist, observing the activities in the field as if from a distance and comparing them to other parts of her data and to other cultures she had read about in anthropological books and articles. In hindsight I can trace the anthropologist's self not only to my academic training but also to my father's Northern European roots. Being from a small family himself (most of which was exterminated in the ghettos of Lithuania), my father brought me up to appreciate rugged individualism and rigorous critical inquiry. Throughout the text I refer to my individuated scholarly self as "the anthropologist." Sometimes in the text, Smadar and the anthropologist converse with each other. At times, the anthropologist instructs Smadar how to conduct herself and her research to optimize the rate of data return, but at other times, Smadar has to remind the anthropologist that there is much more to the "field" than fieldwork.

Another problem in textualizing the field experience was verb tense. Traditionally, anthropological data, interpretation, and cross-cultural analysis are all written in the present tense. But since what was true of the Mzeina in 1975 or 1985 may not be eternally "true" of them, I have chosen to use the past tense whenever I provide anthropological interpretation or analysis. All the dialogic narratives, however, and some other narrations of the field experience, are in the present tense because I want the theater-like script to preserve the immediacy of the field. On the whole, I hope this ethnography "will be a text of the physical, the spoken, and the performed, an evocation of quotidian experience, and palpable reality that uses everyday speech to suggest what is ineffable, not through abstraction, but by means of the concrete. It will be a text to read not with the eyes alone, but with the ears in order to hear 'the voices of the pages'" (Tyler 1986:136).

MZEINA ALLEGORIES OF BEDOUIN IDENTITY UNDER OCCUPATION

The Mzeini paradox of identity was that they could not maintain an independent Bedouin identity beyond the fragments incarnated in allegory, because they were disenfranchised on their own land by continual military occupations. This paradox of identity rarely surfaced in ordinary daily conversation, but if it did, the conversation quickly turned into a heated debate. The ironic paradox was articulated only in the presence of those charismatic creative individuals who might fuse themselves, as persons, with the persona of one of the seven allegory-telling characters. Perhaps the creative individuals served as catalysts for such articulation because each of them was, in him- or herself, a metonymy, reifying the paradoxical tribal reality under occupation. Perhaps they also served as safety valves, because they could playfully act out the tribe's pent-up bitterness about the harshness and absurdity of Mzeini daily life.

Whenever the paradox of Mzeini Bedouin identity was indeed thematized, a second set of paradoxes invariably emerged. Characters belonging to the center of social acceptability, such as the Sheikh, the Symbolic Battle Coordinator, and the Ex-Smuggler, paradoxically found that, due to the external political-economic situation, they could make only marginal contributions to the daily flow of Mzeina life. Their stories expressed the fact that storytelling itself was the most effective form of power they could exert. On the other hand, oddball characters like the Fool, the Madwoman, the Old Woman, and The One Who Writes Us, who were on the margins of Mzeini social acceptability, paradoxically were able to enact allegories that palpably expressed the central issues of Mzeini identity under occupation.

When these two sets of paradoxes—the Mzeina vis-à-vis the occupation, and the character's centrality/marginality vis-à-vis the Mzeina—arose, a person who might enact an allegorical persona sometimes chose to remain silent, and the group might even disperse. At other times, however, such a person would spontaneously speak up, fusing him- or herself with the persona of his or her character-type, and the allegory-telling voice emerged from those fragile interstitial moments of bitter silence that often follow a heated debate. As a liminal persona, who paradoxically conjoined the Bedouin Self with the occupier's Other, the person-cum-persona was able to transcend world politics by means of local poetics, and thus succeeded in forcing the audience to confront hard truths that recomposed the way they conceptualized the political situation outside the framework of the performance. Playfully transforming a quotidian event from his or her own life into an allegory, the teller recounted it following the conventions of the traditional Mzeina "once-upon-a-time" genre of tales, and thus became an interlocutor with the tribal pantheon of Sheikhs, Symbolic Battle Coordinators, Madwomen, Fools, Old Women, Ex-Smugglers, and Anthropologists from the reservoir of communal memory—allegorical types belonging to the tribal folkloric genres that differentiated the tribe's history from that of its occupiers.

Michael Meeker has suggested that "the Bedouin narrative provides a more insightful analysis of the character of the tribe . . . than can be found in the writings of anthropologists" (1979:92). I agree, and after reviewing the recent history of military occupations of the Sinai in chapter 2, I present in chapters 3 through 9 the narratives of the Mzeinis' daily lived experience, which I shared with them in a "we relationship" (Schutz 1962:253, 316), from my awkward position of being caught up in a culture I was rigorously trying to observe.

Each chapter from 3 to 9 starts with a brief anthropological interpretation of the institutional and situational paradoxes forming the background of the character's emergence into his or her allegorical performance. Several vignettes follow, the main one of which is the script of an argument that leads to an individual person's taking upon him- or herself the allegory-telling persona of his or her particular character-type. Each of the vignettes reveals how deeply the experience of being occupied has permanently penetrated even the most intimate spaces of Mzeini private lives. For the Mzeinis, being occupied has become an inner state of mind and soul.

Chapter 10 is an abstract theoretical analysis of the dynamics of typecasting and allegorizing associated with the performances in the previous chapters. Using examples from these, I discuss the poetics arising out of the military occupations that shape Mzeini Bedouin identity. I conclude by arguing that the narratives told by these seven characters may be seen as a processual rise and fall of Bedouin identity in the form of allegory. I hope to show how the seven allegories revealed and temporarily solved the paradoxes immanent in both the structure of each character-cum-persona, and in the Mzeina political relation to their occupiers. I further argue that each character's allegorical performance, because it imposed a nonnegotiable "ritual process" (Turner 1969) on the audience, provided a set of specific answers to existential and organizational dilemmas characteristic of Mzeina life under occupation. This reconstruction of tribal tradition through allegorical performance salvaged the Bedouin identity of the Mzeina from the cultural infringement of Israeli and Egyptian political and economic forces, which tribesmembers could confront directly only at great risk to their lives. The Mzeinis spontaneously transcended their suffering from global political strife by creating local improvised performances that bravely criticized both their occupiers and themselves, thereby enacting, by and for themselves, their own poetics of the military occupation.

2
BEDOUIN IN LIMBO, OR DEVELOPERS OBSERVED

Israeli and Egyptian Policies for the South Sinai Bedouin

"They want an end to the spread of settlements across their land. They want their land back, finally. They want to be free to move about with their flocks from pasture to pasture as they used to." It is not too late to put a stop to the lecture. Instead I hear my voice rise in tone and abandon myself regretfully to the intoxication of anger. . . . "Shall I tell you what I sometimes wish? I wish that these barbarians would rise up and teach us a lesson, so that we would learn to respect them. We think of the country here as ours, part of our Empire—our outpost, our settlement, our market center. But these people, these barbarians don't think of it like that at all. We have been here more than a hundred years, we have reclaimed land from the desert and built irrigation works and planted fields and built solid homes and put a wall around our town, but they still think of us as visitors, transients. There are old folk alive among them who remember their parents telling them about this oasis as it once was: a well-shaded place by the side of the lake with plenty of grazing even in winter. That is how they still think about it, perhaps how they still see it, as though not one spadeful of earth had been turned or one brick laid on top of another."

J. M. COETZEE
Waiting for the Barbarians

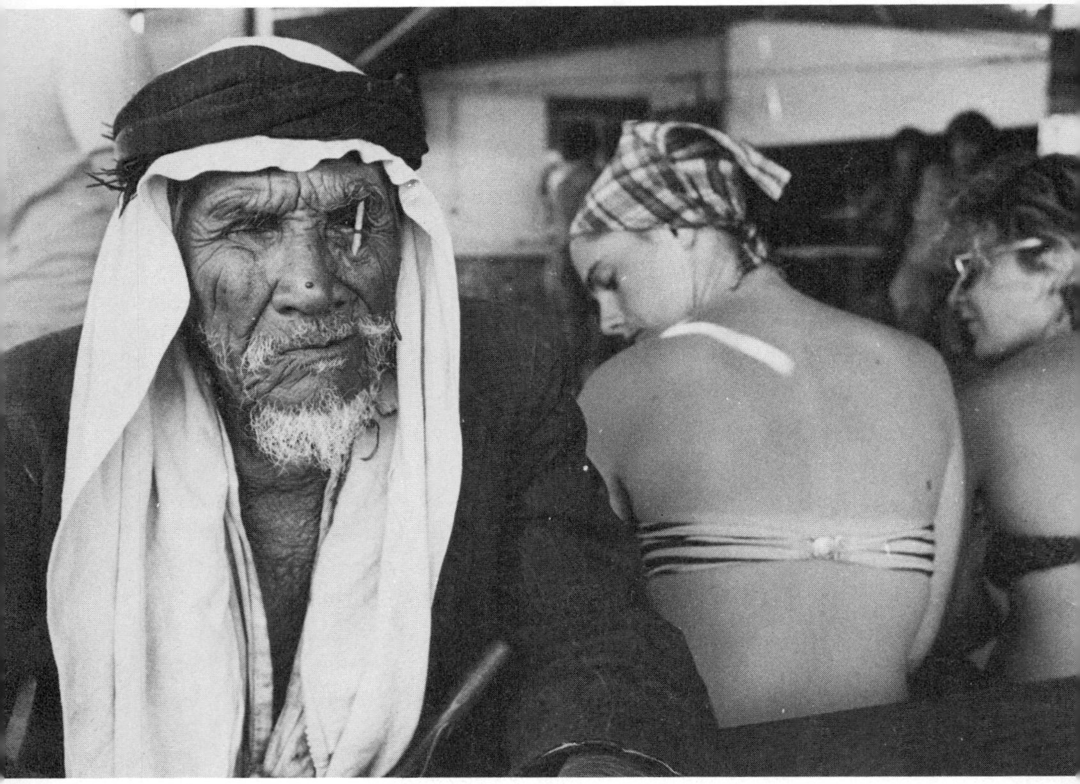

ZEIDĀN *AL-SHĒBA* (THE GRAY-HAIRED)

It was a summer day in 1976. Zeidān *al-Shēba* (the gray-haired) was sitting in his usual place between the crowded cafe of *moshāv* Neviʿōt (an Israeli agricultural cooperative) and the asphalt parking lot where overloaded tourist buses stopped. Zeidān was elaborately dressed in the traditional manner of the Mzeina Bedouin. As he sat impassively, tourists wandered by, wearing only bathing suits, and took his picture. They were attracted by his exotic costume and were astonished by the matchstick inserted vertically between his eyebrow and the wrinkles under his lower eyelid, to prop his right eye open. Some of the picture-takers dropped coins in front of him. He casually picked them up and slipped them into his vest pocket. Fixing his gaze on the nearby sea, he spoke to me at a leisurely pace:

"I was born in Nuwēbʿat Mzeina shortly after World War I. My father earned his living by making charcoal from *ratam* (broom) bushes (*retama roetam*, Latin) near ʿEin Khuḍra. One of my first jobs was in an orange grove near Jaffa. We used to ride our camels as far as Beer Sheba and go by foot from there. When the job was finished, we would use our wages to buy stockpiles of rice, flour, cooking oil, and sugar from the market in Beer Sheba and bring them back to the Sinai.

"When I was a little older and the border with Palestine was closed because of Israel, I worked in the shipyards in Suez. I used to repair and paint the ships going through the canal and stayed there three years without seeing my family. Then I went back to Nuwēbʿat Mzeina and got married. I spent a whole year with my wife, and we migrated with our few animals and made some money selling charcoal. Then I went back to Suez and worked another year. I came back to Nuwēbʿat Mzeina only for the Ramaḍān month and for the date harvest.

"I kept working like this until the war of 1956 broke out and the Egyptian border was closed. There was no work then. For a whole year we lived only on my orchards and on the staples we had stockpiled. Early in 1957 the large fishing boats arrived. I used to fish for an Egyptian boss in the Gulf of Suez. My wife and children moved to the Abu-Rodeis area. We could get food there but not many jobs. Sometimes I used to work a little while in the oil fields and manganese mines, but there wasn't always work. So I invested some of my time and money in caring for and expanding my orchard in ʿEin Khuḍra, and also started a new orchard on the Tih Plateau.

"Then came the war of 1967. For a whole year we had to live only on the staples I had accumulated and on my orchard. After that my eldest son went to work for the *Yahūd* (Jews) on the new road connecting Sharm al-Sheikh and Eilat. We all went back to Nuwēbʿat Mzeina. That's where the jobs were, and that's where we would buy our food. My son got to be a foreman on the road crew because he was a good worker. He bought an old pickup truck with the money he earned, and now he uses it to take tourists from Dahab to the Santa Katarina monastery. He's a really good tour guide.

"I'm getting old. The tourists come to take pictures of the matchstick in my eye and that's how I make my living. I still take care of my orchards in ʿEin Khuḍra. The Israeli doctors sent me to a big hospital near Tel Aviv to have an operation for my eyes. I can keep my eyes open now without using matchsticks to prop up the lids. They even gave me glasses. But I put the matchstick back in anyway so I won't lose my income. Who knows what the tourists see in it."

"But you are a Bedouin. Why bother with all these jobs when you could have more orchards and animals?"

Zeidān shrugs. "*Jebāl Sīna—ma lehum ʿaida wa-mafīsh minhum faida.*" The Sinai mountains—good for naught: can't be used, can't be bought.

*

Zeidān's life history was the consequence of a collision between the ecological and social realities of the South Sinai peninsula and the policies imposed on the region by two occupying governments. To review the historical sequence discussed in the first chapter, during the fifty years of Arab-Israeli conflict, the occupier of the South Sinai has changed no fewer than five times. From the 1940s until 1952, the Sinai was under the rule of King Farouq of Egypt. From 1952 to 1956 it was controlled by the Arab Republic of Egypt under Gamal Abdul Nasser. In 1956 the Israelis, backed by Britain and France, occupied it, but soon returned it to Egypt, which, aided by the Soviets, held on to it until 1967, when it was again occupied by Israel. In eight stages between 1974 and 1982, following Henry Kissinger's shuttle diplomacy and Jimmy Carter's Camp David talks, Israel again returned the Sinai to Egypt. Policies effected by the Egyptians were altered by the

Israelis, and vice versa. The South Sinai Bedouin have seldom had a voice in formulating any of these policies, which have nevertheless often drastically altered their lives.

This chapter documents and interprets how Egyptian and Israeli development policies affected the Mzeina Bedouin of the South Sinai, and how the Bedouin responded. I argue that the broader economic and political interests of the Egyptian and Israeli governments have generated their Sinai policies. Yet Sinai and its inhabitants imposed ecological and social limits on the implementation of these policies. To overcome these limits, each government had to try to redirect the wage-earning activities of the South Sinai population.[1]

South Sinai Bedouin economic activities were of two kinds: domestic and wage labor. Wage labor was the main source of income; the domestic economy served as a safety net for surviving the conditions caused by political and economic oscillation between Egypt and Israel (Marx 1977*a*, 1980; Perevolotsky 1979, 1981). With every change in administration, the Bedouin had to adapt to the new policies imposed on them. In both the Egyptian and Israeli cases, government strategy for implementing policy was to coordinate force with negotiation. The forms that negotiation and compulsion took were congruent with the structure of bureaucracy in each respective state. Thus each administration won the acquiescence of the South Sinai Bedouin and then established rapport with them. Moreover, each government thereby earned legitimacy and approbation from its own public.

ECOLOGICAL BACKGROUND

The South Sinai is the mountainous southern portion of the Sinai peninsula. It covers a triangular area of approximately 17,000 square kilometers and has well-defined natural boundaries: on the north, the Tih Plateau; on the west, the Gulf of Suez; and on the east, the Gulf of ʿAqaba. The Ras-Muḥammad juncture of the two gulfs at the tip of the peninsula opens into the Red Sea. The arid, mountainous country is cleft by many *wadī*s (dry river beds), providing routes that lead from coast to coast. A few wadis are accessible by motor transport, but others can be traversed only with camels or donkeys, or on foot. In 1979, when I completed my initial four-year period of fieldwork, only two asphalt roads existed. One, paved by the Egyptian government in the late 1950s, ran along the coast of the Gulf of Suez. The other, built by the Israelis between 1970 and 1972, ran along the Gulf

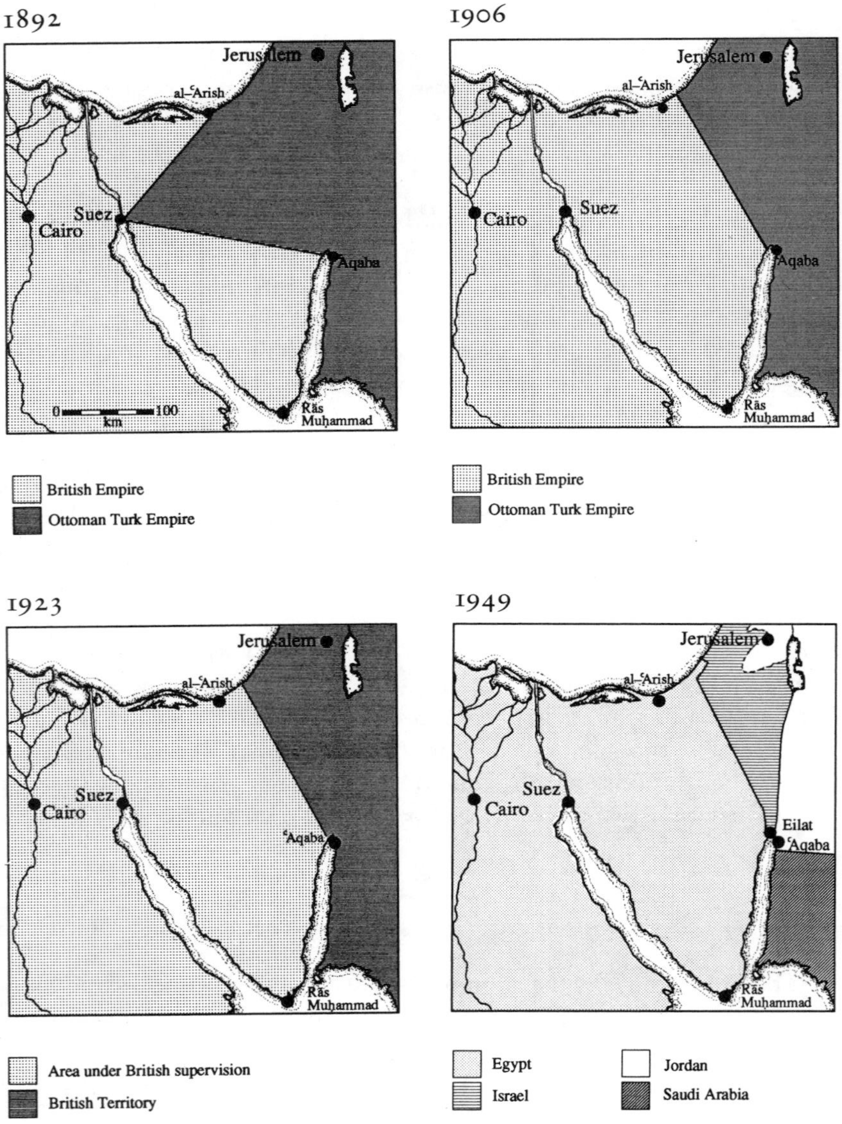

SOUTH SINAI INTERNATIONAL BORDER SHIFTS: 1892–1982

1956

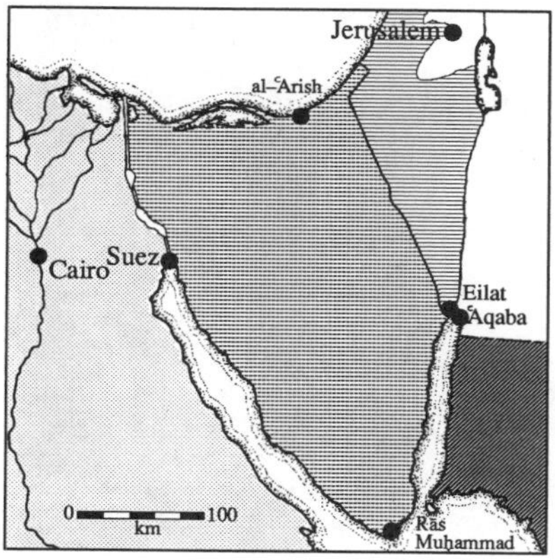

1967

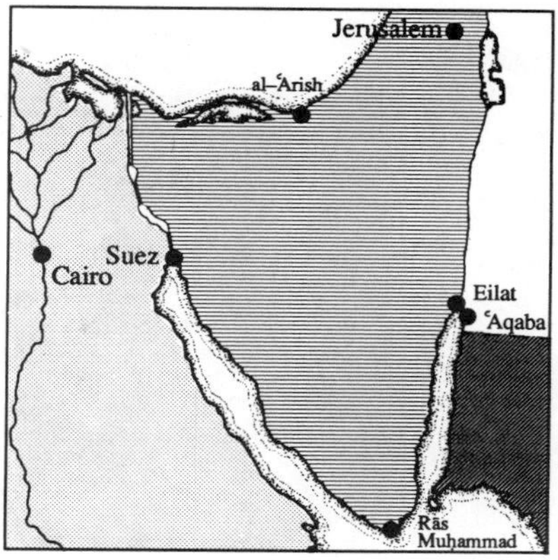

1970—ALLON PLAN

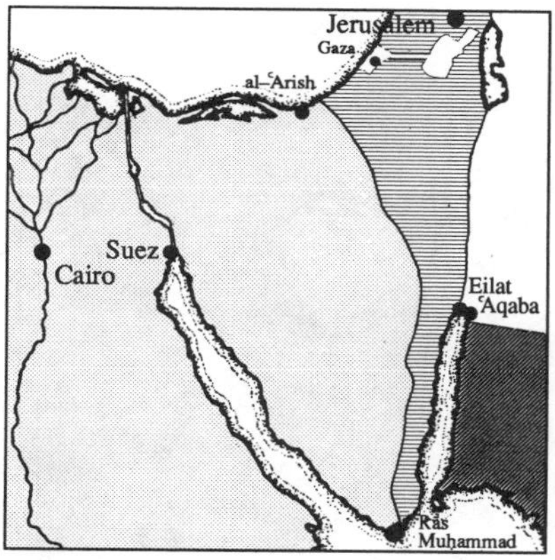

24 OCTOBER 1973 TRUCE

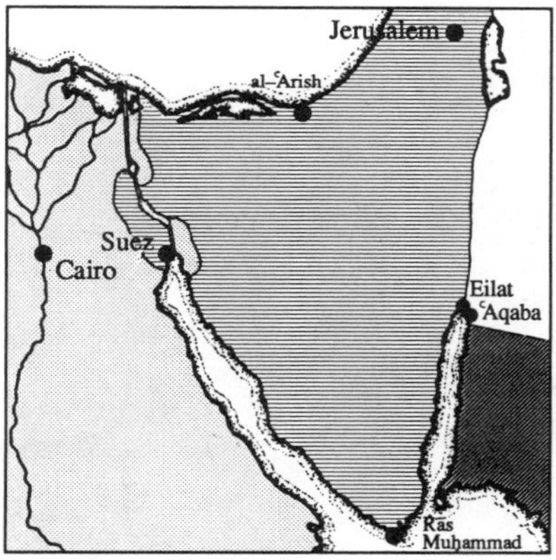

Egypt
Israel
Jordan
Saudi Arabia
Territory temporarily occupied by Israel

JANUARY 1974—
SEPARATION OF FORCES

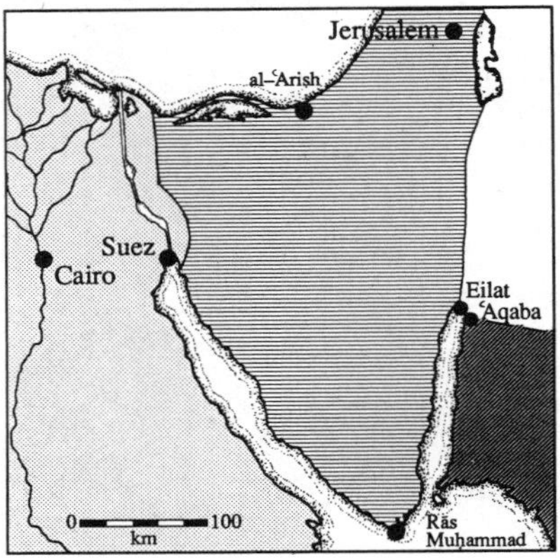

4 SEPTEMBER 1975— KISSINGER
DISENGAGEMENT AGREEMENT

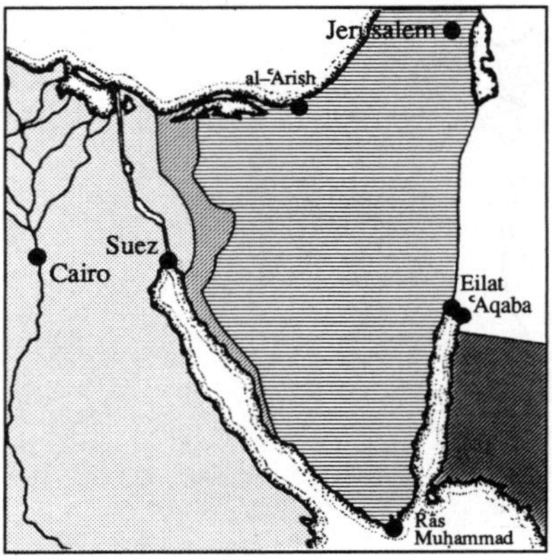

THE CAMP DAVID ACCORD

MAY 1979

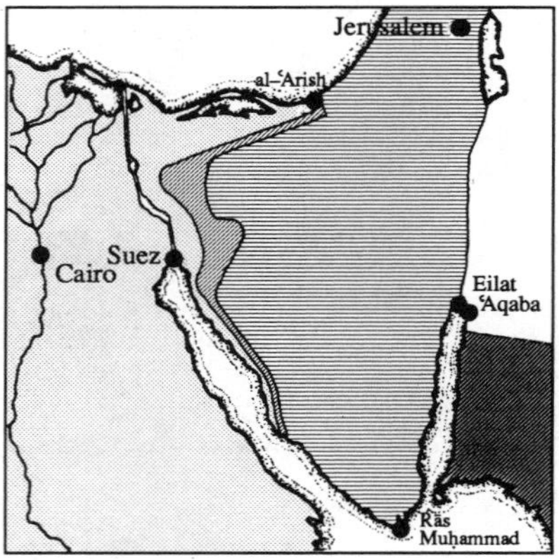

JUNE 1979

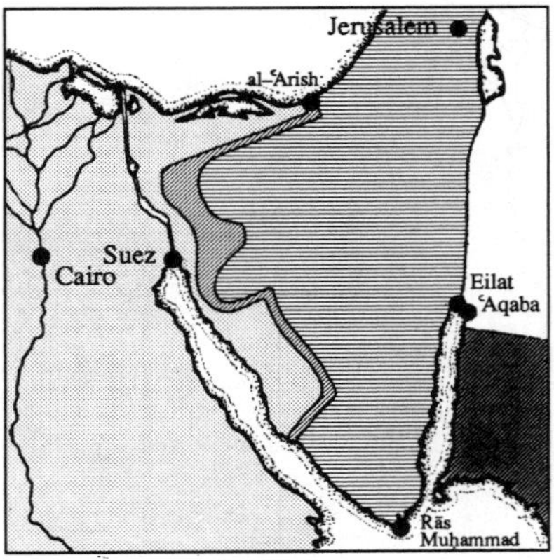

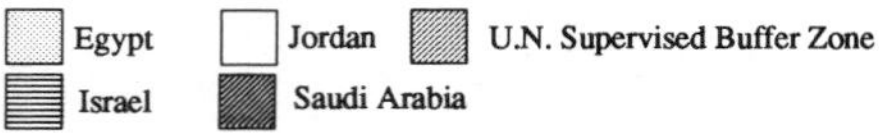

AUGUST 1979

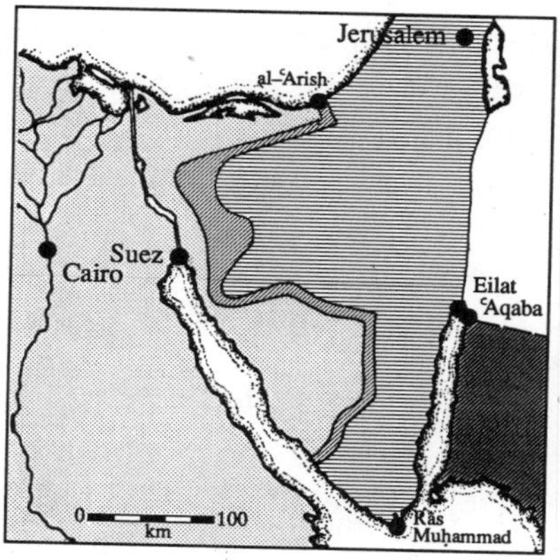

OCTOBER 1979

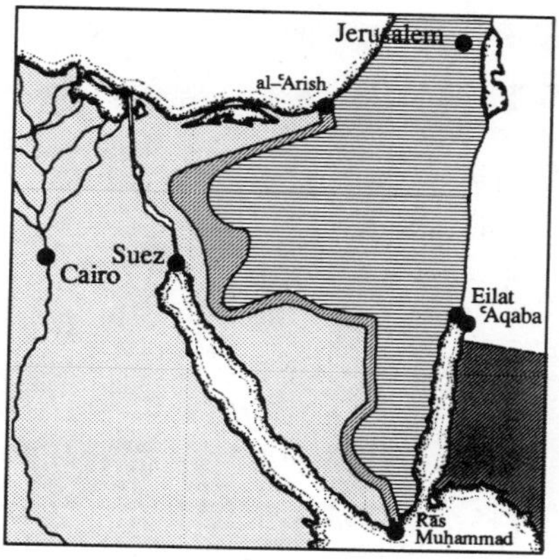

JANUARY 1980

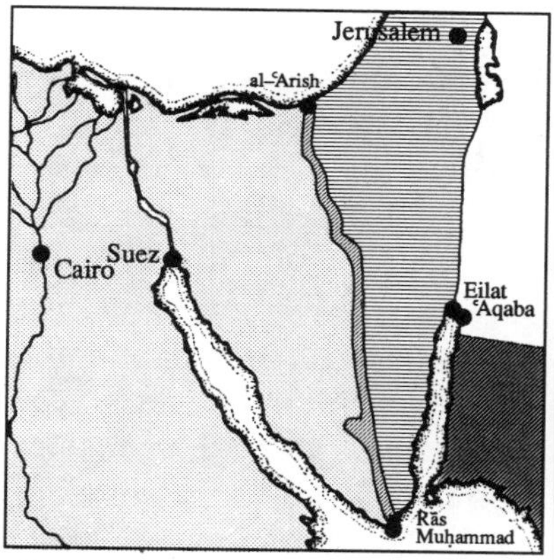

25 APRIL 1982

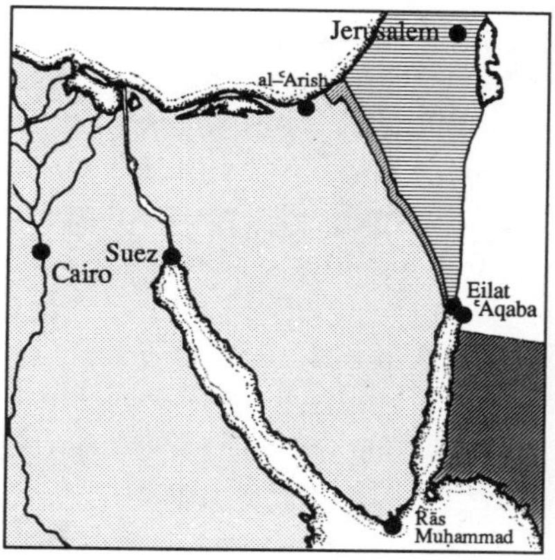

Egypt
Jordan
U.N. Supervised Buffer Zone
Israel
Saudi Arabia

of ʿAqaba coast. After the Sinai was returned to Egypt in 1982, the Egyptians paved over two other dirt roads with asphalt. One connected Abu-Rodeis with Nuwēbʿa through Wadi Firān, Santa Katarina, and ʿEin Khuḍra. The other connected Nuwēbʿa with Suez through the Tih Plateau.

Each time the gray-haired Zeidān crossed the peninsula from the East Coast, he first saw the high cliffs falling precipitously into the ʿAqaba Gulf. He then had to travel up steep, rocky wadis and pass through a ring of mountains 800 to 2,000 meters high to reach the lowest levels of the Highland Watershed Plateaus, 800 to 1,200 meters high. Above the plateaus tower the highest mountains, those of the Santa Katarina region, 2,700 meters high and at the very heart of the South Sinai. Traveling farther west, Zeidān would come to the desolate Gaʿ, a gutter 15 to 20 kilometers wide filled with dust and pebbles, separating the steep drop of the peninsula's western mountains from the Gulf of Suez.

Rainfall is scant and irregular. The average annual rainfall is only ten millimeters, but the region can go several years with no rain at all and then suddenly suffer a tremendous flash flood. It sweeps down from the high watershed plateaus to both gulfs, uprooting trees, dislodging boulders, tearing big chunks of asphalt out of the roads, drowning camels, donkeys, sheep and goats, and even people like Zeidān's old mother who are not quick enough to run or climb up the wadi cliff walls. The precipitation in the highest mountains at the very heart of the peninsula is more regular, averaging sixty millimeters per year. The temperatures in the coastal lower elevations range from 15°C in winter to 43°C in summer. At high altitudes, in contrast, winter temperatures can drop as low as −15°C, and in summer reach only 26°C. The peninsula's relative humidity is very low, especially in summer, when it can be below 10 percent. Because of the latitude, the sun is often directly overhead (Assaf and Kessler 1976; Eshbal 1976).

Vegetation is sparse and mostly perennial, and, due to the hot dry climate, specializes in uniquely effective techniques for water storage and regulation. After sufficient precipitation, a blanket of short-lived annual plants springs up on the Tih Plateau, its surrounding sand dunes, and other high-altitude areas (Danin 1978). But due to the undependable precipitation patterns, Zeidān and the other Bedouin could not trust these skimpy pastures to support a pastoral economy. The average family flock consisted of four to six goats, two or three sheep, and at times one camel (Glassner 1974).

The majority of dependable water sources are wells the Bedouin have dug to reach the water table. After several rainless years water table might drop until some wells go dry. After a flash flood, on the other hand, natural waterholes might form in narrow shady pits in the normally dry tributary streambeds. Some hold water up to five years, if not used up by people (Issar 1980). A few wells have diesel-run mechanical pumps.

Most of the South Sinai soils are unsuitable for cultivation, even with irrigation. They cannot hold water because there is virtually no organic matter among the sandstone or igneous rock detritus composing them. Only in the Santa Katarina Mountains and in a few oases do the Bedouin cultivate small permanent orchards like Zeidān had, with fruit trees and vegetable garden plots, barely adequate to provide a subsistence living. Along Wadi Firān is the largest oasis on the peninsula—ten kilometers of densely planted date palm trees and orchards of both deciduous and tropical fruit trees. In 1979 the Firān Oasis had over fifty wells of sweet water; the water table could be reached almost anywhere around by digging three meters down. On the ʿAqaba Gulf coast are three large oases, Nuwēbʿa, Dahab, and Nabeg, situated on the large dry deltas of the three main wadis draining the high mountains of the peninsula toward the East Coast. The water table is quite high, but the water is salty—minimum concentration of sodium chloride is a thousand milligrams per liter (Kolton 1980). The largest oasis on the coast of the Gulf of Suez is al-Ṭūr, where the water table is also high, but the water is sweeter.

The fish population is not sufficient to support large-scale commercial fishing. The Gulf of ʿAqaba is the northernmost coral reef in the world, on the edge of the Desert Zone, only 200 kilometers south of the Mediterranean Zone. The gulf is isolated from the Red Sea by the shallow Straits of Ṭirān, no more than 200 meters deep, and therefore many of its spectacular corals are endemic species, growing only near the narrow coastal shelf, which drops into sheer depths, at places deeper than 2,000 meters. It has less plankton than any other sea in the world except the Sargasso, which means that this ecological zone has low biomass in general, and especially few larger fish suitable for human consumption (Dafni 1969; Fishelson and Philosoph 1981). The Gulf of Suez is slightly more productive.

At the heart of the peninsula is the Santa Katarina Monastery, reputed to have been continually occupied since the fifth century by Greek Orthodox monks (Tsafrir 1970). In the late 1970s between ten and twenty monks lived there, some permanently and some for a few years, all affiliated with the Greek Patriarch of Cairo. The monastery

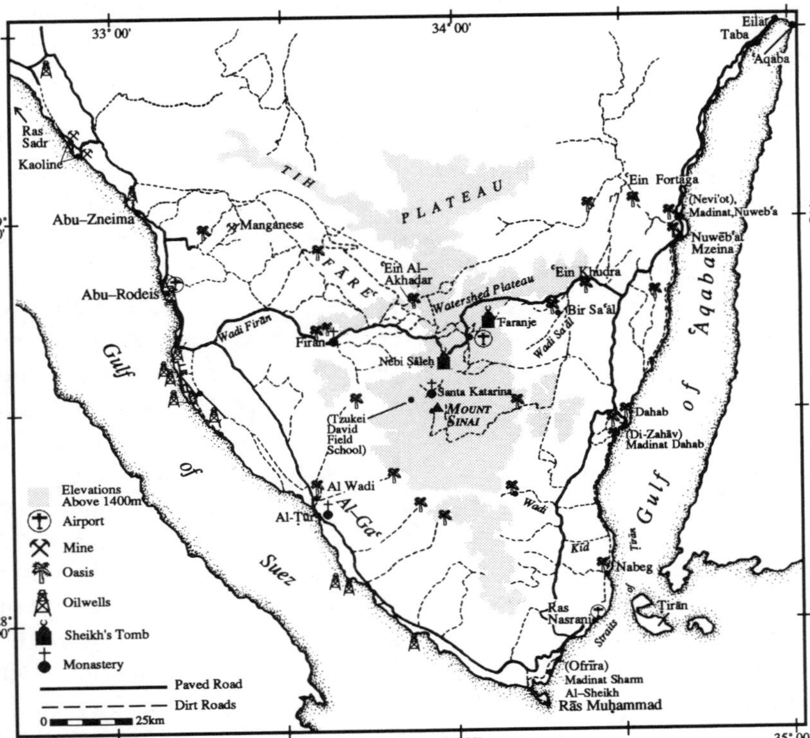

THE SOUTH SINAI PENINSULA

had two smaller branches, one in the Firān Oasis and the other (closed in 1967) in al-Ṭūr. The Bedouin consider this monastery to be the only stable foreign agency inside the Sinai.

TRIBAL STRUCTURE AND ORGANIZATION

The approximately 13,000 South Sinai Bedouin see themselves as members of a tribal alliance called Ṭawara, a name derived from the word *ṭūr*, meaning "mountain," but implying "the holy mountain," Mount Sinai. The tribes that compose the alliance are divided into two groups. The first group consists of the Mzeina tribe, about 5,000 people scattered throughout the South Sinai except near the monastery, with most living in the east, and on the shores of the Gulf of ʿAqaba and the Gulf of Suez; the ʿAleigāt tribe of about 2,100, residing mainly in the northwest of the peninsula, though some live in al-Ṭūr, or in the peninsula's southeast, or in Egypt; and the Ḥamāda, a tribe of around 550 that resides with the ʿAleigāt in the northwest. A very small tribe of 80, the Bani Wāṣel, at times joins this half of the alliance and at other times remains neutral; they live in al-Ṭūr and the southwestern mountains.

The other half of the Ṭawara alliance consists of the Wlād Saʿīd tribe of around 1,000 people, the Garārsha tribe of around 1,250, and the Ṣawālḥa tribe of around 500. The Garārsha and Ṣawālḥa control most of the mountain passes and routes from the Firān Oasis north and northwest to the Suez Gulf. Most of their members live in Egypt proper, west of Suez Canal. The Wlād Saʿīd control the mountain passes and routes from the Santa Katarina Monastery to the southwest and southeast.

According to the Mzeina myth of settlement, these two tribal groups warred against each other until 400 years ago, when, with the help of the monastery, they negotiated a truce. Despite the rigid assignment of most Bedouin to one or the other of these two groups, members of both were relatively intermingled in space and were linked by marriage and local relationships. Two tribes were not assigned to either of these two major divisions. The Jebaliyya, a tribe of around 1,450, were said to have originated as monastery servants, allowed to farm monastery lands, but not to own them (Ben David 1981). The other tribe was the Ḥeweiṭāt, about 450 people who lived in the Firān, al-Ṭūr, and the northwest. They had fled a feud in northwest Saudi Arabia early in the 1930s. Despite the fact that these two tribes were not traditionally partners in the mythical Ṭawara alliance, they were accepted in everyday life and as proper marriage partners for all the other tribes.

All tribes of the alliance except the Mzeina had a more or less defined territory composed of a small exclusive core plus marginal areas shared with neighboring tribes (Marx 1977b; Nir 1988). Having no core, the Mzeina considered their territory to be the whole South Sinai peninsula (except for the Santa Katarina Monastery area). Tribal dominance over an area was shown by the fact that only its own members had the right to use its mountain passes, build permanent structures (anything other than a tent), dig wells, use other water sources without permission, and own date trees within the oases. Most of the members of a tribe stayed within the territory claimed by the tribe. One could not go far in the Sinai without crossing a tribal boundary, and yet one shortly would be back in the territory of the tribe whose land one had just left, so irregular were the territories (Murray 1935; Shoukair 1916).[2]

It is surprising that, though the South Sinai Bedouin considered themselves pastoral nomads, they departed from the otherwise typical practice of defining territorial dominance through access to pastures. Every Ṭawara member was permitted to send his daughters to graze his flocks wherever he wished on Ṭawara land, but not to build any structure more permanent than a tent on lands not of his own tribe. This was another indication that the Ṭawara were not the typical classic Arab nomadic pastoralists. Many Mzeinis confirmed this with their oft-repeated remark, "We are not like the rest of 'em, The Bedouin."

Only the Mzeina, largest of the tribes, were spread almost everywhere throughout the South Sinai, and they gave as the boundaries of their territory the natural boundaries of the South Sinai. According to their myth, they first settled on the East Coast upon their arrival in Sinai, probably around the seventeenth century, but through intertribal marriages and by purchasing shares in date trees in the various oases, they acquired other rights. During my period of research their dominance over strategic mountain passes and wadi routes throughout the peninsula, either exclusively or in alliance with other tribes, was generally acknowledged.

When I asked Mzeinis how they conceived of Bedouin organization, they responded with the ideal type of a segmentary lineage system (Evans-Pritchard 1940). Each tribal segment was represented in a tribal "supreme court" composed of three judges.

Mzeinis also recognized a second mode of organization, however, which they associated with governmental administrative agencies, both Egyptian and Israeli. For administrative purposes, external regimes as far back as the Ottoman empire have utilized the post of sheikh and appointed respected leaders to such posts. Despite their official position, however, sheikhs as such were not respected or recognized as societal leaders by the Bedouin themselves.

A third form of organization also existed. When asked to describe residential patterns, Mzeinis divided the South Sinai into geographical districts, each with its own name.

When I asked individual Mzeinis to explain how these modes of organization worked in daily life, some of them threw up their hands and said resignedly, "Oh, God! Mzeinis are scattered all over the world," or "Mzeina, like goats—all over the place." Probably they could not define their social organization because they were intertwined simultaneously in many different organizational networks based on dyadic relationships: kinship, marriage, neighborhood, smuggling partnership, wage work, friendship. These networks were ego-centered and the only thing they had in common was precariousness (Hart 1970).

LIFE IN THE SOUTH SINAI UNTIL 1956

Prior to the 1956 war, life in the South Sinai was shaped almost exclusively by the ecological and social factors described above. The Egyptian government had not implemented policies that significantly affected the Bedouin. If anything, Bedouin contacts with Egypt were initiated by the Bedouin themselves, due to their need for paid employment. During the British Mandate over Palestine and Egypt, for example, Zeidān went first to Jaffa and after the 1948 war spent three years working in Suez. Other men went to the Nile Valley and delta for the same purpose. Still others worked in the Egyptian quarantine station in al-Ṭūr, open only during the months of pilgrimage to Mecca.

Until 1956 many Bedouin still partially followed the traditional pastoral migratory cycle throughout the peninsula, as Zeidān did. During the summer portion of the cycle, coastal fishing groups would exchange dried fish for dates and other fruits grown further inland by Bedouin who cultivated gardens. During the fall and winter, Bedouin would make charcoal from acacia trees (*acacia rediana*, Latin) and ratam (broom) bushes. This would either be consumed locally or sold in al-Ṭūr or Suez (Al-Jabarty 1879, vol. 4:315; Rabinowitz 1985).

Due to the relative absence of Egyptian agents in the South Sinai before the 1956 war, the role of the Santa Katarina Monastery in providing medical care and in mediating between the Bedouin and the outside world was greater than after 1956 (Field 1948; Forsyth and Sisson 1964). Thus the problem of government policy implementation did not arise.

EGYPTIAN POLICIES AND BEDOUIN RESPONSE: 1956-1967

It is striking that no development policies dealing with the land of Sinai have ever been formulated without the stimuli of destructive conflict and war. In 1956, as in later wars, the plans for Sinai development were in part a means of emphasizing the value of the peninsula to the Egyptian public (and later to the Israeli public), and thus justifying the military costs of acquiring it.

Egyptian development policies were constrained by the geographical features of the South Sinai. A new asphalt road was paved along the West Coast to connect the city of Suez with Sharm al-Sheikh. This route was chosen because it was close to Egypt and because its level terrain presented the fewest and least complex engineering problems. The road was used for transporting ores and was also of strategic value for moving troops to Sharm al-Sheikh in the event of conflict with Israel.

Development took the form of mineral and petroleum exploitation and was largely carried out by private Egyptian companies. The manganese and kaolin mines at Umm-Bujma and Ras-Malᶜab, which had been operated sporadically on a very small scale in previous years, were dramatically expanded with foreign aid from Yugoslavia and the Soviet Union (Glassner 1974). Six oil fields in the Abu-Rodeis/Ras-Sadr region were discovered and exploited. But the search for minerals and oil was not carried into the more distant and inaccessible districts. The opening of these enterprises constituted a redirection of Bedouin wage earning. Many men like Zeidān, who had previously gone to Egypt for long-term employment, could now seek paid jobs inside the South Sinai, albeit only along the northwest coast. Opportunities for the South Sinai Bedouin to work were reduced, however, by competition from Egyptian and Sudanese migrant workers, who had come to the South Sinai because of job shortages in their own countries. Egyptian policy encouraged importing these migrants into the Sinai as a way to reduce unemployment and its attendant political unrest in volatile areas such as the Nile Valley and the Sudan, Egypt's immediate neighbor to the south. Heavy manual labor was done mainly by the Sudanese—especially tall, muscular young men from the South Sudan. The local Bedouin refused it because it was low paying and did not help them build socially useful networks within the Sinai. The better-paying skilled jobs were taken by Egyptians who had the necessary qualifications. Thus the Bedouin found themselves in an occupational limbo despite Egyptian efforts to redirect their labor.

Another aspect of Egyptian policy dealt with smugglers. Before 1967 the South Sinai was the site of a lucrative narcotics traffic. Until 1952 drugs had been smuggled into Egypt by the northern Bedouin from Jordan and Saudi Arabia via the Negev and the North Sinai. After 1952, when the Socialist revolution overthrew Egypt's King Farouq, Gamal Abdul Nasser fortified the whole North Sinai against Israeli invasion, so the drug traffic shifted to the rugged South Sinai, virtually inaccessible to large military vehicles. As a result of the 1956 war, smuggling became even more attractive because United Nations authorities in control of the ʿAqaba Gulf prohibited Egyptian military presence in the coastal region. Mzeini and other Bedouin entrepreneurs hired fellow tribesmen to transport hashish and opium by camel. The entrepreneurs came to form a new elite of wealthy Bedouin, and this led to a broad polarization of Bedouin society. The Egyptians wanted to eliminate smuggling because of its harmful consequences for Egypt. They could not eradicate it by force alone, not only because of the fiscal impossibility of patrolling the large inland regions, but also because the Bedouin's temptation to risk illegal smuggling was great due to their having so few feasible alternatives for employment. Hence the Egyptians governing the South Sinai felt they needed to negotiate further with the Bedouin and tie them more closely to their development projects. This was done with attempts to provide the Bedouin with some public services in the Abu-Rodeis area, such as a few clinics and schools, and several stores that sold subsidized basic food staples such as flour, sugar, rice, oil, and tea.

As Zeidān related, "My wife and children moved to the Abu-Rodeis area. We could get food there, but not many jobs." Indeed, a complex of shanty towns developed in the Abu-Rodeis area. A few residents in these towns (Sil Firān, Wadi ʿAbūra, Wadi Gharandal, and others) worked in the mines and oil fields. Most combined occasional work there with smuggling, commercial fishing (encouraged by the Egyptians), and domestic economic activities. Pastoral migration routes were changed to harmonize with smuggling.

The intent of the Egyptians to gain Bedouin compliance was frustrated by the persistence of smuggling and subsistence agriculture, two activities that permitted the Bedouin to make use of Egyptian services without surrendering their independence. Therefore the Egyptians employed a new negotiating tactic. They endowed the office of sheikh with more authority by using the sheikhly hierarchy to distribute a bimonthly charity called *ṣadaga*. The ṣadaga consisted of flour, sugar, cooking oil, and other basic staples provided by the United Nations Relief and Works Agency (UNRWA). Sheikhs were charged with transporting the ṣadaga from the Egyptian administrative center in Abu-Rodeis and then distributing it. Thus they were expected to act as mediators linking the administration with the inland population. Unfortunately, many sheikhs preferred to stay near Abu-Rodeis and sell these staples to the people of that area.

Using the sheikhs as intermediaries greatly retarded the development of dyadic ties between individual Bedouin and the various Egyptian administrative agencies and private companies. The Bedouin conceived of all Egyptians as belonging to a monolithic governing entity and referred to them as simply *al-ḥakūma* (the government). This notion of a monolithic "ḥakūma" was congruent with the structure and operation of Egyptian bureaucracy. The Egyptians also viewed the South Sinai population as an undifferentiated mass. They dealt with only a limited number of sheikhs and referred to the majority of the people with the collective noun *Bedu* (Bedouin). There was no direct communication between administrators and individual Bedouin. As the Bedouin put it in their own words, "The sheikhs lick the ass of the government (*al-mashāyikh yalḥasu mabʿar al-ḥakūma*)."

THE ISRAELI OCCUPATION OF THE SINAI: 1967–1979/1982

It took the Israeli government approximately one year to formulate policies for the South Sinai. During this period, Zeidān and others depended on their stockpiles of food and cash that they had built up from 1956 to 1967.

Soon after the 1967 war, Israeli interests in the South Sinai were primarily administrative. They felt it was necessary to gauge the extent of Bedouin nationalist identification with Egypt and then take steps to combat it. Israeli fears of a Bedouin nationalist resistance, however, proved groundless.

The first step toward creating a Bedouin administration was to discover what existing tribal structure could be useful to Israeli authorities. Traditional modes of Bedouin social organization were recognized as conditioning factors when the policy for the region was designed. Teams of Arabic-speaking Israeli internal security agents who were to specialize in military administration in the Israeli Occupied Territories visited Bedouin encampments throughout the peninsula. The agents found that legal rights and obligations among the Bedouin were ascribed to genealogically defined groups. Therefore the Israelis tried to elicit the names of potential leaders for all genealogical groups. Approximately thirty sheikhs were appointed. Some of the sheikhs who had held administrative office under the Egyptians were allowed to continue. Additional offices, however, were created by the Israelis. This meant a diminished share in power for each individual sheikh. Sheikhs who objected to this new arrangement decided to go to Egypt or Jordan, or were exiled. Some of the new sheikhs were appointed on the basis of their ties with the Israeli security services prior to 1967.

At the same time that Israeli military officials were building a new administrative network, they were also working to gain rapport with the Bedouin. They did this by personally distributing basic food staples to every encampment in the south. The sheikhs were no longer intermediaries in the distribution of the ṣadaga, now from the American charitable organization CARE.[3] Each nuclear family's share was given directly to its head, who carried a record book with him for collecting it. The Israelis also began a program of inoculation against epidemic diseases. The Bedouin, who had expected to be dealt with impersonally through the newly appointed sheikhs, were astonished by this new direct style. Some of the Israeli officials who contacted them were of very high rank. This informal style of negotiation was and still is typical of the Israeli bureaucratic structure and operation. The Bedouin responded to it by discarding the notion of "ḥakūma" (the monolithic government) and replacing it with the concept of a collection of governors and their military aides.

This preliminary administrative effort of organizing the new Israeli military government culminated, perhaps, in August 1968, when Zeidān and all other South Sinai Bedouin men were ordered by the military government to extend their hospitality to their new occupiers by gathering in Wadi Firān and holding a formal reception for the military governor and his staff. The reception was lushly described in the good old Orientalistic tradition (Said 1978) in *Yediʿōt Aḥaronōt*, the most widely circulated Israeli newspaper, in an article bearing the amazing title, "The Revelation on Mt. Sinai to the Twelve Tribes":

> A family atmosphere is gradually forming between our military men and the innocent tribes of the desert. . . . The chiefs of the Bedouin listen very well to the demands of the military. . . . The sheikhs feel indebted and grateful. They expressed this by presenting a feast for the masses in Wadi Firān, to which they invited the heads of the army and the military government.
>
> It does not matter that the military actually financed the feast, and even provided the lambs that were slaughtered, and organized anything that required organization for the mass gathering. One way or another, it was a very impressive spectacle, not only in the assembly of brotherhood between the occupiers and the occupied, but also in the fact that it was on the very occasion of the Bedouin tribes meeting each other. . . . They gathered in a valley enclosed on all sides by granite cliffs, and the speakers' voices echoed between its walls like voices from heaven. These pronouncing blessing, and those swearing to be wholeheartedly faithful, and promising without even being asked, "We will do and obey. . . ."
>
> Afterwards, a movie was screened for the generation of the wilderness, "The story of ʿAli Baba." For the first time since the desert was created, they [the military] placed a small screen in the foothills of the mighty mountains and all the people perceived the thundering and the lightning.
>
> They sat like thrilled children, their heads between their palms, their eyes wide open, frightened, and their lips held back their excitement.
>
> How manifold be Thy wonders, O God of Israel! (Oren 1968)

This peroration, overblown as it may be, well illustrates the hegemonic, even though dyadic, character of Israeli-Bedouin relations. This style of negotiation, established after 1967, continued until the Sinai reverted to Egyptian control. Two phases in this period have to be distinguished. The first, from 1967 to 1972, was characterized by low investment in development. The second phase, from 1972 to 1979, was sharply marked by the opening of the Eilat-Sharm road, and from then on by large-scale financing of development.

The 1967–1972 Phase. The four years following the 1967 war were marked by intermittent hostilities between Egypt and Israel. Shelling, bombardments, and commando raids were carried out by both sides along the length of the Suez Canal. The Israelis, on their part, made use of the Sinai narcotics traffic as a weapon against Egypt. The military governors allowed some Bedouin smuggling boats to cross into Egyptian waters. They had no fear that the drugs would float across the Israeli border because transportation in that direction was far too difficult.

During this period Israeli government exploitation of the Abu-Rodeis oil fields increased, but commercial enterprises in the South Sinai came to a halt. The Egyptian and foreign businesses which had been operating the mines in the Abu-Rodeis area were evacuated to Egypt. Their machinery was just left in place. Israeli developers made use of whatever equipment they found suitable for their own development projects. For example, a desalinization plant was taken from the Egyptian development zone and moved to the Israeli army headquarters in Sharm al-Sheikh. Later, this plant served the newly built city of Ofīra, and then it was moved again to Moshāv Di-Zahāv. The migration of this equipment vividly illustrates the gradual shift of the economic center of gravity from the West Coast to the East Coast of the South Sinai (Marx 1980:117). The culmination of this shift may be seen in the decision reached by both civilian and military developers of the region to construct a road connecting Eilat with Sharm al-Sheikh. They reasoned that such a road would facilitate rapid military movements by land to the strategic points of the south: the Straits of Tirān, Sharm al-Sheikh, and Ras-Muḥammad. It would also make transportation possible around the entire South Sinai Peninsula, along its coastline. From the civilian point of view, the road would stimulate tourism to the majestic red and black mountains facing the eastern coast, sharply descending into the Gulf of ʿAqaba and its coral gardens.

The new road was carefully designed to be in harmony with the pristine landscape around it. Aesthetic considerations overrode monetary ones, since the road was intended to be an international tourist attraction. Moreover, labor costs would be low if local Bedouin, such as Zeidān's eldest son, could be hired cheaply. Yet the road posed a major threat: once it was opened, drug smuggling by the Bedouin into Israel proper would be possible and indeed likely, given the higher prices that hashish would bring there. Force and negotiation were used once again to solve the problem. As soon as road construction began, severe measures were taken against smugglers. Boats and camels loaded with narcotics were blown up, and informers were required to report in great detail on the drug traffic. With this source of income destroyed, the Bedouin had no choice but to turn to the Israeli developers for blue-collar wage work, which Israelis preferred not to do.

The recruitment of road workers was congruent with the hegemonic-dyadic style of negotiation that had arisen between the Bedouin and the Israeli officials. Labor exchanges were opened, and individual Bedouin could often apply for work without sheikhly mediation (Glassner 1974). Gradually the polarization between wealthy smuggling entrepreneurs and their impoverished employees leveled out, because all had equal access to employment. Zeidān's eldest son, for example, began his career as a simple laborer, rose to the position of foreman, and used his earnings to capitalize his own business.

The opening of the Eilat-Sharm road markedly increased the flow of Israeli government investment into the South Sinai. This initiated a new phase in development, which lasted until Israel started relinquishing the region in 1979.

The 1972–1979 Phase. Suddenly, in 1972, Israel's frontier was pushed 275 kilometers south, from Eilat to Ras-Muḥammad, and it had to be tamed. In accordance with the Allon Plan,[4] one town and two *moshavīm* (agricultural cooperatives) were established as way stations to the Straits of Ṭirān. The town was named Ofīra, and the moshavīm were called Neviʿōt and Di-Zahāv. The moshavīm were established on lands bought for a song from the Mzeinis, who thought they got a very good deal because the lands were deluged with flash floods once a decade and literally buried in mud. The economy of the two moshavīm was based on both agriculture and the tourist industry. In contrast to the moshavīm, Ofīra was far from Bedouin oases and had no water for agriculture. The Bedouin were astonished to see the Israelis build an air-conditioned town in what even they thought was the middle of nowhere. The Israelis, however, were passionately determined to pursue the Zionist dream of building greater Israel. The location of these three settlements followed the Allon Plan in moving Israeli civilians into militarily strategic points, such as Pit'ḥāt Rafīaḥ (in the Gaza/Rafaḥ Jewish settlement zone), the Golan Heights, and the Jordan River Valley. To attract such civilians to the South Sinai, Israel offered them tax relief, heavily subsidized housing, and salaries supplemented with hardship pay. Military personnel in Sharm al-Sheikh were encouraged to bring their families to live in Ofīra.

The development of the Santa Katarina area took place despite the fact that it was not in accordance with the Allon Plan for civilians. The impetus for the civilian projects built there came from Israeli environmentalists, nature buffs, and academics. Development began with the spontaneous founding of a field school operated by some of the staff of the Israeli Society for Nature Protection (a voluntary association like the Sierra Club, but financed by government subsidies as well as memberships). The school was named Tzukei David (David's Cliffs) and was a complex comprised of a tourist hostel, classrooms, and staff living quarters. Although the school was a fence away from a small army base, it was agreed that the choice of its location was based solely on the natural beauty of the area, with its high red granite cliffs rising steeply to 2,700 meters above sea level, its cascading streams, and the small Jebaliyya Bedouin orchards nestled between the curves of the wadis. The castle-like monastery of Santa Katarina provided a unique backdrop for the school's activities, which combined ecological research with guiding Israeli tourists on backpacking, camel, and four-wheel-drive truck expeditions. Throughout the entire period of Israeli occupation, little was done to facilitate convenient access to the area by private car.

Tourism was selectively developed so as to avoid harming the environment. Among the hikes the school offered for high school students was an "observation tour" of the nearby Bedouin village, al-Milgā. The students were taken to the hills surrounding the village, and, just as zoologists observe an ibex herd, the students observed the curious activities of the human species in their natural habitat. Further, they were to document these observations on special forms prepared by the school staff, and to discuss their findings when they returned to the classroom (Lavie 1988).

Other Israelis, employees of Haminhāl Lepitūaḥ Merḥāv Shlomō (the Administration for the Development of King Solomon's Wilderness), also moved to the Santa Katarina area. They were in charge of providing community services for the Bedouin in the southern interior. In contrast to the earlier concentration of public services in Abu-Rodeis under the Egyptians, the Israelis distributed services throughout the major encampments and settlements of the region. Egypt's interest had been in concentrating the Bedouin in Abu-Rodeis in order to control smuggling. The Israelis, after completely eradicating smuggling, did not want to concentrate the Bedouin in any one place and certainly not around Israeli settlements.

Beginning in 1967, Israel had allocated a small amount of money for civilian development on a very small scale in the Santa Katarina zone. A local civil administrator, who in theory was responsible only for water surveys, in practice took charge of supervising development. He decided to install much more permanent and costly facilities than those originally envisioned by his superiors in Tel Aviv, out of his own personal concern to avoid hasty and ecologically destructive development. He was able to violate administrative directives from Tel Aviv and yet continue in his post, and even get more funding, because he gained the support of the Santa Katarina Bedouin, whose labor and cooperation the government needed because they were skilled mechanics and construction workers who could be hired cheaply for building the Israeli settlements on the East Coast. This situation illustrates a challenge to the bureaucratic hierarchy on a dyadic basis, a process common in Israeli politics. The typical style of people's interactions with the government in Israel is very informal and direct. Individuals can cut through red tape by going directly to the top and demanding what they want, and get it after convincing the authorities of facts that support their position.

A visitor to the South Sinai could clearly see the contrast the two different modes of development followed by Israel in the Allon zone, on the East Coast, and in the Santa Katarina zone. Driving along the new road, he would pass Neviᶜōt and Di-Zahāv, exact replicas of other moshavīm inside Israel—mass-produced prefabricated white matchboxes. Then came Ofīra, a typical small Israeli town with modernistic prefabricated cement architecture completely dissonant with the contours of the landscape. These settlements were obvious declarations of Israeli dominance over the physical and social environment. On the dirt road to Santa Katarina, however, the same visitor would be hard-pressed to distinguish the Israeli houses from the Bedouin ones. Although modern facilities had been installed inside, the exteriors of new Israeli homes had been built in the traditional local style. The architecture of the new Santa Katarina housing expressed the tenuous harmony between the Israeli developers, the Bedouin, and the scenic terrain.

The idiosyncratic, hegemonically dyadic character of administration in Santa Katarina can be further contrasted with the development on the East Coast, directed from above, by examining the interests of settlers there. The financial inducements the Israeli government offered East Coast settlers attracted young people who wanted quick profits. Some of them were also motivated by the Zionist ideology of supporting one's country by populating its frontiers even when those frontiers lay in territories belonging to other states. For such Zionist pioneers, settlement in the South Sinai was less troublesome than elsewhere because the local population was seemingly cooperative. The Israeli press described the occupation of the South Sinai as "humanistic," in comparison with the aggressive settlement of Pit'ḥāt Rafīaḥ in the North Sinai, where Bedouin were expelled from their land (Chomsky 1974:47). The Israelis living in Santa Katarina received no economic incentives from their government. They accepted a lower standard of living only because of their scientific curiosity and their commitment to protecting the beautiful land and its native species (human and other) from the destructive effects of rapid development and commercial tourism. On the whole, Israeli society wanted to hold up the shining example of Israeli-Bedouin coexistence in the South Sinai in order to cleanse its conscience, which was somewhat troubled by Palestinian resistance in the West Bank and the Gaza Strip, and Druze resistance in the Golan Heights.

During the Jewish holidays, rows of colorful camping tents would stripe the coast of the Gulf of ʿAqaba, and clouds of smoke from portable barbecues would darken the blue horizon of sea and sky. After each holiday, the rows of colorful tents were replaced by organized linear rows of Bedouin men walking side by side to stuff all the dirty toilet paper, used tampons, discarded tin cans, and other trash into huge plastic bags. Goats would scatter along the beach campgrounds, chewing orange peels, rotten tomatoes, newspapers, and other organic refuse the tourists had left behind. Herding activities and East Coast migration cycles were modified to take advantage of the heaps of trash now available.

The interest of the Israeli government was to create a tourist industry that could endure without damaging the ecological balance of the desert. By special legislative action, the nature conservation laws of Israel were extended to the South Sinai and were enforced by nature reserve rangers. They prohibited large-scale commercial fishing by Bedouin, with the aim of maintaining the delicate balance in the gulfs between the rare tropical corals and the species of fish unique to these waters. Mzeinis who dared to sell sea shells or pieces of coral to tourists were made to pay enormous fines. The Bedouin were also forbidden to collect firewood or make charcoal from most of the desert plants, which the Israelis declared protected species. Although the Bedouin were compelled to give up such occupations, they acquiesced in this insofar as substitute sources of income were provided by the nature reserve authorities themselves. Bedouin were hired as guides for the nature reserve rangers and as guards for archaelogical sites.

When the Bedouin discovered that the tourists would pay them for food, drinks, and articles of clothing, and even just to take their "exotic" pictures (not everyone has a matchstick in his eye), they quickly grasped that a profit could be made from them. Using the capital they had accumulated from wage labor, Mzeini entrepreneurs started providing Bedouin-style hospitality for money. They built and rented out huts in fake Bedouin villages they established between the coastal Israeli moshavīm and their own homes. Some Mzeinis, like Zeidān's eldest son, organized a shuttle service to the monastery of Santa Katarina, charging inflated prices, but undercutting the prices charged by their Israeli competition. This excursion was very much in demand among the hippie backpackers floating around the Sinai. Mzeinis also initiated so-called desert safari tours by camel and provided taxi service between Eilat and Ofīra, driving vintage Mercedes sedans. The beaches along the Gulf of ʿAqaba soon became an internationally famous pilgrimage site for naked sun worshippers, who came from throughout the world. This brand of tourist was totally bewitched by fantasies about the Bedouin way of life and became the major clientele for paid-for Mzeini hospitality (Lavie 1984).

The Mzeinis soon found themselves in a double bind. They were attracted by the high profits and independence of their work with the tourists, but were revolted by their unexpected, despicable behavior. The tourists, for their part, saw no reason to wear clothes in "the wilderness." The Bedouin organized delegations of respected men who went to the administrative and military headquarters in Sharm al-Sheikh to complain and to request that the obnoxious behavior of the tourists be regulated. The topic was discussed endlessly in every conversation between individual Bedouin and Israelis living in the Sinai. All negotiations, however, proved fruitless. The Israeli authorities had no wish to assume responsibility for regulating enterprises started by the Bedouin themselves. Yet the Bedouin were not permitted by either Israeli or Egyptian law to impose their own laws on non-Bedouin. Hence the problem could not be resolved.

Large-scale sedentarization occurred in the east as an adaptation to the expanding tourist business. Semiportable huts were erected using palm fronds and scrap materials such as thin plywood boards, pieces of corrugated sheet metal, disassembled vegetable boxes, and cardboard taken from Israeli construction sites and the city dump of Eilat. Shanty settlements inhabited by families appeared in the oases of Nuwēbʿa, Dahab, and Nabeg (near Ofīra). Each new settlement was physically divided into quarters by degree of wealth, ranging from rich

ASPHALT ROAD MAINTENANCE. PROTECTING THEMSELVES FROM THE HARSH SUN, THE BEDOUIN MEN USED ISRAELI VEGETABLE CARDBOXES AS HATS.

to middle-class to poor. This new form of residential organization emerged due to the differentiation among individuals in their ability to accumulate cash.

Because Israeli law prohibits non-Jewish workers (mostly Arabs) from staying overnight in Israeli settlements, shanty towns composed of discarded army tents as well as shanties, and housing only men, sprang up near the large-scale Israeli development projects in Eilat and Sharm al-Sheikh. Since tourism was a seasonal business, men would leave home for extended periods to work for the Israelis as mechanics, gardeners, hotel cooks, busboys, construction workers, street cleaners, custodians, hotel "maids," and trash collectors. Workers needing trade skills were taught in trade schools at government expense. The best workers were rewarded with free, organized trips to major Israeli cities. The climax of each trip would be a visit to a Tel Aviv night club to watch a strip show. Other Bedouin made trips at their own expense to visit their employers' homes in Israel.

"I'm getting old," said Zeidān. "The tourists come to take pictures of the matchstick in my eye and that's how I make my living. [But] I still take care of my orchards in ʿEin Khuḍra." Although all the Bedouin seemed fully committed to wage labor, they continued to invest time and money in maintaining orchards and in stockpiling food as insurance against unemployment, just in case. They also prepared for other eventualities by accumulating small quantities of hard foreign currencies such as American dollars, German marks, and Swiss francs, which they added to their existing small reserves of Egyptian pounds and gold coins.

At the same time, a third type of sedentary settlement sprang up in the mountainous interior of the peninsula, built with the help of the Israeli civil administrator in Santa Katarina. Acting on his own responsibility, he responded to the Bedouin's requests and had deep wells dug, some as deep as sixty meters. This initiative provided the Bedouin who dug the wells with work and also motivated them to settle nearby. Motorized pumps were installed to make drawing the water easier. The Bedouin took advantage of this and developed subsistence gardens near the Israeli wells. The Israeli administration in Santa Katarina also built Bedouin community centers near the wells as further incentives for settlement. Each center was composed of a small clinic with its own resident medic, trained by the Israelis, and an elementary school staffed by a more or less literate local teacher. Although this settlement initiative was consistent with the tenuously harmonious nature of development in Santa Katarina, it nevertheless served the aims of the authorities in Tel Aviv. After settlement, administrators could predict more accurately where the interior population could be found.

Another Israeli method of establishing rapport and gaining the cooperation of the Bedouin was to provide them with superlative medical services. This also served to maintain the self-esteem of the Israelis back home, because it seemed to demonstrate the "humanitarian" character of their military occupation in general. By the end of 1972 the Israelis had established eleven small clinics of the type mentioned above. There were also a few Israeli nurses in Abu-Rodeis and Santa Katarina who treated civilian Israeli and Bedouin patients. Israeli doctors were sent by the Ministry of Health to the South Sinai for one-month tours of duty. Each Bedouin clinic would be visited by a doctor for a day or two every seven to ten days.

No hospitals, civilian or military, were built in the Sinai, but all serious cases were immediately evacuated by ambulance, airplane, or emergency helicopter to hospitals in Eilat, or even further to Tel Aviv or Jerusalem. One adolescent Bedouin, for example, was bitten by a deadly desert viper and was brought to an Israeli army base while the soldiers were in the middle of Yom Kippur prayers. Although the boy's father had traveled eight hours by camel and car to get him there, within one hour the patient was diagnosed and flown to an Eilat hospital by helicopter. All medical care provided to the Bedouin, including expensive transportation such as helicopter service, was paid for by the state of Israel.

The Sinai Bedouin had a form of traditional medicine based on elaborate theories and practices (Levi 1978). To convince them of the value of modern medicine, a physician working with the Bedouin had to gain their confidence through long-term personal interaction. He also had to know the traditional medicine, its practitioners, and the social context in which it was used.

The Israeli doctor who brought about a major shift away from folk medicine to modern medicine, without belittling the role of the traditional system, was hired by the Israeli administration in late 1976 as resident physician for the peninsula. He took responsibility for the health care of all Bedouin and tourists in the South Sinai. He would make a three-day journey by jeep every week, passing through the major Bedouin settlements along the East Coast. Bedouin who were not living close to these clinics would come by camel or car, sometimes traveling as far as seventy-five kilometers. Every month the doctor would tour the very remote areas by camel. In case emergencies arose in his absence, patients would be admitted to the nearest army or civilian clinics and if necessary would be transported to Israeli hospitals.

Israeli medical projects in the South Sinai demonstrate again that Israeli policy could be generated idiosyncratically and that hegemonic dyadic interaction between individual officials and Bedouin could modify the implementation of this policy.

BEDOUIN IDENTITY AND THE RELATIONS WITH OUTSIDERS

Defining a Bedouin Self in contrast to the identities of outsiders was always a problem in the Sinai—such a major one, in fact, that I have selected it as the central issue of this book, and therefore will discuss it only briefly here in this historical overview. Defining a Bedouin Self became an immediate and urgent issue when relations with outsiders ceased to be conducted through sheikhs. From 1967 on, the Mzeinis gradually experienced a crisis in cultural existence and identity. They knew what "real" Bedouin were supposed to be, from their depiction by the tourist guides who frequented their encampments, as well as from their own traditional folk narratives. Yet, after prolonged personal interaction with Westerners, they doubted that their own being-in-the-world could properly be termed Bedouin existence. All Westerners, whether tourists or soldiers, Israelis or Europeans, Jews or Christians, intruded into and challenged their privacy. In response, the Bedouin categorized all these intruders (even Palestinian tourists) by means of the general term *al-Yahūd* (the Jews). The dichotomy between "us" and "them" was stated by the Bedouin in terms of "We are the Muslims, they are the Jews."

This formulation provided the cultural clash with wider meaning and triggered an Islamic revival throughout the South Sinai. Money made through trade in "sins," or the selling of Bedouin hospitality to naked tourists, was purified by lavish expenditures for building mosques and for restoring the shrines of saints. Many people who used to pray only on major holidays started praying punctually at the prescribed five times a day. They tuned the antennas of their transistor radios to Egyptian and later Saudi radio preachers and also to programs that interpreted Islam in terms of modern life. People constantly juxtaposed their values as pious Muslims to the moral chaos of their heretical occupiers. For the Mzeinis, religious revival reduced the tension of adjusting to the changes that the Israelis imposed on their life. It provided a clear reply to the cultural challenges of the West, and it also made clear to the Israelis the limits of Bedouin compliance.

EGYPTIAN ADMINISTRATION OF THE SINAI AFTER 1975

When Egypt and Israel signed the Kissinger interim agreements on 4 September 1975, the Bedouin prepared themselves for yet another change of government. Social and political relations with the Egyptians had to be reestablished. The most important issue was that of the Bedouin's political reliability. Would the Egyptian officials regard Zeidān and his fellow tribesmembers as fellow Egyptians returning from exile, or as treacherous collaborators? Perhaps the Muslim identity of the Bedouin, which they themselves had recently revived as a means of stressing their differences from the Israelis, could have served to bridge the gap between the predominantly Muslim Egyptians and the tribes of the South Sinai. Religious developments within Egypt, however, ruled out this solution.

At the end of 1975 the Egyptians controlled only the northwest coastal area between Suez and Abu-Rodeis. Access to the coastal road was divided equally between Egypt and Israel under American supervision. Egyptian vehicles would use the road for six hours and then turn it over to Israeli vehicles. Bedouin living in Wadi Firān had already concluded in mid-1978 that this state of affairs would soon come to an end. Sifting through gossip collected from Egyptians, Israelis, and radio broadcasts, they predicted that the peninsula would shortly be divided equally between the two opposing states along a north-south line from al-ʿArīsh to Ras-Muḥammad. Accordingly they began to convert more of their assets into hard currencies, gold coins, and Egyptian pounds. Their prediction was fulfilled by the Camp David Accord. In the early summer of 1979, Egypt regained the mountains east of Abu-Rodeis. In midsummer 1979, it regained the western and central Tih Plateau and the mountains northwest of Santa Katarina and south of Abu-Rodeis. In October 1979 it regained al-Ṭūr, the Gaʿ, and the mountains of the southwestern tip of the peninsula. Finally, on 25 January 1980, the Egyptians had arrived in Santa Katarina, exactly as the Bedouin had foretold two years in advance. By 25 April 1982, the whole South Sinai was once again part of the Arab Republic of Egypt.

It was during the period from 1979 to 1980 that the Egyptians first began to think seriously about developing the Sinai (*al-Ahrām*, 8, 15, 16 July 1979). This was also when the first significant contacts between Egyptian officials and Bedouin began. These officials had to decide what Egypt's obligations were toward a population that had lived in the company of her enemy for almost fifteen years. Egypt was faced with the conceptual problem of how to expunge the memory of an occupier that many Egyptians perceived as an arm of Western colonialism. Were the Bedouin part of this problem, or part of its solution?

As it happened, both Egypt and the Sinai had been subjected to intrusive contacts with the West. The South Sinai Bedouin had unanimously responded to this challenge by means of an Islamic revival. In Egypt, however, two responses had emerged, each built on a previous social and intellectual movement. On the one hand, the Egyptian government and the supporters of President Anwar Sadat appealed to the tradition of Egyptian secular nationalism and argued that Egypt should open its doors to the benefits of the West. State-supported Muslim institutions, such as al-Azhar University, invested this official policy with an Islamic sanction. Opponents of the regime, on the other hand, were sharply critical of this "institutional" Islam which, they said, served only the interests of the governing elite. Nevertheless, popular opposition to the regime began to express itself among Egyptian Muslims in the form of an "alternative" Islam (Guindi 1980).

In the context of this polarization of Egyptian Muslims into the institutional and alternative camps, the Bedouin of the South Sinai could not demonstrate their loyalty to Egypt simply by asserting their religious identity. Public discussions of Islamic values had acquired an intensely ideological character in Egypt. The Bedouin's insistence on their Muslim identity might have been perceived as a challenge to the government's institutional Islam. Hence a different, nationalist basis for solidarity with Egypt had to be stressed.

Bedouin identity accommodated itself only slowly to government interests. At first the government did not recognize the Bedouin per se but assimilated them into a wider category, "natives of Sinai," which included both the urban and the Bedouin populations of the peninsula. For example, when heavy floods hit the northern region in 1975, Egyptian newspapers reported the deaths of twenty-one "Bedouin" but stated that government aid was being sent to the "natives of Sinai" (*al-Ahrām*, 11 June 1975). By 1979, however, the tribes of the South Sinai were taking part in popular demonstrations organized by the Egyptian government to show support for Sadat's foreign policies. Finally, in 1982, the "sheikhs of the South Sinai tribes" as well as "crowds of people from the Bedouin tribes of the liberated areas" were included in official celebrations in Sharm al-Sheikh on the day that Israel formally evacuated the Sinai (*al-Ahrām*, 24 April 1982).

In the same year educational teams were sent to the South Sinai to "raise the religious and nationalist consciousness" of the Bedouin (*al-Ahrām*, 25 January 1982). These teams, under the direction of the establishment's al-Azhar University, clearly strove to channel Bedouin religious identity and wed it with institutional, progovernment Islam. Under such conditions the original grassroot ardor of Islamic revival in Sinai cooled. I speculate that the underlying distinction between Bedouin and non-Bedouin may now be taking a different form. The Egyptian plans for developing the South Sinai have clashed sharply with Bedouin interests. The Bedouin must respond to them on both the pragmatic and the ideational levels. Perhaps the traditional opposition between the Egyptian peasant and nomad has reemerged with new ideological content.

EGYPTIAN DEVELOPMENT POLICIES: 1979–1988

The Egyptians viewed the Sinai as an appropriate site for expanding agriculture, mining, and petroleum production, and for employing not only Egypt's growing population, but also that of the Sudan, to bolster regional stability. At first they saw no need to divide the peninsula into northern and southern districts, even though the north and south are quite distinct geographically and socially. It was administered as a single province under the direction of one civil governor. In addition, policymakers did not take geographical differences between the north and south into consideration when planning development projects. For a time the capital of the South Sinai Province was Ras-Sadr, apparently chosen due to its proximity to Egypt. Although physically convenient, this location was inappropriate socially because Ras-Sadr lay outside the territories claimed by the Ṭawara tribal alliance. This may be one reason the capital was later transferred to al-Ṭūr.

Initially there was no policy-making body in Egypt specifically concerned with the development of the Sinai. Prior to 1979, when Egypt had regained only a narrow strip of land adjacent to the Suez Canal, practically no policy existed. As Egypt regained more territory, the governor of the Sinai began to formulate plans for development. These plans reflected the input of various political and economic interest groups that had access to the provincial governors, including the military, Egyptian industrialist families, directors of various government ministries, President Sadat, and members of the political parties both in Egypt proper and in the Sinai. In 1975 the office of the governor of the Sinai was so deluged by requests, petitions, and demands from families who claimed property and other interests in the Sinai that the governor published an open letter in a Cairo newspaper asking for moderation (*al-Ahrām*, 9 December 1975). Once a consensus was reached about a particular project, however, the governor unilaterally announced the plan for it, without conducting any public debate. The interplay of elite interest groups that had generated the plan was totally masked by the government's monolithic behavior in publicizing and implementing it.

Further plans were made public in March 1980. They included proposals which have had far-reaching consequences for the people and ecology of the Sinai. First, it was proposed that Law Number 104, providing for state ownership of desert land and thus making the whole Sinai government property, be changed to permit private ownership. This passed and has lifted government controls on land use and exposed desert land to hazardous and injudicious exploitation.

Second, it was suggested that water be piped from the Nile Valley to agricultural villages to be established in the Sinai on land expropriated from the Bedouin and populated by relocated Egyptian peasants, and that roads, housing, and school buildings be expanded (*al-Ahrām*, 15 July 1979; 25 January, 24 April 1982). Currently, Nile water is pumped as far as the city of Suez and its vicinity and matchbox apartment houses have been built in al-Ṭūr, Abu-Rodeis, and Ras-Sadr. This is an intolerable burden on the fragile Sinai ecology, especially since provisions for sewage and sanitation were insufficient. President Sadat himself had a villa built near Santa Katarina and severely strained the area's water resources by irrigating his impressive front lawn.

Third, plans were recommended for encouraging mass tourism in the Sinai. Two additional roads spanning the peninsula were paved with asphalt, and a ferry terminal was dug out of the corals at Nuwēbʿa to encourage tourism between Egypt and Jordan. Because of this terminal, Zeidān's eldest son lost the family beachfront fishing territory. When he and other fishermen organized to request compensation from the local civil governor, they were told that, according to Law 104, the land had always belonged not to their families, but to the Egyptian authorities. A *mukhabarāt* (Secret Police) agent threatened the fishermen with jail if they pursued their claim.

Near the Santa Katarina Monastery the Egyptians built two large hotels, depleting the water resources the Bedouin need for their garden agriculture, and in Sharm al-Sheikh they expanded the Israeli hotels.

They continued to operate the scuba villages the Israelis had established near their moshavīm along the ʿAqaba Gulf coast. As of today, no Bedouin have been hired to guard the priceless archaeological sites throughout the peninsula, and no Nature Reserve Authority has been established.

Tourist numbers have been declining since the Egyptians started administering the Sinai again. The kind of tourists attracted to the area were rugged backpackers, whom the Egyptians have done little to encourage. Maps and trail guides are hard to come by. Signs were erected on the few asphalt roads, warning tourists not to leave them. No regulations are enforced regarding littering, stealing of antiquities, or destruction of the ecology and coral reefs. Large-scale commercial fishing, including fishing with the use of dynamite, is not outlawed. The Tourist Police and the Secret Police keep constant tabs on the tourists, and on the Bedouin who interact with them.

Finally, new mining and oil-drilling ventures have been initiated. Kaiser Aluminum, an American corporation, has carried out a geological survey of the Abu-Zneima district and reopened the manganese mines there. Egypt was to contribute 100 million Egyptian pounds (probably from its U.S. foreign aid) to this joint venture. One can only assume that no environmental impact studies were ordered to guide planners in designing these mining operations.

In October 1980, the agricultural policy for the South Sinai was announced. A "land reclamation" policy was also formulated in response to the demand by Egypt's educated classes for employment (*al-Ahrām*, 16 July 1979; 25 January 1982). Currently an enormous surplus of students has graduated from state agronomy colleges in Egypt and cannot find employment in the public sector. Rather than creating jobs for them, the government turned over "reclaimed land" to them and encouraged them to develop it further. But these lands had no adequate irrigation facilities, and no loans were available to finance housing construction, production costs, crop transportation, and marketing. The Egyptian recipients of "reclaimed lands" in the Sinai published their demands for improved services in Cairo newspapers, and the government was forced to respond and make some improvements.

Some 214,000 *faddans* (acres) of land were reclaimed in three regions: the Gaʿ area north and south of al-Ṭūr, the coastal area stretching from Ras-Sadr to Abu-Rodeis, and the area between Wadi Firān and Santa Katarina. Egypt aims to increase the population of the whole Sinai from its current 40,000 to 4 million inhabitants by the year 2000, to relieve population pressure on Nile Valley lands. The first steps toward this goal were taken when the government offered financial aid to former residents of Sinai who wished to return to it. Some 60,000 people were reported to have returned to the area between Ras-Sadr and al-Ṭūr. In April 1982, a "standing commission for the population of the Sinai" was formed (*al-Ahrām*, 29 April 1982).

Egyptian grand designs for settling the Sinai with its own relocated population have been largely unsuccessful. Many Egyptians still think of the Sinai much as Muscovites think of Siberia. On the whole, it seems that the abundance of media reports on new development projects in the South Sinai was announced purely for public consumption. Only a very few desert lands around al-Ṭūr have been irrigated or planted. The agricultural fields of the Israeli moshavīm have been abandoned to the sand, wind, and voracious Bedouin goats.

The generating and implementing of agricultural policy, both in Sinai and in the rest of Egypt, well illustrated the monolithic style of the Egyptian government. The various elite groups who formulated policy were always quite distinct from the working class, peasant, and Bedouin groups affected by it. Implementation should have taken the form of dialogue and negotiation between the administration and the population targeted for development. Popular protest succeeded only when the target population managed to unify itself and gained access to the national media. In the absence of protest, state policies were carried out unchanged and hence tended to benefit only the national elite. This was particularly true of the South Sinai, since most of the lands targeted for "reclamation" were and still are populated by Bedouin.

THE RETURN OF THE EGYPTIAN "ḤAKŪMA"

Egyptian plans for the South Sinai Bedouin are necessary consequences of the goals of the national elite. If large numbers of Egyptians were to be settled in Sinai, the Bedouin had to be displaced from their jobs and their lands. Such actions would probably stimulate protest. Hence the administration of the Bedouin had to be designed to blunt their capacity to organize themselves and to attract media attention.

The administration followed three strategies to accomplish this. First, they dramatically increased the number of sheikhly offices. In 1980 the government recognized some 200 sheikhs as spokesmen for the tribes of the Sinai (*al-Musawwar*, 7 March 1980). Since there were

AT THE TEMPORARY BORDERLINE, FEBRUARY 1980. BEDOUIN FROM THE EGYPTIAN SIDE OF THE BORDER DEMONSTRATED LOYALTY TO EGYPT BY WAVING THE EGYPTIAN FLAG AT THE BORDER POLICE STATION. THIS PERMITTED THEM TO SPEAK WITH THEIR RELATIVES ON THE ISRAELI SIDE OF THE FENCE.

about 40,000 Bedouin in all of Sinai and about 13,000 of them lived in the south, I estimate (due to the difficulty of obtaining official government statistics) that at least fifty of the new Sinai sheikhs belonged to the southern tribes. Under the Israelis only thirty sheikhs had been recognized. This meant that each sheikh now had a smaller share of power. Secondly, the Egyptians deposed ten of the southern sheikhs that the Israelis had appointed and replaced them with former tribal sheikhs and other dignitaries who, as a consequence of the 1967 war, had left the Sinai or been exiled by the Israelis and who had now returned as clients of the Egyptian administration.

Finally, the Egyptians created two entirely new offices that had absolutely no relation to existing social groups. The first was "head sheikh of all the Sinai tribes," a post filled by Sheikh Suleiman al-Yamāni of the al-Bayadiya tribe of the North Sinai (*al-Musawwar*, 7 March 1980). He was decorated by Egypt for having assisted the Egyptian army during the 1973 war. Probably he was in contact with the Egyptian army before 1973 and continues to be a client of the Egyptian government. Many Mzeinis were baffled by this appointment, arguing that he had had very little contact with the tribes of the South (*al-Akhbār*, 17 January 1981; *al-Musawwar*, 7 March 1980). The second office was "advisor to the governor of the South Sinai Province for tribal affairs" and was held by Sheikh Samḥān Mūsa Mṭeir. He is from the Wlād Saʿīd tribe, a small tribe unable to provide a broad popular base for protest activity.

As early as 1981, some indications of Bedouin protest appeared in the Egyptian media (*al-Akhbār*, 17 January 1981; *Kashshāf al-Ahram*, May 1982). Newspaper interviews with some other sheikhs recorded their requests for new stone and brick housing, more paid employment for their sons, adequate medical services, and new wells to replace the sources of drinking water formerly provided by the Israelis (*al-Musawwar*, 7 March 1980).

Egypt had a different set of problems at home than Israel had, and these accounted for the choices its elite made about how to dominate the Sinai frontier. One of the main problems in Egypt, as in Israel, was inflation, but their strategies for dealing with it differed. In inflation-ridden Israel, prices were raised to compensate for the decline of Israeli currency in relation to the American dollar. Taxes rose accordingly, especially taxes on foreign-made products such as automobiles (over 200 percent) and electronics. Therefore Zeidān's sons gradually found out that, even though they were employed, they could not afford to live under Israeli rule. The Egyptians feared that such measures would backfire by causing unrest among their vast lower classes, so their policy was to keep taxes low and to subsidize basic food staples. So Zeidān's sons were relieved to discover that their meager savings in hard currencies went much further under Egyptian rule. Food costs dropped to 10 percent of what they had been under the Israelis, and they were able to replace their dilapidated pickup trucks with newer models. Household budgets were not so tight, but this happiness was short-lived.

The high unemployment rate in Egypt,[5] and the willingness of Egyptians, unlike Israelis, to do blue-collar labor, displaced the South Sinai Bedouin from being the first hired in the new Egyptian development projects. Even Sudanese migrant workers had preference over the Bedouin, because once again Egypt wanted to bolster its own regional stability by alleviating unemployment unrest to its own south. Zeidān's eldest son, who had been a tour guide during the Israeli occupation, found that his opportunities for employment in the tourist industry were also drastically reduced. The Egyptian administration in the South Sinai was not able to provide the Bedouin with realistic employment opportunities. But when the sheikhs complained to the Egyptian newspapers, the administration argued back that the Bedouin were lazy by nature and character. To give them incentive to work, in spite of the fact that jobs for them were conspicuous by their absence, the administration arbitrarily took about half the Bedouin, including Zeidān's old brother, who had no sons to support him, off the ṣadaga (CARE charity) list, and reduced by approximately 50 percent the benefits of those who remained.

As for medical services, Egypt, despite its well-intentioned plans for the Sinai (*al-Ahrām*, 15 July 1979), already had a severe shortage of personnel and facilities for its own large, dense population. Very few well-trained doctors were willing to leave the comforts of Cairo or Alexandria to help the South Sinai Bedouin, whom the Egyptians, in contrast to the Israelis, did not regard as living Biblical specimens. So, no more helicopters for snakebites.

The human consequences of the dramatic cut in medical services under the Egyptians can be illustrated by the case history of one twenty-five-year-old Mzeini woman, mother of two, whose family in January 1988 had to pay for her to be hauled in private taxis from one of the ʿAqaba Gulf coast sedentarized communities to a low-cost Moslem revivalist clinic in Cairo. The Egyptian doctor back on the East Coast of the Sinai had judged that her severe, painful ear infection and very high fever did not justify use of the regional ambulance. (Some Mzeinis said his lack of interest in the woman's case might be related to her family's inability to give him additional monetary incentive for his work.) When the woman returned in late January from her surgery in Cairo, her ear started bleeding. Her family took her back to the same local doctor, who said her recovery was normal. When she got worse, he suggested they take her to a traditional healer to exorcise the demons from her body. But the efforts of the enlightened Israeli doctor who had learned folk medicine had had one unfortunate side effect: the Bedouin had accepted modern medicine so well that a whole generation of traditional healers had died without replacement. When the woman was at death's door, the doctor finally prescribed aspirin (and the family had to buy it from him). Her family decided again to pay for taxis and were on their way with her to the city of Suez, when she died en route. On 14 March 1988, I attended her funeral and learned this whole story firsthand. She was a very dear friend of mine. During the week of mourning that followed, I heard of other similar stories.

Housing was another area of tension between the Bedouin and the administration. In 1980 the press reported that the government had constructed new housing for the Bedouin of the Santa Katarina area and of al-Ṭūr, but they refused to live in it. Rather, they preferred to remain in the shanties they had constructed out of scrap sheet metal, plywood, and stone (*al-Ahrām*, 31 March 1980). This rejection of government housing can be interpreted in two ways. It could be a tactic adopted by the Bedouin to claim rights to plots of land by refusing to move from those plots. This was the strategy followed by the Negev Bedouin in 1979 when they were resisting Israeli expropriation of their land. On the other hand, it could stem from the Bedouin's lack of confidence in the Egyptian-Israeli Camp David Accord about Sinai. In 1988 they strongly felt that a new Israeli occupation was not impossible. They predicted that the Israeli suppression of the West Bank Uprising, coupled with the instability of Mubarak's regime in Egypt, could kindle another regional war. Therefore they thought it would not be wise to commit themselves to life in only one location—and especially in housing built by a government. The family of Zeidān's maternal niece, for example, has moved its semiportable shanty four times since 1962 to allow the head of the household to adjust to the vagaries of the job market. He had been employed by the Egyptians in Abu-Rodeis but lost his job when the Egyptians evacuated the Sinai in 1967. He moved to al-Ṭūr where his friends were also living in a shanty town and waited for other opportunities. In the early 1970s he found work with the Israelis in Dahab and moved there. When the Israelis left Dahab, he returned to al-Ṭūr to seek employment with the Egyptians. Clearly, living in portable housing has been a rational adaptation to economic and political instability.

The Bedouin rejected the Egyptian government housing for their own good reasons, but the administration had a strong interest in sedentarizing these seminomads and keeping them near the main asphalt roads so they would be easy to reach and control. (This contrasted with the Israeli approach of wanting the Bedouin's flimsy shanties well away from the scenic asphalt tourist route, but refusing permission for permanent housing in order to keep the alluringly nostalgic shanties, as relics of Moses' forty years in the Sinai wilderness.) So in 1983 Zeidān's sons and other Bedouin sighed with relief when the Egyptian government finally agreed to permit residents of the main sedentarized oases on both coasts to independently build their own permanent housing—but not out of the plentiful, cheap local granite, which blends beautifully with the landscape. The houses had to be made of cinderblock, a material the Bedouin had not learned how to use, so those who could afford it had to hire Egyptians or Sudanese to make the cinderblock and build their houses for them. Even these better-off Bedouin kept their disassembled shanty materials in reserve, just in case. A desperate building boom ensued, because the Bedouin feared that any land not physically covered by some sort of permanent structure would be declared government property and so reclaimable by non-Bedouin Egyptian citizens. As of 1988, the Egyptian government has started providing electric and telephone service, but still no running water or sewage systems.

In education, the Egyptians built more schools, added high schools to the local system, raised teaching standards, and encouraged the Bedouin much more forcefully than the Israelis had to send their daughters to school. The curriculum was the regular Egyptian one, designed to foster Egyptian nationalism even among the Ṭawara Bedouin, who not only had a longstanding primary loyalty to their own family and tribe, but who were afraid of the consequences of being strongly identified with Egypt, in case the Sinai again returned to Israeli rule.

The Bedouin were now considered Egyptian citizens (except for the right to a passport, unless they could afford it), so the young men were expected to serve in the Egyptian army (unless they could afford to buy their way out). This made no sense to them, or to their parents, and many of them fled to the rugged mountain interior where only some of them could be captured by the Egyptian Secret Police and turned over to the draft enforcement agency. In 1988 one of Zeidān's grandchildren told me such a story: "Yesterday, they came and took my friend Ramaḍān to the army around midnight. A [Bedouin] informer told the Secret Police where he was hiding. They beat him up and loaded him on the jeep. Today he's on his way to Zagazīg [the main Nile Valley base for South Sinai recruits]. Perhaps I will be next. . . . I know we are Egyptian citizens now. But only the rich Bedouin benefit from the return of the Egyptian ḥakūma. I—this country, just like Israel, doesn't give me anything. Why should I give it two years of my life?"

THE MEANING OF DEVELOPMENT: OCCUPATION AND ACQUIESCENCE

One of the aims of this chapter has been to point out that the pristine South Sinai wilderness and its Bedouin inhabitants have been pawns in the power games of the Middle East for over forty years. Outside agencies have manipulated the land and people of the South Sinai to further the interests of two nation states, Israel and Egypt. The policies implemented by Israel did not harm the environment, although they significantly disrupted Bedouin life. On the other hand, if absence of stratification is deemed a desirable feature in social existence, it could be argued that Bedouin wage labor under the Israelis was beneficial insofar as it reversed earlier tendencies toward forming polarized classes in Bedouin society. This internal leveling was accompanied, however, by the encapsulation of the Bedouin into the wider Israeli state as low-status dependents. Certainly the medical services provided were praiseworthy. Yet the most beneficial policies did not automatically accompany the Israeli occupation. Sometimes the interests of the Israelis and the Bedouin happened to coincide, as was the case when the Bedouin were employed by Israeli enterprises short of unskilled labor, and sometimes certain administrators, prompted by their own idiosyncratic motives, were able to make their own policy and respond to Bedouin needs. In no case, however, were any policies adopted that favored the Bedouin over the essential interests of the Israeli state. If political conditions had been different and harmful policies had been implemented, the Bedouin would have been powerless to stop them, since they could not truly become Israeli citizens.

Egyptian policies are now permanently disrupting the fragile ecological balance of the peninsula and are once again turning the Bedouin into very marginal migrant laborers in their own homeland. Mistakes made now in haste will certainly be extremely costly to correct and will plague the peoples of Egypt and the South Sinai for years to come. Only with patience and careful thought can the long-term interests of Egypt and her South Sinai Bedouin population be harmonized.

Having reviewed the South Sinai peninsula's ecology, social structure and organization, recent history of political turmoil, and the effects of all these on the Ṭawara Bedouin and particularly the Mzeina, you now have sufficient context to shift your point of view to the words and lives of individual Mzeinis. In the chapters to come, you will meet Sheikh ᶜAlwān, ᶜAlyii the Madwoman, X the Ex-Smuggler, Hajja Ḥmēda the Old Woman, Shgēṭef the Fool, Shaᶜabān abu-Srayaᶜ the Symbolic Battle Coordinator, and also, surprisingly enough, the one Mzeinis call "The One Who Writes Us." All these people use their various talents to allegorize the vicissitudes of a life under military occupation into spontaneous theatrical performances, as outbursts of protest against forced change, and as creative attempts to preserve their Bedouin identity and tradition during the clash between tribe and state. Before embarking on this discursive exploration of Mzeini life as mirrored by this cast of characters, however, let us return to Zeidān al-Shēba at the end of his day.

EPILOGUE

When dusk fell, Zeidān al-Shēba removed the matchstick from his eye and tottered from his customary seat between the crowded cafe of Moshāv Neviᶜōt and the asphalt parking lot where the overloaded tourist buses stopped. He said to himself, "Work's over." Leaning on his walking stick, he dragged himself toward Nuwēbᶜat Mzeina, his vest pocket full of the day's take. As he sat to rest on a sand dune overlooking the sea, a group of tourists waving the Japanese flag passed by. They marched along the beach to the beat of a snare drum, barking out militaristic-sounding slogans in Japanese. Startled, Zeidān rose from the dune and peered at the marchers, unable to see them clearly. He asked his anthropologist, "Has the Chinese army arrived?"

"No, these are just tourists from Japan."

Zeidān did not believe this reply. "Impossible. These are not the voices of tourists."

The anthropologist teased him: "What makes you think this is the Chinese army?"

Zeidān paused and said in a seemingly blase tone, "The Turks were here and went. The British were here and went. Then came the Egyptians, with them came some Russians, and then came the Israelis with the Americans, Scandinavians, French, Australians, and the rest of the world. Only the Chinese have not shown up yet, and China is a rising power in the world, so I'm waiting for them."

3
THE SHEIKH

Al-Sheikh

[The] chief . . . stands in high esteem among the Rwala. Such a one has a brave, strong heart, *qalbeh qawi*; knows how to wrestle with the greatest danger, *ma^ceh fetel*; has a broad outlook, *ma^ceh ^cerf*; thinks of the future, *shofteh ba^cide*; and never acts hastily, *leh sabr.*

ALOIS MUSIL
The Manners and Customs of the Rwala Bedouins

The [South Sinai] desert community is of necessity a poor one. . . . The power of the Sheikh, exaggerated as a matter of course to strangers, was originally very limited. He was not a law-giver, unless he united with his office that of the judge, still less was he a law-maker. . . . [T]he effect on a tribe of contact with the outside world is to exalt the power of the Sheikh, since it is through him that the decrees of government are transmitted to the tribesmen . . . But the Sinai Arab tribesmen still stand in little awe of their sheikhs.

G. W. MURRAY
Sons of Ishmael

"But what can we do? We are *ahl al-dageʿa*," the people of the land. "They"—the potential or previous occupiers, whether Turks, British, Egyptians, Israelis, Americans, or Soviets,—"are *shughlīn al-siyāsa*." They are the people of politics. "So what can we do?"[1]

This was the answer I was given many times as I talked with individual Mzeini men while we engaged in such everyday activities as fishing, sitting in cafes, visiting households, or traveling by camel. Thinking about the heroic rebellion of the El-Shabana Bedouin (R. Fernea 1970) or the extremely successful economic war that the Rwala Bedouin fought against the Syrian government (Lancaster 1981), I often wondered why the Mzeina did not protest against the external powers controlling their lives. When I confronted the Mzeinis with their helpless situation vis-à-vis the international political processes directly affecting their daily life, I was struck by the attitude expressed in their rhetorical question, "But what can we do?" Older men would then distinguish between Those of the Land and Those of Politics, shrug their shoulders, and dismiss it with a bitter smile. Younger men said it with a raised voice and wide-open eyes, and then they chuckled in a nervous staccato.

The ironic paradox "People of The Land/People of Politics" is useful in analyzing Mzeina Sheikhs. The Bedouin of the South Sinai are not the region's political governors, nor do they control their own political fate. The governors of the South Sinai have their centers of political power outside the peninsula, in Cairo or Tel Aviv. They come and go. They have neither maintained a long lasting interest in the Sinai, nor lived there permanently like the Bedouin.

Interestingly, I rarely heard this paradoxical distinction made as Mzeinis or members of other tribes conversed among themselves in the everyday settings mentioned above. In such situations the men

◄SHEIKHS AT THEIR MONTHLY MEETING WITH THE ISRAELI MILITARY GOVERNOR, ABU RODEIS

articulated the distinction only when speaking to me. Was it irrelevant to their daily life? Or was it perhaps a well-internalized, "taken-for-granted province of meaning?" (Schutz 1962:229–234; Berger and Luckman 1967:19–28).

I have already argued in the previous chapter that the Israeli and Egyptian governments perceived the Mzeina as *both* obstacles *and* resources for implementing international peace agreements and South Sinai development policies (Lavie and Young 1984). In itself, this is yet another insoluble paradox. To gain Bedouin compliance, these regimes endowed the post of sheikh with some degree of authority. In contrast to the Rwala or El-Shabana sheikhs, however, the Mzeini sheikhs did not lead rebellions or successfully conduct economic wars against their occupiers. Nor did they arbitrate disputes or hold traditional feasts (cf. R. Fernea 1970; Lancaster 1981). They had little power in local affairs and did not protect the independence of their tribe. A man did not become sheikh among the Mzeina through tribal consensus; sheikhs were appointed by the foreign governors, and the Bedouin were to comply with the decision. But like the El-Shabana or the Rwala sheikhs, the Mzeini sheikhs were also involved to some extent in mediation. Their sole role was that of go-between, creating a bridge between the People of Politics and the People of the Land.

While thus circumventing this existential paradox, sheikhs exhibited yet another conundrum inherent in the structure of their position. In the eyes of Mzeinis, they were agents of the occupier and therefore were respected by their fellow tribesmen not as sheikhs but only as human beings. The Mzeinis, however, were fully dependent on their sheikhs to obtain permission from the state authorities to engage in or change any aspect of their economic and political lives.

Perhaps this explains why the Mzeinis, when asked who their leaders were, always pointed to judges and sheikhs. They nonetheless obliquely ridiculed the "backwardness" of their judges, and many said of their sheikhs: "Eh . . . they have no honor. They lick the ass of the government." They said this in spite of the fact that, in keeping with colonial tradition, both the Egyptians and the Israelis conducted careful intelligence inquiries and were cautious in selecting "their" sheikhs. These men usually belonged to honorable, affluent families of extensive lineage that were said to be able to trace their descent directly to the Mzeina ancestor. Some sheikhs were sons, grandsons, or other family relatives of previous sheikhs. One man told me, "Our sheikh, he has a pure origin (*aṣl*). His roots can be traced straight to our father,

Faraj." But, after a moment of reflection, he added with a sigh, "Well . . . who cares?"

While the scholarly literature's Arab sheikhs are centralistic, forging tribal consensus on the basis of correspondence between descent and territoriality (Antoun 1972; Dresch 1984; R. Fernea 1970; Lancaster 1981), there was little correspondence between Mzeina descent and Mzeini territory. A few of the fishermen lineages were the only ones for which a correspondence between territory and descent obtained. Members of most Mzeini lineages were usually found in different regions of the peninsula. Noncorrespondence of this kind limited the extent to which Mzeini sheikhs could achieve consensus with, or exert authority over, lineage members. When appointing sheikhs, the external authorities failed to realize that, for the Mzeinis, the more important organizational form was regional. Most sheikhs attempted to mitigate the problem of noncorrespondence (between descent and territoriality) by taking one or two additional wives. These wives were members of the sheikh's lineage, but did not reside in his region. One old Mzeini I spoke with joked that, "Our sheikh loves women a lot. But his route to his younger wives' hearts was not the written [i.e., truthful] one."

In the *mag*ᶜ*ad* the sheikh usually sat quietly, seldom participating in the flowing conversation or otherwise interacting with others. If they were intimately acquainted with each other, Mzeinis usually looked each other in the eye; otherwise (or if they were speaking with someone of the opposite sex), they looked down, sneaking glances at the other person when she or he was not aware. The sheikh, on the other hand, gazed above the men's heads. When I sought an explanation of the sheikh's behavior in the magᶜad, some of the men said with respectful voices, "Well, he's above all our small talk." Yet at other times the same people belittled him, saying, "Well, what can he say?" or, viciously, "Our sheikh—he has nothing to say."

The paradoxes built into the sheikh's position—first, the Mzeina disrespect for, yet dependency on, their sheikh; and second, the sheikh's embodying of the Mzeina in the eyes of the occupiers, and the occupiers in the eyes of Mzeina—placed him at the center of Mzeina tribal ideology, which has always been associated with external agencies (cf. Lavie 1986). But as it has no material substance in terms of real administrative power, the sheikh's central ideological position isolated him from the everyday experiences shared by ordinary Mzeinis.

The People of the Land/People of Politics paradox rarely surfaced in ordinary daily conversation; if it did, the conversation quickly turned into a heated debate. If the ironic paradox was articulated, it was only in the presence of the sheikh. If this paradox was ever thematized, a second set of paradoxes, that of the sheikh's position, invariably emerged. When these paradoxes were discussed, the sheikh sometimes chose to remain silent, and the argument ended with the men and the sheikh quietly leaving the magᶜad. Sometimes, however, the sheikh spoke up spontaneously, his voice emerging from those frail moments of bitter silence which often follow a heated debate. As a liminal persona, who paradoxically conjoined his Bedouin Self with the occupier's "Other," the sheikh was able to transform world politics into local poetics. He playfully transformed a mundane event of his daily life into an allegory, which he then recounted in the traditional genre of Mzeina storytelling.

The narrative constituting the sheikh's allegory entailed the paradoxes of both the Mzeina and their sheikh. As curious as it may sound, in *being* a paradox, the sheikh's allegorical narrative solved itself as a paradox—as I will show in the following three narratives.

What follows may be seen as the processual rise and fall of leadership qua allegory. Indeed, the sheikh's allegory revealed and temporarily solved the paradoxes immanent both in the structure of his persona and in the Mzeina's political relation to their occupiers. In his allegorical performance, the sheikh provided a set of specific answers to existential and organizational dilemmas characteristic of Mzeina life.

1.

Bīr Njeima, Ramaḍān, 2 September 1977

End of summer in Wadi Njeima, at the margins of the Highlands Plateau (*Fareᶜ*). Strong sun in deep blue skies beats down on the worn-out hills of red granite, striped by black veins of volcanic dikes. Along the wadi are a few ancient green acacia trees. Several black goats find a crowded shelter in the small spots of shadow created by one of the trees and chew its dry, curly bean-like fruit, fallen to the ground. A heat-fatigued camel monotonously devours the thorny top of yet another acacia.

Twelve summer tents made of flour sacks, and ten huts built with military ammunition storage boxes, stand several meters from each other on an ancient alluvial terrace embracing the wadi walls. The terrace is elevated from the main river bed, thus protecting the dwellings from a long-hoped-for flash flood. Several winter tents woven of brown-black goat hair, neatly folded, hang from ropes tied to acacia trees. A rough-hewn "mosque," a square of black stones laid flat on the ground, partially buried on the pink arcosis, is so positioned that the *miḥrāb* points southeast, to Mecca. Near the mosque, a circle of dark stones delineates the magᶜad. Woven bands of black goat-hair and white sheep-hair, sewn together, form a striped sheet, half the size of a winter tent wall, casting a partial shadow over the magᶜad's circle. In the wadi's deep center stands an old well. From its sweep dangle two buckets riddled with holes. It is surrounded by a small trough. Beside the well, a barbed wire fence protects a stand of tall date trees and their bushy offshoots from the voracious appetite of the goats. Nearby stands the new well with its generator-operated pump, encircled by a large cement trough.

Burning afternoon heat, visible, wavering up the wide wadi on this Ramaḍān day of fast. Like a ghost town, the encampment is still, quiet, seemingly barren. I notice two old men in white caftans, Ḥmēd and Shtēwi, napping and then moving, napping and then moving, as the striped shadow cast upon the magᶜad progresses with the waning day. Most of the eleven men have gone to the annual intertribal date harvest in Wadi Firān, exchanging dates for the dried fish brought by Mzeinis from the shores of the Suez and ᶜAqaba Gulfs. The anthropologist was told that younger Mzeinis are disinclined to take a date-season vacation from their work in Eilat or in Israeli development projects on the peninsula's east coast.

In the encampment seven women have gathered inside two summer tents. There they nap, their babies cuddled in the soft, curved niche between their breasts and stomachs. In response to the mothers' request, I play with the children, gathered together in the last tent of the row. We play quietly, with hushed yet unleashed energy, allowing the fasting mothers to rest. Plants, rocks, trees, people—everything seems to hover in anticipation of the evening breeze.

Suddenly a jeep bursts into the silence and stops almost inside the magᶜad. Three young men enter the circle. After the customary exchange of greetings they give one of the old men three dried fish, tied together by the gills on a thin rope.[2] They leap back into the jeep and disappear in a cloud of dust, heading west to Wadi Firān. The kids and I peek out from our tent.

Ḥmēd totters towards me, the three fish hanging from his hand. He hands them to me and says: "Go to the ḥajja, the sheikh's wife, and tell her that Khḍeir abu-ʿAṭṭallah, and Rāshed abu-Salīm, and Rashīd abu-Mnēfi, from the People of Dahab, bestow their peace on her husband."

The anthropologist notices that, in introducing the names to her, Ḥmēd uses the regional affiliation of the three men, not their agnatic descent.

I approach Sheikh ʿAlwān's tent, surprised to find his wife there and not with the rest of the women. She lies on her side, half-awake, half-asleep, her baby suckling at her breast. I cough outside, indicating that I would like to be invited in.

"Is it you, ya Smadar?"

"Yes, it's me, Ḥajja Rbaiʿa, dried fish in my hand, a gift to the Sheikh's wife from Khḍeir abu-ʿAṭṭallah, Rāshed abu-Salīm, and someone else, I think it's Rashīd abu-Mnēfi, all from the People of Dahab."

"Come in, please," she encourages me. As I enter her tent, she whines, "But what am I going to do with all these dried fish? Since the date season has started, so many men have stopped here and given me fish, God bless them. . . . But how many thanksgiving dinners (*ṭahawa*) will the sheikh, my husband, give this year? He spends more time with his younger wife, the one who lives near the [Israeli] Military governor's office. He has forgotten me, 'the mother of the sons' (*omm al-wlād*)."

I feel uncomfortable at this sudden outburst of emotion. I expected to exchange the customary greetings, to refuse (because of the fast) an invitation to a cup of tea, to chat a bit, and to return to my Ramaḍān daytime job as the kids' "pacifier." I tell the anthropologist not to forget to later write in her fieldnotes that the sheikh's wife used the term "the mother of sons," usually describing the wife in a polygynous marriage who bore her husband his first sons. I hesitate in her tent, wondering if she'll confide more of her personal affairs. And the anthropologist is well aware that Bedouin women usually express their emotions in highly formalized poetry, not in personal talk (cf. Abu-Lughod 1985).

Rbaiʿa sighs. She lifts her veil (*ṭarḥa*)[3] from the ground to wipe a tear. I try to ease the tension by talking about the heavy heat. She talks about the Ramaḍān fast. The smell of the dried fish tickles our hungry nostrils. We talk about how wonderful it will be on the day of ʿId al-Faṭr, the feast ending the fast at the beginning of the next lunar month. She tells me of her pilgrimage to Mecca two years ago.

I am alarmed by the kids' joyful shouts and am about to leave when she says in a choked voice, "The sheikh my husband doesn't fast any more in Ramaḍān. He doesn't even pray. It's all because of Israel. When his great maternal uncle was a sheikh with Egypt, this uncle, he used to pray five times a day, and he used to fast during Ramaḍān. This was in the days when we were all still half pagans (*juhul*) and didn't pray much. Now, with Israel, we all pray, and my husband has become a pagan."

Rbaiᶜa's brief outpouring moves me. But the anthropologist suppresses her scholarly curiosity, choosing instead to maintain politeness. I leave Rbaiᶜa's tent to resume my childcare duties.

By now the young children are prancing up and down the wadi. I hear a clear soprano voice booming out, "Silence! If you don't shut up, the sheikh will come and hand you over to the military governor!"

II.

Bīr Njeima, 16 September 1977

It is the morning of ᶜId al-Faṭr, after the main prayer of the holiday. Yesterday all the men returned either from Wadi Firān or from working with the Israelis and anxiously waited for the new crescent moon. With relief, they watched it arrive at dusk. The fast is over. Rejoicing, the children skip up and down the wadi dressed in new holiday clothes, and the whole encampment bursts into color. From their storage boxes (*kushk*) the women draw their heavily coined veils (*burguᶜ*) and shake the dust of forgotten times from the weighty holiday clothes, hand embroidered with bright reds, greens, blues, and yellows. They wear these now. The men dress in new pastel and white terylene caftans,[4] on top of which they wear black vests (*ṣdēri*). In addition, some wear a gray or blue gabardine coat. Their white headdresses almost seem to glow.

Men and women enter each other's tents and huts. They hug each other, each placing his or her hands on the back of the other's neck, kissing the air three times, bodies bobbing to the rhythm of the kisses. One says in greeting, "You, the celebrators, may all things good happen to you this and every year, in health and peace (*al-ᶜaydīn, kul sana ṭaybīn, beṣaḥḥa wasalāme*)," and the other answers, "May good be also bestowed upon you every year (*kul ᶜam weintum bkheir kamān*)." Groups of jubilant boys or girls enter each residence, asking for candies.

Around eleven in the morning the men gradually gather in the magʿad, each carrying an empty food can (*dalla*) filled with water, shedding his thongs or sandals before entering. There are eleven men present, related by agnatic and/or cognatic ties. The eldest, Ḥmēd and Shtēwi, recline on their left elbows, resting on a pillow. Their sons-in-law, Freij and Nūr, age thirty and fifty, sit cross-legged beside them. Freij's community of origin is in the Flatlands (*al-Ṭāref*), and Nūr has come here from the town of Suez. Nūr's parallel cousin, Rāshed, silently rolls his prayer beads. To his left sits Slimān, also about thirty, and Shtēwi's brother's son. He rolls his tobacco-stuffed cigarette paper one last time and licks it shut. Shtēwi's younger brother, Sālem, flicks pebbles from the rug on which he sits. He is married to his parallel cousin, whose natal community is in al-Wadi on the Gulf of Suez. Nūr's oldest son and Sālem's friend, Saʿīd, as the youngest present, tends the fire and prepares cycles of bitter coffee and sweet tea, which he serves to the men. His alert eyes observe the others as he hands tea to ʿAbdallh and Raḍwān, both middle-aged; their wives are from the ʿAleigāt and Ṣawālḥa tribes. These two men are included in the encampment because some of their agnatic kin live in nearby settlements. Ḥmēd's youngest son, Ḥamdān, sits near Saʿīd. He is divorced and in his early twenties.

I also sit with the men. We sit in a circle, in the shade, and converse quietly while eating sweet dates and drinking water. Saʿīd serves us coffee. Every once in a while someone looks at his watch, waiting for noon.

Four men from a nearby encampment arrive in a vintage jeep. As they take off their shoes, we all stand up. They enter the shadowed area, and we shake hands and exchange holiday greetings, counterclockwise. We sit again. Rāshed, age thirty, opens the radio transistor and adjusts the long antenna and dial. As we talk, we half-listen to scratchy, evasive Qur'an chants broadcast from Saudi Arabia.

Fifteen minutes till noon. Some men look again at their watches. They take their water and walk out of the shaded circle into the sun. Purifying themselves for the noon prayer, they wash their hands, their arms up to their elbows, their feet, and then legs up to the knees. The anthropologist stays inside and continues writing. When the men return, Ḥamdān teasingly reminds her of her gender: "I can't shake your hand again till prayer is over." She is reminded of the taboo against men and women shaking hands or having any other physical contact following the preprayer ritual washing.

Ten minutes before the noon prayer. Nūr murmurs, "Our Sheikh ʿAlwān hasn't arrived yet. Who knows if he will arrive or not. He spends more of his time in one of those Bedouin cafes, the ones near the office of the military governor in al-Ṭūr, than with us. God help the Ḥajja, his wife, 'the mother of sons.'"

At five minutes to noon we notice a cloud of dust rising from the wadi. Some say the tourists are coming. Others think it is the sheikh. The children break the news to us, running after the jeep as it enters the encampment's outskirts, shouting gaily, "The sheikh is back! The sheikh is back!"

The sheikh, a man in his fifties, applies the brakes only a few meters from the magʿad. This is an act of trespassing, especially since the circle is still occupied. He appears tall and light-skinned, red from the sun, unlike most Bedouin and myself, who are dark olive from the sun. He sports a bushy mustache and genuine Ray-Ban aviator sunglasses, not the cheap imitations worn by young Bedouin men on occasions of foreign-tourist skirt-chasing. He is veiled within a heavy aura of Old Spice After Shave, not the burnt charcoal scent of nomads who sit around open fires. His footwear is not the decrepit thongs or sandals of most Mzeinis, but white socks and dusty, pointed, black shoes. Instead of a pastel-colored caftan like the men have, he wears a jaunty turquoise one, embellished by a black gabardine coat. Older Mzeinis of means carry a pocket watch nestled in their vests, but he wears a self-winding Seiko wristwatch with English/Arabic day/time.

The anthropologist is taken aback as she watches the sheikh enter the magʿad without shedding his shoes and socks. Saʿīd quietly protests, "eh-hey," but the others ignore both him and the feet of the sheikh. Once again we all rise, shake hands, and exchange greetings with the sheikh, counterclockwise. We sit down again.

Two minutes to twelve. Ḥmēd hauls himself up with difficulty, grimacing from old pains. He limps to the nearby mosque. A piercing sun illuminates his face as he cries out the holy verses, exhorting the believers to pray. One by one all the men, except Sheikh ʿAlwān, enter the mosque, arranging themselves into two wide rows, and pray, their faces full of reverence. Meanwhile, taking the communal eating bowl, the sheikh scrapes cold, dessicated breakfast leftovers into a ball. After eating he fixes his gaze on the red granite cliffs on the horizon. He reminds me of a sphinx, so very still and motionless.

Suddenly he says, "Write in your notebook: since the last government changed [from Egyptian to Israeli], the Mzeina play with God. I—I don't play with God. It's enough for me to play with the government." The anthropologist writes. "Just like that," he abruptly ends, and retreats back into himself.

MAGᶜAD REJJĀL (MEN'S CLUB) IN A SEDENTARIZED SETTLEMENT

The men return and quiet conversation begins to flow again. The sheikh still gazes silently at the horizon. The assembled company, intentionally or not, weave into their statement criticism of the Israeli authorities. The anthropologist assumes that they hope the sheikh will transmit their views to the powerful authorities above him.

FREIJ: They said, my brother Swēlem from the Flatlands, they released him from the jail in Sharm [al-Sheikh] for the holiday . . . Praise be to God.

SHTĒWI: Yeah . . . people said that Swēlem sits in jail. A good guy, your brother. What happened?

FREIJ: In the [full] moon of [the month of] Rajab, he fished for lobster in Ras al-Ṭanṭūr. That snake from the Reserve came and took away his fishing license.

The people had nicknamed one of the rangers working for the Israeli Federal Agency for Nature Reserves "the snake."[5] The agency had been trying for some time to protect the ʿAqaba Gulf lobster, which it declared an endangered species. The commercial fishing for lobster was prohibited, yet lobster was in great demand by the black market food supply of Israeli gourmet restaurants. Aside from the fact that lobster is an expensive delicacy, it is also non-kosher, hence the demand.[6]

The anthropologist watches Shtēwi, who doesn't quite understand, perhaps because his agnates and cognates all live in the Highlands?

SHTĒWI: And then?

FREIJ: Then, after a week, my brother joined some men who fished for *Ḥawāja* (Mister)[7] Ronni [an Israeli fish marketeer] in the area of Ras Muḥammad. The command car of the military government arrived there, and the Druze sergeant came down and checked the fishing licenses of the people. My brother didn't have his. That "snake" had taken it. So they put him in jail because he didn't have a license.

NŪR: But . . . people said . . . in Ras Muḥammad, no one fishes for lobster.

ḤAMDĀN: No. That doesn't matter any more. The Coast People know that the Reserve can't arrest Bedouin who fish for lobster. The Reserve can only write the Bedouin a fine. The fine doesn't help. The Jew who buys the lobster just pays it. This is why "the snake" took Swēlem's license. It isn't part of his job, but Swēlem, what can he do? So he gave it to him. So how can he not fish? And his kids—what will they eat?

SHTĒWI: So what happened after that?

FREIJ: He sat a week in jail. Someone found our Sheikh ʿAlwān in Mnēfi's cafe, but the Sheikh said he didn't understand much about fishing. So the brother of my brother's wife went to Sheikh Ṣbeṭān [one of the sheikhs who lives on the ʿAqaba Gulf]. Sheikh Ṣbeṭān went to the military governor and was angry with him. He told him, "How come the Bedouin are not allowed to make a living from the sea, isn't the sea theirs?" The military governor said only that Sheikh Ṣbeṭān couldn't speak for my brother, since my brother is of Sheikh ʿAlwān. So Sheikh Ṣbeṭān told the governor that my brother's wife is from the family of Sheikh Ṣbeṭān's wife, and then the governor shut up.

The circle of men bursts into laughter. Perhaps people laugh, the anthropologist speculates, because the European Jewish governor doesn't understand the intricacies of Bedouin kinship. This is ironic, since colonial administrations have always tried to control the Bedouin through a strategy of divide-and-conquer on the basis of lineal segmentarity (cf. R. Fernea 1970). As Freij spoke, he mentioned two sheikhs—his lineage sheikh, ʿAlwān, who lived in the mountains, and Ṣbeṭān, a sheikh of another Mzeini lineage, who lived by the sea. Because he lives by the sea, Sheikh Ṣbeṭān is familiar with the wits and wiles of fishing regulations, whereas Sheikh ʿAlwān knows nothing about them. Sheikh ʿAlwān is the only one who could bail Freij's brother out, however, since he represents the lineage vis-à-vis the Israeli administration. But the military governor was too smart by half. Hebrew does not distinguish between agnates and cognates, and although he spoke some Arabic, the Israeli governor did not understand the cultural significance of the distinction made in Arabic. Ṣbeṭān played upon the governor's ignorance, telling him that Freij's brother's wife was in fact from Ṣbeṭān's wife's lineage—and therefore that Freij's brother could be represented by Sheikh Ṣbeṭān vis-à-vis the Israeli authorities.

FREIJ: Sheikh Ṣbeṭān also told the governor that the Reserve is not allowed to take away Bedouin fishing licenses, and that he will discuss the matter at the next sheikhs' [monthly] meeting with the governor and his aides.

Pause.

ʿABDALLAH: Why does the Reserve care if people fish for lobster in Ras al-Ṭanṭūr?

NŪR: Those guys . . . they love mountains and animals more than people . . . even if the people are their own. Once they brought a chubby guy and told me that he's from the university, a doctor for mice. They said, he would pay me if I'd take him on my camel to the top of Wadi Mandar, and then help him carry his things on my back to the peak of Mount Ṣabbāḥ . . .

SHTĒWI [*interrupts Nūr, eyebrows pinched with puzzlement*]: Really?! To the peak of Mount Ṣabbāḥ [one of the steepest in the peninsula]? . . .

NŪR: Un-huh! Every evening he used to dip bread in something that looked like baby shit. It tasted like nuts. He put it in the tin boxes I carried for him. The next morning, he had all sorts of mice and gerbils caught in those boxes. He talked to them and measured them and wrote about them as if he were a physician, and then . . . by my life! . . . he would let them go. Ha! . . . And he told me that the government pays him money to do this. That was his whole job. And really, he sounded like he was someone big there. But he's crazy, and the government which sent him must be crazy, too.

Laughter.

RAḌWĀN: And there is another one, crazy like your mice doctor. He is a *jolōji* (geologist). He doesn't put his heart with animals. He puts it with stones.

SHTĒWI: Stones?!

RAḌWĀN: Jolōji, that means, someone who climbs around on mountains to collect stones . . . Once ʿAṭṭallah came to me and asked me if I was looking for work. I said, "What kind?" and he said, "There are two *jolōjiya* (geologists) and they need people to go with them and carry their stones when they are high up on the mountains." I said, "Whaat? The Jews also have monks who build chapels on tops of mountains?"[8] He said, "No, you fool. They said they'll check the stones and tell us how old our land is . . ." They paid us quite well. They were sweet people, religious, like us, skullcaps on their heads. They carried half the stones and left ʿAṭṭallah and me with the other half. They gave us half their food, and we made them bread and tea. They were also from some university, Beer Sheba, maybe.

Pause.

ḤMĒD: Well, in the beginning, when all these *ṭawaṭīt* ("turkeys") started coming, I said, "They must be looking for manganese or oil, even gold, maybe." But after a while, I wasn't so sure. They didn't change anything, they just took a little of this, a little of that, maybe a souvenir for their government. But they continue, each time taking just a bit. Who knows, maybe this desert has some things hidden in it.

RĀSHED: Not hidden and not a watermelon (*mush madsūs wala baṭṭiḥ*)! Once a guy from Nature [The Israeli Society for the Protection of Nature][9] told me that our land's pretty, and that's why they have to guard its beauty.

FREIJ [*immediately responding*]: What is this?! Our land is *our* land! Those guys—is it any of their business?

Most of the men look at Sheikh ʿAlwān. His sphinx-like gaze is still fixed on the mountain tops. Only his cheek muscle twitches.

SAʿĪD [*cynical intonation*]: Our land is our land? Ha ha . . . [*then seriously*] Now it's not allowed to gather *arāk* [bushes] (*salvadora*, Latin) as firewood (*ḥaṭab*) in the Shurā [the mangrove area north of the straits of Ṭirān]. The Reserve said that many Bedouin from all the tribes come there with their pickups, and use all the arāk. Why do they care?

Pause.

RĀSHED: And do we care? . . . Once, when we were moving (*lamma raḥalna*—when we had a full migratory cycle), we were going from one place to another, collecting firewood, a bit here, a bit there. Now, everyone who can't find a job gets a pickup, and *hayya* (let's go), to the Shurā or to the Farsh [the Highland Plateau], to load his pickup with arāk or *ʿajram* [bushes] (*ochradenus*, Latin), to wander from community to community and make money. One day they [both kinds of plants] will be finished. It's good that *someone* cares. So what if he's not from here?

FREIJ [*interrupts Rāshed with a raised voice*]: But because that "snake" from the Reserve guards our sea and our bushes, my brother has to sit in jail?

ḤAMDĀN: Patience, my dear Freij . . . The jail in Sharm is like laughter. One ʿAlēgi [an ʿAleigāt tribesman] with whom I worked in *kelīm* (dishwashing, Hebrew) at that restaurant in Sharm sat in that jail because he had stolen two empty barrels from the army.[10] He said the food was good, and the policeman slapped him, only on his face, and only twice. The other policeman, the one who speaks Arabic and has a mustache, he gave him cigarettes . . . The paternal cousin of that ʿAlēgi stole ten, and he didn't go to jail. Instead, that redhead master sergeant tied him to a date tree and beat him with his belt. If they catch you doing something, two to three days in jail, even a week, are better than that. And if you go to jail, the sheikh will help get you out.

SĀLEM [*shaking his fist*]: But a jail's a jail, sitting there for empty talk about bushes or lobster or selling corals and shells to tourists?![11]

SLIMĀN [*shaking his head in disagreement, his voice lower than Sālem's*]: No, man! These things are no nonsense! Once, our fathers and grandfathers, even some of us here, didn't they use to make money from the tourists who came to the Santa Katarina Monastery?

SEVERAL MEN: Yes, they did.

SLIMĀN [*to Sālem*]: See how? And today, don't we make money from those who come to these mountains and bushes and corals? [*pausing for a second; since no one answers, he continues*] We do and we do. Now if we take fish and stones and corals and bushes and . . . you name it . . . to sell, all of it, what would be left for our sons and grandsons to show the children of those tourists when they all grow up?

NŪR [*shouting*]: Both of you, you foolish asses . . . Your land is never yours, never! It was under the Turks, and then under the English, then under the Egyptians, and then under Israelis, and then, under the Egyptians, and then, under the Isra—

RĀSHED [*gesturing with his hand*]: Enough, enough! We all know that. And for that we have sheikhs who talk with them for us. We are the People of the Land and they [the occupiers] are the People of Politics.

On other occasions, I heard people bitterly laughing about this dichotomy. But now, in the heat of debate, no one thinks it is funny. Only the sheikh manages to smile, though just barely, and everyone looks in his direction. But his gaze remains fixed on the faraway mountains.

ḤAMDĀN [*furiously*]: But the sheikhs . . . are they any of *our* business? . . . Every time the government changes hands, the new government replaces half of them. The other half replaces one face with another. The Israelis kicked out to Egypt some of the Egyptian sheikhs. And when the Egyptians return, they may jail some of the Israeli sheikhs. I told you before. Sinai's land is like Sinai's sheikhs, sometimes with Egypt, sometimes with Israel.

FREIJ [*very loud*]: With a sheikh or without a sheikh—it's all the same. The sheikh, [*louder*] what is he? He "is" a nice salary without working; he "is" a meeting with other sheikhs and the military governor once a month; he "is" a "hanging around" in the Bedouin cafes of al-Wādi. [*He pauses for a second, then slowly, in a quieter, though rancorous voice, uttering the oft-repeated cliché*] The sheikhs lick the ass of the government!

By now, Sheikh ʿAlwān's cheek is twitching even faster.

SĀLEM [*with sarcasm*]: And you—don't you lick the ass of your sheikh? We saw you, how you brought a skinbottle full of dates to his wife the Ḥajja and his children from the Firān . . . If not, who will get you an ID? Who will sign you with the [CARE] Relief? Who got your brother out of jail? And who will help you to put your thumbprint in the right place, so that you can go on the Ḥajj to Mecca next month?

SAʿĪD [*screaming, pointing with his index finger to Sheikh ʿAlwān*]: This sheikh?! Say whaaat?! He knows very well how to explain to us what the government says. But does he know to explain to the government what *we* say? . . . And his poor wife, "the mother of sons" . . .

Once again all eyes are focused on the sheikh. He fiercely stubs out his cigarette in the ground. The muscle of his right cheek twitches even faster. Choked by his tobacco-saturated cough, he shouts: "Shut up, all of you, you sons of bitches! How wonderful Bedouin talk would be if it were not redundant (*maḥsan kalām al-ʿArab lo ma taradīdo*)! And never forget that, for the Israelis, your worth is no more or less than the corals and the mountains and the mice that they have found here. As for the Egyptians—you are nothing but Bedouin. You're not the fat city dwellers (*mudunnīyya*), not even peasants (*fallaḥīn*), just Bedouin, OK?"

All eyes, focused on the sheikh, widen. Some veiled faces peek out from inside tents. Even the children stop playing down in the wadi. I tell the anthropologist to recall the hierarchical trilogy of urbanities, peasants, and nomads that was drilled into her when she studied the Middle East. Then I remember the woman who warned the kids two weeks ago that if they didn't shut up, the sheikh would hand them over to the governor.

"Aakh . . ." continues the sheikh in feigned disgust. With a sigh, he slowly repeats the proverb: "How wonderful Bedouin talk would be if it were not redundant . . ."

"If it were not redundant," some of the men repeat.

*

"Not long ago, when the crescent moon of Ramaḍān had just risen, the big boss of the Reserve in Sharm al-Sheikh, Ḥawāja Assāf, asked me to join him for a trip to the Highlands and their people."

The sheikh talks to us in a distancing voice, marking the start of a story.

"I told him, 'Now that people are fasting, you want to visit them? Who will knead dough for you? Who will serve you tea?' He said, 'OK, we won't visit the people, just the mountains. But you've got to come.' And do you think I could say no? But I teased him, 'For you guys—the people, the mountains, there's no difference [between them] . . .'"

"There is no difference," some men echo, signaling their active participation in listening.

"So the next day, the Reserve boss loaded his jeep with a carton of food cans, fuel and water jerrycans, a small gas stove, a backpack, and a sleeping bag. I loaded on the jeep a little bundle made of my two blankets. In it I put little bags of flour, sugar, tea, a few dates, a salt crystal and a can of sardines. I tied the goat waterskin to the side of the jeep."

The anthropologist observes how the sheikh juxtaposes the traditional Bedouin equipment for overnight trips with the traditional Israeli equipment for back-route surveys. She is surprised that the sheikh does not conceal from the audience the fact that he ate before sundown during Ramaḍān.

"So before we went on the dirt route, we stopped at Jabali's cafe. The big boss bought a pack of Farīd cigarettes, and I bought Marlboro. I poked fun at him for that. I told him, 'I get a small salary from the government, and you get a large one.' He said that he puts his money in the bank so that the money will grow, like corals, and make more money. I told him that it didn't make sense, and that I put my money into basic food staples (*ʿeish*) which I store in a cache (*garia*) in the mountains. If another war should start, my children will have something to eat till the new government starts giving us work. He laughed, and we entered the bumpy dirt road (*dagadīg*)."

"Money makes money?" asks Nūr, "What ugly thinking! A man needs to store basic food staples in his cache!" he adds, and the others nod their heads in agreement.

"And I wanted him to be happy, so that he'd put his heart in the way, so I sang him a *hejēni* (caravan song) and explained to him what it was. But I told him that it would sound better without the sound of the motor, with only the sound of camel hooves on the arcosis (*saḥasīḥ*) of the wadi. See?"

The sheikh pauses, thinking his audience would laugh. I chuckle, but notice that no one else seems to have picked up on his mocking reference to what Israeli nature buffs see as "authentic desert travel."

"Late in the afternoon we arrived at Faranje [the central highland of the plateau]. The Reserve guy stopped his jeep and asked me to join him in climbing one of the mountains he found on his map. I teased him, saying, 'Climb a mountain? Why? Have you lost one of your goats?' 'No,' he said. 'I just want to see the plateau from above. I also want to see how the sun sets beyond the mountains of the monastery area."

"What's his business with the sunset? Does he pray at dusk?" asks Freij, disbelief in his voice. The other men laugh.

"So we climbed up the mountain, him, running to the top like I did when I was a kid, and me, with the bones of an old man, and no walking stick . . . But could I say no to that child? . . . And we sat there, high up. He looked at his map and said, 'This mountain, what's its name?' And I told him, 'Why do you always ask us names of mountains? You think every mountaintop has a name? Well, let's call this one *Ras Ghābat al-Shams* (the peak of the sunset), because we climbed it to see how the sun sets."

"Ras Ghābat al-Shams," repeats Shtēwi slowly. "*Ya salām!* (Wow!) It even rhymes." We roar in laughter.[12]

"And we sat there, high up, and we saw all of Faranje, all of the plateau (*ʿilu*), all full of ʿajram and *shīḥ* [bushes] (*artemisia herba alba*, Latin), and in the middle, the Israeli airport. Then he told me, 'You know, now that your people work for us around Faranje, they live there most of the year. So now they gather their firewood only in Faranje, and it isn't good for the ʿajram.'"

Sālem blurts out, "What kind of talk is this?" We turn our heads towards Sālem, but the sheikh doesn't wait, saying,

"So as I told you, that Reserve boss said, 'I think that, just as I forbade the gathering of arāk in the Flatlands after you started living there permanently, I will also outlaw gathering ʿajram here, in the plateau.'"

"He'll outlaw gathering ʿajram here," echoes Shtēwi, leaning forward.

"'Ahh . . .' I moaned, 'the days of the past . . .' That kid didn't answer. He just sat there, and enjoyed his soul. I offered him one of my Marlboros, and lit one for myself. And we were smoking our cigarettes like that, without talking. So I repeated, 'The days of the past . . . Once we lived without all this mess.'"

The anthropologist makes a note to herself that this is the beginning of a new story, a story within the sheikh's story, signaled by the word "once."

"True, without all this mess," some report, nodding their heads.

"'Once, even as near to the time of my grandpa . . . My grandpa made his cash when he made and sold charcoal (*habsh*), and also when he sold a few young lambs and kidgoats. In the spring, he would climb to the Tih Plateau and burn *ratam* [bushes], and in the winter he would burn *sayyāl* (acacia trees) down in the wadis. Two, three times a year he loaded everything onto his camel, and went on a *khaṭīra* (a trip to buy basic food staples) to Suez. There he sold everything and brought back flour, wheat berries, sugar, tea, rice, oil, some fabrics and clothes, and other small things.'"

"Food and other small things," repeats Rāshed.

"And Ḥawāja Assāf knit his forehead, and asked me, 'Was it enough for all the family? the men and the women and the children?' And I answered, 'No. My father and paternal uncles worked in Suez and Qantara before they got married. But after they got married, they made charcoal, and sent us to work with the Egyptians, in Abu-Rodeis.'"

"In Abu-Rodeis . . . We all worked for the Egyptians, in Abu-Rodeis," Ḥmēd adds.

"And then, that Reserve guy, like a scorpion had just bitten him, said, 'Wait, wait! I want to understand something. How is it that you didn't consume all the sayyāl and ratam? I always thought they were here, just the way they are, because they are holy with you . . .' So I said, 'You know, this was when we were moving around, before the Egyptians wanted us all to live near Abu-Rodeis and work in the oil fields and the manganese mines—before your term, before now, when we all want to be near the main dirt-roads.'"

And the anthropologist will note that during the Israeli occupation Bedouin gradually chose to relocate in order to be near the main truck routes of the peninsula. Since the Suez market ceased to exist, El-ʿArishian merchants who traveled in trucks sold the Sinai Bedouin basic food staples and other household items and bought their excess animals from them.

"'You know,' I told him, 'Today we have plenty of everything, and we have little money, so we can't buy all this plenty. In those days, when we had just a little of things, we had to respect those things, and save them, so that everyone would be able to make a living from those little things. You can't measure the little of those days in money. It came from our land.'"

"From our land," Ḥamdān says.

"Our land, we sit in it!" adds Nūr.

"So I told him more about our land. I said, 'Those days, we used to e agreements (ᶜ*anwa*—intertribal legislation) between the different phratries (*rubaᶜ*) of the Mzeina, and between the Mzeina and the rest of the Ṭawara. You know, it's like your Israel has agreements with America and Britain and France. We used to have the agreement on pastures, and the agreement on camels, and the agreement on charcoal.' So he asked, 'What exactly are these agreements?' And I told him about our agreements."

"And our Sheikh ᶜAlwān told Ḥawāja Assāf about our agreements," Ḥmēd, the eldest, echoes, slowly accentuating every word.

These are intertribal agreements discussing the boundaries of the South Sinai tribal alliance with regard to pasture, the return of lost camels that wandered into the North Sinai, and the use of plants needed for making charcoal. The charcoal agreement prohibits the destruction of whole plants for the purpose of charcoal making and gives tedious instructions for pruning the parts made into charcoal (cf. Levi 1982, 1988:371; Rabinowitz 1985). The anthropologist hypothesizes that the sheikh does not spell all this out since everyone in the audience is familiar with these agreements.

"By then, it was dusk. That Reserve guy didn't say anything. He just stared at the red clouds. Later he said, 'Look, how beautiful!' I teased him, 'Eh . . . so you, too, talk like the tourists? But you have been here for a while . . .' The moon rose, and we went down from the mountain. And I hummed to myself the *gaṣīda* (poem) of my maternal uncle as a hejēni."

This is a poem composed by ᶜAlwān's maternal uncle, who was also a sheikh, to the father to whom ᶜAlwān's wife referred earlier. The poem criticizes external governments and the way they use the sheikh to exert control over the Bedouin. The poem is known to the audience as "The Gaṣīda of the Sheikh."[13] The anthropologist notes that the sheikh does not recite the poem to his Bedouin audience, probably because they all are familiar with it, but the words of the poem flash through her mind:

Bigūl: Al-bārḥan bil-leil bayyatt saharān,
Al-nōm lajlaj fi ᶜeini ma ghashshāha.
Wmseit ṣāḥi, wṣbaḥt ghathyān;
Wzkān al-ᶜīsha zay hēdhi— balāha.
Ḥat al-jamal bat ᶜindi gawyān,
Ghār al-jarīda teᶜashāha.
Wugshoṭ ghabīṭi min faug Hadlān,
Wḥanto fi galbi ma nasāha!

Warkab min fōgo, wbel-māshi ʿajlān,
Weilfi ʿala ḥbayib ḍamīri ghalāha,
Weifi ʿArabna fi dirt al-aḥsān,
Lau al-ḥajar wal-gashsh bigit māha.
Wal-ḥamd l-Allah min al-rāʿi shabʿān,
Lau beẓlām al-leil baṭno malāha.

Al-yōm jad al-maraḍ kul ḥay wujʿān;
Ḥatta nafsī kazzat ʿashāha.
Hādha biwīn, wadhāk ghathyān;
Uṭlubu illi maʿaṭali fi samāha.
Jāt al-mōt ṣar yākhod min al-ʿArbān;
Jāt al-ḥakūma zawwat ghathāha.
Sārat al-ḥakūma tejībna min kūl el-arkān;
Taṣīb-al-Bedu mīhi bhawāha.
Ḥaṭatna fi ṣūr min fōgna sheikhān—
Al-ḥakūma ghadhab! Allah daʿāha!
Wazkān lelmʿāyesh ma ṣār sheiṭān—
Yidhīʿok al-wagt min kuthur ghalāha.
Zamān khaṭirna min faug baʿarān;
Wel-yōm ʿarabi teḥarāha.

As they say of old: Last night I camped without sleeping,
My eyelids unyielding to sleep's restless teasing.
All night sudden wakings, worn out at dawn;
If this is life—God, let me go on.
Even my camel knelt irate to sleep,
One withered palm frond all he had to eat.
When I lifted the saddle around Hadlan's tail,
I will never forget his heart-rending wail!
Now I ride in haste, his massive back above,
Again to make the rounds of all those I love,
To visit each oasis, grassy and lush,
Where even among stones cool springs do gush.
And my camel there content, Praise be to God,
All night in the pasture chewing his cud.

These days all things live in illness and pain;
Even my own soul cannot bear to eat again.
Here the people whine, there they are groaning;
Ask heaven why all things on earth are moaning.
The Bedouin's losses started with Death;

Governments moved in to seize what was left.
They rounded us up from every side;
They forced us to forfeit our way of life
In permanent encampments, put sheikhs on top—
What arrogance! cursed forever by God!
And just to make a living, you must grow a devil's ears—
It's frightening how the value of money disappears.
In olden times food came to us on camel caravans;
Nowadays on dusty roads in shabby trucks and vans.

But soon the anthropologist has to go back to her dedicated note-taking, as Sheikh ʿAlwān continues his story: "'Why don't you make an agreement for the ʿajram with the rest of the sheikhs, just like the one you already have for the sayyāl and the ratam?' said the Reserve boss, 'It would be better than a law that I would have to enforce.'"

"That he would have to enforce!" Shtēwi gasps.

"I laughed and said, 'The sheikhs don't make agreements. The sheikhs are only good for talking with the government. The *ʿurfi* (customary) judges make agreements.' So he wanted me to talk to the judges. I told him, 'They won't talk to me about such nonsense. You can't make charcoal from ʿajram, so you can't make money selling it to strangers. So there wouldn't be any agreement. The ʿajram, there was never an agreement on it, and there never will be an agreement on it. It just grows."

"That's right, it just grows," says Raḍwān.

"The ʿajram, it can't have an agreement," Rāshed assures us.

"So as I told you, we were going down from the mountain. That Assāf looked like his head was still in those red clouds."

Some men laugh. The sheikh doesn't wait for the laughter to die down, but chides them,

"No, ya folks (*jamāʿa*), don't laugh. That guy really loves our land of mountains. He just doesn't know how . . . And when we were near the jeep, just before getting in, I said to him, 'Look, ya Assāf. You're as young as one of my sons, and it's really great that your government pays you for just playing "Nature" or "Reserve," and with red clouds and lobster, and God only knows what else . . . And you even said that you put your money in the bank. But we have no bank. All we have ever had is this Sinai and that's it. And for our life, we have to take from it. Your government says it's hers, and the Egyptians may say it's theirs, but *we* are the people of the land.'"

"Ya-ha, see how?" says Freij with a smile.

"See how?" others join in.

Pause.

"And power be bestowed on you (*wal-gūwwa*)!" says Saᶜīd.

"And God will bestow power on you (*bigawwīg*)!" answers the sheikh.

This utterance of "gūwwa!" and the answer of "bigawwīg!" was a traditional exchange of greetings. However, someone in an audience might sometimes exchange such a greeting with a storyteller during a dramatic turning point in the story, to show that she or he understood that the point just expressed was to be emphasized.

"So after I told him that, he started the jeep's engine, and lit himself another cigarette. We sat. He looked like his mind was working fast. He said, 'One pickup-truck load of ᶜajram for a family twice a month would be OK?' And I had to say OK. It's better than nothing. And we drove to the Monastery. He went to his friends in the house of King Farouq.[14] And I took my things and went to be a guest in the magᶜad of Mūsa al-Jebāli [from the Jebaliyya tribe]."

"So our Sheikh ᶜAlwān drank from the coffee of Mūsa al-Jebāli. One of his family is married with one of my wife's family," adds Raḍwān.

"Two days after that, I got a ride with the Israeli captain of the people of the Monastery [area] back to al-Ṭūr, and that's what happened."

"And that's what happened," repeat all the men in unison.

"That's what happened" is one of the many statements to signify that the storyteller has reached the end of his story.

"Bravo (*taslam ᶜīdok*), ya Sheikh ᶜAlwān!" some add.

A peaceful silence reigns over the wadi. Shtēwi furrows his forehead, thinking. He then pipes up, "But even in the old days, charcoal alone was never enough for making money. Old folks always had to work for some government."

"So what?" says Sālem. "We had those agreements, which we still have, and the rest belongs to the story that the sheikh told that Reserve guy. And now, Saᶜīd, serve our Sheikh ᶜAlwān coffee. He must be thirsty after this long story."

The soft silence embraces everything. Then someone asks, "When are the pilgrims leaving for Mecca?" and a new conversation is born.

III.

Once a month, the Jewish military governor of the South Sinai, usually a major or lieutenant colonel, together with other, lower-ranking military personnel, met with the sheikhs. In these meetings, the sheikhs and officers discussed the implementation of Israeli civil and military laws and regulations, as well as any administrative problems that had arisen. From 1967 until early 1975 the monthly meetings took place in the oil town of Abu-Rodeis. After the return of the Abu-Rodeis area to the Egyptians (following the 1975 Kissinger disengagement agreements), the meetings were moved to al-Ṭūr.

Several times I requested permission from the military governor to attend the monthly sheikhs' meeting. I also asked several sheikhs to ask him for permission. In spite of the fact that the sheikhs explained to him that "she has a body of a woman, but talks politics like a man," the military governor refused my request. He explained that I was of the wrong gender *and* politics.

There was only one asphalt road along the western coast of the Sinai peninsula, connecting Sharm al-Sheikh with the town of Suez via al-Ṭūr and Abu-Rodeis. Ever since Abu-Rodeis had been founded by the Egyptians, the Bedouin had been permitted to work there, but not to settle. They, however, were allowed to live in Abu-Zneima. So when Abu-Rodeis became the Israeli administrative center for Bedouin affairs, several Bedouin cafes quickly sprang up, side by side, along the asphalt road. These cafes, built of dried palm fronds and scraps of thin plywood, served tourists and soldiers. They were also gathering points for the sheikhs and their entourages. Unlike magᶜads, they had tables and chairs. In them one could order Israeli versions of Coke and Sprite as well as waffles, candies, Bedouin tea, and Israeli coffee. The Bedouin would surreptitiously buy the ouzo, vodka, brandy, whiskey, and beer that non-Muslim tourists and soldiers bought openly. By buying liquor under the table, perhaps the Bedouin made a feeble gesture towards their Muslim conscience. Following the monthly sheikh's meeting, some of the sheikhs, especially those appointed by the Israelis, would go to the cafes, openly and despondently drinking away their frustration.

When the military administrative center was moved to the town of al-Ṭūr (where Bedouin had not been allowed to live since the time of the previous Egyptian occupation), the whole complex of monthly meetings, roadside cafes, and drunken sheikhs migrated to the road leading to the neighboring al-Wadi.

Al-Wadi, 5 November 1978

Mnēfi's cafe, 10 o'clock at night. The shanty town sleeps. I sit at a corner table, drinking a cup of hot tea, smoking a cigarette, and tell the anthropologist to write a summary and analysis of the day's events by the light of a small, dim lantern.

A military command car stops, brakes squealing. Out jump five Israeli reservists in their forties, dressed in olive-drab army shirts and dripping swim suits barely restraining their bulging, neglected bellies. The wet towels draped around their necks and the unloaded M-16s slung over their shoulders sway as the men fling themselves around a table. With them are two Israeli hippie-type women, clad in calico-patched jeans with bead necklaces around their bone-thin ankles, their flimsy T-shirts tented by their cold nipples. I assume they have just come from nocturnal skinny-dipping in the nearby hot spring.[15]

"Mnēfi, we want your *real* Bedouin coffee," orders one of the soldiers in Arabic.

Mnēfi vanishes into the kitchen and probably concocts some boiled water mixed with prepackaged Elite Turkish Coffee [Israeli brand name] that someone bought for him in the supermarket of Eilat or Sharm al-Sheikh. He serves the coffee in small cups imported from the West Bank, and says in Hebrew, "This is authentic (*aṣli*)[16] Bedouin coffee."

Sheikh ʿAlwān sits with two other sheikhs at another corner table. One is from the Mzeina, the other, a sheikh of another tribe. They huddle in their woolen wraps, enveloped in a cloud of cigarette smoke. They chat about the monthly sheikh meeting that took place that afternoon, while they drink cycles of beer followed by sweet tea.

"Look, there's that weirdo who lives with the Bedouin," one of the soldiers says in Hebrew, pointing at me. "Why do you study Arabs? Aren't Israelis good enough for you?"

"Hey you, leave this girl (*bint*—unmarried virgin) alone. She's of us now," responds in Arabic Sheikh ʿAlwān, who also understands Hebrew. "Come, join our table, ya Smadar, have beer with us," the sheikh says to me.

I hesitate for a moment. The anthropologist tells me that she is already full of the day's events and wants to be left alone for a while, but . . .

"If three Muslims invite me to drink with them, who am I to refuse?"

I joke. "I am not a Muslim. The people of this land are Muslims, but what are their sheikhs?" I ask in a cynical intonation.

One sheikh responds in drunken laughter, "Muslims? This is all new. Islam has once again become the fashion. Before the time of Israel, no one prayed regularly five times a day . . . This is all new. Before, with the Egyptians, only our sheikhs prayed."

The anthropologist is curious, so she permits herself a difficult question. "And don't the sheikhs dictate fashions?"

"Who puts his heart with the sheikhs?" ᶜAlwān asks sarcastically, and the rest join in with alcohol-induced laughter.

Another sheikh points at ᶜAlwān and says, "How can this one, for example, be a sheikh who lives on the Highland, while half of his [lineage] people dwell in the East [Coast]? Why won't the government give him a command car with a chauffeur?" We laugh some more, and he continues half-seriously, "And how can I be a sheikh, while most of the people I am supposed to sheikh for are now in Egypt?"

Since no one is able to answer, we are silent. The cloud of cigarette smoke above our heads thickens. The soldiers and their two women have drunk their fill of coffee and smoked their cigarettes. The sheikhs and I exchange meaningful glances as all these middle-aged straw-widowers depart at this late hour with the two women.

"You know, my lineage had another sheikh during the Egyptian period. The Israelis exiled him to Egypt. Write it down. Write it down," says the non-Mzeini sheikh. "Write that he didn't know how to play his *shīza* [a complicated cross between checkers and "go"]. He knew how to go between the Egyptians and us. When you [the Israelis] arrived, he just didn't know how to explain you to the Bedouin, or how to explain the Bedouin to you. Your government is different, but he was too old to learn another way to play the shīza. And you know, when the Egyptians return, we are all going to go. Of course, we must all go."

Silently we finish sipping our beers and order sweet tea. After a while, the third sheikh adds, "Well, gentlemen (*jamāᶜa*) that's the way it is. For every government, the sheikh is a Bedouin, and for every Bedouin, the sheikh is the government. These two will never meet."

Gloom fuses with our cloud of cigarette smoke and the alcohol. Sheikh ᶜAlwān gathers himself. Suddenly, he pounds his fist on the table and says vigorously: "But we know damn well how to play our stories!"

It's very late. We sip our next round of cold, bitter beer, then pucker our lips to the sweet tea. And the night breeze carries the crow of an anxious cock.

CODA: ON GOD, POLITICS, AND RED CLOUDS

In accordance with the Camp David Agreement, Sheikh ʿAlwān's encampment was returned to Egypt at the end of 1979. Over the summer of 1981 I returned to the Sinai for a short period of fieldwork. I joined a group of Bedouin from the eastern peninsula, still under Israeli control, and together we crossed the temporary borders, heading west for the annual date harvest in Wadi Firān.

On the Egyptian side of the border there were *no* environmental laws and regulations. In addition, the grandiose Egyptian development projects planned for the Sinai made me fear for the desert's fragile ecological balance—fear that it could be permanently destroyed. The development plans also threatened once again to turn the Bedouin into migrant laborers in their own homeland (cf. Lavie and Young 1984).

In Wadi Firān I met Sheikh ʿAlwān. He was still a sheikh, in spite of the change in governments. In one of the magʿads, he reclined on a colorful handwoven rug, rolling his prayer beads between his fingers. Later, he prayed in the mosque with everyone else. The next day, in one of those liminal moments when the sun is still setting and the moon has yet to rise, he told me a proverb strikingly similar to what Musil had written in the 1920s: "The sheikh must be a man of vision and knowledge, of understanding and fear (*Al-Sheikh lāzem yikūn shawwāf waʿarrāf wafakkār wakhawwāf*)." We looked at each other, and two sighs emerged from the depths of wishful thinking. He added, "Yeah . . . now your friend, Sheikh ʿAlwān, has made his wife happy, and also joined the ones who play with God. Nice friends God's got here. To the west, Anwar Sadat plays with him, and the Muslim Brothers, too, but theirs is sort of different. And on the other side of the earth, Ronald Reagan, he also has his God. And to the east, Menachem Begin, he has his God, too. Even [the West Bank settlers of] Gush Emunīm, in the countries of the north (*bilād al-shām*), have some God who wants them as they are. See, God is a good thing for the People of Politics." He coughed his tobacco-saturated laugh and pointed his index finger to the skies. "Look," he said, perhaps unaware (perhaps not) that he was imitating the Reserve boss, "Look, how beautiful! Here are the red clouds . . ."

4
THE MADWOMAN

Al-Majnuna

Madness [was] the result of our incapacity to control or to moderate our passions. Instituted by the unity of soul and body, madness turned against that unity and once again put it to question.

MICHAEL FOUCAULT
Madness and Civilization

Unlike men, [women] are categorically denied the experience of cultural supremacy, humanity, and renewal based on their sexual identity. In different ways, some women are driven mad by this fact. Such madness is essentially an intense experience of female biological, sexual, and cultural castration, and a doomed search for potency. The search often involves "delusions" or displays of physical aggression, grandeur, sexuality and emotionality. Such traits in women are feared and punished in patriarchal mental asylums.

PHYLLIS CHESLER
Women and Madness

"Women—they say in Islam that they are like beasts, just like goats. We, men, should guard their *nafs* (soul)." So said Hajj Slimān, a furrowed, pious old man who volunteered every Ramaḍān to wake up his neighbors for the late night meal. The men around him hummed in agreement.

When I told his wife what he had said about her kind, she responded, "Well, you know, men have *ʿagl* (rational mind). They know Islam, and understand how to pray to God and Muḥammad his prophet. We, women—Allah blessed us only with nafs."

Indeed, Mzeini ideas about gender did not differ much from the general Muslim ideology of gender—a hierarchical order where women are to be controlled because of their emotional, passionate, and capricious souls, capable of bringing shame (*ʿeib*) on the whole family, whereas men, with their ability to think and act rationally, acquire religious honor (*sharaf*, *karāma*) for exerting authority over women.[1] Ideally speaking, Mzeini marriages were said to be as stable as other Muslim Arab marriages. Stability in marriage was to be achieved by a utopian compatibility between the husband's ʿagl and the wife's nafs. This stability was greatly enhanced by arranging the young man a patrilineal-patrilocal marriage, preferably to a *bint ʿam*, a father's brother's daughter.[2]

But the Mzeinis had another pair of concepts describing the essence of manhood and womanhood. When I asked many married women about their opinions about men, Ghānma gave me the most succinct answer, saying bitterly, "Men—how could you trust someone who erects immediately? They have *ghayii*—sexual lust." And Silmi, sardonically grinning on the day of his third wedding, muttered to me, "Women—better watch out for them. They have *ṣabr*—patience, endurance, tolerance, equanimity. And their ṣabr can destroy even the toughest of guys." This common wisdom of everyday life emphasized

◀ A MARRIED WOMAN OF CHILD-BEARING AGE

a quality opposite the Muslim idea of male rationality, namely, male sexual desire, even as the Muslim emphasis on female sexual passion was juxtaposed with its opposite quality: the ability to endure and manipulate. And I wondered what kind of juncture these two sets of oddly paradoxical inversions would form in a marriage.

During my thirteen years of fieldwork I observed many Mzeini marriages that ended in divorce within their first year unless children were involved. These marriages were not merely based on the harmonious compatibility between ʿagl and nafs, but were driven into conflict by the husband's fear of what he perceived as his wife's power to manipulate him, and by the wife's distrust of her husband because of what she perceived as his insatiable, shifting sexuality.

Perhaps because the men were responding to the vicissitudes of life in the Sinai with its frequent geopolitical and economic changes (cf. Marx 1980), ghayii, rather than ʿagl, was the concept of manhood that typified quotidian discourse. Men, in order to maximize their options while constantly preparing for external governmental changes, had economic and political interests that were numerous, broadly defined, ephemeral and multifocused. Ṣabr, rather than nafs, was then the concept typifying the everyday discourse of womanhood in order to develop the women's sense of their inherent ability to cope with their men's transient interests.

Mzeini marriages therefore differed greatly from the classic Bedouin marriage described in the anthropological literature. Though they maintained patrilineal descent, Mzeini residence after marriage was usually not patrilocal or virilocal. The fathers of the spouses-to-be would negotiate the newlyweds' residence, which could variably be with the kin of the bride or the groom.[3] Furthermore, unlike other Arab pastoralist cultures, the Mzeinis did not have any long- or short-term bridewealth customs to demonstrate the respective families' deep commitment to the marriage bond (cf. Fortes 1949; Kressel 1977; Lewis 1961). The only things given to the newlyweds equally by the families of both the bride and the groom were a few blankets, storage boxes, sacks of basic food staples, a pot or two, and other rudimentary household goods. Perhaps the lack of any significant symbolic or monetary exchange between the spouses' families prior to and after the marriage signified that the Mzeinis did not view marriage as a life commitment. Maybe it stemmed from the fact that these people, in spite of their pastoralist tradition, had always been migrant laborers. Or perhaps it was just due to their relative poverty as semisedentary nomads.

As among other Bedouin tribes, the bride played a pivotal role in forming an alliance between the spouses' fathers. But in the Mzeina case, the bride also played an important role in the eventual break-up of this alliance and the serial start of other alliances of the same sort.

Mzeini marriages had an interesting, and to my eyes, also devastating dynamics. Usually, in adolescence, a girl or a boy would develop a platonic love relationship with someone from his or her encampment or from a nearby settlement. In spite of the strict purdah code, the lovers would usually sneak out to meet and exchange small presents. The girl would unveil for the boy, revealing her mouth and nose, two extremely sensual organs, and they would embrace. This first love was their most precious relationship, to be longed for and reminisced about for the rest of their lives.

But few were the lucky first lovers who got married to each other. Since they were from the same vicinity, their respective fathers were already woven into the same network of friends. When the girl reached fifteen, and the boy eighteen, the father would search for a prospective spouse who was the child of someone residing where the father had no immediate paternal or maternal kin or close friends. Seemingly for securing the future of the newlyweds, but actually for their own benefit, the fathers would discuss ventures such as sharing an orchard, acquiring water rights in a well, or just being friends for the days to come. And the children were expected to obey by accepting their fathers' choice of spouse for them.

But the bride, being not so bound by patrilineal considerations as the groom was, rebelled against the marriage. Because the wedding ceremony took place in her natal community, she was already nestled among her supportive girlfriends. Even if she moved to a different community, or at worst, to her in-laws', she was always surrounded by a supportive group of unmarried or freshly divorced women. These women friends helped her arrange and cover up the surreptitious though still platonic meetings with her adolescent sweetheart, where she found emotional refuge from her marriage.

Usually, the father's interest in his daughter's marriage lasted for around a year or two. During this period, the father might beat his daughter with the *ʿasā*, the stick used for disciplining camels, to ensure that she acquiesced in the marriage. But as soon as the friendship or partnership of the husband's and wife's fathers was growing strong, they no longer needed the bonding role of the daughter.

Soon after the fathers lost interest in the marriage, the daughter, unless she had become pregnant, would start playing a serious game of hide-and-seek with her husband, to avoid his sexual demands when he returned from a period of migrant labor. Eventually getting tired of this irritating game, the husband would call for divorce. About six months after the divorce, the woman's father would already be showing renewed interest in marrying her off again. This time he would select other people with alliance potential who had children of marriageable age. And once again, the daughter could fulfill her pivotal role in achieving a new alliance.

On the average, young Mzeinis remarried one to three times. Each time, the young woman hoped the groom would be someone she would love, and every time she was disappointed, she rekindled her smoldering platonic relationship with her first love. But bitterness crept into this first love relationship, in spite of closer physical interaction short of intercourse, because the adolescent sweetheart had also married. Most women feared that if their first love's wife showed any sexual interest, he would fall in love with her.[4]

The remarrying cycle stopped when the woman became pregnant. A divorced woman's child belonged to the ex-husband's patrilineage, and therefore she had almost no chance of remarriage. The woman also started thinking about who would provide for her in her old age and was therefore interested in bearing sons. Similarly, single women other than widows were looked down upon and were sometimes classified as "mad." Most women, then, submitted to their fate and stayed with the husband whose children they conceived. When a young woman reached the precise moment of being pregnant and recognizing her dependence on her husband, Mzeinis said that "ṣabr had begun to reside in her nafs." Most marriages were characterized by a tension between husband and wife because the wife resented losing her early womanhood's relative independence to manipulate her emotional relationships within the boundaries set by the patrilocal system and the purdah code. Only after years of married life, from menopause on, could a strong bond of friendship, mutual caring, and a "teasing relationship" (cf. Howell 1973) develop between the husband and wife.

Although the woman lost her independence after pregnancy, she did gain a new power. Women believed they could endure the vicissitudes of their early marriages and tolerate their husbands because of the *ṭuhūr*, female circumcision. The tip of the clitoris (*ʿanṭūr*) of girls between three and six years old was amputated to help them control their nafs and thus avoid bringing shame on their families. The Mzeinis' traditional belief was that if the clitoris tip were not removed, it would develop into a penis. Mzeini women argued that female circumcision prevented them from being burdened with ghayii—the insatiable lust of men. It is interesting to note that young boys were circumcised around the same age as young girls, and their circumcision was also termed ṭuhūr. But both men and women said that the sole function of male circumcision was to keep the tip of the penis clean.[5]

Women further argued that the removal of the clitoris tip, resulting in the lack of ghayii, meant that they had minimal interest in sex with their husbands. An old woman said, "My marriage could have been so wonderful if my husband hadn't kept doing his thing on me. The childbirths I didn't mind, they came once every two years or so, and now in my old age my sons provide for me. But whenever my husband came home [from migrant work], he had to do it twice a night. I fought, I bit his wrist, but when I got pregnant I realized I needed him, and therefore I had to let him do his thing. My skin there was red, and it used to hurt a week or two after he went back to work."

Tending to a man's household needs and children gave the wife an immense source of power. Because their husbands viewed sex as coming with marriage in a "package deal," women were able to assert their domestic power and manipulate their men by granting or withholding sexual favors. A middle-aged woman told me, "My husband quit buying enough basic food staples [for storage in the family's cache]. He thought that changing his inflated Israeli salary into dollars was a better way to save money. I told him I didn't like it, and he didn't listen. I told my eldest son [age fourteen] to tell him that all moneys are paper and only storing food will get us by [in case of a change in government in the Sinai]. My eldest son told him this in front of the men in the magʿad [an act considered a challenge to the man's honor]. Even then he didn't listen. Then I stopped sleeping with him when he came home. I screamed at him, 'Go to the female donkey!' He was stubborn for two more vacations, and then he started buying us things to store in the cache."

Mzeini women seemed to believe that clitoridectomy fulfilled both ideological and practical roles: it was a religious measure to control the woman's passionate nafs, and by eliminating the phallic ghayii, it also helped the woman better tolerate her everyday life.

Men therefore found themselves with unwilling or uninterested partners. A romantic yearning of adolescent boys was to have a "sweet sleep" with a woman, but the newlywed husband often had to struggle physically with his wife to get her to engage in sex. Among the metaphors used by Mzeini men to describe their penises was the ʿasā or *ʿasāya*, the stick used to discipline camels. Derived from this, the phrase for the coital act was "to hit her with the camel's stick" (*ḍarabha bil-ʿasā*).

Many young men expressed to me their fears about returning from migrant work, their insecurity in not knowing whether their wives would be home waiting for them, or away, having escaped. They abhorred their sexual struggles with their wives in the early years of marriage. To the best of my knowledge, female prostitution was not available to these men. They therefore resorted to bestiality. As one short, chubby man who owned a female donkey confided to me, grinning, "For us the donkey is like a prostitute is for you Israelis."[6]

Approximately one-third of Mzeini men I talked with told me that they experienced periods of impotence lasting from one month to one year during the first fifteen years of their marriage. Describing impotence, they used the metaphor of "falling off the camel's back" (*ṭāḥ min al-jamal*, or *wagaʿo al-jamal*). To remedy his impotence, one man even traveled 450 kilometers to Bethlehem, seeking psychiatric help in a mental hospital. In the spring of 1978 Dahab was the largest semisedentarized settlement in the South Sinai, a community of eighty-nine nuclear households, where six men were pointed out to me by both men and women as complete impotents. In January 1979 I hired one of these men to accompany me while I conduced a demographic survey in the remote, rugged southeastern mountains of the peninsula. Riding our camels sometimes as long as two days between encampments, we had all the time in the world to meander in wadis and in conversation. He confided in me and told me that the point came in his life when he got so emotionally burned out over struggling with his wife to get sex that he indeed became impotent. Similar conversations with three other men of the six pointed at similar dynamics.

The actual and metaphorical use of the camel's stick suggested that men were expected to exert physical authority over their wives, and one of the means they were supposed to use was sex. But since men were usually absent from their homes, the authority they exerted was to a large extent symbolic. On a day-to-day basis, women ran the life of the encampment.

The Israeli doctor who regularly tended most of the major settlements in the South Sinai told me that many of his men patients came and asked him to prescribe them *ḥbūb guiyāt*, "empowering pills." And to my surprise, a man from Wadi Naṣb cynically called his work as a street cleaner in Ofira, the southernmost Israeli settlement in the peninsula, "vacation" (*ajāza*). When I asked him why, he lamented, "Every time I come home, my wife complains about this and that and wants me to buy her and the children this and that . . . And at night she says she's tired, and when I come home from the magʿad, she wakes up the baby to make him start crying . . . This is such a headache . . ."

In the last decade, rumors had spread among both Mzeini men and women that the clitoris, if not cut, would not become a penis. Such rumors were based on the Mzeini participant-observation of the nude hippie culture that forced itself onto their beachfront territories along the ʿAqaba Gulf—a handful of young men had even had firsthand experience of the Western female genitalia (of European and American hippie women or Eilati prostitutes). Conversations the Mzeini had with Israeli nurses, physicians, and physical anthropologists further confirmed the rumors. One of the Mzeini sheikhs even offended the purdah code by daring to demand from his wife that their two young daughters not be circumcised. In a loud argument heard all over the neighborhood his wife screamed, "We are not of those from abroad, whose blood is heavy! This is still the desert, and we need our blood to be light! If I don't take my daughters to the circumciser to have their clitoris removed, their health will be weak and you won't be able to marry them to anyone." Two days later, after the sheikh left for his monthly meeting with the military governor, I asked her why she was so opposed to her husband's idea. She frowned and said, "What are these men thinking? If our daughters keep their clitoris, not only will their health be weakened, but also their minds."

Perhaps only temporary or permanent impotence allowed the men to suspend the paradoxical "double-bind" (Bateson 1972) caused by the dialectic conflation of male ʿagl/ghayii and female nafs/ṣabr, and the women could override it only through temporary or permanent madness.

Madness (*junūn*) was a behavior the Mzeinis attributed only to women. A woman became mad when she deviated from the strict code of conduct designed to help her maintain shame. To protect the family honor, women were not allowed to talk about their painful romantic emotions except in a highly metaphorical, rigidly formalistic genre of poignant poetry (cf. Abu-Lughod 1986). When a woman broke down emotionally and cried or talked about her problems in straightforward language, people around her claimed that she had become possessed by *jinn*s (demons). Such a woman would usually burst out with a public monologue, heard only by other women, where she explicitly described her painful experiences. Mzeini women called such monologues "talking about one's wounds of the heart" (*jurūḥ al-galb*). It was common for women to enter and leave states of possession during their early years of marriage, although very few women remained mad permanently. Everyone considered permanently mad women free of the restrictions of honor and shame and allowed them to wander about the settlement. Their fathers or elder brothers took minimal care of their needs for food, housing, and clothing. Other community members also assisted, and no one but occasional Western tourists harmed them.[7]

The Madwoman who is the focus of this chapter had three ex-husbands, one of whom explained why she was a perfect example of an uncontrolled woman. I asked, "Aren't you ashamed that your ex-wife, the madwoman, talks about her 'wounds of the heart' in front of all the rest of the women?" After a long pause he said, "She [the madwoman] carries on her back the fate of all women . . . And praise be to God that when they see her, they understand that if they want to live well, they should be exactly on the other side. They have the rationality that she refused to acquire."

In fragile moments when married women of childbearing age gathered to confide in each other, the paradoxes of passionate/enduring women and rational/lusty men surfaced. During such conversations, the women gradually came face to face with the absurdity of these paradoxes and the volatile juncture they created in their marriages. These conversations were openended, because the existential paradoxes were unsolvable, so the meandering dialogue reached a stalemate. At that point, a Madwoman, if present, might have chosen to rise up, assume an expressive role, and allegorize her "wounds of the heart" experience into a story. By publicly acting out her marital grievances, the Madwoman, using the "allegory of desire" (Fineman 1981), forcefully persuaded her audience to see her "truth" (De Man 1981). In a moving monologue, tragic to her but comic to her audience, she conveyed the melodramatic story of her life, focusing around the paradoxes of male rationality/lust and female passion/endurance. She told her audience that she was so true to her female nafs that it transformed into the insatiable masculine ghayii. Possessed by ghayii, she could not mold her self to mature into having ṣabr. Lacking the ṣabr, she could not act rationally as women do after they have children in their marriages. Convoluting the logic of Mzeini manhood and womanhood, she overrode this pair of paradoxes. Her experience, told as an allegory, showed the women that in the here-and-now of occupied Sinai, women normally were forced to develop not only endurance but also inherent rational capabilities, ideally attributed to men. And they needed both endurance and rationality to cope with the demands made on Mzeini relationships by the reverberations of Middle Eastern and global politics.

1.

Sil Waᶜar,[8] 12 February 1977

A very early morning in a fleeting spring that leaves one yearning for more. The desert celebrates, scattering the clay-brown dust with its few blossoming plants—red, orange, lilac, and white. The fragile white flowers of the *ratam* bushes remind me that we are at the threshold of the wedding season, beginning in April or May and marking summer's arrival.

From the dried delta walk ten girls, none over seventeen except myself. We walk eastwards, away from the huts on the deep blue beach hugged by the mountains. Before us the black metamorphic cliffs smoothed by centuries of flash floods stand so sleek one wants to stroke them. Deep burgundy dikes fissure the black cliffs. Through the wadi's mouth we enter the narrow canyon—nine black silhouettes and one blue and turquoise, all stepping in pink-black arcosis.

Rāḍiya, Salīma, Sālma, and Rāshda are the youngsters, about ten years old, unveiled. Loose, long-sleeved dresses of bold floral prints drape to their ankles and are covered by plain black *ḥirga* shawls.[9] Their foreheads are dented by the straps of woven wool bags (*kharīṭa*) dyed in reds, blues, greens, and those of waterskins or small orange jerrycans slung over the bags. The girls lean forward to compensate for the weight, and the water sloshes with each step.

Four older girls, fourteen to seventeen, wear foot-long black *lathma* veils, sparsely decorated with silver sequins, embroidery, and white bead fringe. They wear the same shawls and floral dresses as the younger girls, but cover the dresses with black full-length sleeveless tunics (*thōb*). The seemingly modest tunics accentuate the girls' breasts and hips due to the presence of a stiff wide *khzām* (sash) of shiny white, signifying that they have begun to menstruate but are still virgins. The glossy paper of a rolled magazine juts out of Maḥamūda's bag, and a flute peeks out of Nādia's. Khaḍrā's shawl is dusted white with flour, and Kāmla walks beside me at the rear of the group.

Lastly there is Salwa, seventeen, who prances and hums with the energy of a young child-free woman recently divorced. Her dress is like that of the menstruating girls, but her *ṣufīyya* (woolen belt) is fuchsia-red, signifying that she is no longer a virgin. Salwa's yellow *nugba* veil is short,[10] reaching just to the chin, completely covered with tear-shaped silver-coated metal pieces (*dmeiᶜāt*) and lined at the top with red embroidery and white and blue beads. She has daringly hiked the veil up just a bit so that her chin peeks out.

A flock of thirty-five black female goats and ten brown-spotted white sheep patter in front of us with a mincing gait. The herd belongs to the girls' and their neighbors' families.[11] The two billy goats, their genitals stuffed in jockstrap-like pockets sewn from old army-tent canvas and tied to their butt and short tail, skip among the female goats, who walk straight, like soldiers, obedient to the barking of a bone-thin female dog. The billy goats ignore the dog. The wadi's arcosis squeaks monotonously beneath our feet and the goats' hooves—step-tsick, step-tsack. At times, the dog stiffens up, sharpens her ears, sniffs the air, and runs after imaginary prey. Rāshda and Khaḍrā yell out, "*Ḥaii, ḥaii! Ḥagg-kisht, ḥagg-kisht!*" to a disobedient goat who deviates from the canyon towards the cliffs. In goat language, these expressions mean "go straight with the flow!"

We continue climbing. I wipe sweat from my forehead, look back, and see through a black canyon window the horizon with light blue sky and deep blue sea, holding the pink delta in its bosom.

Salwa, the new divorcee, hums a jumpy *hejēni* (caravan song) to the rhythm of our steps. The anthropologist identifies the melody as a fisherman's song she has tape-recorded several times, and the words flash in her mind:

> *Tiz ᶜAlyii sabᶜat ashbār,*[12]
> *Wzubb abu-Zāyed al-mayshūm ma-malāh.*
>
> ᶜAlyii's vagina is seven handlengths long—
> Even awesome Abu-Zāyed's cock can't fill it up.[13]

Salwa just hums. She does not sing the words. Kāmla, stepping near Salwa, giggles quietly, pointing at the billy goat vigorously rubbing his locked-up masculinity against the buttocks of a female goat. We all giggle now, and soon our giggles become a roar of laughter. But tears gather in the corners of Kāmla's eyes and soak into her veil.

"What's with you?" Salwa asks Kāmla with a straight face.

"Nothing. It doesn't matter." Kāmla sniffs, swallows her tears, and marches brazenly on. We follow.

Around two weeks ago, rumors spread in the encampment that this summer Kāmla will be given in marriage to Swēlem, the son of Kāmla's father's friend. He lives with his parents in Wadi Saᶜāl. Like most of us, Kāmla learned about her future marriage from gossip. The rumors abound, but her parents have not told her a thing. The rumors say Swēlem and Kāmla have met only twice within the last few years.

Once, when they were just entering adolescence, they met when Swēlem's family went down from Wadi Saᶜāl north, to the date harvest in Nuwēbᶜat Mzeina. That was when Kāmla's mother's sister lived in Nuwēbᶜa, and her mother loaned Kāmla to the aunt to help with the goats.

And the second time was three years later, when Kāmla's family spent the summer in Nuwēbᶜa. Swēlem was a trash collector for the city of Eilat, and his Israeli boss gave him a three-day vacation—welcome, but not long enough to find a ride to his parents' encampment in a Bedouin four-wheel drive vehicle that would return him on time to the only paved road leading to Eilat, where he could flag down a bus. Nor could he have gotten there any faster by hitchhiking on a desert safari truck, which would give him a ride in exchange for showing him off to the tourists. So on his father's advice, Swēlem spent the early evening hours at one of the magᶜads of Nuwēbᶜa, where his paternal uncle usually sits. But after the red moon of evening had set, he crept away to the *malᶜab*, the plaza of the taboo dancing at the outskirts of the settlement.

The elders say that in the old days, when only Bedouin were in the Sinai, dancing was the thing to do when one was young and restless. But these days the same elders say that parties and dances belong to the nude hippies on the nearby beach. Muslims should not dance, they say. But everyone Swēlem knows goes to the malᶜab: adolescent girls about to be married, freshly divorced young women, all the men his age, married or not, and nearly pubescent boys and girls who curiously watch the rest, hoping to grow up fast so that they, too, can join in.

While in the malᶜab, Swēlem danced *marbūᶜa* and *redēḥi*[14] and tried to seduce the girls with cigarettes, inexpensive perfume, and Camay soap that he bought in the supermarket of Eilat. He knew the girls might run away in elated embarrassment, but he didn't give up hope. Maybe one or two of them would be grateful and brave enough to reveal their unveiled faces, if only for a splinter of a second, and with Allah's will, he would chance to press a pair of breasts to his heart. And so it was that Swēlem tried to hug Kāmla and she bit his wrist.

So the rumors that arrived from Wadi Saᶜāl say that when Swēlem's father asked him if he would agree to marry Kāmla, the daughter of his friend, Swēlem shrugged his shoulders and said, "I saw her once or twice at the malᶜab." The father thought that was good enough, and off he rode on his camel to Sil Waᶜar to discuss the marriage arrangements with Kāmla's father. The fathers negotiated where the wedding ceremony would take place, who would buy the newlywed couple blankets, pots and pans, wooden storage boxes, and other household goods, and where the couple would live.

These rumors from faraway lands also tell us that Swēlem's first love, whom we shall call his sweetheart (*ṣāḥiba*),[15] is the daughter of a maternal relative of Nādia the goatherd, who lives in Swēlem's encampment. The rumors say her eyes are like almonds and her skin is as white as milk. And we all know Kāmla's sweetheart, Samīr *al-ganzūḥ* (the dandy), a mischievous, pushy neighborhood boy.

The heavy sun now beats on our heads as we keep trudging up the wadi, with the herd ahead of us. The two billy goats, deep in despair, having given up biting at their canvas pockets, trail behind the herd. Salwa once again hums the fisherman's song, and once again, tears drop from Kāmla's eyes. Salwa stops humming and snaps at Kāmla, "Enough, you girl! Shame on you! Fear your father's words!" Kāmla sniffs and sweeps her eyes with her shawl.

The anthropologist contemplates the power of the statement "Shame on you!", one capable of causing a total freeze in discourse, whatever it may be, perhaps because honor and shame are categories taken from the realm of the Holy. But despite her scholarly gaze, I freeze for a second. When my Yemenite grandmother does not approve of my words or deeds, she also whispers from between her teeth in sharp Arabic, "Shame on you!"

Around 10 A.M. we arrive at our customary lunch spot, a billowing old acacia tree. What a relief to dump our bags and carefully lay our brown waterskins down in the shade to refill them from jerrycans.

"The sun has worn us out," sighs Salīma, sinking down in the shade. The older girls remove their veils and wipe the sweat drops from between their noses and lips. The black goats disperse in all directions, leaping towards plants hiding in soil pockets in the fissures of the red and black rock. The heavy white sheep amble about, chewing the few flowers in the wadi. I lament inside to see these last few spring flowers systematically devoured.

We laboriously prepare our lunch. Khaḍrā and Maḥamūda knead dough on a smooth boulder. Nādia asks younger Salīma and Rāshda to help her gather firewood, while Kāmla lights another fire and places the teapot on it. I wash the small tea cups.

After the meal we lie in the shade, listening to Nādia improvise on her flute in a minor key. Since flute music was considered a symbolic sexual stimulation, women played the flute only when they were sure that no man was within listening range. In the encampment, married women who gathered and played the flute in an inner yard of a hut or in the private domain of a tent often asked a prepubescent girl to watch outside for men and to warn them if a man approached. There was no such danger when girls played while herding their family flocks. But in the pastures, young men would dare to visit their goatherd sweethearts and the girls would gladly play the flute for them, a standardized way of violating the rigid purdah code.

Nadia's melancholy melody wafts among the black shawls, carrying its minor key like the dry air carries tingles of moisture from the nearby sea. In the window between her headdress and her veil, Kāmla's large brown eyes glaze over with wellsprings of tears. Nādia lays the flute down, and Kāmla, taking a long breath, starts reciting a poem as if she were quoting scripture:

Beini wabein al-ḥabayib
Jabal ʿāli webʿīd bilād,
Wabaḥar jāri,
Washōgi al-ḥabayib zadd.

Ya katebīn al-wàrag,
La tiktebūsh walā waʿād!
Iḥna iftaragna—
Wuṣubḥān al-mejammʿa ʿād.

My beloved and I
By high mountains kept apart,
And by stormy seas,
But longing just grows in our heart.

Oh ye scribes, touch not
The wedding-paper with your pen!
Our ways have parted—
Blessed be He who joins us again.

"Who joins us again," we repeat in unison, as is the custom.

Kāmla sniffs and wipes her tears as she chants the metrical lines.

"Enough, you girl! Shame on you!" Khaḍrā scolds.

Kāmla sulks and turns away.

Maḥamūda's hand reaches outside our circle and draws from her bag the magazine she found two days ago in an Israeli Nature Reserve trash can near the encampment. She unfolds it, and my eyes open very wide when I see the naked couple on the cover. I notice it is written in some Scandinavian language—perhaps thrown out by Scandinavian scuba divers, who come en masse in winter to dive in the encampment's coral reef.

Maḥamūda leafs through, and we all congregate around her. We sit close together, thigh touching thigh, shoulder rubbing shoulder. We dwell on each page. Maḥamūda tells us a story about each picture. With fascination she conjures up the frightening worlds of male and female witches living in the hellish faraway countries beyond the White Sea [the Mediterranean], full of devilish blond people with sea-blue or satanic-cat-green eyes.

"They probably live in hell, because they don't remove their pubic hair, and run around totally, totally naked, like those hippie tourists in Dahab and Nuwēbᶜa," Nādia says firmly.

"But in hell, the color of such people turns black from sins, and on our beaches, the sun burns them and they turn red and full of blisters.[16] So why is the color of these people in the magazine as white as goat's milk?" Khaḍrā asks.

None of the girls can answer. They giggle, embarrassed. As long as we look at men with women, or women with other women, Maḥamūda's stories flow in a stream. But things get complicated when dogs and women, or horses and women look at us from the magazine pages.

Maḥamūda tries to explain: "Maybe it's the reverse of what we have. With us, I've heard some say, when a *khurma* (a hole—a married woman) doesn't want to sleep with her husband while he is dying in his penis [i.e., when he has a strong sexual desire for intercourse], he beats her up to make her submit (*bikawenha*),[17] and then he gets his thing from the female donkey. Now these women of hell are not circumcised, and so, when their vaginas kill them [i.e., when they have enormous sexual passion] they go to the horses and dogs. *Ikhsī* (Yuukk)!" Maḥamūda spits on the ground, and the girls giggle, perhaps because men having sex with donkeys is in the realm of the possible, but women submitting to sex with horses and dogs is bizarre.

Salwa grins and says to me, "When are your people going to circumcise you, ya Smadar? You are already an adult. Your clitoris has grown so much, it probably covers the mouth of your vagina."

I blush. My ears feel boiling hot. "I don't think my people will circumcise me. We don't do that. My clitoris is very small."

"Maybe it is indeed small. But doesn't your vagina kill you [with sexual passion]?" Salwa pushes further.

"My vagina kills me only when my heart searches for love." I feel like an overripe tomato, and the anthropologist tells me she is not sure how to handle the fact that *she* is now a subject for Mzeini inspection.

Kāmla responds, "Wow, then you lust like men, fear Allah. With us, because of the circumcision, we have ṣabr. Almost never do our vaginas kill us . . . We love, but wounds are in our hearts."

We are silent. The conversation is stuck. The group disperses, and we each go about our own activities. Salwa washes her long, thick hair, Salīma helping, pouring water from the jerrycan and disentangling the knots. Rāshda and Sālma embroider and bead goatherd veils. One can see that their breasts are budding. Soon, when these are rounded, they will have to cover their faces in public. Nādia and Khaḍrā bead the tops of head-covers (*malab*), which they will wear after their weddings, probably this summer. Rāḍiya and Kāmla together embroider the shawl that Kāmla will wear during holidays after she marries.

The anthropologist writes her fieldnotes and then plays the goatherd flute. After she finally succeeds in imitating some Bedouin melodies, Nādia teases her, telling the others, "This Smadar has big lust. Only three weeks have passed since she has returned from Jerusalem, where she saw her sweetheart . . ."

The anthropologist instructs me to keep my scholarly cool, but I can't, so I levy a rebuttal: "I heard the longing in your flute playing. Three days we have been grazing the flocks in Wadi Waᶜar, and your sweetheart has not yet visited. Maybe he has fallen in love with his wife."

We laugh. I expect a spunky response, but instead Nādia decides to recite a short poem, and I can hear the pain in her voice:

Walla laḥalef leṣāḥibi—
Sādeg, walla kadhdhāb.
Masṭūr zai al-maṭar,
Nāzel maᶜa saḥḥāb.

Oh I can't swear by my sweetheart—
True or false, I have my doubts.
He's faithful as the desert rain
Disappearing with the clouds.

"With the clouds," the girls repeat sadly.

"Men—I wish they were like this billy goat," Maḥamūda remarks, pointing out an exhausted billy goat who slowly chews his cud.

"Oh, don't we wish!" some answer, groaning.

Around 3 P.M. we stretch and start talking about the walk back to the encampment. Kāmla asks me to go with her to gather her goats from the canyon cliffs. We climb on the black-red rock exposures, and call the goats, "Ḥaii! ḥaii! Ḥagg-kisht! ḥagg-kisht!" while we throw small pebbles at the stragglers. We sit on the hot rocks, gasping from the effort, and the goats gradually gather around us. We are silent, listening to the echoes of many hooves. Our breasts heave until our breath stabilizes.

*

KĀMLA: Ya Smadar, that's it. In a month or two you won't see me here. The good days of herding have come to an end. In two months, Kāmla will no longer be one of a white belt, a lathma [veil] and a *gibleh* (the hair style of a virgin) . . .[18] [*She moans, then gazes at the distant Gulf*] . . . Ah . . . if only I were like ʿAlyii, the Madwoman . . .

SMADAR [*interjects immediately*]: ʿAlyii the Madwoman?! Allah and not His replacement! Why?

KĀMLA: Because she is the only one among us here who talks about her wounds of the heart in front of all . . . She has no shame . . . And since the day she got crazy, they stopped trying to marry her off . . . And who knows how many times I am going to marry and divorce and marry and divorce . . .

We are silent for several moments.

SMADAR: The wounds of the heart . . . what's this mean?

KĀMLA: The wounds of the heart . . . [*struggles to avert tears*] The wounds of the heart are [*tries to speak as she weeps*], for example . . . things like a forced marriage (*jīzat ghaṣab*) . . . You know . . . when you get married because your father wants you to, and your beloved one marries [someone else] also because his father wants him to . . . The wounds of the heart [*her shoulders shake from crying*] . . . it's all the things to yearn for, and not to talk about . . . It's . . . it's the lust deep inside the soul . . .

It's very hot. Kāmla cries. I think about my wounds of the heart.

ADOLESCENT GOATHERDS RESTING ON THEIR WAY BACK TO THE ENCAMPMENT ▶

Past relationships. Arguments with parents. Tears roll down my cheeks and dry very fast. It's hard to tell the difference between the salt of sweat and the salt of tears burning both our faces.

Kāmla says in a high-pitched voice: "If I only had the freedom of the mad . . ." and her lament increases.

I try to find words to soothe her. Strangely, I repeat Salwa's magic formula: "Enough, you girl! Fear your father! Shame on you!" and am left wondering at my words.

Kāmla abruptly stops crying. She just sniffs several times. Then, her whole body shakes, ceases, shakes again, then stops. But no more tears.

We go down from the cliff surrounded by the goats. Now Kāmla hums the smutty fisherman's song. This time, I dare sing the words,

> ʿAlyii's vagina is seven handlengths long—
> Even awesome Abu-Zāyed's cock can't fill it up.

Between the tears, Kāmla manages to smile. "Well, ya Smadar . . . you may not be from the People of Shame, but you are definitely not from those people of the magazine."

I join her smiling. If only she had known that my grandmother is of the People of Shame.

II.

Dahab, 12 December 1978, a year later

Around nine o'clock on a winter morning. The stormy wind howls among the shanties and the palm trees. The huge foamy waves of the deep blue Gulf of ʿAqaba beat the coastline. Even the sun feels cold.

The settlement looks like a ghost town. Two hours earlier, the unmarried and recently divorced women goatherds drove their flocks to the nearby mountains. A few men have gone to sell their artifacts and hospitality to the few tourists who dare sunbathe on the beach. But in winter most men of this settlement leave for longer periods to work at underpaid jobs in Eilat or in the Israeli settlements of the South Sinai. The older children attend the local elementary school. At the outskirts of the settlement, a group of younger children ride the curved stumps of date trees, their imaginary camels.

As I approach Ghānma's hut, the hubbub gradually sharpens. Six married mothers, carrying their babies and marching their toddlers, collect in Ghānma's inner yard every morning. They all wear dresses with long sleeves and bold floral prints, covered by black tunics with elaborate embroidery along the hem. Their dresses are belted by wide fuchsia-red wool sashes indicating their status as married women. Their hair is gathered in *masāyeḥ* or *guṣṣa*,[19] two kinds of special braids also designating their married status. Bright orange or yellow veils covered with tear-shaped silvery pieces, embroidery, white shells on the sides, and colorful beads on the bottom conceal the women's noses, mouths, and necks. The veils are long, reaching the women's midriffs. Black shawls heavily embroidered with colorful thread and silver sequins drape over their backs.

Jamīla, the oldest, is forty and the only woman whose eldest son and daughter are married. The fact that her eldest son is married and has a family of his own elevates her status. Ḥabūba, the youngest of the women, has been carrying her first pregnancy for eight months. Everything in the yard moves rhythmically. Sitting in a semicircle on the ground, Rābᶜa and Freija churn yogurt, passing waterskins back and forth between their knees. Zuhra sways, swinging her crying baby who hangs at her back, wrapped in the white cloth strapped to her forehead. The toddlers play and prattle. Ghānma's sewing machine taps. The women chat in *kalām ṣabāya* (women's talk), a staccato style, typical of women's conversation in the absence of men.

Meanwhile, the sad voice of Umm Kalsoum undulates from the transistor radio, contradicting the rhythm and atmosphere of the scene.

The women gossip about Kāmla, whose natal community was Sil Waᶜar. Kāmla married for the second time last summer. As with her first marriage, to Swēlem, Kāmla's father made arrangements without considering her opinion, as is the custom. During negotiations for her first marriage, Kāmla's father agreed with Swēlem's father that the newlywed couple should live in Kāmla's natal community. This time, however, the spouses' fathers agreed that Kāmla should move to Dahab, the community of her second husband and some of his paternal kin.

The conversation is quiet, each woman taking her turn without interrupting the others.

*

RĀBᶜA: Kāmla *dākhel ᶜindi* (Kāmla entered with me, i.e., Kāmla has taken refuge in my hut). They say, Khḍeir abu-ᶜĪd [Kāmla's second husband] may come for a short vacation tomorrow from the hotel in Eilat where he works. There's not much work this winter in Eilat, they say, so many men get unpaid leave.

While the literal meaning of "dākhel" was "to enter," in the context of disputes between a newlywed husband and wife without children, "dākhel" or *shāred* (to escape) *ʿind* (with someone) meant that the wife wanted to avoid her husband. She did this by asking for refuge at a neighbor's household. These neighbors could not be either her own or her husband's paternal or maternal kin because it was within the honor of these respective kinship units to foster the success of the marriage. When the husband came home after a long period of migrant labor, one of the wife's duties was to have sex with him. As an authoritative male figure, the husband had to keep his honor, and hence, it was beneath his dignity to look for his wife's shelter in the neighborhood.

Women kept the hiding places of "dākhel" or "shāred" women secret from men. Gossip, though, leaked into the magʿad. There the newlywed husband behaved as if things were normal, and sometimes, using metaphorical language or reciting a suitable poem, he even boasted about how many times he had had intercourse with his wife the night before. Other men, knowing that the wife was absent from the hut, nodded their heads in sympathy when they listened to the husband's story, but no one verbally responded unless he wished to challenge the young husband's honor. The husband might well have known where his wife was hiding, but, protecting his honor, he did not dare ask assistance from the male head of that household to return his wife to him. At times, to redeem his honor, the husband would catch his wife when she left her refuge for errands. If caught, the wife would not try to escape, but would go along with him to their hut. Once the husband had her back in their home, he or her father might beat her up.

FREIJA: This is her second marriage. The first time, I think, she got married to one of the sons of Rabīʿa from Wadi Saʿāl, I think with the shy one, Swēlem. Khḍeir is nicer, but his father is not as beneficial to Kāmla's father as Rabīʿa's husband was.

ZUHRA: Well, she's still so young . . . So her father does not think he should consider her opinion of the man he wants her to marry.

ḤABŪBA [*with raised eyebrows, feigning astonishment*]: Why does he need to consult her? Everyone knew that just before the second marriage, the fathers of the two were about to start an orchard in upper Wadi Naṣb. Kāmla's father couldn't do it alone. He had money, but the land there is of ʿĪd's lineage [ʿĪd is the father of Kāmla's second husband].

GHĀNMA [*raises her head from the sewing machine*]: But isn't poor Khḍeir the one who wants to eat the orchard's apples?

We burst into laughter. A common theme in men's love poetry was a man smelling the sweet perfume of fresh apples, or a man picking large, juicy apples. Men explained to me that apples were a metaphor for women's breasts.

FREIJA: But she—why does she need to take *their* marriage [the one the fathers arranged for her] so harshly? She can be married and also have her free life. Tell me, how many times did she see Khḍeir? It isn't hard to be patient with the husband when he comes home three–four days in a month or two . . . Anyway, marriage has always been forced.

ZUHRA [*cynically, half-smiling*]: Marriage or not, they say she still plays with her old sweetheart, Samīr the Dandy, who never really kept it secret that he visited her when she was herding her mother's goats . . . Eh, let me tell you, some people have no fear of Shame . . . Khḍeir knows about it, they say, but he waits until ṣabr will prevail on her nafs and she'll start to tolerate the marriage.

RĀBʿA: My husband says, every time this Khḍeir abu-ʿĪd returns from Eilat, he wants people to know he has brought Kāmla lots of gifts. I wish my man had been like this Khḍeir. Mine just brings home the gossip from the magʿad . . . And they say, this son of ʿĪd hopes people won't dākhel Kāmla when he's back for vacation. They should see how dear she is to him.

GHĀNMA [*her face brimming with a smile*]: Ho-ho . . . that sucker . . . a year ago he divorced his first wife. That marriage lasted only eight months. She was never home when he needed her after returning from a month's work, and he was too shy . . . [*then folding her smile into a straight face*] What a pity . . . he's a good man, indeed, and he really served his first wife well (*khadamha khidma*). Had she gotten pregnant from him, she would have sat with him, and acquiesced to her fate.

JAMĪLA [*fixing her gaze on the radio, from which the voice of Umm Kalsoum laments on*]: Oh, the sweet days when I herded my mother's goats in the mountains . . . The freedom of the mountains . . . Playing sweet music on the flute . . . the mind empty, the heart open . . . By now, childbirth pains have made me ugly . . .

GHĀNMA [*interjects*]: Right, they say you have even stopped putting your daughter on guard when you play—soon we'll name you *ʿAjūz* (the Old Woman).

JAMĪLA [*continues anyway*]: Men don't lust after me any more, just my husband still wants to do his thing. Let me tell you, girls, [*giggling*], his penis is still firm . . .

Some join the giggling, then, a pause. No one knows what to say.

ḤABŪBA [*timidly*]: Ah . . . why can't marriage be a pleasure (*keif*)?

GHĀNMA [*snaps immediately*]: You don't gain anything from a marriage of pleasure. Look at Salwa. The third time she got the one she wanted. Today, everything *he* does, she approves of, with no arguments, without dākhel at the neighbors', and she's still not pregnant . . . It's like she has no ʿagl of her own.

The anthropologist abruptly stops her hasty note-taking. She is surprised that Ghānma wants to attribute the male quality of ʿagl to Salwa, even though Ghānma's comment is negatively phrased.

ZUHRA [*sighing*]: That's the way it is in a marriage of love, my dear. The woman loses her ṣabr because of her nafs, because of her heart. Then she can't make her husband do what *she* wants . . . [*shaking her head from side to side, clicking her tongue*] Tsk, tsk . . . There is no gain in a marriage of pleasure . . . Eh! Leave love to men's poems and to Umm Kalsoum.

The oldest woman in the group, Jamīla, starts, leaning forward.

JAMĪLA [*raising her voice*]: By the life of God! You young women! It looks like your husbands are your servants! *You* are the ones who should serve *them*! Men—they go to the mosque, they know the Qur'an, they have ʿagl, so they work and bring money. We women—we serve our children and work at home. We women—our minds are like goats' horns, short and twisted. That's what men always say in court.

GHĀNMA [*jumping in, louder*]: But tell me, you, the mother of Rafīg [Jamīla's only married son]. Tell me! . . . Who spends the money? Who invests the money in a man's children? Who tells the man what the needs of his house are?

FREIJA [*interjecting, also loudly, turning to Jamīla*]: And ya Jamīla, you were no different. We all know that once, when your husband beat you up, you told your sons he was a thief and a liar, whose heart was black and whose blood, heavy. When he got back from work, the younger one told him this to his face in front of all the men in the magʿad.

GHĀNMA [*also turning towards Jamīla*]: So tell me, who has ʿagl? It's women who have it! [*shouting*] Let's pray that Allah will bring us all the ṣabr to tolerate *them*!

The anthropologist looks up in shock from her scribbling and stares at Ghānma. Is she hearing this right? Does Ghānma really assume that if women fine-tune their ṣabr carefully enough and long enough, it will make a qualitative change into the masculine ʿagl?

ḤABŪBA [*slyly*]: But darling, what do *you* understand about money? How can *you* earn it? Are *you* able to work as a construction worker? gardener? hotel cook? custodian? At best, you can bake some flatbread and sell it to the tourists. This is little, very little money. And do you think that an Egyptian or Israeli employer would hire *you*?

RĀBʿA: You youngsters—Of course men go to work and make money . . . They need it, too. They feel they need to marry immediately after they've divorced. They have to screw, and better not the female donkey . . . Don't they say, *ana tejawazt thintein: ḥmārati wamarati* ("I've been married to two: my donkey and my wife"—a Mzeini proverb)?

GHĀNMA [*cuts her off*]: And the donkey always comes first!

The anthropologist recognizes the proverb Rābʿa has just quoted. It was often cited by men in the company of other men when talking about sexual dissatisfaction with their wives or the absence of a female sexual partner.[20] On many occasions, when men or women mentioned this proverb in one-gender conversation, the response was laughter. But she notices now that the stressed atmosphere in Ghānma's inner yard does not allow a pause for laughter.

RĀBʿA [*goes right on talking*]: Men have ghayii in their nafs! That's why they die in their penises. And thank Allah who commanded us to be circumcised. Thanks to that, we have ṣabr with men until they are the way *we* want.

I look at Rābʿa intently. I am amazed that in a quirky fleeting way, just in passing, Rābʿa has attributed the female quality of nafs to men, and has said their lust resided there, rather than with the male ʿagl.

And the anthropologist frowns at the thought that the binary oppositions she has cleverly extracted from her data are being turned topsy-turvy by her informant. But soon enough she is relieved to hear Zuhra call her ideas back to order.

ZUHRA [*yelling, agitated*]: The way *we* want?! Impossible! First of all, on your wedding night, you run to the mountains. The next day, he boasts in front of all the men about how sweet his night with you was. But this gets him so angry, that after a couple of weeks, he climbs the mountains, where you're still with your goatherd friends, and . . .

GHĀNMA: . . . And he takes you somewhere, and forces sex on you. And finally, if you're lucky, and your father doesn't beat you up on top of it all, you can dākhel with people. Only if you get pregnant do you calm down.

ZUHRA: So tell me, tell me in the name of the Prophet, is this the way we really want it to be?

FREIJA: And when men take you to [the customary] court, they say you have no ʿagl at all, so of course your father has to speak for you in front of the judge, and your husband's elder brother tells the judge that you also didn't have any ṣabr to deal with him!

GHĀNMA: *Sidd rizg al-gāḍi!* (Allah block blessing from the judge—God damn the judge!)

JAMĪLA [*the oldest of the eight, jabs her fists in the air and shrieks*]: Shut up! Shut up! . . . Fear God, you heretics! . . . Shut up! *Shame* on you!

Silence descends like the silence of the believers after the muezzin has just finished calling the people to prayer. Like Honor, Shame belongs to the realm of the Holy.

But Umm Kalsoum is still singing on the radio about her love, her melancholy voice fusing with the howling wind.

Suddenly, as if carried by the wind, a slovenly figure bursts into Ghānma's inner yard, violating all rules of etiquette. She neither knocks on the wooden gate to the outer yard of the shanty, nor coughs outside to wait for an invitation to enter.

This is ʿAlyii, the Madwoman.

Some distant fear creeps into the back of my mind while the anthropologist accelerates writing her notes. But the six women erupt in boisterous laughter on seeing ʿAlyii. The Madwoman's attire is an incongruous mixture of styles: her guṣṣa hair style is that of an old menopausal woman, whose sons are all married; her lathma veil is of an adolescent goatherd; her fuchsia-red ṣufīyya waist belt is the type worn by a married woman of childbearing age. Her robe and shawl are spotted with grease and chunks of dried dough and full of holes and patches, in contrast to the dress of the other women—neat, clean and proper. Three sickly goats, who are not supposed to be herded inside the settlement, totter behind her.

*

"Have you seen my goat? Have you seen my goat?" the Madwoman cries out. "My goat has escaped to the mountains, and has taken my life with her . . ."

"By the life of the goat," Zuhra mockingly swears, and we all giggle.

The anthropologist recalls that when men talked among themselves about married women of childbearing age, they frequently called them goats, and complained about their lack of discipline.

"Oh, my God! Why didn't I serve my husbands?" the Madwoman asks.

ʿAlyii pauses and in a gesture of sorrow, claps her hands together, clasps them tightly to each other, and rocks back and forth over them. Even as we keep snickering, Ghānma asks her, "Tell us, ya ʿAlyii, why didn't you serve your husbands?"

"Three husbands I've had," the Madwoman continues, "and my father chose them for me. The three sons of my father's dearest friends. And I behaved like a fool. I refused to serve them. Why? . . . Why? . . . Because I wanted the freedom of the mountains . . . The empty mind . . . like the goats . . ."

The Madwoman again claps her hands together and rocks.

"The freedom of the mountains . . . The freedom of the goats . . ." parrots Ḥabūba, simulating the Madwoman's agitated voice, and once again we crack up.

The anthropologist now reminds me that, while I was learning how to herd, I noticed the paradox between the Mzeini concept of the goat as a free animal and the severe disciplining process used to make the kidgoats walk in a herd formation, not get lost in the mountains, and learn which plants to avoid eating. But the kidgoats were given names, usually of the goatherd's dear girlfriends who had married and moved to other communities.

The Madwoman waits till the laughter dies down and then reminisces with nostalgia. "Oh, my husbands . . . how they used to beat me . . . How I refused to serve them even with the camel's stick . . . How I refused to serve them . . . They wanted me to wear my nicest clothes for them, put on perfume, to *kuḥul* (line) my eyes . . . They wanted . . . They wanted me to carry their children in my womb . . . and then . . . they thought I would love them."

Freija produces a feeble moan and utters, "Ya Allah . . ." The rest of us laugh while Jamīla and Zuhra nod their heads and chuckle, "By the Prophet, it's all true!"

ʿAlyii is elegant as she sweeps around the yard, smiling proudly. "But I won out over them," she proclaims.

"*You* tell us, how did you win out over those men?" Ghānma asks, eyes shining.

"I dressed up with rags and sent them all in turn to my father. I said to them, 'He picked you, so spend your nights with him. You can recite lust poetry all night. You can recite on apples and peaches and on the sea and on your camel's stick. You can screw each other with poems or any other way.'"

Our eyes light up and our shoulders shake from laughing.

In their poetry of desire, men often used the metaphor of a peach to describe the fuzzy feeling of a woman's skin between the times when she removed her pubic hair. Since Mzeinis considered pubic hair a pollution, women removed it about once a month with sticky leaves of *libeid* (yellow gromwell, *alkanna orientalis*, Latin). When it grew back afterward, it was very soft and short. Men shaved off their pubic hair (cf. Levi 1978). In the men's poetry of desire, a stormy sea often referred to sexual arousal, and the camel's stick was the erected penis. Interestingly, women did not have any sets of metaphors to describe the sexual organs of men, and they were not supposed to know men's love or lust poetry.[21] Always after I would collect men's poetry, women often asked me to turn on the cassette recorder or read from my notebook men's love or lust poetry. To the anthropologist's surprise, the women recited the poems with me or with the recorder.

"Look at my men—they're thrown away . . ." asserts the Madwoman. "They're like trash."

"Like trash," echoes Freija.

"They fell off the camel's back like trash," Jamīla expands.

We roar with laughter. Everyone knows that ʿAlyii's husbands became periodically or fully impotent, and they all experienced a series of divorces after their encounter with her.

"But I paid with my life." The Madwoman's voice breaks. "The life of ʿAlyii is the life of the goat. She is never satisfied. She is always restlessly looking in this desert for the green, juicy grass of the north (*al-shām*) . . . the green of the north . . ."

Ḥabūba warns, "Watch it, ya ʿAlyii! The green grass is with men!"

The women all burst into laughter while the Madwoman stands frozen, teary-eyed.

"Only a dead child was in my womb," she continues, choked up. "Men's ghayii rooted in me killed the child . . . Men's ghayii killed the child . . . killed, killed . . . killed the child."

Ḥabūba's hand covers her eyes, the only exposed part of her face, and she giggles in a nervous staccato. Recently she confided in me and told me that two years ago, she found herself pregnant by her first husband immediately after their divorce. By drinking herbs and running up mountains, she succeeded in causing a miscarriage. She felt she had to do it because having a child after a divorce would have reduced her chances of remarrying.

ʿAlyii loudly accuses us: "You . . . you have taken unto yourselves all endurance in the whole world! You know Shame, but you have no souls! Look at the ugly, ugly ways you use to make your husbands behave as *you* want! They buy you food and dresses . . . They buy you 'tears' to put on your veils. And you don't cry. You laugh. You laugh when they take you in their taxis and pickup trucks to visit your girlfriends and kin. You laugh when they buy you sewing machines . . . You laugh, and they will do everything so that they can be with you, and not only lust after you in their poetry. You whores! You get what you want in the very way of ʿagl. Indeed, you have your mind working! And what do you do to get all that? . . . You lie to your souls! You whores! You lie to your nafs!"

Everyone but the Madwoman and myself suppresses giggles. Are they all laughing at the madness of this outcast woman, or are they nervous with embarrassment because what she says has hit a raw nerve? Ghānma kiddingly attacks her: "We deny our souls?! We are whores?! But it's you, ya Madwoman, you're the one who is lusty!"

And Jamīla adds, "They ought to circumcise you again!"

But ʿAlyii does not wait for the giggling to die down before she resumes her tirade. "And me? . . . My lust destroyed my soul. My soul destroyed me. I didn't have patience. I didn't have the rational mind. When men say in court that women's minds are short and twisted like goats' horns, they only talk about me. Oh . . . My goat . . . My goat! Have you seen my goat? . . . Have you seen my free goat?"

The Madwoman totters out of the shanty, followed by raucous laughter and her three sickly goats. But the anthropologist senses that the subtext is not so funny as the text. The last chuckle fades to a moment of agitated silence.

"Poor ʿAlyii," Jamīla murmurs. "How men ruined her."[22]

All the while, Umm Kalsoum still laments from the radio to the wind about her ardent love.

And the conversation soon flows again, shifting smoothly to the description of a new style of veil embroidery that Ḥabūba's mother saw when she went on pilgrimage to Mecca. Observing the scene, however, the anthropologist is taken aback by the disjuncture between this conversation and the previous discourse.

III.

In May of 1979 I returned to the Sinai after an absence of almost a month. By the end of March, I felt an urge to run north, to friends and family. I felt need of emotional support after witnessing in March, for the third year in a row, the simple but in my eyes devastating circumcision ceremony for the girls of Dahab's northern neighborhood. During April, I was still shocked by the scene: the parade of eight girls, aged three to six, holding between their teeth a new razor blade still in its wax paper cover; a mother opening her daughter's legs and honoring me by asking me to hold her arms tight; the oily laughter of the obese circumciser after amputating the clitoris tip; the girls running panic-stricken, red threads of blood on the insides of their thighs, from the circumciser's inner yard to the shore, where the salty sea water might cleanse their wounds and stop the bleeding; my fainting, now an annual attraction of the ceremony; the hand slaps and cold water on my face; the *ṭahawa* (thanksgiving) meal of dried fish and rice; the murmur of *Sūrat al-Fāt'ḥa* (the first chapter of the Qur'an); my escape to the outskirts of the settlement where, all alone, I stop being an anthropologist, and throw myself upon the shore, vomiting and crying, vomiting and crying, all the while wondering whether I cry because of pleasures never known and already lost by the girls, or because of their mothers' firm belief in the power the circumcision gives a woman over a man by removing lust, or perhaps because my own sexuality seems diminished as I carefully walk the thin rope stretching between the worlds of Mzeina men and women.

Back to Dahab. All this trauma seemed to send my mind back to Kāmla's words of two years ago: "If I only had the freedom of the mad . . ."

Dahab, still, 2:00 P.M., 7 May 1979

Afternoon heat enough to make the air faint. Everyone naps. These

YOUNG GIRLS RUNNING PANIC-STRICKEN, FROM THE CIRCUMCISER'S YARD TO THE SEA, RED THREADS OF BLOOD ON THE INSIDE OF THEIR THIGHS

are the hours when I interpret the first half of the day's events. I take my notebook and walk a kilometer north, even farther than the limbo space of the settlement's outskirts. I find one of my regular retreats, a rare sandy spot on the rocky beach, and sit down.

Low tide. Parts of the reef are exposed. I notice the dark turquoise tails of parrot fish sticking out of the water while their beak-like mouths chew on coral. Like tree bark, the white acorn-shelled crabs (*tetradyta*, Latin) cling in groups to the black boulders. A hermit crab (*anomura*, Latin), carrying the shell of a snail it ate and now resides in, runs from the dry part of the reef towards the hot water puddles. The wet breeze stirs up ripples in the puddles.

I spot ʿAlyii, the Madwoman, her dresses rolled up and tucked into her fuchsia-red waist-belt, T-strap plastic sandals on her feet, a basket woven from dried palm fronds hanging from the back of her head onto her back. She walks on the reef leaning on a thin, rusty iron stick. In her right hand she holds a wide blunt knife.

Women usually walked on the reef during low tide and used these tools to open giant clams (*tridakna*, Latin; *buṣra*, Mzeina vernacular), one-third meter long, that were clinging tenaciously to the reef. The women would let the clam close on their iron stick underwater, twist it to open the shell, then remove the clam with the knife and empty its shell into their baskets. They also caught slippery, half-meter-long octopuses (*garnīṭa*, Mzeina vernacular), which they grasped firmly by a couple of tentacles and beat many times on the seashore rocks to kill.

But ʿAlyii?

To my amazement, she empties several giant clams, one at a time, into her basket. Suddenly, she catches a medium-size octopus and hurries to the shore, holding the center part of its body to prevent its tentacles from gripping her hand. She vigorously whaps the octopus over and over again on the acorn-crab-dotted boulders until it is dead. All the time she is humming a jumpy hejēni, matching the words of a fisherman's proverb to this craven melody:

> *Nīka, ya ma betnīka,*
> *Abadan ma betistanīka.*
>
> Screw her yes, screw her no,
> Never will she wait for you.

After she has fussed with organizing her catch, she sits down near me. I am somewhat intimidated by her nearness, but my anthropological curiosity wins out. I tease her, saying, "This song must be shameful to sing."

"Eh-hey," she banters back. "Who are *you* to talk about Shame? Your women in your countries know no shame . . . Look at me! I'm like the tourist women on the beach, see?" She holds the bottoms of her breasts in her hands, and wiggles them. I laugh at this grotesque imitation of the nude hippies' bouncing breasts.

I compliment the Madwoman on her catch. Giant clams and octopuses are haute cuisine items. "Who are you going to eat all these goodies with?" I inquire.

She straightens her back and announces, "After I salt and dry all these, I'll give them to my brother. He's my guardian. We'll all eat this with *fatta* (shredded flatbread) and *samn shīḥi* (clarified herb butter) on the morning of ʿId al-Faṭr."

Something interesting crosses my mind. I say, "You know, ʿAlyii, men always go fishing. Women go a little. But what women catch is what Mzeinis love the most to eat. Women, then, must be valued fishermen too."

"Oh, you, don't believe what you hear about what women do." She cracks up with laughter that soon becomes hysterical and goes on and on. Suddenly she stops laughing and remarks, "Women—they're all mad."

"All of them?! Mad?!"

There is a moment of disturbing silence. ʿAlyii starts humming the hejēni, but without the smutty text. Then she abruptly interrupts herself: "Stink! they all stink! The *shaiṭān* (satanic spirits) visit them . . . , sometimes for a long time, and make them stink!"

Mzeini men and women had explained to me many times that the shaiṭān were one kind of jinns. Menstrual blood was related to the jinns, and women tried to mask its smell by pouring perfume on themselves or washing more often with a perfumed soap in spite of the constant lack of water. The smells of other vaginal secretions, pubic hair, and dirty nails were also associated with the jinns. But I was curious to get the Madwoman's explanation of the shaiṭān.

"Why do the shaiṭān visit women?"

"They want to test how well ṣabr has caught their nafs. And you know what? Men want to know it too. That's why they beat their wives if they want to screw them. They want to force the shaiṭān to leave their wives' bodies from here," she explains, pointing at her second toe, next to the big toe. "Without the shaiṭān, she will wait for you [her husband] at home. She won't dākhel. She'll have ṣabr. And patience is good, it's the key to salvation (*al-ṣabr ṭayyeb wamiftāḥ al-farrāj*—an oft-repeated Mzeini proverb)."

I had heard this interesting explanation for wife battering from several Mzeini men and women healers. They argued that a rebellious wife was possessed by demons and therefore needed to be beaten to exorcise them. In cases of women who could not physically engage in sexual intercourse due to severe vaginal contractions, expert healers prescribed that the woman sit on an ant hill, her genitals exposed to the ants, as a measure of shock therapy (Levi 1978).

"But the shaiṭān live only in women's bodies?"

The Madwoman chuckles bitterly. "No, young girl . . . No . . . Yes . . . *al-ʿomār* . . . These are the good jinns, those who know the Qur'an.

Men, they are good. The ʿomār only tickle their bones, and that's it. Men have ʿagl . . . [A male healer] just reads the Qur'an to the jinn, or writes something [in an amulet], and the ʿomār leaves [the man's body] right away. The ʿomār also have ʿagl . . . [The ʿomār] doesn't want any pain."

"So men don't stink?"

"They think they don't. Ha-ha. They think they don't . . . But you—don't believe what they think . . . You . . . Don't write what they tell you . . . They are lying . . . They have no ʿagl . . . You . . . They screw the donkey . . . Ha-ha-ha. And they think they don't."

The Madwoman now mirthfully points her index finger from side to side like a metronome while uttering the last line of the old proverb: "My female donkey and my wife; my female donkey and my wife; my female donkey and—"

I interrupt her, asking, "When did the jinns enter your body?"

ʿAlyii does not answer. She gazes at the sea. I gaze at her and realize I am terrified of this Freedom of the Mad. Everything makes sense and yet does not make sense at all.

Suddenly she rises, loads her basket onto her shoulders, snatches her rusty knife and stick, and marches off into the high tide sea. I cup my hands around my mouth and yell after her, "High tide, ya ʿAlyii, high tide!" But she keeps stomping along the reef. The water reaches to her thighs, and she screams at the wind, "Ḥaii, ḥaii . . . Ḥagg-kisht, ḥagg-kisht . . . Oh, my goat! My goat! . . . Who has seen my goat?"

5
THE EX-SMUGGLER

X

". . . So then, yours is truly a journey through memory!" The great Khan, his ears always sharp, sat up in his hammock every time he caught the hint of a sigh in Marco's speech. "It was to slough off a burden of nostalgia that you went so far away!" he exclaimed, or else: "You return from your voyages with a cargo of regrets!" . . . These words and actions were perhaps only imagined, as the two, silent and motionless, watched the smoke rise slowly from their pipes. The cloud dissolved at times in a wisp of wind, or else remained suspended in mid-air; and the answer was in that cloud. . . . It was beyond that screen of fickle humors that [Marco's] gaze wished to arrive: the form of things can be discerned better at a distance . . . [T]he jam of past, present, future that blocks existences calcified in the illusion of movement: this is what you would find at the end of your journey.

ITALO CALVINO
Invisible Cities

ISRAELI NATURE BUFFS AND THEIR BEDOUIN CAMEL DRIVERS AT A LUNCH BREAK

"What kind of question is that?" Every Mzeini was baffled when I asked what the meaning of *Bedu*, or Bedouin was. After a pause, he or she would answer "*al-Bedu raḥḥāla*," the Bedouin are nomads. This answer was uniform, and it was announced with pride. But only a handful of old people born around World War I proceeded with a detailed description of their memories—specific places and incidents of the *riḥla*, the complete classic annual nomadic migration cycle. These people had spent their childhood autumns and winters on shielded alluvial terraces near oases in lower altitude wadis. In the spring they would gradually climb to the Tih Plateau or to the highland plateaus of the peninsula watersheds for annual pastures, changing camp twice a month or so. During the summer, they would harvest their date trees in Wadi Firān and in the large oases on the coasts. They would end the summer with the pilgrimage to Faranje, the site of the Mzeina ancestral tomb on the central highland plateau, then proceed to Nebi Ṣāleḥ, the neighboring shrine overlooking the most strategic crossroads on the peninsula. After the pilgrimage, they would start descending to the lower altitude oases, and then the cycle began again (cf. Levi 1978, 1988).

People born in the 1940s would mention the riḥla, but explain it only in general terms. When I asked for details, they would list a series of mountain passes in a particular region of the peninsula, but unconvincingly, either through evasion or perhaps just from ignorance.

People born in the 1960s just uttered, "al-Bedu raḥḥāla," and remained silent thereafter. When I asked for details, they said, "It's of our parents' time." If they were from the coasts, they said that since 1972, the year the Eilat-Sharm asphalt road opened, they had migrated only twice, after the two huge flash floods in 1973 and 1975. The migration was by pickup trucks, only to one campsite in the highland watershed plateaus, and then back to the coastal oases. Some moved every year during the winter months from the coastline into wadis near the coast, seeking shelter from the winter winds. But these short moves were not considered a riḥla, they said.

It took me four years of fieldwork to realize that this was an important question to ask the Mzeinis. During my first two years in the field, as a devout young student of Arab tribalism, I thought that one couldn't ask "the natives" questions such as "What is a Bedouin?" or "What is the meaning of a tribe?" I believed I should have reached the answers to such problems on my own, relying on the gathering of ethnographic details. Being a serious student of tribal nomadic cultures, well versed in the canon of scholarship discussing the classic tribe,[1] I lovingly collected genealogies and kinship classifications and tried to form a model that would describe how descent and kinship affect matters of territoriality and migration—one of the issues central to the study of nomadic cultures.

But such an approach soon led to anomie. In retrospect I can see why: the Mzeina were not the typical Bedouin tribe I had read about in the literature. With a population far beyond the carrying capacity of the desert, and with a long history under military occupation, they were no longer classical nomads, if they ever had been. They were wage workers, who tended gardens and raised goats only in their spare time. Consequently, issues of segmentarity, important to other Arab tribes, were irrelevant to their daily lives. The Mzeina presented a paradox as to their Bedouin identity. Salīm, an angular young man, expressed it succinctly. Answering my question about what being a Bedouin meant, he said with a bit of chutzpah and sarcasm: "*al-Bedu raḥlīn wal-Mzeina shaghalīn*"—"whereas the Bedouin are nomads, the Mzeina are laborers." I liked this rhyme. When I said it to other Mzeini men and women, many laughed and said, "This is our life." Salwa, a feisty woman in her midthirties, added, "Our men are laborers. We are not free like the Bedouin on that radio program from Saudi Arabia.[2] Our men work for whatever government occupies the Sinai. Wherever there's work, we move to be near it." Adding another layer of punning to the raḥlīn/shaghalīn discrepancy, she said, "Other Bedouin are raḥḥāla, our life is a *shughla* (a hassle)."

But it was the anthropologist who initiated all these conversations. In the course of their daily life, Mzeinis rarely worried about who a Bedouin was or what constituted a tribe. These were questions asked by outsiders: tourists, soldiers, developers, settlers, and anthropologists. Interestingly, the standard answer of the Mzeina sounded like a facsimile of the standard official tourist guide explanation. "Let me tell you why we are called Bedouin," I overheard ʿĪd, a lanky teenager in patched army pants and a red-and-white-checkered headdress, explaining in broken English to a sunburned Scandinavian couple who had tried to strike up a conversation with him as he sat nearby, watching them sunbathing in the nude. "In Arabic, *bādia* means desert. We, Bedouin, are people of the desert." "Really?" I challenged him in Arabic. ʿĪd did not answer me. From the look on his face I gathered that for me there was a different explanation.

Still, despite the seeming irrelevance of the topic, every once in a while during a mundane conversation about life in the Sinai, I would casually drop the remark, "Bedouin are nomads, whereas the Mzeina are laborers." Once, sitting at the private magʿad of Silmi, a wealthy ḥajj from Bir Zgheir, in a circle that included several elegant ḥajjes in their midfifties, I was corrected with a sardonic smile: "The Bedouin are raḥlīn while we Mzeina are *shayyalīn* (couriers)." I suspected that Silmi was making a point about smuggling, an activity attractive to many South Sinai Bedouin between 1952 and 1972. People like Silmi and his circle of friends put to good use the discrepancy inherent in the fact that the Mzeina were nomads who depended on wage labor. They offered their fellow tribesmen an occupation that overrode that discrepancy. They could be nomads and make money at it. The Mzeinis thus could work as migrant laborers on their own terrain.

Egypt at that time had the largest consumer market for hashish in the Middle East. Turkey, Lebanon, and Syria were the largest regional producers of the drug. Prior to 1952, the narcotics route ran through the more accessible desert areas of the Middle East, crossing the Trans-Jordanian Plateau, the Negev, and the North Sinai to Egypt. After the overthrow of King Farouq in 1952, the Egyptian army under Gamal Abdul Nasser started to fortify the North Sinai, to prepare for nationalizing the Suez Canal. As a result, the smuggling route had to change. For the hashish to make its way into Egypt, it had to go through the mountainous, inaccessible southern portion of the Sinai.

Young South Sinai entrepreneurs quickly took advantage of this shift and took charge of the South Sinai leg of the drug route. Concurrently, they took advantage of the Bedouin's relative unemployment and their intimate knowledge of the complicated South Sinai terrain. "If the smuggler trusted you," said a weatherbeaten Mzeini who once worked for such an entrepreneur in the early 1960s, "his man in your land would have told you to go on a certain day to a certain spot, usually near a mountain pass. There you would meet someone from the neighboring land. You just had to load your camel with whatever was on his camel, and then you could sing *hejēni*s (caravan songs) while riding, have fun visiting encampments along the way, and then, after the last mountain pass of your own land, someone from the next area would be waiting for you. You would unload your camel, and he would load the stuff on his, and that's all there was to it. After the delivery arrived in Egypt, the money would come back from Egypt on the return trip." When I asked him whether he was worried about the Egyptian army, he said, "The Egyptians were afraid of us Bedouin, not the other way around. They are river people. In the desert, they never left the main motorized transport roads. Things got a bit tougher when they brought in their *mukhabarāt* (Secret Police), and people started telling about other people. They even established a camel patrol . . . But the few Egyptians who came here were just hungry peasants. Give them some money or some hashish to sell on their own, and it was as if they hadn't seen a thing."

While providing a way to combine the ideology of free-spirited nomadism with paid cash labor, the smugglers also overrode the Mzeini paradox between tribal agnatic segmentation and practical individual-based networks (cf. Hart 1970). They were members of lineages who were said to be ideologically powerful, tracing relatively pure descent from the Mzeina's ancestor. Membership in these lineages gave them not only greater access to territory, but also greater obligations to cooperate economically with their kin. Smuggling, however, was dangerous and illegal. Smugglers could not risk cooperation with untrustworthy or inept kin. Instead, they employed, for meager wages, people they could trust to come up with creative solutions in moments of crisis. In selecting these people, they emphasized wits and wiles over segmentary concerns.

The smugglers skillfully exploited the Bedouin, who preferred smuggling to other migrant work, although wages were paltry for both. Smugglers spent little on overhead and made a reasonable profit when the hashish arrived in Egypt. As a major employer, they became central to Mzeini daily life. Ironically, to play down the importance of their illegal activities, they cited their lineage purity as the reason for their social position.

After the 1967 Israeli occupation, until the Eilat-Sharm road opened in 1972, the South Sinai attracted very few developers, settlers, or tourists. During those years, the Israeli authorities had a good relationship with the smugglers. Assuming that the Egyptian border guards would be given a cut of the drugs as a bribe, they chose to allow the smugglers to continue operating the drug traffic to Egypt, on the logic that drug use by Egyptian soldiers could only benefit Israel. When the Eilat-Sharm road opened, however, the Israeli authorities feared that the relatively inexpensive drugs might find their way into the lucrative

Israeli drug scene, so they started intensive helicopter patrolling of the South Sinai. Fishing boats and camels they caught carrying hashish were literally blown up with dynamite. Smuggling was effectively ended when the Israelis offered the Bedouin all the blue-collar jobs in the many development projects they started in the Sinai. The Bedouin preferred these jobs to smuggling since the wages were slightly higher and there was no legal risk. Between 1972 and 1975 some smugglers left for Jordan or Egypt, and some even made friends with the military government by promising to remain within the law. Those who did not were forcibly exiled.

Ex-smugglers who remained in the South Sinai lived off their accumulated wealth. They became very religious, making ostentatious pilgrimages to Mecca, and praying punctually five times a day. Some, however, started drinking, and sat around reminiscing about their heyday. They rarely frequented the communal magᶜads. Instead, they had their own magᶜads in their inner yards, where they sat silently, letting their few visitors talk, and only nodding their heads to agree or disagree. By choosing when they would or would not talk, they enacted their power to "define the situation" through silence (cf. McHugh 1968). If the Ex-Smugglers refused to talk, a silence of power ensued, and their visitors would continue talking with each other in order to avoid an embarrassing lull in the conversation, as long as no argument stalled the flow of the dialogue.

Two paradoxes were inherent in the composition of the Ex-Smuggler persona. He was ideologically powerful because of his membership in a pure lineage, where agnation and corporation partially overlapped, and yet he had accumulated his economic power by totally disregarding segmentary concerns. Second, the smuggler had used the territorial strategies of nomadic pastoralism, yet only to underpin a system of wage labor. By being himself paradoxical, the smuggler had been able to offer a temporary solution to the Mzeina paradoxes of nomadism/wage labor and agnation/individually based networks—conundrums he himself contained. Whenever these collective paradoxes surfaced in daily discourse as existential dilemmas, the conversation soon disintegrated into an argument. The catalyst for such an argument was often the Ex-Smuggler's presence, but he was able to override, even while reifying, the collective paradoxes by acting them out. And this he did by being silent. Such a silence was not his ordinary silence of power, but rather, an allegorical silence, performed as if it were a story his guests did not dare interrupt. The Ex-Smuggler's silence imposed liminality on those unresolvable contradictions. Like the allegories told by other Mzeini personae, the Ex-Smuggler's silence acknowledged yet transcended the inconsistencies between framed domains of traditional knowledge and the vagaries of daily life.

I.

I don't know how to write about you, Smuggler. Here I sit, in the Berkeley serenity of gourmet food and salon politics, an old pine tree branching in front of my window, and a pair of squirrels affectionately grooming each other on one of the branches. If I leave my study and go to the kitchen to make a cup of tea, I see the Golden Gate from the balcony. Sitting at my desk in this pastoral scene of quiet and refuge, I live amidst the focused concerns of academic life, and the vicissitudes of life in the Sinai are difficult to conjure up.

In my memories you wander around in a place that once, I thought, was pastoral and pristine. But that illusion faded together with my naive desert wanderlust after about a week of fieldwork. So here I am. Bent over the desk. Brow furrowed. My thoughts far away. In the Sinai. On you.

Maybe on nights lit by the full moon you sneak to some steep *nagb* (mountain pass) to recall with nostalgia those sudden forays into the "field," when you checked how things were going with the shipments. Maybe during those burning afternoons you sit in one of your shining white caftans under that thorny, frizzy-topped acacia in that same geographically remote yet strategically central oasis, your deep wrinkles etched by your time and place. You cough your tobacco cough, close your cataract-filled eyes, and recall those days when you were young and cunning. And when you open your eyes, at those soon-to-be-sacred moments before the *ʿaṣr* prayer, you probably mumble in your ironic tone: "*Maṣr bit'ḥayyi maʿa al-ḥashīsh*"—"Egypt comes alive with hashish." After the prayer, despite your cancer, you probably roll a cigarette and spit a curse, cynically resigned to the mentality of peasants and city dwellers.

And here, in Berkeley, I try to write about your illegal past, about events that occurred before you retired to the comfort of Muslim piety, hoping to expunge your "sins," all but forced upon you by circumstance. I want to write about your exploring eyes, shining beneath the bushy silver brows, and about your goatee, sharpening your angular face. I want to write of your cynicism when you talk about your various cancers, and of the daring gambles of your marriages and divorces, all aimed at gaining greater access to territory. I wish to describe the deep voice you reserve for analyzing the political situation. And write of your anger at the Sheikh or the Galīd when they forget that despite your newly acquired humble piety, you might still be the director of the show "Daily Life Among the Mzeina." Most of all, I want to write about your silences, more thunderous than your angry rebukes.

Once, the anthropologist was able to expose the nameless objects of his study—those "informants" with whom he lived—for the sake of science. The anthropologist assumed a discontinuity between the real life of field experience and the academic enterprise. Once, he was able to generalize from the data and write about a particular Self as a generalized Other. But this approach has become problematic.

I will have to transform you from being your Self into being a typified Other. I have no clue how to write about you as a typical Other. You are not typical, despite the fact that you are a prominent Mzeini persona. I am in a real dilemma. You are hurt enough—the cancer and the politicking. Shall I censor? Shall I disguise? Create a composite? What if your enemies read the final text and guess your identity? Perhaps the solution is to make you into a timeless creature and write in the voice of the natural historian, "describing," "comparing," "classifying," "generalizing"—all in the dull present tense.

Perhaps the solution would be to discuss my dilemma with you. You will instruct me what to say and when to keep silent. Could we write the text together? Orally, of course, but into the tape-recorder. You might decide against entering into the pantheon of anthropological fantasies. I would be disappointed, yet respectful. But if you choose to enter into "the literature," I am afraid I will still have to have the final say.

II.

Winter 1985, South Sinai

Forest and I cross the desert driven in an elegant Peugeot taxi, headed toward you. In 1981, the last time I visited you, I crouched in the back of a dilapidated pickup truck, sandwiched between a woman holding her baby and a crying goat. With every bump on the dirt road and every heave of the truck, sacks stuffed with stinky dried parrot fish fell on us. Now we ride on a smooth, two-lane asphalt road arbitrarily breaking through the lip-shaped sand dunes that flow down from purple sandstone cliffs.

The taxi driver carefully picks out his library of cassettes one bearing Michael Jackson's picture. This in spite of my clear interest in another, bearing Umm Kalsoum's.

"Times have changed," he smiles. "Four years ago, a trip from Dahab to Wadi Firān took around five hours. Today less than two."

We get off at a midsized oasis. "Could you pay in dollars?" he asks. "That's the best way we have to fight inflation." We nod our heads. His Peugeot glides toward the Gulf of Suez.

We load our heavy backpacks on our shoulders and start the climb to that geographically remote yet strategically central oasis where you still live. This part of the journey has not changed. Smooth red granite cliffs caress the soft horizon in the late afternoon. We sweat, almost breathless. Forest reminisces about less strenuous hikes in the Sierra Nevada.

Dusk. The cliffs merge with the darkening skies. Two adolescent goatherds in soft dresses walk down our trail. "Smadar!" one of them shouts excitedly. "Smadar has come back from America!" I am touched that they do not veil, a sign that even after four years of absence, I am not a stranger.

"You must be climbing up to visit Ḥajj X," her friend says.

"How is he doing? Has he changed much during my years in America?" I ask with concern.

"X—instead of the cancer eating him, he eats his cancer," the two smirk.

*

And here we are in that oasis on a crossroad of wadis, known best to those wishing to avoid what pass for the main roads of the South Sinai. A crisp clear night. With sore muscles we squat over a large platter overloaded with rice and cooked dried parrot fish. "Burp loudly," I whisper to Forest, to remind him how to show that he is fully satisfied.

"Our Lord's alliance with you," I thank Ḥajj X in the customary way.

"Health and well-being on us and on you," answers Ḥajj X, as is the custom.

The four men who are also visiting echo my blessings, and the ḥajj repeats his. Finally, we can recline on a colorful narrow rug and let our aching muscles recover.

Ḥajj X winks as he pours what passes for vodka in Israel into seven small tea glasses.[3] Half-smiling, he toasts, "We only live once."

I get my notebook and pen from the pack. Ḥajj X tells the others, "She went to America, and got a husband there, but instead of bearing children she still writes about the Bedouin, true?"

"True," I chuckle. We are silent for a bit.

SMADAR: Well, you know that now in America, I am writing the book about the time I lived with the Mzeina. When I finish, God willing, the University will grant me a doctorate.

ḤAJJ X: And then, will you be able to work for the government?

SMADAR: No, but I might get a job at a university.

ḤAJJ X [*leaning forward*]: They may give you a job in America because of us, here?

SMADAR [*raising one shoulder, a Mzeini gesture meaning indifference or doubt*]: Who knows? They might not . . . My work is kind of . . . a bit convoluted (*muʿawwaja*). Hmm . . . how could I say it . . . Well, they don't look at the Mzeina themselves, they look at my writing.

I utter this acknowledgement quietly, embarrassed by its truth.

ḤAJJ X [*flings his arm out and lets it drop dismissively*]: Ah . . . all of you Westerners . . . you are all . . . well . . . kind of convoluted.

The darkness helps me hide my blushing face. I look at the ground. We are silent for several long moments.

SMADAR [*almost in a whisper*]: In the book . . . I wanted to know if it's OK for me to write about you and about others like you.

ḤAJJ X [*smiling*]: Health and well-being! Of course! [*He then laughs heartily, to the rest*] See? I learned about America from the radio and soon they'll learn about me in the books.

Everyone laughs.

SMADAR: Tell me something, the truth. By Allah's strength, the truth. I want to know if you think I could write about the Smuggling Period. You know, 'til '72, when they opened the asphalt road. You think it would be safe?

ḤAJJ X [*knitting his brow, then looking me straight in the eye*]: I think it's a nice idea. It's fine.

Our long silence is punctuated by the distant sound of an owl.

SMADAR: Are you sure? One hundred percent? Books in English don't have international borders.

ḤAJJ X: I am really sure. But you, tell me, why does your soul feel guilty?

SMADAR: Perhaps I feel guilty because with the words of the Mzeina, I create my career. I don't want my work to cause you harm.

ḤAJJ X: Harm? No, it's the Christians who are harmful, *al-Naṣāra khasāra.*

Everyone laughs at this good rhyme. In the Mzeina proverb, "al-Naṣāra khasāra," "al-Naṣāra" (the Christians) refers to the superpowers, who can harm the ḥajj or his tribe. Ḥajj X uses this idiom to convey to me that this cannot happen in my case.

ḤAJJ X [*deeply inhales his cigarette smoke, then continues*]: My words—they're all history. *Illi fāt māt.* Whatever happened died [meaning, it's water under the bridge]. Write it down. Illi fāt māt. See? I even roll my eyes to the sky when I say this.

"Is this yet another 'show' of the fatal Bedouin savage in front of his exotica-hunting anthropologist?" I think to myself, while Ḥajj X continues to play with this cultural expression.

ḤAJJ X: Illi fāt māt. Gosh, what a nice Arabic saying. Everyone who came here wrote it down. You—write that everything finished in 1972, when they [the Israelis] opened the asphalt road and brought jobs. Now, times have changed. It's all history. If one wants to smuggle these days, he'd better have a small private plane, not a camel [*winking*]. Buy me a plane, and we can write real stories of the present.

SMADAR: Yeah. Smuggling is now part of the past. Illi fāt māt.

ḤAJJ X: And anyway, who would care? America—despite the movies [that American film producers shot here], they don't care about us. And if we weren't cheap labor or better than the [topographic] maps, neither the Egyptians nor the Israelis would care about us either.

Silence.

SMADAR: But people still talk about the Smuggling Period . . .

ḤAJJ X: Eh . . . Well . . . They tell stories . . . Don't you know by now that the Bedouin always have to sit near the fire and tell stories?

SMADAR: Maybe . . . like this . . . we'll compose some story about you? Here we are, sitting by the fire.

ḤAJJ X [*laughing*]: Fine. I will tell you things from my memory, and you . . . you have a weak memory. That's why you write everything down [*laughter*]. So you will tell me things from the memory of your notebooks. And we'll write this story.

SEVERAL MEN: Neat idea. Indeed. Let's do it.

ḤAJJ X [*to the audience*]: Indeed? By the time we are done with this story, my mind might start getting convoluted like the minds of those Westerners.

Everyone cracks up at Ḥajj X's well-aimed jibes. I also join in.

SMADAR: Who knows, maybe when we finish telling our story, my mind might be straightened out. It might become like yours.

The laughter rises. I share the amusement, but my academic self has taken a beating.

ḤAJJ X [*pointing his index finger at me*]: But patience, my friends. We'll tell the story not about me, but about someone else, also a smuggler. But someone we'll make up . . . Someone really tough . . .

Silent pause.

ḤAJJ X: But . . . but those like you who come here and measure things on our land, they want everything precise and true, no?

SMADAR: Well, yeah . . . That's what they teach us at the university . . . [*looking at the ground*].

ḤAJJ X [*focuses bright eyes and bushy eyebrows on me*]: So for the sake of Science (*ʿilm*), let's say . . . that the guy, *our* guy, usually lived in Wadi ʿEin al-Ḥsi (The Spring of the Pebbles).

Everyone roars with laughter, not just because no such place exists, but mostly because in a desert full of rocks, the fabricated name is absurd.

ḤAJJ X [*continues seriously, in spite of the laughter*]: Once . . . long ago . . . like in the stories . . . And let's call him . . . hmm . . . Ḥajj *Khantarīsh* . . .

SMADAR [*feigning shock*]: Ḥajj Khantarīsh?! Allah and not His replacement! You must be kidding!

ḤAJJ X: Yeah . . . with precision just like that of the university. Ḥajj Khantarīsh!

Khantarīsh is the worst quality hashish. It is also a nickname given to someone or somebody whose worth is negligible. Now, as if we are narrating a Kundera novel, we're all enmeshed in layers of absurdity and circles of laughter. The anthropologist has abdicated her authority and joined in her "informants'" laughter about the anthropological enterprise. Together they are all now writing a story onto a tape, about a place that can't exist and a man whose name just can't be.

THE STORY: PART ONE

We choose just an ordinary Tuesday at a small encampment near a remote yet tactical crossroads of two wadis. Perhaps the encampment ought to be semisedentary, that is, having both wooden shacks and woven goat-hair tents. Of course, there ought to be a well of the old style, its single bucket attached to a poplar trunk by a rope and weighted with a stone. Here the collaborating storytellers have their first textual dilemma. Ḥajj X insists that despite the romantic location, we should also toss in a new well with a motor pump. It is true that retired smugglers were the first to invest in motorized water pumps. But after a moment he reconsiders and asks me to delete the mechanized well from the notebook. "ʿEin al-Ḥsi is a place to reminisce about," he sighs, "not an oasis that keeps up with modernized times."

We discuss background details. The mountains towering from the wadi could be blushing red granite or black volcanics. The weather should be heavy early autumn heat. The vegetation sparse, aside from four well-manicured date palm trees near the well.

"I really don't much care about the color of the mountains, I leave that to you," says Ḥajj X with a shrug of his shoulder. "Write whatever. What's important is that no one could reach there except on a camel."

Our hero, Ḥajj Khantarīsh, Ḥajj Lousy Hashish, arrived back at his own oasis last Saturday, yet his back still hurt from the long ride. "He who marries two wives does not sleep at night, and carries the whole world on his back" (*jōz al-thintein ma yenām billeil, waḥāmel al-ẓahar kulho*), or so says the proverb. And Ḥajj Khantarīsh was married to four wives.

As with other Mzeini smugglers, one of the most important goals to be achieved through Khantarīsh's marriages was territorial access. Mzeini men acquired territorial access through descent lines. If a man did not have a lineage member living in a place, the best way to gain access was through marriage. The more marriages, the greater access. So the smugglers often had more than one wife. Like other Mzeinis, smugglers usually violated the ideologically vaunted *bint ʿam* (parallel cousin) marriage in favor of one that would bring them greater territorial access. But Mzeinis also divorced frequently, because of their shifting political and economic interests that depended on which foreign government occupied the Sinai. Smugglers divorced even more frequently than other Mzeinis because, once friendship ties were established with the residents of the wife's oasis, the wives were no longer needed, unless there were several children involved. The wives did not mind this since it was not their, but their father's interests that were at stake. Many times the divorce was more welcome to the woman than the marriage was.

Ḥajj X and I decide that Ḥajj Khantarīsh whiled away most of his days riding high in his pickup truck or atop his camel, crossing the desert expanse between his various wives for short honeymoons, stopping at will in each community en route, drinking tea, socializing, talking politics—always the guest.

But the story began on just a plain Tuesday morning. Ḥajj Khantarīsh, this time not the guest, was sitting in his own magʿad, shaded by the proverbial acacia—the only magʿad at the Spring of Pebbles Oasis. Since his third wife's father died, he has been the only man in the oasis this time of year. The rest of the men have gone down the mountains to their temporary employment at the oil fields of Abu-Rodeis. Some, regularly paid by the civil administration, begrudgingly cleaned the main dirt roads. Being surrounded only by women and children was an awkward reminder for Khantarīsh that his heyday was long gone.

Ḥajj Khantarīsh was perfectly shaved. The pleasing scent of fresh soap surrounding him would have revealed to anyone (had there been anyone) his tender night last night. Dressed in his Friday best, a shining white caftan and a headdress almost whiter than the peak of Mount Hermon in winter, the ḥajj sat and waited for guests. Sat and waited.

But the horizon was blank. No one had passed by here for the last three days. As a matter of fact, since the new road had opened, everyone knew that if he were caught smuggling, he'd see his camel's soul flying up to the sky while its body was blasted to bits by dynamite. Naturally everyone preferred to work for the Israelis.

Ḥajj X and I decide that Ḥajj Khantarīsh will also have an anthropologist of his own, and she should be frustrated.

"ʿEin al-Ḥsi is not what it used to be," she thought to herself.

"Where's the action?" If she had wanted to document the cops-and-robbers the Bedouin played with the Israelis, she should have done her fieldwork ten years ago.

This anthropologist finally overcame her initial embarrassment about talking to the powerful Ḥajj Khantarīsh, entered his magʿad, and seated herself before his honor. She was silent. He was silent. They remained wrapped in their own silences for about an hour, until ants began to crawl into the anthropologist's brain. She was getting fidgety. She sketched one camel after another in her notebook, retied her headdress, scratched her knee, poked her ear, drew more camels. Suddenly, our composite Ex-Smuggler, Ḥajj Khantarīsh, turned to her, and spoke with measured words:

*

ḤAJJ KHANTARĪSH: Why don't you write my genealogy?

ANTHROPOLOGIST: Why do you think I should write it?

KHANTARĪSH: Because everyone who conquered this land, the British, the Turks, the Egyptians, the Israelis, they all thought that tribes are like maps. If you understand the map you won't lose your way. Nice idea, huh? . . . Since '67—who hasn't written it? The military, the *Minhāl* (the Israeli civil development authorities), official tourist guides . . . They all wrote my genealogy. [*He grimaces a smile*] By God, what stupidity!

Silence. Khantarīsh was rolling a cigarette.

ANTHROPOLOGIST: Really? . . . I read that one guy, he's from Canada and his work is like mine . . . he recorded an old Arab proverb that said, "I against my brother; I and my brother against our cousin; I and my brother and my cousin against the world" (Salzman 1978a:53). You know about this?

KHANTARĪSH [*shrugs both shoulders*]: They say so. But this Canada guy doesn't know *my* brothers . . . The eldest amounts to less than nothing. He just wanders around with his few goats. And the younger—he always worked with the Egyptians and then with the Israelis. Now he works for the Egyptians again.

ANTHROPOLOGIST: What's wrong with that? There are many Bedouin like them.

KHANTARĪSH [*reflective*]: What's wrong with that? Well, really, nothing's wrong with that. It's just a certain size of mind, like for example, a lamb's.

At this point in the improvised narration process, Ḥajj X, his four

Mzeini guests, and I have to laugh, because lambs are considered very stupid.

Our story continues:

ANTHROPOLOGIST: If your brothers are only lambs, what are you?

KHANTARĪSH: I heard everyone who visited Tel Aviv talking about the zoo. I don't think we have one here. But if you insist, I can tell you that I named the youngest son of my youngest wife Nimr—Leopard.

I tell Khantarīsh's anthropologist to note that, from her experience with Mzeini naming patterns, parents rarely used names connoting power or beauty, due to their fear of the evil eye. "Apparently," I instruct her to write in her fieldnotes, "Ḥajj Khantarīsh is not afraid of the evil eye."

KHANTARĪSH: If he had to, Nimr would bite his cousins.

Like other Bedouin tribes, Mzeini tribesmembers had an ideology in which patrilineal agnation and political-economic corporation overlapped. Therefore, one had to depend on one's cousins. But almost always, Mzeinis cooperated with neighbors and friends, a pattern of networking essential to ex-smugglers. Here, when Khantarīsh talked about the possibility of his son hurting his own paternal cousins, he acknowledged the discrepancy.

At this point, X and I direct Khantarīsh to laugh to himself. But he should soon draw into himself, quietly playing with his prayer beads.

ANTHROPOLOGIST: Do you trust your brothers?

KHANTARĪSH: My father didn't trust them . . . You know, when we were little, I was the one who went with him to visit from one Bedouin encampment to the other . . . My father, he used to say about my elder brother, "He who teaches the idiot finds out that the next day everything is forgotten" (*bitʿallem fil mitballem beyaṣbaḥ nāsi*—a Mzeini proverb). And he [my father] married my brother to his cousin. So after all this you want me to trust my brothers? . . . No! all they want is my money.

ANTHROPOLOGIST: And do you give them any?

KHANTARĪSH: Sometimes. They're my brothers, no?

Silence. We tell his anthropologist to light a cigarette.

ANTHROPOLOGIST: So who do you trust?

KHANTARĪSH: Men. Real men. Anyone who knows what *amāna* (trust) is. Any man who understands what *kalām rejjāl* (a man's word) is.

ANTHROPOLOGIST: And their *aṣal* (roots, i.e., tribal affiliation)—do you care about it?

KHANTARĪSH: Why should I care about their lineages (*fruᶜ*, plural, literally meaning "streams")? [*then firmly*] A trustworthy man is worth ten stupid brothers.

A pause. I tell the anthropologist to worry about whether this is a Mzeini proverb that needs to be specially recorded in her proverb book. She has never heard this one before. Then I suggest to Ḥajj X that now the conversation between Ḥajj Khantarīsh and his own anthropologist ought to be redirected into hard-core anthropological concerns.

ANTHROPOLOGIST: Let's talk some more about that guy from Canada and his Arab proverb. I was taught at the university that the Bedouin tribe had to be a united yet divided collection of brothers and cousins. And here you tell me that this is mouse talk (*kalām farr*—nonsense). So maybe you could tell me . . . [*pauses innocently*] what is a tribe?

KHANTARĪSH [*loud*]: What kind of question is that, "What is a tribe?" Can I ask you, "What is the state of Israel?" Why do you think that the first question is easier? Is it because "a tribe" is something you didn't grow up with?

Khantarīsh here should stop his rebuke and take a long breath.

KHANTARĪSH [*slowly, smiling*]: But because you're my guest, and because I really want to help your research, I'll give you the names of our ancestor and his sons, and how we trace our roots to them . . . You know, the Mzeina's ancestor's name was Faraj. Write it down. Write. Faraj had two sons, ᶜAli and Ghānem. Let me repeat so that you can write without rushing. Rushing, you probably know the proverb, is from the devil (*al-ᶜajal min al-shaiṭān*).

Frustrated, the anthropologist politely wrote "her" tribe's genealogy for the umpteenth time.

At this point X requests Ḥajj Khantarīsh to wink at "his" anthropologist and then to sharply turn his face and gaze at the horizon. Khantarīsh and his anthropologist ought to sink back into their own silences.

With all his experience of backpacking nature buffs, X makes sure that Khantarīsh in his white caftan will be placed against the striking image of sunset and red rocks when he performs his *maghreb* prayer. I make sure that his anthropologist, though duly impressed by the beautiful scene, will open her notebook and start writing some introductory remarks about the activities in which Khantarīsh, the research object, was involved. X leaves this task completely to me while he elaborately rolls a cigarette. So I tell his anthropologist to write:

The Smuggling Period, 1952–1972: As a result of the military fortification of North Sinai since 1952, the narcotics traffic shifted to the southern mountainous area with its inaccessible topography. South Sinai entrepreneurs immediately made use of this shift. Further, the intertribal organization of personal friendship networks was put into action, facilitating the drug trade. These entrepreneurs gradually formed a new elite of wealthy Bedouin, leading to a large-scale polarization of the otherwise egalitarian society. The Israeli military government, having intensively studied issues of tribal structure and organization between 1967 and 1972, was able to eradicate smuggling. To recruit Bedouin as labor for their development projects, they exploited the same intertribal networks the smugglers used. An even more effective incentive to entice the poor Bedouin to work for the Israelis rather than the smugglers was the Israeli Defense Force antidrug "iron fish."

THE NARRATORS: CRITIQUE OF THE STORY, PART I

Somewhere in the Sinai, sometime in Winter 1985. It's late at night. I've just now finished reading to Ḥajj X what I've written in my notebook from the ideas and parts of text we tossed to each other and into the night.

The ḥajj says, "I like it. Ḥajj Khantarīsh is not so much of a khantarīsh, despite the fact he's trying to present himself as one. Well, this is typical. But you, why did you finish this part of the story with so much khantarīsh [contextually, meaning bullshit] that sounds just like the lessons in Islam that come from the transistor radio?"

"We have agreed that I should write some general remarks about smuggling. Well, this is how we tell stories in my work," I answer, and the anthropologist in me feels chagrined.

Ḥajj X laughs. "You and your work . . . And the university . . . Since Israel occupied these lands I've seen so many people from universities—collecting stones, plants, mice, rain, even hyena dung . . . God! You make me laugh!"

"What can be done? To each his own song of heart (*kul wāḥad waḍamīro*)," I answer with a proverb.

"Let's have another drink," Ḥajj X proposes as a temporary textual solution. "You learned from us a good way to look at life. To each his own song of heart."

The general hum of agreement is Forest's lullaby. The earlier glass of vodka overcame his desire to stay awake, and since he doesn't understand Arabic anyway, he has fallen asleep midway through the story, cuddled into a ball, his head in my lap.

"Back to work!" Ḥajj X is full of pep. "I like this serious nonsense we're doing. Let's continue our khantarīsh of a story."

I suggest we start a new chapter, in which our Ḥajj Khantarīsh will meet with guests, perhaps a brother or a friend, people with whom he can talk under his acacia about the good ol' days.

Ḥajj X corrects me, pointing out the fact that ex-smugglers, when meeting with family, neighbors, or friends, do not say much. "Knowing how fast gossip spreads, their silence is their wisdom," he remarks perceptively. "But it's no great wisdom for you to write about somebody who does not say anything."

"Why not?" I inquire. "Since this is a story anyway, why not try composing some silences like this?" It seems to me that on this fantastic night, anything could be in our story.

"But before the silence there ought to be a *big* argument . . . of everyone . . . but . . . our retired smuggler has to remain silent," Ḥajj X warns me.

"OK . . . OK . . ." I succumb. "But what will they argue about?"

"About what is always argued when there is a big argument," Ḥajj X responds, as if I am supposed to know the answer.

"About what?" I insist, though in the back of my mind I begin to remember several arguments I witnessed in which ex-smugglers, despite unspoken demands, maintained their authority of silence.

"Well, ya Smadar, one could think that you arrived here only yesterday," teases Ḥajj X, annoyed. "Ex-smugglers argued with other people about themselves, of course!"

Ḥajj X would have made a great anthropologist or Muchona the

Hornet lookalike (Turner 1967), I think to myself. His perspective sharpened by having been both an outlaw and at the center of Mzeini daily life (because of access to capital), Ḥajj X demonstrates a well-developed capacity for cross-cultural reflection. But he cuts short my scholarly ruminations, ordering:

"So now write that . . ."

THE STORY: PART II

Ḥajj X and I want the guests to arrive at ʿEin al-Ḥsi at midmorning in autumn, two days after the first conversation between Ḥajj Khantarīsh and his anthropologist. Khantarīsh would be seated as usual, leaning on the acacia's wide trunk, still dressed in his Friday best, though it was only Thursday. He will shade his eyes, habitually red from the campfire smoke, and squint at three clouds of dust approaching from the east side of the wadi.

"These are probably two foreign tourists and their Bedouin tour-guide." Khantarīsh considered how much the guide might be making in approximate figures if he were a middleman for the camel owners as well. When he finished calculating the interesting monetary aspects, he concluded: "Soft-skinned Westerners!"

X dictates to me the words that Ḥajj Khantarīsh would think to himself: "Since the Jews have arrived, the mountains are no longer a place of refuge. These tourists—the more they reach places it is very hard to get to, the more they enjoy themselves. Stupid people! Why do such modern creatures who live in pleasant cleanliness suffer their vacations in the desert when they have enough money for better things?"

X wishes that now Khantarīsh close his eyes and daydream about his pre-1967 pleasure journeys to Cairo, the capital of *omm al-dunya*, "the mother of the universe," Egypt. His drunkenness in a dim nightclub in Shareʿ al-Ahrām, sinking deep into lush burgundy velvet; his blushing at the smug laughter of a high-class prostitute while she compliments his desert virility; a bed on a frame and a box spring, and the whiteness of bed sheets in al-hotel; the packed humanity in the streets; riding taxicabs and feeling rich and powerful; then returning to his oasis solitude, now feeling like a desert bumpkin, yet still the clever Bedouin.

We tell Khantarīsh to notice three white headdresses. "Bedouin!" His heart jumped with joy. "No," the cynic in him admonished. "These are those camel-buff tourists who try to dress like us." Squinting his eyes, he hoped to identify at least the Bedouin guide.

Suddenly he noticed the conspicuous absence of colorful sleeping bags and backpacks that tourists would have dangling from the saddles. "Three *real* guests!" Khantarīsh was thrilled.

"Women—knead! knead dough! Pound! Pound salt in the mortar! Pound! Guests are upon us!" the ḥajj shouted happily from beneath his tree.

"Ho, you, The One Who Writes Us!" Khantarīsh ordered his anthropologist. "Come with your notebook! Allah has sent us trustworthy guests! Men!"

The silhouettes grew larger. The ḥajj looked eastward, toward the midmorning sun, shading his gaze with his palm, opening and squinting his cataract-clouded eyes, straining to identify the riders.

"Here is Fteiḥ," he told his anthropologist. "Fteiḥ is a good friend from the smuggling days. He organized my business on the ʿAqaba Gulf, and shipped things." She wrote this down, noting his excitement.

"And here is Ṣbayyel."

"An ex-smuggler too?"

"Ṣbayyel the Fisherman. You don't know him? He lives near Fteiḥ and married Fteiḥ's daughter. They're really good friends."

His anthropologist wrote all this down, adding that one of the most preferred marriage partners for a smuggler was the daughter of the head of a fishing lineage. The old fisherman had the most desirable of assets, a sailboat and a safe harbor.

"And this must be Ḥusein, if my eyes do not betray me. Aakh, ya Ḥusein, ya Ḥusein. He also lives in Bir al-Tamar, the Well of Dates, near Fteiḥ and Ṣbayyel."

X and I laugh at our joke—all wells have date palms around them. Yet another name that cannot be.

"Have you heard about his brother? Ḥajj Ḥamdān?" we allow Khantarīsh to continue. "He's a famous *ʿurfi* (customary law) judge," he added, filling his anthropologist in on the information. She wrote this all down. She thought it a good idea to know people in high places.

The closer the silhouettes came, the greater Ḥajj Khantarīsh's agitation. But by the time the guests arrived at the edge of the encampment, his face was a mask of poised tranquility, his smile restrained. As he helped the three men to kneel their camels around the magʿad, he and his anthropologist exchanged the hugs and kisses-in-the-air greetings with the guests, according to the hospitality protocol. The old mother of Khantarīsh's wife entered the mag'ad, thin rolls of flatbread in her right hand, a bowl of salt in the left.

Ḥajj Khantarīsh tore off a piece of the bread. He folded it neatly into a two-by-two-centimeter square, dipped it in the salt, and blessed his guests. Then he poured coffee and tea from the kettles he prepared every morning in case guests might come. Everyone drank, thanking him for his generous hospitality.

X tells me that now it is important for everyone to be silent. Each was waiting for someone else to initiate the conversation. Fteiḥ took a long breath. He forced a smile onto his face and cleared his throat, but for some reason, he did not say anything. To cover his embarrassment and to distract himself from the tension of the long silence, he busied himself with rolling a cigarette. Finally, he said something. The rest could hardy hear it since he was mumbling to himself. But our anthropologist thought she heard him say, "The world goes round. One day we sleep on silk, on sand the other." Fteiḥ's companions, Ṣbayyel and Ḥusein, repeated more loudly, "One day on silk, on sand the other."[4]

The conversation began to flow, but only among the three guests. Ḥajj Khantarīsh did not participate except by nodding his head. His anthropologist wondered why these three men, who had had all the time in the world to talk to each other when they were riding in the wadi, were speaking just among themselves.

At this point in our improvised narration X asks, "Remember the Ṣabbāḥa scandal from the year after the last big flood [1976]? Let's toss it in as the topic of conversation." I leaf through my fieldnotes and find the episode. Reading it quickly, I suddenly realize that this story is perfect. It contains all the elements important for my argument: that a smuggler's silence reifies yet solves Mzeina discrepancies between the temporal enactment of tribal ideas of agnation and these ideas' irrelevance to both smuggling and the mundane flow of Mzeina life. X and I decide to select from my notes an argument that three men and an ex-smuggler had about the Ṣabbāḥa scandal, but we change the speakers' names to Fteiḥ, Ṣbayyel, Ḥusein, and of course, Ḥajj Khantarīsh.

"That was a long story. Could you please tell me its essence?" I ask. So X summarizes the events at the trial we had witnessed together:

> Raḍwān was the only son of an ex-smuggler named Silmi. Ṣabbāḥa was the wife of Raḍwān. One hurried day she packed up her belongings and left the nest she and Raḍwān shared. This in spite

> of the fact that, according to the ʿurfi, women cannot divorce their husbands. This was after five years of what everyone had assumed was a marriage of doves. Raḍwān, insulted in his manly pride, sued Ṣabbāḥa in the ʿurfi court. Manshaḍ, Ṣabbāḥa's father, and ʿŌda, his eldest living brother, were forced to protect their shining family honor and, since women are not allowed to speak for themselves in the court, they represented the fleeing wife. To everyone's shock, Manshaḍ and ʿŌda revealed that Ṣabbāḥa had no choice but to leave her husband. Raḍwān, may Allah redeem his sin, had been impotent from day one of the marriage. And why had Ṣabbāḥa decided after five years of happy, sexless marriage to leave? One day she thought of old age: "Who will feed me? Where will I live after my husband dies? I have no sons. If I want sons I must go through the pain of sex and of bearing children.[5] I need a husband whose penis stands up." Although not yet declared officially impotent, Raḍwān preferred not to represent himself in court. His father, Silmi the ex-smuggler, and his father's only brother, Khnēbish, spoke for him before the judge. "Ṣabbāḥa doesn't know what she's talking about," they said. "She's simply gone mad."

Now let us see what Ḥajj Khantarīsh and his roaring silences of power will do with this story.

The conversation between Khantarīsh's three guests continued to flow without his participation. His anthropologist, though baffled, was still gamely taking notes.

*

ṢBAYYEL: They said yesterday they gave the verdict in Wadi Kīd. Times have changed, guys. The judge decided in favor of the woman. He said her husband should divorce her.

FTEIḤ: Poor Silmi. Now everyone knows that his eldest son, who arrived after many daughters, his beloved son, fell off the camel's back . . . Akhh . . . What a shame . . . big shame . . .

Pause. The three guests looked intensely at Ḥajj Khantarīsh, hoping he would say something. Everyone knew that Fteiḥ, Hajj Khantarīsh, and Silmi [the husband's father] were not only business partners in the 1950s, but friends of heart and soul.

But the ḥajj was silent.

ḤUSEIN [*hesitating*]: Well . . . What could you expect of Khnēbish

[Silmi's brother]? He's just lucky that all his life, no one needed him in court before. He never—

FTEIḤ [*cuts Ḥusein off*]: It's his brother's luck, too.

ḤUSEIN [*ignores Fteiḥ, continuing*]: He never had to talk in court . . . So his tongue is heavy [meaning, lacks eloquence].

FTEIḤ [*shaking his head from side to side*]: Poor Silmi. Really a shame. What a *khazūk* (shafting) his brother gave him. There's nothing worse than someone's brothers, if they . . . like this . . . [*Ṣbayyel and Ḥusein focus their eyes on Fteiḥ. He hesitates, carefully choosing his words*] . . . if their blood isn't light [light blood is a metaphor for eloquent social skills]. What else can we say?

ṢBAYYEL [*raised voice*]: Maybe it's better if you shut your mouth. I do not like the way you talk about this case. Your brothers *are* your brothers. Look—Manshaḍ [Ṣabbāḥa's father]—didn't he appear in front of the judge with ʿŌda [his brother]?

ḤUSEIN: *Aii-wallah* (c'mon), how can you compare? ʿŌda is a man among Men. He has amāna (trust). He has *ʿagl* (rational mind). He knows the ʿurfi's language. His words [are] like swords.

At this point in our dialogue, I realize and tell X that my non-Mzeini readers will get lost unless I supply them with more information about the inner workings of this customary court.

X gives me a funny look, but then says, "Sure, why not? You can even write it in your convoluted university talk." So I write in my notebook:

In ʿurfi trials, the disputant men or their representatives presented their most important arguments to the judge and audience in improvised rhymed poetry. The rhymed court poetry was very dense, and therefore short and pungent. In order to perform well, good court representatives had to have a perfect command of the court terminology coupled with creative, poetic talents.

Before or after an important statement was made by a disputant or by one of the disputant's representatives, he would reinforce it by pointing at another representative of the disputant, saying, "*wahādha kafīli*" or "and this is my guarantor." The *kafīl* (masculine) or guarantor would be the one who would then stress the point even more before the judge, presenting it as the absolute truth.[6]

FTEIḤ: What can I tell you? . . . The trial was not fair. Go prove that Ṣabbāḥa is right . . . You think she opened her legs and showed the judge and the rest that she's *bint benūt* (the ultimate virgin)?

All the men were snickering. The anthropologist felt obliged to produce a feeble smile.

FTEIḤ: Here—everything was dependent on the kafīl. The root of the problem is, that the kafīls of the two sides didn't talk to the judge with the same skill.

ṢBAYYEL [*a bit louder*]: Don't talk mouse talk, my dear fellow. The trial was like all trials. And during the years Allah gave me from the time I was created, I have attended quite a few trials. What's important is who talks to whom before the trial. Especially in a problem like this that you can't see with your own eyes, right?

Expecting some sort of a response, the three stared at Ḥajj Khantarīsh. But the ḥajj gazed wordlessly. His anthropologist and I agree that this conversation was weird. I tell her to listen to the wind whistling down the wadi and the ringing bell of a faraway goat to reassure herself that she is in the field, even though this conversation violates the analysis of face-to-face interaction she has already written down on her topic cards. Ḥajj X instructs Ṣbayyel to drum his fingers nervously on the top of a rusty food can, his tin of green home-grown tobacco. Suddenly, Ṣbayyel opened it, his sharp elbows moving abruptly, rolled a cigarette and passed the rusty can and the rolling paper around. All, the ḥajj included, nodded their heads in a silent thank you, and they rolled cigarettes. Ḥajj X suggests that they might even have rolled their eyes to the sky.

The silence was as heavy as the early autumn heat.

FTEIḤ [*pointing a withered finger at Khantarīsh*]: I swear by Allah! If it were I instead of Silmi, I would have brought *you*! [*pointing at Khantarīsh again for emphasis*] I would have brought you to represent my son in front of the judge as a *rāʿi*.

Literally, "rāʿi" was a paid male shepherd. But this was not the case in the South Sinai, where herds were and still are small, and herding is done by girls. Among the South Sinai Bedouin, "rāʿi" was a legal term referring to a man who was given permission to act as if he were a member of the *khamsa*, the five-generation-depth lineage that constituted the blood vengeance group (cf. Marx 1967; Peters 1975).

ḤUSEIN [*eyes squinting beneath raised eyebrows, face grimacing into a smirk of disbelief*]: Really? . . . How could you bring the ḥajj to court as rāʿi?

FTEIḤ [*looking Khantarīsh in the eye*]: I would have paid you. Wouldn't you come?

Ḥajj Khantarīsh gingerly adjusted the way his woolen cloak wrapped his white caftan. He did not answer. But Ṣbayyel did not allow the silence to grow. He changed his sitting position so that he was less comfortable. Soon he blurted out:

ṢBAYYEL [*to Fteiḥ*]: *Mush mumkin* (impossible)! How can you call yourself a Man (*rejjāl*—men)[7] when you pretend not to know the Law? [*He slows to a didactic tempo*] When you go to the judge, you must bring with you men from your khamsa who will talk to him for you! You must! A rāʿi—it doesn't work!

FTEIḤ [*raising his voice, almost overlapping Ṣbayyel*]: The rāʿi works!

ṢBAYYEL [*cuts a swath through the air with his right arm, shouting*]: Impossible! Doesn't work! Never!

FTEIḤ [*shouts over Ṣbayyel's voice, punching his fist into the guests' rug*]: It works! Of course it works! [*lowering his voice, his contemptuous smile stretching his thin mustache towards his ears*] Don't you remember, guys? Three years before the '67 war, when Ḥajj Khantarīsh sued that other Ḥajj—damn it—I forgot his name . . .

ḤUSEIN: Ḥajj Ḥasan, maybe?

FTEIḤ: Yes, Ḥajj Ḥasan. That was a very complicated case. Ḥajj Ḥasan didn't let Ḥajj Khantarīsh pass through his land. Remember? In that trial our Ḥajj brought two rāʿi as kafīls. See how?

Fteiḥ's eyes beseeched Khantarīsh for support. But he met the brick wall of silence. Ḥajj X wants Fteiḥ the ex-smuggler to wink at Khantarīsh the ex-smuggler, hoping it will help. Khantarīsh was still silent. Fteiḥ's fixed gaze grew sad. Knowing that ex-smugglers can afford to smoke both the homegrown green tobacco and the heavily taxed imported American filtered cigarettes, X and I agree that Fteiḥ should fidget to release the tension. We tell him to reach into his caftan pocket to verify that the soft pack of Kents is still there, and then to repeatedly open and shut his silverplated box of homegrown tobacco placed on the ground in front of him. Fteiḥ should slowly turn his head towards the others.

ṢBAYYEL [*quietly, with a smile*]: Just between you and me, ya Fteiḥ—yesterday, Silmi was judged according to Matrimonial Law. Our Ḥajj Khantarīsh and Ḥajj Ḥasan were judged according to Smuggling Law. And you are all my guarantors that we ourselves had disputes about how to deal with Smuggling Law.[8] Only Mūsa abu-ʿAteish judged smuggling. Honestly, ya Fteiḥ—why do you make the sounds of someone who doesn't know? You well know that in Smuggling Law, unlike all other Laws, your kafīls don't have to be your blood. So you tell me, ya Ḥajj [*leaning towards Khantarīsh*], isn't that right?

The lines on his forehead contracting, Khantarīsh appeared to be listening intently, but still said nothing. Fteiḥ scratched his knee, spitting a curse at the camel's fleas that sucked his blood. Accelerating the tempo, he whipped out the pack of Kents from his caftan pocket, flipped out four cigarettes, tossed one to Khantarīsh, and after several hesitant seconds, tossed one to everyone else. The four Mzeinis and Khantarīsh's anthropologist lit the cigarettes with small embers. Silence again.

FTEIḤ [*quietly*]: Listen to me, guys. We are not like the rest of 'em. The Bedouin. The Bedouin are raḥlīn (nomads) and we are shaghalīn (laborers).

Khantarīsh's anthropologist quickly noted this great binary opposition that even rhymed, underlining it several times in her notebook.

FTEIḤ [*louder*]: I swear to Allah, for us Mzeina, the world has changed! Since the days of Mūsa abu-ʿAteish's Smuggling Court, I play with the thought that if, God forbid, I have to go to court, for whatever kind of problem, I'll get a rāʿi instead of my stupid cousin. Why not? We are not like the rest of 'em, the Bedouin. Really.

ḤUSEIN [*quietly, but with authority*]: Impossible! Perhaps we are only shaghalīn, but our laws are like the laws of the rest of 'em, the raḥlīn. The ʿurfi is just the same.

FTEIḤ: No, my dear Ḥusein. We are different. Look, a woman, Ṣabbāḥa, won her case. [*He spits on the ground*] Here, people say that a woman's value is that of three men.

This was a cynical proverbial remark often made by Mzeini men to express their frustration at feeling like guests in their own homes. Because men were forced to work as migrant laborers, their mothers, wives, or eldest daughters ran the everyday life of the encampment.

ḤUSEIN: Ṣabbāḥa won her case because her kafīls convinced the judge that her husband's impotence was not her fault. And everything was [in accordance] with the ʿurfi, not against the ʿurfi. And [*emphasizing each word*] the ʿurfi is the Bedouin's ʿurfi, *Gaḍīyyat ʿArab* (The Law of the Arabs)! Listen to me, ya Fteiḥ, hold tight to my words! You can have many, many friends who will help you more than your brothers. But you are a Bedouin. If you have no blood relatives, if you have no khamsa, you have no justice. And Ḥajj Khantarīsh is the kafīl of my words.

FTEIḤ [*firmly, in a quiet voice*]: No! the ḥajj is the kafīl of *my* words! By Allah, you people, hold tight to the words of your friend Fteiḥ. [*Louder*] The smuggling period changed our world. The rest of 'em, the Bedouin, are raḥlīn, and the Mzeina, shayyalīn (couriers).

Here X and I stop our retelling of the argument taken from my fieldnotes. I tell Ḥajj X that when I heard this argument in August 1976, I was surprised that no one laughed at the self-critical rhyme. The usual Mzeini saying is that the Bedouin are raḥlīn (nomads) and the Mzeina are shaghalīn (laborers). The person whom we here named Fteiḥ punned instead that while the Bedouin were raḥlīn, the Mzeina were shayyalīn. Listening to that 1976 argument I expected that, following one of the typical Mzeini formulas of how to end an argument, this shaghalīn/shayyalīn pun would be taken as a punch line and bring the argument to a humorous, harmonious end. But that did not happen. Everyone was silent and the tension in fact increased.

ṢBAYYEL [*flinging his arm out and letting it drop dismissively*]: Cut it out, ya Fteiḥ. Really, cut it out. So the rest of 'em, the Bedouin, are raḥlīn, and the Mzeina, shaghalīn. And some of us were also shayyalīn. So what? Have they [the occupiers] made us into peasants? Have they made us into city dwellers? We are still the people of the desert! We are still the real Arabs, the Bedouin!

*

Unexpectedly, Khantarīsh smiled. His smile was spontaneous and warm. Everyone's face turned toward him. But he still said nothing. Acknowledging the attention, he just nodded his head. Khantarīsh's anthropologist and his three guests all wondered: does he agree with Ṣbayyel or with Fteiḥ?

Khantarīsh kept smiling. The fading tension softened the marks of time and place engraved into the four men's faces. Everyone sank into the deep silence. But unlike the preceding silences, this one was ritually performed by him, and his three guests willingly partook of it as if listening to a magical story. Wordlessly Khantarīsh offered not the Marlboros tucked in his caftan pocket (which he had bought because he liked the cowboy ad he saw in a magazine he found), but the green tobacco from his silver box decorated with etched verses of the Qur'an. Immediately, Ṣbayyel offered everyone his rolling paper. Soon all were wreathed in the sweet smoke of homegrown tobacco.

Khantarīsh's anthropologist counted out eight full minutes. She was sorry that nothing was said, but she also toyed with the idea that this silence might be a representation of Victor Turner's "liminality" (1967). She drew some more camels in her notebook. It took five camels before it occurred to her that Khantarīsh had somehow transformed his silence of power into allegorical silence.

Ḥajj X and I are building up to the big moment. We have to get the poetic setting exactly right. It must be dusk. Exactly ten minutes prior to the maghreb prayer, Khantarīsh should slowly remove his gaze from the tops of the red cliffs that form the walls of the wadi. He should focus his cataract eyes on his anthropologist. Breaking the silence, almost whispering, he will say: "I heard . . . Well, they say . . . that there is one . . . a guy . . . he wrote, 'I against my brother; I and my brother against our cousin; I and my brother and my cousin against the world.' It came out from some faraway country, they call it Canada. But the man said it is a hoary Bedouin proverb. Well, he knows what he's talking about . . . he's from the university. He is a professor of Bedouin."

Ḥajj Khantarīsh focused his forceful eyes on his anthropologist. She winked at him. He returned the wink, pointing at her with his short, chubby index finger. "And this is my kafīla," he proclaimed.

Everyone laughed. Grammatically, the word kafīl can have a feminine form, "kafīla." However, women were not allowed to serve as legal guarantors. The courts were run according to patrilineal segmentarity—only men could be guarantors.

With peals of laughter the story's four Mzeinis and their anthropologist shook the argument's leftovers out of the magʿad. Khantarīsh tilted his head slightly in Fteiḥ's direction, and they both went to the trough to perform their preprayer ritual washing. Ṣbayyel and Ḥusein,

A HOST SMEARING BLOOD ON THE NECK OF THE AUTHOR'S CAMEL, BLESSING IT FOR A SAFE TRIP

following the order of precedence, waited until the other two finished and washed themselves immediately thereafter. Each of the four men cleared the pebbles of the wadi with his right foot to reveal the coarse sand beneath, then each lovingly drew with his right foot a small *miḥrāb* pointing towards Mecca—a pious transformation of small sections of desert into a sacred space. They prayed silently. After the prayer, the ḥajj rose stiffly, holding his swollen knee. Despite the vocal protest his guests made according to etiquette, he walked towards the herd that had just returned from the skimpy pasture. He grabbed a plump young lamb and dragged it over near the magʿad. Deftly slitting its throat in one stroke while whispering "*bismallah*" (in the name of God), he slaughtered the lamb. His anthropologist hypothesized that his casual skill revealed that he had done this many times, a sign of his wealth in his heyday. He gathered the warm blood into a small pot. He then limped to the three camels, dipped his right hand into the blood, and smeared it on each camel's neck, blessing it for a safe trip later.

Over dinner, Ḥajj Khantarīsh jokingly began a quasi-theological discussion of some unanswerable questions having to do with *ḥarām*, all the religious "don'ts," and *ḥalāl*, all the religious "do's." Why was the smoking of hashish not "ḥarām," but the drinking of alcohol was? Why did so many Muslims drink alcohol who did not smoke hashish? And if hashish were "ḥarām" and alcohol "ḥalāl," would people then smoke it more often than they drank alcohol? Ḥajj Khantarīsh drank his fill of vodka, and his guffaws were the loudest. The wadi walls echoed.

Late at night the crickets chirped his anthropologist a lullaby, the rhythm blending with the staccato whispers of Khantarīsh and Fteiḥ. Blankets thrown over their woolen cloaks to protect them from the cold dry wind, they breathed gossip into each other's ears. Struggling against the webs of sleep, his anthropologist heard two sentences echo in her ears like contradicting mantras. "If you have no blood, you have no justice." "A trustworthy man is worth ten stupid brothers." "If you have no . . . trustworthy men . . . stupid brothers . . ." In this way the contradictions immanent in the tribal reality accompanied her into the land of dreams.

THE NARRATORS: CRITIQUE OF THE STORY, PART II

Somewhere in the Sinai. Late at night, winter 1985. X stretches and says, "Ya Smadar, enough of telling stories to your notebook. Now tell our whole story from the notebook to all of us here."

I read the final product of our collaboration. X smiles with islands of teeth between pale gums. "That argument I made up and told you to write, [the one] between Ṣbayyel, Ḥusein, and Fteiḥ, it's almost like what was in real life. It might have happened somewhere . . . but it might not have," X muses.

"That argument—it sounds really good!" some of the men reassure us.

I pause to think about what X means by "that argument I made up and told you to write . . . it's almost like real life." He refers to this as made up even though all we did was change the names of the participants and emphasize certain already fantastic qualities in the story, a standard ethnographic practice. Perhaps for X, a "real story" would be to leave unchanged an account of events that occurred in a real time and place. But for me, the field experience is a process of lived events becoming a text that I can remove from the field and in my office continue to manipulate and mold.

Ḥajj X is aware of my textual obsession. It begins to dawn on me that this is why he suggested that we work on this particular dispute about the Ṣabbāḥa scandal and that we work from my notes. Even though I flipped through them and decided the dispute was perfect for my thesis, I missed the significance of Khantarīsh's anthropologist to the story. Philip Salzman's proverb served as an honorable face-saving device for a fictitious ex-smuggler too proud to admit that in a time of legal crisis his two stupid brothers would have been worth ten trustworthy men. But by making use of Khantarīsh's anthropologist's presence and of her imports of Arab proverbs from Canada, Ḥajj X enabled Khantarīsh to demonstrate how his long allegorical silence could ritually violate ordinary etiquette, because the use of the proverb to break the silence allowed both Khantarīsh and Ḥajj X to avoid violating the tribal ideological code.

As I muse upon this while X and I consider our story, I realize that in pursuing Bedouin proverbial truth, I had literally missed the proverbial presence of myself.

After a long pause, now uncertain as to my interpretation of this evening's textual construct, I say to X, "But you know, I was the one who decided what to write at the end. Once more I had the final say. Did you like it this time?"

"This time the end is good. It still has the university in it, but the words are nice. You too wrote something that is almost like real life. It's what you wrote about Khantarīsh's hospitality. Smugglers always had to be much more generous to their guests than other people did. But they could not be showy about their generosity. They had to do everything quietly."

"Quietly, indeed," the small audience and I agree.

"It's good that you marked all the places in the story we told where I said there should be silence," continues X. "I didn't expect this from you. I just thought that you'd take a break from writing while the cassette recorder was still rolling on."

"Why so?"

"Because everyone who comes here to learn about us wants us to talk all the time so that his cassettes and notebooks fill up quickly so that he can return to where he comes from. What these people do not understand is that, sometimes, silence could finish arguments much better than a proverb or a story."

X pauses to pour himself another glass of vodka. "Just like our Khantarīsh from the story," he adds.

But wait a minute, I think to myself. Khantarīsh *was* silent. He did not tell a story. X is about to refill my glass, but I cover it with my hand. He drinks in one gulp and hugs himself in his blankets.

"Sometimes, silence can solve arguments better than proverbs or stories," I echo. "Could it be that silence, sometimes, *is* the story?" I say to the others, while actually talking to myself.

There is a long pause.

"The silence *is* the story," I answer my own question.

No one speaks. I listen to the quality of the silence—the bleating of a kidgoat searching for his sleeping mother's nipple, the hissing of the wind through the many date palm fronds, and the sound of Forest's peaceful breathing, his head still in my lap. I look at X, thinking how much I will miss him. Will I see him again? X looks at me. This is our shared silence.

"The silence *is* the story?" X asks unexpectedly.

"In our story, I think the silence actually tells the ex-smuggler's story," I answer, making no attempt to interpret.

"It's late. Let it be so," X chuckles. "We swear on it by Allah, the university, and the honor of Men," he adds with faint solemnity.

Everyone laughs at this. Forest wakes up suddenly. "Where are we?" he asks.

"You'd better watch it, ya X," says one of the men, choking with laughter, "or else, you'll find yourself collecting hyena dung for the university."

"At my age and with my health, I can do anything. Tell me, now that we've written a story that pleases both of us, will they give me work as a professor in your university?"

I choose not to answer, thinking how sadly ironic X's unanswerable question is. I put on a laughing mask to join the rest.

6
THE OLD WOMAN

Al-ʿAjūz

Prototypical for Georgia O'Keeffe's early period is a mouse-eye view of the world . . . her "flowers" theme: Twenty-seven percent of the early sample shows the interior world of invaginated, richly colored, sensual blossoms. But there are no such "flower" paintings after age 55. In old age, O'Keeffe's paintings are of vast spaces, arid desert regions, unpeopled but full of light. With age, she moves from the sexual, richly furnished, interior microworld into a vast domain of dry sands, sharp edges, and roads that knife through the high plateaus . . . Seventy-five percent of the later paintings are of this spacious and hard-edged variety, in which sensuality—to the degree that it is still present—belongs to rounded rock spires and sand dunes rather than to the soft inner flesh of flowers. Whereas older male artists typically undo the hard-edged line of their youthful paintings, O'Keeffe moves the other way: from the diffuse, pulsing color of her youthful flowers to the sharp contours of mesa and arrowing road in her later years.

DAVID GUTMANN
Reclaimed Powers

AN OLD WOMAN (ʿAJŪZ)

"Each Bedouin community that has more than fifty families living there more or less permanently has an *ʿomda*. The government appoints him. They want him to be a mayor of sorts. But for us, the title 'ʿomda' is nothing but a joke. Any man who fusses and acts bossy, we call him 'the ʿomda.'" This was an answer I received when I talked with Mzeini women and men about the official local conductors of their everyday life.

ʿOmdas won their appointments because of their public collaboration with the occupiers. They received a very small salary from the civil government. In exchange, they acted as local figureheads, providing the illusion of a consultation with the local-level authority before the civil or military administration took local action.

Here are three excerpts from the 1977 logbook of the Dahab ʿomda:

- One windy winter morning. A Swedish tourist accompanies a policeman from the station of the nearby Israeli moshāv, Di-Zahāv, to visit the settlement's ʿomda. The tourist complains about the theft of his elaborate underwater photography gear. After the visit, the policeman and the Swede conduct searches inside randomly picked Bedouin huts.
- A month later, just before the Passover holiday. The ʿomda and his extended family have a late afternoon "high tea" for a group of twenty or so American Jewish donors on a visit to Di-Zahāv. Stage managed by two Israeli civil administrators, they perform a ceremony of Mzeini hospitality that includes coffee grinding, tea drinking, and bread baking. The donors write fat checks that are to build a school for the Di-Zahāv children. The Bedouin provide the tour's local entertainment and later, they will be the labor for building the school.
- A summer day of the same year. The local ranger drops by. He complains that the settlement is overpopulated by cats. An hour later we hear scattered shots. The next day, on the outskirts of

> the settlement, I see the children playing with the corpses of eight dead cats and the empty pistol shells around them.

Often, because his official salary was too small, and despite the fact that he was always supposed to be in the settlement, an ʿomda would be away for several days, working at one of the better-paying migrant labor jobs in the vicinity of his settlement. "Who fills in for the ʿomda when he's away?" I asked. "Don't worry," people soothed me with slightly amused expressions. "The ʿomda has a *wakīl* (deputy), the *ʿAjūz*." The Old Woman. Seeing my surprised face, someone added, "No. Women can't have official appointments. But she acts like it is anyway."

I was baffled. Mzeinis explained to me many times that men and women were to have strictly separate domains of action. All domestic issues were to be handled by women, while all public issues, including interaction with foreigners, were to be handled by men. "In our family, the man is like a foreign minister, and his wife, the interior minister." This separation, Mzeinis argued, stemmed from the strict code of honor and shame.[1] The scholarly literature agrees with the Mzeini explanations.[2]

The Old Woman as the unofficial deputy of the ʿomda posed an ideational paradox. How could a woman hold a public, even an informal public position? Yet this inconsistency was congruent with the constraints of the Mzeina's lived reality. Most men were periodically absent from their sedentarized settlements or season encampments due to migrant labor. Women thus found themselves in situations where despite the strict purdah codes they had to deal by themselves with all sorts of intruders into the normal flow of life, ranging from tourists to Israeli military reservists on patrol. The simple presence of outsiders roaming through Mzeini settlements, in effect exploiting Bedouin hospitality, which provides no way to exclude these "guests," exposed the Mzeinis to the Western model of gender relations. And much of what they saw violated the traditional code of gender separation and female modesty.

Due to the high cost of living, exacerbated by high inflation rates in Israel, the wages earned by the male heads of nuclear families were barely adequate. Some women in heavily toured settlements used the discrepancy between the purdah codes and the transnational reality of the South Sinai for supplementary income. In their husbands' absence, female entrepreneurs hosted organized tour groups in their inner yards. They demonstrated Bedouin breadmaking and sold the bread with hot sweet tea for sums of money they negotiated with the tour leaders. Usually, in a one-hour visit, an average group would pay a woman the equivalent of her husband's wage for the day. The sum was high since the woman made sure the tour leader and his group were aware of the fact that she was violating the modesty taboos by letting a group of tank-topped and shorts-clad male and female strangers into her inner yard. The tour guides recognized the profitability of viewing forbidden, exotic women in their cloistered habitats, and so benefited as well.

While the absent Mzeini husbands were working, gossip reached them through passersby, often neighbors who on their way to work had witnessed the tourists entering the couple's inner yard. When the angry husbands returned home, they reminded their wives of the taboos.

"Why not?" protested a woman. "Even though their clothes are shameful, many tourists are nice people. And I see them half-nude on our beach anyway. And they can take my picture from afar without my permission anyway. So why not make money off them?" Her friend added, "My husband calls me a prostitute when I let tourists in and show them things from our old ways of life. He hit me on my back once for it. But when it comes to the tourists' money, he spends it without a qualm."

The older a woman grew, the looser grew the ideological taboo on her public actions. A woman became officially old at menopause. The actions of a postmenopausal woman could therefore be in contradiction to Bedouin ideas of purdah without posing a direct challenge. "I still have many years to wait until I have the freedom my grandmother has," said a woman who was about to get married. "She even sits in the magʿad and smokes cigarettes in front of everyone." Indeed, during regular evenings anyone could see one or two of the neighborhood's postmenopausal women sitting in the magʿad, the center of male public action. These women sat slightly apart from the men's circle, and only rarely did they participate in conversations or discussions. But when they did choose to speak, their concise observations carried great weight. During holidays, when all the settlement's men were in the magʿads, old women avoided them. But for me, the mere fact that there was a regular female presence in this bastion of masculine power was striking.

In the Mzeina vernacular, "ʿajūz" was the name for a postmenopausal woman. It is interesting to note that this is the masculine form of the word. It should have been "ʿajūza," with the vowel "-a" that typifies the feminine ending. Mzeinis called the husband of a postmenopausal woman a *shēba*, an old man. This word referred to a male even though it ended with the female suffix "-a." Apparently, in old age, the man took his title from his wife's reproductive status. When I pointed this linguistic discrepancy to younger Mzeini men, they said that an old man should indeed be called a *shāyeb* and an old woman should be called *ᶜajūza*. A daughter-in-law of a feisty ᶜAjūz chided me, "Can't you see that they swapped temperaments?" A symbolic gender reversal in old age, perhaps (cf. Gutmann 1987)?[3]

But these reversals were more evident in the women than in the men. Older men just mellowed, their gestures softer, their faces more relaxed. "Their penises get soft and their minds follow," explained an arrogant young man in his thirties. It seemed that old men stopped arguing vehemently in the men's club. They did not try to impress their friends with self-winding watches, loud after shaves, aviator sunglasses, or cassette recorders. Most importantly, they mitigated their attempts to impose their authority over their wives' domestic power.

The change in status of old women was more noticeable since it concretely signaled the role reversal. Old women stopped wearing the wide, fuchsia-red belt that proclaimed a woman's childbearing status, the only external expression of her sexuality she was allowed. Old women no longer had to strictly veil in mixed gender company, but could choose when to veil (cf. Anderson 1982). The veil and belt were symbols of the sexual control society had over women of reproductive age. While female sexuality was the source of women's shame and therefore had to be controlled through purdah, postmenopausal women were stripped of their sanctioned sexuality. It was assumed that they should not have any.

The ᶜAjūz was especially stripped of her sexual role by a genre of "ᶜajūz" smutty stories, jokes, and songs recited by adolescents in mixed gender company. Any sexual expression by adolescents, especially by adolescent girls, was strictly taboo. In sedentarized settlements, however, boys and girls danced every night on the outskirts. Unable to express their own sexuality directly, they sang and danced out sexual themes relating to the Old Woman. In this genre, the Old Woman's libido was larger than life. "Our Old Woman can eat a young man if she wants," said one of her sons. "How come?" I asked. "She just looks him straight in the eye," he said with a knowing look. I made a face at him to indicate that I didn't understand. "She has no shame," he pronounced.

The contradictions inherent in the persona of the Old Woman—a woman referred to by a masculine term; a woman stripped of the visual symbols of controlled womanhood; a woman who is and is not subject to purdah—gave the ʿAjūz the ability to maneuver in both the public and private spheres of action. The presence of a challenging model of Western gender relations, the absence of men due to migrant labor, and the need for additional household income—all stood in direct contradiction to the purdah taboos and practically forced the women to violate Bedouin tradition.

The Old Woman was able to dramatically enact her set of paradoxes in the interstices of the conflict between Mzeina tradition and the challenges forced upon the tribe by the transnational state of the South Sinai. Because of the publicly effective charisma of a few Old Women, they acted as informal community mediators. They were the ones who set the trend of women posing for tourists to make money. Old Women were also the first to invite tourists for an "authentic" Bedouin show in the inner yards of their married daughters or daughters-in-law. They were the spokespersons for women whose husbands were away, when they had to deal with soldiers or civilians looking for their husbands.

At times, when Mzeinis conversed in mixed gender company about the daily experiences of living under occupation, the dialogue arrived at a narration of events and feelings stemming from the men's periodic absence and the women's resultant necessary interactions not only with strangers, but even with nude male strangers. This was partly due to the lack of a local-level official to represent genuine Bedouin concerns and partly for the reasons discussed above. An argument might develop, exposing the rift between the ideas of purdah and the reality of the military occupation. Sometimes, the argument might become irreconcilable. The men would blame the women for loose behavior. The women would blame the men for their absence. At the moment in which nothing made sense any more, when reality became irreal, if a charismatic Old Woman was present, she could choose (if she wanted) to rise up and allegorize an experience she had had which touched on these problems. Because of her constant liminality, narrating an experience told as an allegory, the ʿAjūz was able to temporarily disentangle and illuminate the paradoxes inherent both in the composition of her Self and in the pragmatics of Mzeini gender relations. Her performance, a simultaneous acknowledgment and defiance of the occupation, reestablished the validity of the Mzeina purdah tradition through a vivid portrayal of its contested change.

1.

Nuwēbʿat Mzeina, April 1979

The week after Passover. The hordes of tourists are gone. An unusual *ḥamsīn* storm pants from the east, bringing coarse particles of white quartz and golden black mica, shaking layers of dust from the palm tree tops. The wind pushes waves of heat before it from the ovens of the canyons, breaking free from the narrow walls, spiraling in a wild dance down to the dry delta. The wind blows the waves back out to sea, into the dark blue depth becoming red, reflecting the late afternoon hue of the Saudi and Jordanian mountains. Two flimsy wooden dinghies are trying to return from the sea. The wind is pushing the Mzeini fishermen away from the coast, and because of Israeli restrictions they have only wooden oars to struggle with. Riding on the white foam, they manage to tie the dinghies to the tidal zone boulders in the turquoise shallows and load their meager catch into large baskets of woven palm fronds. They heft the baskets onto their backs, leaning far forward for balance. Long date-trunk-rope straps on their foreheads. With bent elbows they grasp the coarse rope just under their ears, where it cuts into their shoulders. Ḥajj Ḥamdān al-Shēba, the oldest fisherman, grimaces as his old body protests the weight of the almost empty, heavy basket. A thin crust of dried sweat and sea salt glistens in tiny crystals on the men's tanned skin, refracting rainbow colors to my sunglasses.

Five o'clock. A bright neon sign automatically turns on in the settlement's outskirts. "Fishermen Village," it declares in English and Hebrew, ignoring the indigenous Arabic. The fishermen are headed toward the Israeli village's restaurant. An air-conditioned tourist bus glides down the slope from the main road to the tourist village's parking lot. Forty or so Israelis and Americans in colorful tank-tops and shorts pour out. A notebook in my lap, I sit on the coastline, feet immersed in the cool water, hoping to alleviate the stormy heat. But the anthropologist informs me that the tourists' arrival disturbs her tranquil field note-taking.

The guide announces the program: "a short, do-it-yourself tour of the Bedouin settlement followed by a fish dinner at the village."

The anthropologist decides to follow the tourists into the settlement. She is curious how the encounter between tourist and Bedouin will develop, so I give up my late afternoon cooling pleasure. The sun, a tired red ball, deflates upon the cliffs of the Jordanian-Saudi border.

A thick-armed bleached American, her makeup dripping from her face into the folds of her neck, sighs: "How hot."

"It's not so bad, honey, the view is worth the trip," her friend soothes her.

"Hey, buddies," I hear a man's voice in Hebrew, "take a picture *now*! These fishermen really give a good perspective to the mountains and the sea!"

Click. The dripping blond takes a snapshot.

Before the group starts exploring the settlement the guide warns the tourists that they are not allowed to enter Bedouin homes without an invitation, and that they can photograph everything *but* women. "If you take a woman's picture, her jealous husband might kill her," he warns and continues with a brief explanation about what he perceives to be fundamentalist Muslim modesty and women's inferiority.

The more eager explorers join the guide and arrive at the southernmost cluster of huts. The farther from the parking lot, the more pristine the experience. The anthropologist is still following them. A bunch of runny-nosed kids welcomes the tourists, shouting avidly in a mixture of English and Hebrew, "Money! Money! *Kessef! Kessef!*"[4] The kids become silent abruptly when they see Ḥajja Ḥmēda al-ᶜAjūz emerging from her hut. Her arms akimbo, looking the guide straight in the eye, she asks in broken Hebrew, "*Yesh zberīm*?" Are there any explanations?[5] This is the question Israeli tourists typically ask the guide when they arrive at a new place. The surprised Hebrew speakers, shocked at this appropriation of their role by the native, begin to laugh. The guide and the ᶜAjūz shake hands, gripping firmly in the Western gentlemanly manner instead of the Mzeini hugs and kisses or the featherlight handshakes. The first time I witnessed such an exchange, a young ethnographer seeking pristine indigenous experiences, I was stunned. Now, in my fourth year in the field, I have learned to accept such exchanges as Bedouin–tourists daily routines.

The guide solemnly introduces the old ḥajja to the tourists in both Hebrew and English: "This is the neighborhood's boss." After hearing the guide's lecture about the inferior status of Muslim women, several tourists raise their eyebrows, staring at this tiny wrinkled woman in her rumpled clothes, disbelief in their eyes. But to me—she looks tall. She stands firm. Her hair, gathered at the peak of her forehead, braided and wrapped around a twig to stand up, adds a couple of centimeters to her height. Decorated with a few tear-drop silver ornaments, her yellow veil drapes from the beaded loop that hangs from her unicorn-like braid. Despite the cataract, her lively eyes shine from the exposed rectangle framed by her head-cover and her veil. On her small feet she wears rope sandals, the soles made from automobile tires. Most importantly, the old ḥajja does not wear a waist-belt, indicating to me and to the Mzeinis that she is no longer subject to the female modesty code.

"Tell them," the ʿAjūz goes into her pitch with the guide, "that if they want a picture of me, every shot costs two shekels."

"This is expensive," the bleached woman complains, getting out her camera anyway, "it's double the rate men charge for a picture on their camel."[6]

Covering the exposed rectangle of face with her hand, the ʿAjūz snaps in a Hebrew-Arabic mixture, "Money first." The bleached woman hands her two shekel bills.

The ʿAjūz lovingly folds the bills, then slips them into the pocket of her head-cover that hangs below her waistline down her back. After a short pause, she delves into her pocket and takes out her tobacco pipe, given to her by an admiring German magazine photographer two years ago instead of a fee. A tourist pipe-smoker gasps as he looks at her fancy pipe, made of dark hardwood, with an ivory mouthpiece, its silver lid pierced in an arabesque pattern. Pushing her veil up over her head-cover and sticking the pipe in her mouth, she carefully delves into her pocket once more and lifts out her prescription eyeglasses. Ceremoniously placing them on her nose, she poses, standing stiffly, seeming taller, and says in English, "OK."

Click.

"How sweet," a tourist gushes.

The tourist group returns to the parking lot. Ḥajja Ḥmēda invites me to her inner yard. "*Yahūd* (Jews)," she mutters under her breath, "can't live with them, can't live without them."

The old ḥajj has just risen from a late *maghreb* prayer, his face still quiet. Despite the fresh scent of soap there are still the ever-present delicate white threads of salt in the crevices of his wrinkles.

"Ya wife, have you become an Eilati prostitute? Aren't you ashamed of letting these foreigners take your pictures for money?" I hear the pain in the Shēba's voice.

"Ya ḥajj, tell me, ya ḥajj," the ʿAjūz immediately snaps back at the challenge, "knowing that the Jews at least triple the price when they sell fish in their restaurant, aren't you ashamed of selling them fish so cheap?"

Another unanswerable question.

The Shēba sits down next to me so that I am sandwiched between the two. I wish I could disappear. I have heard these exact lines countless time throughout the last couple of years. This was an ongoing argument. Aware of my shrinking, the Shēba turns to me wearing a sardonic smile. "I heard on the radio that women in America have something called 'the liberation of the wife.' Would they take my ʿAjūz among them?"

"What they have there is for young women, you fool," the ḥajja snaps again, "And I had to have lots of patience until my time arrived."[7]

The old man does not answer. He becomes immersed in rolling his prayer-beads. Gender role reversal, the anthropologist thinks. Perhaps for Mzeini women growing old has always been a liberation from the traditional woman's role (cf. Gutmann 1987).

II.

"Grandpa! Grandma! Smadar! Dinner is almost ready!" calls Nādia. She is the adolescent daughter of Ṣāleḥ, the couple's middle son. Following the voice, we walk through a narrow corridor and enter the main inner yard of this extended family compound.

Ḥajja Ḥmēda al-ʿAjūz and Ḥajj Ḥamdān al-Shēba share this large yard both with Ṣāleḥ's family and with the family of Rāda, their oldest daughter. Rāda sits in front of the small Swedish gas camping-stove, inspecting the fish and rice. Nōra, Ṣāleḥ's wife and the neighbors' daughter, adds the final seasoning of salt, pepper, and ground cumin. Rāda's husband, ʿŌda the ʿomda, is absent. ʿŌda is the local ʿomda of the Darārma clan—some of the men in this family belong to it. He inherited the ʿomda's title from his father, who was the local Darārma ʿomda under the Egyptians. His title brings him only a meager monthly salary and also makes him the butt of many jokes, because both the Israeli officials and the Mzeinis poke fun at his inability to exercise power.[8] Although his position demands his presence in the settlement, ʿŌda is not here this evening. He is moonlighting, helping the Israeli ranger in an intensive garbage collecting operation, following the Passover migration of Israelis to the campsites along the coastline between Nuwēbʿa and Eilat.

This is a typical fisherman family, the anthropologist observes. Unlike many Mzeinis who prefer exogamy to maximize economic and political options, Ḥajj Ḥamdān married his children to neighbors or parallel cousins.[9] This family therefore formed an almost classical agnatic-corporate unit, enabling it to keep its beachfront territory to itself. Male members of fisherman families were able to fish both within the settlement boundaries *and* along the uninhabited parts of the ʿAqaba Gulf coastline. Fishing within the settlement boundaries was used for casual provision of daily meals. Any extra fish was sold to the Israeli village's restaurant and to those families who had no beachfront rights because they had moved to this community as part of the sedentarization process that took place after 1972. Expeditions to the uninhibited coastline were made for larger catches sold to Israeli fishmongers.

Nādia carries a large platter above her head, placing it in the center of the circle of men. The aroma of spices and fish permeates the yard, only to be blown away by the eastern ḥamsīn. The men, squatting on their hamstrings, waddle toward the platter. With their right hands, they grab the rice, kneading it in their palms into egg-shaped balls. Then they press into the ball succulent chunks of parrot fish from the mound of fish in the center of the platter. They eat the best parts of the fish, its tail and middle.

As is the custom at these communal fish and rice family dinners, passersby from all over the peninsula can join in. Ramaḍān, though, hesitates. He has just been released from the hospital in Eilat after an appendectomy and is on his way to his encampment in Wadi Saʿāl, in the mountains southeast of here. Umbārak is sitting cross-legged near him. Trying to be the polite guest, he takes only a few handfuls of rice and fish, but these are enormous, bursting through his fingers. Umbārak's family encamps in Wadi Islā, in the southwestern mountains of the peninsula. Tomorrow he will take the early morning bus to Eilat, returning to his job as a Bedouin busboy working for Jewish immigrants from Morocco who serve an imitation of French haute cuisine mainly to Scandinavian tourists. Between bites Umbārak imitates the owners' North African Arabic accent and everyone laughs appreciatively. Sallām, a young man in his early twenties, obnoxious although from this settlement, is another nonfamily diner. He is the youngest son of the Shēba's best friend. A week ago, Sallām's wife finally succeeded in making him divorce her. Perhaps attempting to alleviate his pain, perhaps attempting to redeem his honor, he goes from home to home in the settlement (his wife's parents' home excluded), telling anyone who can't avoid listening that one day, his ex-wife will come to realize what a great man she has lost.

I eat with the family's wives, Nōra and Rāda. We eat straight from the charcoal-blackened pot. We scrape the burned rice crust from the bottom and suck small flakes of flesh from in between the many bones of the fish's head. Umbesēṭa and Helāla, who are neighbors, eat with us. Umbesēṭa's husband is away, fishing on the tip of the peninsula. He sells his catch to Shimᶜon, the Israeli fishmonger who doubles the price when reselling the fish to Eilati restaurants and hotels. Helāla's husband is in prison for fishing without a license. Commonly in large settlements, when a woman's husband was away, she would not cook, but would eat at the neighbors' while her children combed the neighborhood for leftovers.

Ḥajja Ḥmēda al-ᶜAjūz eats the best food with the men. As long as the guests are present at the dinner circle, she slowly sticks modest handfuls of rice and fish beneath her veil. At last, the guests, maintaining politeness, excuse themselves from the dinner circle after a few enormous bites. The ᶜAjūz tosses her veil up and begins to really eat, revealing her dull silver *shnāf* (nose-ring) in the light of the kerosene lantern. In her youth, it was probably a shiny little sexual secret that no man but her husband was permitted to share, and only at night. Now it lies open to public inspection.

The ᶜAjūz continues to eat long after the family men have burped, washed their hands, and praised Allah as custom requires. Finally, she burps very loud, like a man. Nādia immediately rushes to her, a water can in her right hand and a rather used towel hanging from her left. She demurely pours water over her grandmother's hands and gives her the towel. Then she takes the platter outside. I can hear the kids playing and fighting over the leftovers.

The men and women gather together in a large circle. In the middle, Nōra places the hissing Swedish camping-stove, to supplant the traditional embers, and a kettle of tea. We drink the sweet tea while rolling cigarettes. A mundane conversation begins.

Ḥajja Ḥmēda sits a little out of the circle. She delves into her deep pocket for her German pipe and stuffs it with tobacco. With a pair of delicate cosmetic tweezers that her son-in-law ᶜŌda found in a tourist's trash, she carefully picks up a small ember and places it on top of the silver arabesque lid. Her silence and the smoke curling around in long plumes only accentuate her apparent distance from the group.

*

ḤAJJ ḤAMDĀN AL-SHĒBA: How's your health, ya Ramaḍān? How's your stomach?

RAMAḌĀN: Thank God. Now it's much better. The hospital helped a lot.
HELĀLA: Many people say the hospital helps a lot.
RAMAḌĀN: Immediately, when the ambulance brought me, two doctors rushed to my side. One of them, you wouldn't believe it, his family name was Ḥardoun.
RĀDA [*chuckling*]: Ḥardoun? Really? Like that lizard (*agama*—Latin)?
RAMAḌĀN: Yup. Some Jews have strange names. Also one of the nurses, her [first] name was Rotem. She said it is the Hebrew for *ratam* (broom-bush).
NŌRA [*in fast staccato*]: Disgusting. Ugly.

The South Sinai Bedouin did not think that zoological or botanical names (like those typical of Israeli Sabras) were appropriate for people.

RAMAḌĀN: Nice people, though. They knew I had no family in Eilat and that the Bedouin I know in Eilat work during visiting hours. So they let them visit me whenever they could. That broom-bush brought me a big book full of pictures of us and our tents, and the lizard-doctor talked Arabic with me and gave me good cigarettes. And it was all free.
ḤAJJ ḤAMDĀN: Did you hear about the *taftīsh* (searches)?

The Shēba is referring to the systematic searches of South Sinai Bedouin encampments and settlements by the Israeli Defense Force reservists. The Israelis had been using heavy equipment to grade the foundation for a road connecting the northeast ʿAqaba Gulf coast with the Santa Katarina Monastery and the Israeli civil and military settlement nearby. Expensive Caterpillar bulldozer spare parts stored at the base camp of Nageib Merāḥla, twenty five kilometers south of Nuwēbʿat Mzeina, had disappeared two months before.

RAMAḌĀN: Yes. I heard about the searches. Someone from al-Ṭūr who works in the gardens of the city [Eilat] said something.
ṢĀLEḤ: What happened in al-Ṭūr?
RAMAḌĀN: He said, the army came at night, around two [A.M.], and without knocking, the soldiers just walked into one hut after another. They emptied the contents of every wooden box and food sack.[10] If someone was slow with the keys [to his box], they just broke it. Beasts.
SALLĀM: Did they find anything?
UMBĀRAK: Of course not! That's what people told me when I

passed through al-Ṭūr [on my way here]. They said the army will never find anything anyway. The stolen things are big, and no Bedouin is crazy enough to hide them in his own home.

NŌRA: The same thing happened here, around a month or so ago. They also brought dogs, enormous dogs, to help them search.

RAMAḌĀN [*with a sharp intake of breath, shocked*]: And they let the dogs go into the homes of people?

Ramaḍān is shocked not only because searches by the army were frightening, but also because the dog was a polluted animal for the Mzeinis. They raised a few dogs in order to herd their few goats. But dog owners maintained a physical distance from their dogs. Furthermore, dogs were not allowed in either the human living space or the goat and sheep area of a hut or a tent.

UMBESĒṬA: Yes. The dogs—you'd say wolves—they followed them into homes of people. Allah save us from the devil! But let me explain to you what's in their minds: they know that most of the time there are not many men around here because they go to [migrant] work. I once even heard that the nicer military governor, the one from the kibbutz, from the days the military government's offices were still in Abu-Rodeis—he told the soldiers never to enter a Bedouin home unless the man is there. So this [current] governor thinks that the thieves probably hide the things at people's homes and make it appear that they go to work, thinking that the army will not enter their homes.

We are silent. The hot eastern storm brings us the distant shreds of young voices singing a jumpy *redēḥi* melody and clapping hands.[11] The energy of youth, the anthropologist thinks. It has the power to override the purdah codes every single night.

SMADAR [*slowly, afraid to present too much of a challenge*]: It sounds like you're quite sure that the thieves are Bedouin.

Pause.

ḤAJJA ḤMĒDA AL-ʿAJŪZ: Who knows?

We all look at her, expecting that this sharp-tongued ʿAjūz will continue voicing her opinion. But she returns to her elegant pipe, her hollow cheeks sinking in further as she sucks on the ivory mouthpiece.

SALLĀM: Honestly, I do not know one hundred percent, ya Smadar, but I think you are right.

RAMAḌĀN: I don't think so. I can swear the thieves are from Eilat. Eilat is full of criminals. It is so far from Tel Aviv, and all the big criminals go there when they feel the police in Tel Aviv are about to get them. One criminal told me this. I believe him. We were in the same room in the hospital. Someone stuck a knife between his ribs when he was drunk. And from Eilat to the Nageib Merāḥla base camp, it's only one hour or so if you have a good jeep.

ṢĀLEḤ: Maybe the thieves are from Eilat. But I think they are from the Fāreᶜ [the Western Highlands]. The searches are all over the place, though, to scare us so those who know something—they'll talk.

Because the Western Highlands were to be returned soon to Egypt, many Bedouin thought that the thieves probably came from that area. The common wisdom was that the Highlands would be returned to Egypt before the Israelis could find the stolen equipment. Under Egyptian rule, the thieves would be free to sell the goods.

UMBESĒṬA: If indeed they are from the Fāreᶜ, how could they steal from foreigners who settle on *our* territory?

SALLĀM: No problem. Everything is in compliance with the ᶜurfi (customary Bedouin law). [*All the men chuckle. The old ḥajja smiles*] Probably someone from here helped them. Three years from now, when Israel returns this place to Egypt, he'll get paid his share. And still, our long bill [with the occupiers] is not settled.

Pause. The ḥamsīn is beginning to subside. We can clearly hear the singing of the teenagers as they dance the jumpy redēḥi on the settlement's outskirts:

Al-ᶜAjūz al-kabīra dana ᶜomrahā—
Kam khuswu wakhuswu gamāṭ shufrahā.

The Grand Old Dame is about to kick off—
Her greedy cunt gobbled countless cocks.

These redēḥi verses are so traditional and mundane, I think, so familiar that no one but the anthropologist pays attention. But soon enough, young Sallām, in his postdivorce obnoxiousness, proves the anthropologist wrong.

SALLĀM [*in a smug voice*]: Ya Smadar, did people explain to you the meaning of the song those guys outside are singing?

SMADAR [*laconically*]: Yes.

SALLĀM [*with a sidelong look at the Old Ḥajj*]: They are singing about this old man's wife, aren't they?

Some people smile. The anthropologist's presence forces to the surface a reflection on the meaning of smutty verses normally taken for granted. I gaze intently at the old ḥajja. She calmly cleans her pipe with a piece of rusty metal wire, ignoring both Sallām's remark and the smirks that follow. She refills it with fresh tobacco. Old Ḥajj Ḥamdān is not among those who smile. I watch his face become rigid with anger, until at last he bursts out:

ḤAJJ ḤAMDĀN: You people—your talk makes me real angry. Since when are the Mzeina thieves? If a Ṭwairi [a member of the Ṭawara tribal alliance] does not steal from another Ṭwairi, why should a Ṭwairi be allowed to steal from a *faranji* (Westerner)?

SALLĀM: You belong to a different generation (*jīl*), ya grandpa. People of *my* generation say that nobody invited the Israelis here. Nobody invited the Egyptians here either. If they want to be here, they should know that not everyone is afraid of them.

RĀDA [*angry*]: You hothead! It's easy for you to talk! You can "collect" things and—

SALLĀM [*does not let Rāda finish her sentence, interrupts demurely*]: Myself—I never "collected" anything.

RĀDA [*continues*]: You can "collect" things, and who suffers? The women. You men always go to work, and leave us here with all the problems.

UMBESĒṬA: With the soldiers. With the dogs. With the tourist buses. With the children. And with the military governor. We can't talk to him. He doesn't want to talk with women. He always comes here to look for the ʿomda.

RĀDA: And the ʿomda—so many times when they come looking for my husband, he's moonlighting. They always come to me when they need something. And I—I really don't know where exactly ʿŌda is. He's somewhere, either fishing or collecting garbage for the Shmurā.[12] What do they want from me?

ṢĀLEḤ [*lecturing*]: I don't know what they want from you. But I can definitely tell you what any husband would want from you. When he returns from a month of fishing or any other work, he does not want you to open your big mouth on him and say, "We need to buy this, and we need to buy that. And the children don't have enough food. And I don't have enough clothes." He wants you to dress nice, put on perfume, and be good to him. Work is tough. After work a man wants to eat the peach, his heart is in the apples.

Despite the pain implicit in Ṣāleḥ's lecturing voice, everyone but he and the ʿAjūz giggle. Ṣāleḥ's last sentence was a direct quote of the last verse of a *gaṣīda* (poem). This lusty gaṣīda describes metaphorically the buildup of foreplay, the last line describing the feeling of the man during coitus. The fuzz on a peach skin was a metaphor for the hair covering a woman's genitals. The apples were the women's breasts.

The anthropologist notes that she has never heard either the full gaṣīda or excerpts from it recited in mixed company. Men usually recited it when they were fishing away from the encampment, often when they were drunk or stoned. This is a cultural incongruity, and she is astonished.

NŌRA [*blushes, raising her voice*]: Ya Ṣāleḥ, shame on you! When you guys go fishing for a month, you say you take a vacation.

UMBĀRAK: Of course! All work for money is a vacation. Vacation from home. Look at this old man, Ḥajj Ḥamdān. He just comes home from work, and here, his ʿAjūz jumps on him with complaints.

I look at Ḥajja Ḥmēda. Poised, she blissfully smokes her pipe. She returns my look, putting her veil back over her face. Is it because of the anthropologist's invasive gaze? Or is it because of Ṣāleḥ's criticisms, compelling her to conform? Perhaps concealing attentive listening? Or is it the purdah restrictions against smut?

UMBESĒṬA: Excuse me, Umbārak, but I also heard what happened. He jumped on her first. He got angry at her because she brings money home from pictures the tourists take of her.

Carefully, self-consciously, the ʿAjūz readjusts the veil on her face.

RAMAḌĀN: But taking pictures of women is taboo!

HELĀLA: Taboo? Up your ass taboo! It's taboo that people get angry with this Old Woman. The tourists know that taking pictures of women is taboo, and this is why Old Women can ask for more money. Even younger women. If my husband does not give me enough money—is it my fault? It's the fault of what they call on the radio "inflation" or so. The last few times, when my husband went to his *vacation* [*Helāla emphasizes the word, pronouncing it rancorously*] I invited home two groups of tourists.

I made *faṭīr* (flatbread) for them and let them take pictures of me as much as they wanted. I am not an ʿAjūz, and I know it's a very big shame, but it's also work that earns very good money.

UMBESĒṬA: The tourists like it. When we let them into our homes, they think it's . . . well . . . as if it's from our hearts, for real. Let me tell you something: whether it's a shame or not, it's better than theft.

UMBĀRAK: Thank Allah this shame has not arrived to us in Wadi Islā. They didn't open an asphalt road to there, so there are only a few tourists who come by foot or on camels. Our women behave like women.

RĀDA [*loud*]: And I thought *you* are also among those who don't belong to the generation of this Shēba [*pointing to Ḥajj Ḥamdān*].

UMBĀRAK: You, listen to me! This old man is a Man, and his wife, a Woman. [*After a short pause, his angry intonation becomes ironic*] Who knows? Perhaps you also expect her [the ʿAjūz] to throw aside her black dress and put on a bathing suit, or even be nude, and join the tourists. Seek Allah's shelter from the devil!

For a moment laughter relieves the tension. Only Rāda and her mother, the old ḥajja, remain unmoved. I can read the insult on Rāda's face. Still strictly subject to the code of modesty, she probably feels her mother's humiliation. But the ḥajja remains unruffled, smoking her elegant pipe as though uninterested in this dialogue.

NŌRA [*sardonically*]: Perhaps this is the best solution for all of us. The tourists, when they come here, the husband always comes with his wife, and the boyfriend with his girlfriend. And if someone does not have a boyfriend or a girlfriend, he [or she] picks one up here, from the tourists who are already here. They are always in couples. [*Then seriously*] And you? You think you are men? You are never home. You work. And when a man finally comes home he can't understand why he can't eat the peach while his heart is in the apples.

No one laughs or giggles this time.

UMBESĒṬA: When the big search was here, no men were here, except for the old ones. Even the ʿomda wasn't here. And he is paid to be here.

RĀDA [*cuts Umbesēṭa off*]: One hundred shekels a month is nothing!

UMBESĒṬA [*ignores Rāda*]: And this Old Woman, she stood in

front of the captain and told him, "I am the ᶜomda." She accompanied him from one hut to another to see that the soldiers and their dogs did not touch the women.

RAMAḌĀN [*to Rāda*]: If so, by Allah, this ᶜAjūz, your mother is worth more than your husband.

UMBĀRAK [*suffocated with laughter*]: They said in al-Ṭūr, that the top military governor himself said, that Ḥajja Ḥmēda al-ᶜAjūz is Golda Meir of the Bedouin.

SALLĀM: Our women—they're all like Indira Ghandi or Golda Meir.

Listening to this freshly divorced young man, his pride still smarting, all the men but Ḥajj Ḥamdān are laughing hard.

RĀDA [*angry, to Sallām*]: What's so funny here? Golda Meir and Indira Ghandi are not circumcised. Their clitorises must be longer than your penis.

Everyone bursts out laughing, the women and the men, including red-ripe-tomato-faced Sallām. Even the ḥajja laughs, her narrow shoulders shaking while she slaps her knee with her right hand.

The eastern storm seems to fade with the laughter. The hot air stands still. Heavy. The sea lies flat. Motionless. Nōra, filling the gap, busies herself making tea. From the settlement's outskirts, we can clearly hear the singing and clapping of the redēḥi. Rhythmic. Voluptuous. Even the irritating hiss of the gas stove cannot distract from the music.

SALLĀM [*trying to assert himself once again*]: Is it possible that like Golda Meir, our ᶜAjūz is also not circumcised?

But Sallām is not sensitive enough to notice the shift in mood. Ḥajja Ḥmēda al-ᶜAjūz decides to respond to this provocation, her eyes glistening with anger:

"Not circumcised? *You* are the noncircumcised! You are the *kaffār* (heretic)! You think it's better that we all suffer from the army just because some Bedouin want to make easy money! And you are stupid enough to believe that if we 'collect' enough from the Israelis or the Egyptians they will go away! Let me tell you something: As much as we need these strangers, they need us."

Everyone is astonished by this sudden outburst from the Old Woman. Her pronouncements are like the eastern ḥamsīn that has just passed. But the wind has shifted back to the customary west. Now we can hear the waves falling on the shore, returning from their bizarre eastern course to bring the humid breeze inland.

"They need us?" Umbārak murmurs uncertainly, careful not to challenge the ʿAjūz.

"What would those Israelis do in the South Sinai if there were no Bedouin here?" the old ḥajja asks rhetorically. "Tourists from all over the world come here. The Israelis make lots of money from it. And we also make money."

The Israeli in me feels ashamed. Tour operators specializing in the South Sinai as well as other businesses catering to the Sinai tourists sprouted both in Israel and in the South Sinai. They employed the Bedouin only for the underskilled, nontenured positions. When the Mzeinis embarked on entrepreneurial ventures, renting Bedouin-style huts to tourists, organizing camel tours, or leading motorized tours from the coasts to the Santa Katarina Monastery, they charged relatively small fees to compete with the Israeli businesses. Bedouin tourist ventures were also subject to bureaucratic harassment by the military government. Indeed, the Mzeinis now had an income much larger than their income during the previous Egyptian occupation. But since basic living expenses were much higher in Israel than in Egypt, they felt deprived of their monetary gains.

"You know, people—once, around four years ago or so . . ." the ʿAjūz continues.

The anthropologist notices here the beginnings of a story. Four years are not a time span that needs a "once" as a formulaic introduction. The "once" here marks the transformation from the linear flow of events-in-time to the cyclical motion of stories about events-in-time.

*

"Once, around four years ago or so," she says, "after the noon prayer, I walked north on the beach, thinking: to whose home should I invite myself for lunch? All of a sudden, a *gobṭar* (helicopter) came from the sky, and landed between Sheikh ʿAṭṭallah's cafe and the Fishermen's Village restaurant. I thought: maybe one of the tourists was bitten by a snake, or stepped on a stonefish, and the tour leader talked with them in the *makrafōn* (microphone, i.e., Motorola radio) so that they get the person fast to the hospital. But no! From the gobṭar came out a man and his wife, almost as old as myself and my ḥajj, and two other young people with pistols stuck in special pockets that dangle from their belts."

"Pistols dangling from their belts," echoes Ramaḍān.

"These must be their bodyguards," adds Ṣāleḥ.

"So one of those young men immediately ran into the restaurant and got *Ḥawāja* (Mister) ʿAmos out. Ḥawāja ʿAmos greeted the wife first, and only then hugged the husband."

The ʿAjūz pauses. Is it because she wants to emphasize for her audience that this greeting is the direct opposite of the way a Mzeini would greet a couple?

"Mister ʿAmos took them to his restaurant," the ḥajja continues, "and I gave up my plans to eat at someone's place and went home to prepare my lunch. Everyone and his work (*kul wāḥad washughlo*—to each his own)."

"To each his own," repeats Nōra.

"So I sat here, where we are sitting now. I ground some wheat and listened to the radio."

Grinding wheat with a pair of grindstones was a typical pastime of old women. Younger women preferred prepackaged whole wheat flour. Old women argued that the ready-made flour was too fine for the cooking of *jarīsha* (porridge).[13]

"So here I cook my jarīsha quietly. The babies are asleep, and their mothers are asleep. Suddenly, here comes Nāṣer, Mnefiyya's naughty son, shouting, 'Ya ḥajja! Oh ya ḥajja! A big minister is coming now with Ḥawāja ʿAmos. He is looking for ʿŌda the ʿomda. They say he is the foreign minister or the minister of the army."

"The foreign minister or the army minister of the Jews was looking for our ʿomda," echoes old Ḥajj Ḥamdān, astounded.

"As far as I am concerned, he could have also been the minister of the moon and stars," the ʿAjūz goes on, clearly unimpressed. "The problem was, he was looking for the ʿomda while the ʿomda was looking after the tourists' garbage. It was after *ʿId al-Baskawīt* (the holiday of biscuits)."

I am again amused by this Mzeini term for the Jewish Passover.

"I went out, and saw that here, all the children of our settlement were leading this minister to the ʿomda's hut. And the ʿomda is always away, collecting garbage."

"My poor husband, oh mother," laments Rāda, "from his ʿomda salary we can't even buy two sacks of flour a month."

"So as I told you, I went out. I said to Mister ʿAmos: 'Come in, please, come in, let's have some tea. *I* am the ʿomda today. If you'd like, I'll make for you some flatbread. Don't be shy. Welcome! Welcome!' So Ḥawāja ʿAmos laughed, and they all entered. When they were in, I didn't make them take off their shoes, and I showed them

MZEINI CHILDREN PLAYING WITH TOYS THEY MAKE OUT OF THE TOURISTS' GARBAGE

everything we have at home: the rugs, the blankets, the wooden boxes, the food sacks, the teapot, the coffee pot, the mortar and pestle, the chickens, the prayer-beads. I even told them that they can take pictures of everything."

While the Old Woman reels off this list, everyone in the audience is roaring with laughter. Those Mzeinis who befriended Israeli tourists or settlers and visited their homes would upon their return constantly retell the baffling story of the strange Israeli custom—showing the guests the whole house, its contents included. They were also bemused by the Israeli lack of respect for the cleanliness of their homes revealed when the hosts failed to remove their shoes when entering. For the Mzeinis, the house was a well-bounded space, marking the private domain of life. Showing a stranger the house and its contents was supposed to embarrass not only the host, but the guest as well, as a major violation of privacy.

"I showed them everything. Just everything," the ʿAjūz continues between bouts of laughter. "And I sat them here, where we are sitting now, and made tea for them, not on the gas stove, but on top of the fire."

"A Bedouin tea," Ramaḍān emphasizes.

"And then Ḥawāja ʿAmos said, just like this, *dughri* (straight out)—like these Israelis talk (cf. Katriel 1986):[14] 'These people want a male puppy Saluki dog.'"

"'These people came all the way from the *barlimān* (parliament) of Jerusalem to the Sinai for a puppy?' I asked, 'Are they out of their minds, or what?' And let me tell you, people," the ʿAjūz lectures us, "ever since the Jews have come here with the asphalt road, I've seen all sorts of dogs who came straight from hell. One kind look like the Tih wolves; and another kind, with long hair and small face like the face of a fly. Another kind, with a wrinkled face, saliva oozing from their mouths all the time, and our Lord made them without a tail. And another kind, also deprived by Allah of a tail, but it is a taller kind, black, with brown face and butt. And this last kind—many times a dog of this kind comes here with his tourist, it eats a whole goat alive. I swear. And these people want *more* dogs? Seek the Lord's shelter from the devil."

"Allah, save us from the devils indeed," some repeat, startled as well as amused.

"Ḥawāja ʿAmos said that the Jews have many kinds of dogs, but they do not have pure Saluki dogs like the ones we have. And the minister wants a real fast dog, like a Saluki, so that he can train him to run in front of his car."

"The minister wants a Bedouin dog to run in front of his car," echoes Ṣāleḥ, incredulous.

"Perhaps he goes to hunt for rabbits with his car," suggests Umbesēṭa.

"No. He must have a servant who does it for him," Ḥamdān al-Shēba contemplates.

"Who knows?" the old ḥajja replies to these theorists and continues: "I then told Ḥawāja ʿAmos: 'Tell this minister in Hebrew, that I am an old woman, older than he or his wife. And if he wants, he can throw me into the jail instead of the ʿomda, because the ʿomda's children have to eat, and so he works a couple of jobs and does not stay here all the time . . . But please, tell this minister too, that if he wants something special from the Sinai, like a pure Saluki dog, he has to do something, even a little something, for the people of the Sinai.'"

"So the ḥajja said to the minister that he has to do something for the Bedouin of the Sinai," repeats Ramaḍān in admiration.

"Our ḥajja is a lioness," Nōra emphasizes the words, smiling with pride.

"Ḥawāja ʿAmos translated. The minister said that he'll do something only if he'll get a male Saluki puppy *today*, a really pure dog, so that he's able to get papers for it, like the papers Jews issue for dogs who have pure roots. And all that time I was thinking of what I could request. So I told them: 'Ever since you came to the Sinai, you have brought many fuel barrels to your army camps, for your command cars and helicopters and jeeps. Many barrels are thrown away empty, outside your military bases, and no one takes them back to your country. We need these barrels. We clean them and store water in them. And if they have holes, we cut off their tops and bottoms to make a *sāj* (griddle), on which we bake bread. Here,' I showed them my sāj. 'Maybe the madam wants me to teach her how to make Bedouin bread? Her husband could take pictures of both of us.'"

"Forgive my wife," the old ḥajj apologizes to the audience, "shame has left her."

"Let her talk, grandpa, she's caught up with our generation," Sallām chides.

"So I baked bread for them on the sāj. The minister's wife just observed. Who knows? Maybe she didn't want to dirty her hands. And the minister took two pictures. I told them, 'You know? the tourist guides say that our bread is like the baskawīt of the Jews. It's thin, and it has no yeast. We make it really fast, and the Jews who ran away to the Sinai from king Farʿūn (Pharaoh) had to bake theirs really fast.'"

"But the baskawīt of the Jews is crisp," says Helāla.

"Does this really matter? What's important is the essence of the story," Rāda answers.

I order the anthropologist to write Rāda's sentence in her notebook: "What's important is the essence of the story." She presses the pen hard, then underlines the sentence, sketching three stars in the space above it.

Just at that point, the ḥajja reaches the essence of hers: "And then I told the minister: 'Listen to me well. Every year, our men go to prison because of these barrels. The army doesn't use them, but doesn't let us Bedouin use them. Our men take them at night, and if caught, they go to prison. I'll cut a deal with you. You'll give us the empty barrels of the [nearby] army base, and I'll find you a beautiful puppy.' Mister ʿAmos translated. Inside, in my heart, I was afraid. I thought the minister might get angry that I have no shame. But he laughed. His wife laughed. Ḥawāja ʿAmos laughed. So I also laughed."

"What's there to laugh about?" Ḥajj Ḥamdān wonders.

"Those people—they don't laugh at what we laugh at, and we don't laugh at what they laugh at," explains Nōra.

"Then Ḥawāja ʿAmos said that the minister said that if he returns today to Jerusalem with the dog, he promises, in *kalām rejjal* (man to man talk—'on his honor'), that the army will give us half the empty barrels. And only then I told them that the real Salukis are with the Ṭarabīn tribe. I told them that I'd heard that my friend, Nāfla al-ʿAjūz, the wife of Ḥmēd abu-Ḥāsi from ʿEin al-Forṭāga—that two moons ago, her dog gave birth to some puppies. I told them that when they go to her, they should say that her friend, Ḥajja Ḥmēda al-ʿAjūz, asked that she give the ministers the most beautiful puppy, and I will give her a water barrel in exchange. And really, ya people," the ḥajja addresses us, "by Allah, they immediately flew in their gobṭar into Wadi Watīr [where ʿEin al-Forṭāga is located], and I have not seen them from that day to this."

"And the ḥajja has not seen them from then until now," Ṣāleḥ summarizes.

"Wait, wait, the story is not finished yet," the ḥajja protests. "That night, the captain with his Druze translator came. Luckily, our ʿŌda the ʿomda returned from his job about an hour before they came. 'The barrels,' said the captain, 'I came to talk about the barrels.' 'What barrels?' asked ʿŌda. 'It's fine. I know about it. I was the ʿomda for the day,' I said. 'How many do we get?' The captain told the ʿomda to come the next day with his pickup and take half of the empty barrels near the army base fence. Eleven."

"Eleven," some repeat, confirming.

"Don't you remember, ya people, how my husband divided them between the neighborhoods?" Rāda exclaims, smiling.

"And all that for one little puppy," the ḥajja produces a feeble sigh. She gracefully raises her chin, nods her head wisely, and bats her eyes—a sequence of gestures perhaps signifying that there is more to this than just one little puppy.

"Your peace," she says decisively, using the expression that marks the end of a recitation of a story or a poem. She tosses her veil up, then delves into her head-cover pocket and draws out a fancy cigarette lighter, to rekindle her German pipe. Her eyes comb the circle of the audience and rest upon Sallām. He smiles nervously.

"*Kathar kheirok* (may God increase your well-being) ya ḥajja," he salutes the ᶜAjūz, forcing a smile.

"Kathar kheirok," everyone repeats, but from the depths of their hearts.

"My mother is a lioness. My mother," declares Ṣāleḥ. "Everyone is afraid of her—the Bedouin, the Jews . . . When the Egyptians return, they'll be afraid too. She even talks back to my father."

"Don't bring the evil eye, my son," Ḥajja Ḥmēda says softly.

> *Khashēt sūg al-kbār lina wujaᶜ gāṣi—*
> *Bighayyer al-lōn, washauf al-ᶜein yistāsi.*
>
> What pain it is to enter the market of old age—
> Colors all are changed, things blur around the edge.

The old ḥajja recites this poem, sadness in her voice. We are silent. From afar, we still hear the clapping hands and stamping feet of the redēḥi dancers. And the anthropologist is struck by the contrast of the redēḥi words that ridicule the Old Woman because of her relative freedom from purdah, and the poem the Old Woman chose to evoke her sense of self. While the adolescents see her as shameless and free, she is painfully aware that her period of freedom is short. Soon, the limits of the body will steal back the freedom of her soul.

"Ya Sallām, you're divorced now. Go dance with the young 'uns (*shabāb*). Go search for the peach and the apples," Ḥajj Ḥamdān al-Shēba winks.

Sallām excuses himself and leaves. We are still silent. The anthropologist anticipates what will follow: someone ought to start talking about something totally different soon. Careful to note the allegorical process just completed, she watches old Ḥajja Ḥmēda. The Ḥajja is silent, coiled within herself. But from the rectangle framed between her head cover and her veil, her eyes shine with the fulfilled glow reserved for an actor who has just completed a long and complicated part.

III.

In the summer of 1981 I returned to Israel after two years of graduate school. I intended to spend one month with my family and two months in the South Sinai. But the day after I had arrived, my father died from a heart attack in the middle of a wedding. Two weeks later I found myself sitting in the dining area of my parents' kitchen with Ḥajj Ḥamdān al-Shēba, Ḥajja Ḥmēda al-ʿAjūz, their oldest daughter, Rāda, and my mother. My family had just risen from the *shivʿa* (the Jewish week of mourning) following my father's sudden death. The Mzeini couple and their daughter made the difficult journey from the South Sinai to the Tel Aviv suburbs transferring from bus to bus in the late summer heat. Just as they would for a condolence visit in the South Sinai, they hauled along their clothes and food bundled in their sleeping blankets. Throughout the journey they depended on the authority emanating from a small, crumpled piece of paper, a travel permit to go from a military occupied zone into Israel. They managed to obtain the permit with abject pleading, despite the military governor's ill-will toward me.

I hadn't informed any Mzeini of my father's death. There had been no time. They had known I was coming because I had sent them a cassette from Berkeley. An Israeli friend had picked up a Mzeini hitchhiker who was on his way to Nuwēbʿat Mzeina from work in Eilat and told him of my father's death. The news spread with the speed typical of gossip in the South Sinai. From the three dilapidated public telephones in the eastern peninsula people called my parents' home to offer condolences while we were sitting the shivʿa.

But this visit from Ḥajj Ḥamdān and Ḥajja Ḥmēda was a complete surprise, and I was touched. I tried my best to be an excellent hostess. Even though I am vegetarian, I served the guests lamb's meat—that rare, expensive Mzeina food reserved for special guests or for tribal gatherings.

So we were sitting around the dining table, plates loaded with thick, succulent, homemade lamb-burgers, parsleyed rice, and chopped vegetables before my guests and my mother. The guests stared at my mother, waiting. My mother stared back at them, waiting. In a moment of cross-cultural comparison, the anthropologist recalled that Mzeina eating etiquette demands that during family or group visits, the oldest host begins eating, then the group of guests thank him for his generosity and start eating. And in Israel, the hostess waits until the guests start eating and after the briefest pause she joins them. The anthropologist managed to suppress her rising laughter. The small electric fan on the table whirled monotonously, interrupting the nebulous embarrassment, trying, with good intentions, to alleviate the humidity and the heat.

Suddenly, Ḥajja Ḥmēda ordered in staccato Arabic: "The meat—bring it here!" Rāda and Ḥajj Ḥamdān's lamb-burgers immediately landed on the plate of the ʿAjūz. She scrupulously packed them one on top of the other, eyes shining. "Now eat. Eat," she encouraged us, sticking a fork and a tablespoon into the lamb-burger on top of the pile, chewing with vigor. Ḥajj Ḥamdān and Rāda lowered their eyes to their pillaged plates.

"The blessings of Allah upon you, mother of Smadar," the ʿAjūz pronounced, lips shining from the meat's juice.

My mom, who remembers very little Arabic, did not know she had to answer the blessing with one of her own.

"Meat brings fat, and fat makes the woman strong. You and Smadar have to put on some weight," she lectured. "Especially now that your husband has died."

The Shēba and Rāda ate slowly, quietly. My mom politely nodded her head when I translated the ʿAjūz's gems of wisdom, her face reflecting bafflement. Meanwhile, the ʿAjūz was well into the second lamb-burger, eating with blissful contentment.

"Ya ḥajja, don't you want a fat, strong husband or daughter?" I teased half-angry, feeling safe in my own home to violate the Mzeini family hierarchy. The ʿAjūz stopped her loud chewing. She lovingly cut the bottom-of-the-pile hamburger into two perfectly equal halves and passed one half onto the plate of her husband and gave the other to her daughter—my mom's eyes still baffled.

The next day we went to the Dolphinarium, a tropical aquarium and two-dolphin show à la Sea World. It had just opened, and I thought it would be fun and appropriate, because Ḥajj Ḥamdān was a fisherman. During my two-year absence, among the cassettes the Mzeinis had recorded for me and mailed to Berkeley was one that mentioned a strange event. Shimʿon, one of the Israeli fishmongers, aided by three Mzeini fishermen and two American friends, had hunted two dolphins—an act the Mzeinis considered taboo. Dolphins are sacred. I collected numerous folk stories about their dramatic rescues of Bedouin fishermen and saw with my own eyes their impressive ability to trap and kill sharks. The Bedouin considered this a superhuman quality. The cassette said that Shimʿon and his friends had put the two dolphins in a huge glass box, had talked with them every day, and then had driven the box, complete with dolphins, to Tel Aviv.

The smell of fresh paint assaulted our nostrils and huge American posters of dancing dolphins confronted us when we arrived at the packed parking lot. Screaming speakers decorated with colorful balloons screeched Hebrew children's songs. We were swallowed by a mass of children and parents moving with the flow towards the ticket box.

Two policemen pushed toward us against the flow. "IDs," one barked in Arabic.

"These are my guests," I answered in Hebrew with calm firmness.

"IDs," the policeman repeated, ignoring me.

The Shēba reached a trembling hand into the inner pocket of his vest, bringing out the crumpled travel permit carefully rolled into a clear plastic bag.

"Purpose of visit?" the policemen barked.

"A condolence visit," I answered with cold politeness. "It's written here, in the travel permit."

The ʿAjūz, understanding only very rudimentary Hebrew, interjected: "We came here to see our dolphins," she shot back. "You took them from our sea. These are *our* dolphins."

The other policeman smiled and gestured toward the long, amorphous line in front of us. We were released. We continued to merge with the crowd. The ʿAjūz looked back. When she could no longer see the policemen she hissed, "Sons of bitches."

Finally, we arrived at the head of the line. "Sold out," apologized the cashier. "We are selling tickets now for shows after next week. Four?"

I explained the situation to my guests. The Shēba looked relieved. We would leave this sweating crowd and go back to Smadar's home. Rāda looked at him and at her mother, as if to say that it could have been a great story to tell back home.

The ʿAjūz grabbed my wrist tightly. "Smadar, *sawwi al-maʿarūf* (do a good deed). Tell this man in Hebrew what I am going to tell you in Arabic. Word for word. Tell him, that all the fish in this place are from our sea."

I translated faithfully, my voice trying to replicate the huff in her voice even though I felt awkward.

"Tell him, that he and Mister Shimʿon are making a business here, making money from our sea. Tell him, that my husband is a fisherman, son of a fisherman, grandson of a fisherman, and we've never seen someone fishing for dolphin. It's taboo!" she wrathfully pointed her right index finger at the cashier.

I translated, the crowd complaining grumpily that the line was not moving.

"Ya wife, we are guests in this land. Shame," whispered the Shēba.

"Shut up!" the ʿAjūz ordered in a roaring whisper. "These people are not Bedouin. Let me handle it!"

She ordered me to keep translating, saying, "Tell this man that the fish from our sea are not a gift. I am in Tel Aviv only today, and I want to see how our fish are doing here."

I translated. The cashier was silent. "I think this old lady is right," I added, trying to keep a straight face while Rāda's suppressed giggles tickled my back.

"Just a minute," the cashier left his booth, walking in the direction of the management building. On such a hot and humid summer day the patience of the families behind us was long gone.

"Arabs—go home," a voice boomed.

The cashier returned, all smiles. He told us that from that very moment we were the official guests of the Dolphinarium, to be entertained by the vice-manager. We hurried to catch the next show—it was to start in ten minutes. The amorphous line breathed in shock down our necks when they saw the vice-manager accompany us, passing the long lines spreading before the doors of the theatre. The vice-manager seated us in the center of the front row. One of the ushers immediately served us icy cokes.

Trumpets screeched from the speakers and the audience quieted down. The announcer introduced the show. Accompanied by a scratchy Strauss waltz, he brightly pitched the audience the story of the difficult operation of moving the dolphins from the shores of the South Sinai to Tel Aviv and their subsequent training. "Today is a special day for us," he announced with a festive air. "We are honored by the presence of Ḥajj Ḥamdān, one of the most famous South Sinai fishermen. He is here with his wife, daughter, and their anthropologist. Give them a hand!"

The audience clapped their hands and whistled with their fingers while I translated what he said into Arabic.

"Our dear guests, please stand up so that people can see who you are," the announcer requested.

"He wants us to stand up," I whispered.

"Stand up! Stand up!" the ʿAjūz encouraged her husband and

daughter, raising her arms to the sky to the sound of a stronger wave of clapping.

After the show, the manager came to our seats to personally accompany us while we toured the aquariums. Indeed, it was Mister Shimʿon. It seemed that the ʿAjūz had correctly guessed that this was his business.

"You've got lots of brains," the Shēba complimented him in Arabic, a language Shimʿon spoke. "You put the sea into glass boxes, and people pay you good money to come and watch."

Shimʿon just smiled. Later, he said to me in Hebrew, "Menachem Begin sold the Sinai to Egypt, so I was left with no other choice but to market the Sinai in Tel Aviv."

The halls with the aquariums were gradually filling with the parents and children emptying from the dolphin theater. A child handed his program to the Shēba, requesting an autograph. I explained the request to the Shēba in Arabic. Embarrassed, he shook his head no.

"He doesn't know how to write," I explained to the child.

The ʿAjūz interfered, asking me to get my pen out of my bag.

"Give me your right thumb," she ordered the Shēba. She smeared ink on the thumb that had been shortened a centimeter and a half by a shark refusing to die. "*Amḍa! amḍa!* (stamp) you, the fisherman!" she proudly requested, "the same way you stamp your thumbprint on those permits. Today, the honor is yours!"

The Shēba put a hesitating thumb on the program, and then shook the hand offered to him by the delighted child. Afterwards, he stamped his thumbprint on many programs and shook the hands of the crowd of children and parents who had surrounded him asking for autographs and handshakes. The ʿAjūz would apply fresh ink to the chopped thumb every once in a while.

We left when the Dolphinarium closed, even though not everyone who wanted one had received an autograph. I drove us home. We were silent. Exhausted.

Rāda suddenly said, "There will be plenty of stories to tell back home."

Evening fell. We drove along the Mediterranean coast, stuck in the end-of-the-day traffic jam of wedding parties. To our left were the cement skeletons of modernist highrises. To our right, Charles Klor Park, a strip of green grass between the road and the sea (probably named after its American Jewish donor),[15] where middle-class newlyweds came to have their pictures taken. There the couples posed between the worn-out sun and garish cardboard backdrops of the

Wailing Wall or an anonymous Alpine mountain scene (hiding the highrises from view). Leaving the young couples behind, we drove through the slums of Palestinian Jaffa. We entered my hometown. Sprinklers watered the manicured front yards, and people in tank-tops played cards and ate cold watermelon on balconies.

"Our deeds today will make your mother laugh. She will definitely laugh," said the ʿAjūz.

I nodded my head. We parked and I locked the doors.

Rāda said something, as if to herself.

"Pardon me?" I politely asked.

"*Aʿaṭu sabʿāt lesabʿīn yekhufūhen wa-aʿaṭu banāt al-andhāl leramāyem.*" "Give the lionesses in marriage to the lions to scare them, and marry the daughters of jerks to scum," she repeated. "It's a proverb."

As I walked to the house I wondered: was this a critique of the kitsch just seen or is this a comment about the old couple's marriage?

7
THE FOOL

Al-Ahabal

FOOL. Truth's a dog must to kennel; he must be whipped out, when the Lady Brach may stand by th' fire and stink . . . Prithee, nuncle, keep a schoolmaster that can teach thy fool to lie. I would fain learn to lie.

LEAR. An you lie, sirrah, we'll have you whipped.

WILLIAM SHAKESPEARE
King Lear

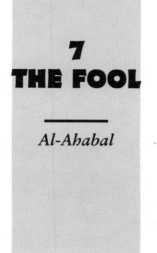

A MZEINI TRIBESMAN, HIS AMERICAN-JEWISH WIFE WHO CONVERTED TO ISLAM, THEIR SON, AND FAMILY DOG IN THE PUBLIC GARDEN OF OFĪRA

"Every dog has its day [to get a beating], and every place has its Fool." So goes the Mzeini saying. And the day young Manṣūr left for Zurich, to marry his love whom he had met on ʿAqaba Gulf nude beach,[1] his father declared him *meshammas*, disowned from both family and tribe by the father's statement that from this day forth, his son was dead. During the week of ritual mourning that followed, the father kept repeating, "The day has come when iron talks back and the Fool rules."

Indeed, the Fool, a Mzeini character present in almost every encampment or sedentarized settlement, was the agent who expressed clearly and succinctly, though perhaps with deliberate awkwardness, the paradoxes of the local South Sinai hybridization of two contradictory cultures: the Mzeina qua traditional Bedouin, with their Islamic religion and nomadic-pastoralist ideology, and the Western culture imposed on them by international politics.

The Fool himself would usually be a reification of this hybridized juncture. He typically looked like a klutz, with a dirty patched caftan and a headdress only half-tied around his head, and with uncut fingernails and beard, which the Mzeinis consider pollution. "We Bedouin are almost waterless, very poor," remarked one Fool, "so we'd better look like it."

"Don't believe him," some who were listening warned me later. "He's made lots of money since the Eilat-Sharm road was opened. He keeps it all in that khaki pouch hanging diagonally from his shoulder."

The handful of Fools I knew were talented businessmen who accumulated wealth from pioneering entrepreneurial activities. If a Fool lived in the heavily toured coastal areas, he would venture into building and renting out traditional-style Bedouin palm-frond huts to the many tourists who wanted to vacation in what they envisioned as authentic desert settings. He also sold them food, drink, and touristy simulations of traditional Bedouin attire imported from the West Bank, and later from Cairo. He was among the first to organize and market Desert Tours on Camelback, and to produce Bedouin-style celebrations for the tourists' amusement and edification. In addition, the Fool would be a money changer, at better rates than the bank, illegally converting the tourists' hard currency (preferably German marks, Swiss francs, or American dollars) into the notoriously inflation-ridden Israeli and later Egyptian currencies. In a case where the Fool lived away from the main tourist routes, he would usually be the one to win the hearts and pockets of Israeli or Egyptian developers, who conceived of him as both nonthreatening, due to his use of humor, and cheap to employ, due to his shabby appearance. So they would appoint him as a subcontractor or labor supervisor, the foreign developers' go-between in their relations with their Mzeini blue-collar laborers.

Unlike the typical nouveaux riches, the Fool did not invest his money in conspicuous consumption of semidilapidated pickup trucks or jeeps. Nor did he buy fancy Japanese transistor radios and cassette recorders, or elegant Swiss watches. Rather, he generously donated the money he made to the building of hewn-stone mosques that mushroomed in all the heavily toured communities. These replaced the spaces on the rough ground made sacred by marking, only with laid-down stones or conch shells, the *miḥrāb* pointing toward Mecca. Perhaps this building of permanent mosques was a response to the presence of so many scantily clad tourists intruding into the everyday life of the Mzeini encampments and settlements, as if visiting some sort of human zoo.

The Mzeinis repeatedly organized delegations that went to plead with the peninsula's Israeli military governor to put up signs requesting the tourists to wear bathing suits. But the military governor merely advised the Mzeinis to make the best of it and learn to enjoy the show, and refused to take any further action aside from choosing an occasional one-night stand from among the naked bodies on the beach. The Mzeinis had no choice but to acquiesce.

When the Egyptians got the ʿAqaba Gulf Coast back in 1982, they immediately responded to the Bedouin request and erected those long-hoped-for signs on the South Sinai beaches. But the more signs, the fewer tourists. Every tourist also had to register with the Egyptian Tourist Police and could be subject to occasional questioning. A few women were subjected to sexual harassment. The Egyptians also outlawed individual and spontaneous small group backpacking by putting up signs along the peninsula's asphalt roads announcing that tourists were prohibited from leaving them. Perhaps the Egyptians, fearing the desert themselves, feared also for the tourists' safety. But the Bedouin thereby lost a relatively hefty source of income. Once again they organized delegations to the governing authorities of the South Sinai, this time requesting the Egyptians to ease the no-nudity and no-hiking regulations. And once again they were instructed to make the best of the new situation and had to acquiesce.

"I am a merchant of sins," confessed one Fool. "I sell the tourists alcohol and rent them huts where unmarried people have tabooed sex." (One of his own brothers later announced, for all but this Fool to hear, "That's why he was the first to sign up and pay the large deposit the first year the Israelis organized the holy pilgrimage to Mecca.") "In Mecca I went to see a holy man. I asked him whether selling alcohol to non-Muslims was *ḥarām* (taboo for Muslims) or *ḥalāl* (religiously permitted). He told me I should cease this at once. But what can I do instead? Make money cleaning toilets in non-Muslim hotels?"

From the remarks I heard by and about the Fool, and given his no-win situation, it is clear that, like other figures of sacred clowns or tricksters, the contradictions built into the composition of the Fool's persona were never resolved.[2] But in contrast to the textually prescribed roles of those other clowns or tricksters, the Mzeini Fool did not make his debut on the societal stage during the spatially and temporally bounded domains that characterize communal ritual performances. Rather, the Mzeini Fool, if present and only if he chose to perform, might spontaneously rise up during awkward breaks in the conversation, interrupting the spatially and temporally unbounded flow of ordinary quotidian discourse. Such fissures would occur when the conversation got stuck in a circular, reductionist argument pitting the Mzeini identity qua Bedouin against the hybridizations in their identity forced on them by their local compromises with Western influences. At this point, the people might all just get up and leave the conversation circle. But sometimes a Fool could save the situation for the time being at least, bridging the textual and contextual discontinuities by embodying them in his own persona and performing a solo ritual with its own farcical logic, allegorizing his own experiences into a moral exemplar that clarified for his listeners their own identity.

The Fool had "ill-formed unity" (Handelman 1987:548): a bright, rich merchant dressed in rags and acting silly, miming the antics of those naked Others on the beach even while his audience was well aware of his conspicuous Muslim piety. His own paradoxical existence enabled him to draw for his audience a clear boundary between themselves qua traditional Bedouin, and themselves qua workers, many of whom preferred the creative, clever job of running their own enterprises marketing their culture to sinful foreigners, when the only apparent alternatives were miserable unskilled jobs in similar enterprises run by their occupiers. The Fool's staging of his own paradoxes, therefore, temporarily solved the Mzeinis' contradiction between their yearning to embody their traditional Bedouin lifestyle, and their reality of having to perform this lifestyle they had never really had in front of exotica-hunting tourists, whom they could not restrain into civility because they were not the ones to decide on the rules and regulations in their own land.

1.

al-Billij, Dahab, Christmas night, 1985

Tourists who started flocking en masse to this spectacular Sinai beach in the mid-1970s wished to live in the authentic conditions of a traditional Bedouin village. Upon getting off the bus, they used to ask, "Where is the Bedouin village?" So the Mzeini entrepreneurs built this fake one and named it al-Billij, imitating the sound of the English word but only as an arbitrary proper name, with no particular significance.

Deep black sea, unusually calm. Beam of half a moon. Aluminum beach chairs half-sunk in sand. Posters of Michael Jackson and Prince glued on the plywood counters of flimsy cafes, their facades sheathed in date-palm fronds so they look genuine from the outside. Some Madonna hit competing with Simon and Garfunkel's "Bridge over Troubled Water," both pouring out of raspy Mitsubishi loudspeakers. An asbestos structure dyed brownish-orange dominating the scene with its big sign: Tourist Police. Five policemen in the station, all crammed behind the small rectangular desk—more than enough protection for the fifteen tourists milling around.

"No nudity," announces the big red print, in English only, on white signs scattered along the beach more frequently than necessary. Strings of Christmas lights, interwoven among the palm fronds, twinkle like cheerful guests from another planet. After Forest and I have waited a long time in a line of three people to see the five policemen, our passports are stamped. We are now under the official auspices of the Tourist Police of the Arab Republic of Egypt.

It's too late to arrive as guests at the home of my adoptive Mzeini family. Not only do they live four kilometers north of here, but after the four and a half years since my last visit in 1981, I am coming with my American spouse and want to introduce him properly. Aside from these considerations, the local scene is sufficiently bizarre to attract the postmodernist scholar's curiosity.

Simon and Garfunkel have won. Madonna's loudspeaker conked out, so now we are listening only to the sound of silence.

"Let's have a cup of tea in one of those cafes," I suggest to Forest, "and then find a rental hut for the night."

"The music isn't bad," he muses, "but my first time in the Sinai Desert, I didn't expect to be celebrating Christmas."

So we stay.

"Hey, Smadar, how you doin', what's up? Who's this handsome guy with you? Remember me? I'm Ṣubḥi." A young Bedouin leaps on me with this barrage in Hebrew, as he approaches me from behind the cafe counter.

I am stunned. I can't quite place this tall tanned young man with long curls down his back, costumed in a tight Speedo swimsuit and a tight tank-top bearing a faded picture of Rambo. Why on earth is he speaking Hebrew to me when he knows I am perfectly fluent in the Mzeini Arabic dialect?

After a long, nebulous moment, he smiles, revealing teeth coated by a patina of brown tar from smoking too many cigarettes. "I am the grandchild of Ḥajj Maḍᶜān the Healer, the one who lives up in Wadi Madsūs," he chatters in very fast Hebrew. "I am the son of Muḥammad, and just before you went to America, when I was still a child, our family moved here from the mountains. This is my father's cafe."

"All right, all right, but why in Hebrew, ya Ṣubḥi?" I inquire in Arabic, feeling hurt that he addresses me in the language of the occupier.

"English they understand a bit, but Hebrew not at all." He points his chin in the direction of the brownish-orange structure. "We could also talk in Swedish—they don't understand any Swedish either, even though they enjoy staring at the blonde Swedish women. Yok tola Svenska?"

"No, but why not Arabic?" I insist in Arabic, while Forest, who understands a bit of Swedish, tries to recover from these hybridized realities.

"Because they—they have big ears. They are snoopy about what everyone says, even someone as young and innocuous (*zarūk*, Hebrew) as me. I don't want any problems with them," he continues in Hebrew under his breath.

Suddenly the anthropologist realizes that the occupier has changed, and therefore so has the language of oppression.

"How is business?" I ask. But Ṣubḥi suddenly freezes. A sleepy policeman, wearing a disheveled wool khaki uniform (despite the warmth of the coastal desert winter) and a submachine gun slung over his shoulder, is patrolling around the cafe. Nonchalantly, Ṣubḥi raises the volume and we sink into the epic of Mrs. Robinson. When the soldier finishes patrolling around all five other flimsy cafes and the four hut clusters of the Billij, Ṣubḥi yells at him in Hebrew, "Hey, go to hell, son of a whore!" The soldier smiles at him and waves back.

"So how is business?" I ask again in Hebrew, and the anthropologist feels very weird.

"No business," he says briskly. "No nudity, no business."

"But during the Israeli occupation, people your parents' age kept complaining that the nudes on the beach were offensive to Islam." I still feel disoriented from speaking Hebrew with this Mzeini.

"Yes, our fathers complained and made money, and complained more, and made more money. We don't get the fat tourists who come to Cairo. The kind we get have beards and backpacks and like the freedom of the desert. For them, freedom means taking off their clothes and screwing all the women in sight. That's what they believe, and it's OK with me. I sell them things and make money, and they teach me their languages. But they don't like to be asked ten times a day where they come from, where they're going, where they've eaten, where they will sleep and with whom. The Tourist Police means no tourists."

I look around and see that the whole place is a stage set to welcome hippie trekkers or stray remnants from "Hair." Political and personal graffiti are scratched in charcoal on the counter plywood: "Make love, not war," "Make love, not babies," "Barbara—see you in Khartoum," "John Lennon," "Nelson Mandela." Here and there are peace signs and hearts.

Ṣubḥi goes behind the counter to change the cassette. "How about 'The Beatles' Best'?" he asks us. "And what would you like to eat? Omelet? French fries? Canned tuna? Mackerel in tomato sauce?"

"Whatever," I answer listlessly. Ṣubḥi gets to work on supper and soon we smell omelets. Forest and I start singing along with the Beatles: "Michelle, ma belle . . ." Meanwhile I notice that two tourists in Bedouin caftans, sporting blond beard stubble and sunburned to the point the Mzeini described as "roasted lobsters," have come into the cafe and are intently involved in a poker game with a Bedouin wearing a T-shirt and jeans. One of the lobsters turns to Forest.

"Hey, man what's happenin'? Where you guys from?" He tries to talk jive, but it doesn't come off.

"Berkeley, California," Forest answers laconically.

"I'm from San Francisco myself, the Haight." Here follows small talk about weather and politics back home. Then he says, "After traveling around the world, the only thing I miss from the good ol' USA is Christmas."

"Well, at least you got a few lights here," says Forest. And he whimsically starts singing "Jingle Bells." The two guys join in, trying to drown out the Beatles booming from the huge speakers. The Bedouin get into the spirit of the thing, clapping their hands in little circles as they would have for the *redēḥi* dance.

Ṣubḥi arrives at our table with a platter bearing two cheap china plates, each with a steaming, elegantly rolled omelet stuffed with "La Vache Qui Rit" processed cheese, accompanied by traditional unleavened Bedouin flatbread. He meticulously sets our places with stainless steel flatware and lays the plates before us.

"S'il vous plait, monsieur, madame," he says with a flourish, then shifts to Arabic. "Eat, eat!"

"We won't unless you join us, because you are our host. But don't worry, we'll pay you anyway." So he pulls up another chair and sits down, and the three of us share the two plates of food.

"Too bad you weren't here yesterday," he says between bites of omelet. "We sacrificed a lamb for Christmas. It was a great dinner."

"We? Who's 'we?'" He has piqued the anthropologist's curiosity.

"All of us young Bedouin who work here for the tourists."

"But Christmas is for Christians," I protest the obvious.

"Look," he says, "when you Jews were here and occupied our land, we all were very devout Muslims. Even Shgēṭef the Fool was. From the money he made renting out his huts here, half of our mosque was built. But now things have changed. The Egyptians are here and they have brought all sorts of government teachers to show us how to be Muslim. They think theirs is the only way. So why not check out Christianity? Most of the tourists are nice people, and now they wear some clothes, of course."

The anthropologist is at first puzzled by this logic. She remembers noticing and writing in her 1978 fieldnotes that during the Israeli occupation, the more hippies there were lolling on the Sinai beaches, the more permanent mosques, built of hewn stone, sprang up around the Bedouin settlements. Perhaps a refuge from, perhaps a defense against, the non-Muslim impingement on Bedouin tradition. Then she suddenly realizes that, just as the language of the occupier has changed, so has their religion.

*

We slept that night on the soft sand floor of one of Shgēṭef's huts, under the lone beam of the half moon, with only twinkling Christmas lights for stars. Ṣubḥi gave us a candle, though, saying it would be more romantic. And the deep black sea was mirror-calm—no storm, as usual, to wake us up in the middle of the night.

In the morning Shgēṭef arrived to collect his fee. "One dollar or two Egyptian pounds per person per night," he announced, poker-faced. Only after he got the money did he give me a big hug and tell me that the whole Mzeini settlement up north was waiting to see me and meet my husband.

When we loaded our packs and walked north on the beach toward the settlement, we noticed a freckled peachy-blonde woman dressed in cut-off pants but also a black kerchief tied in back of her head to imitate a veil.

"Where are you from?" I queried.

"Amsterdam."

"Why the veil?"

"I heard it helps attract a young Bedouin lover. When Israel was here, I bathed here nude, but what the guys seemed really interested in was my nose and mouth. So I'm covering them to make them more mysterious."

The anthropologist sees that the tourists are fine-tuning their long-standing efforts to go native and imitate the Bedouin, who now, in contrast, are acting like an international mishmash of all the various tourists they have had to deal with. Under these circumstances, I can see why, when I asked Shgēṭef "What are you doing these days?", he wryly remarked, "I'm working at being a Bedouin."

Even way out here on the beach the strains of Simon and Garfunkel float from the scratchy loudspeakers:

Slow down, you move too fast.
You got to make the morning last.
Just kicking down the cobble stones,
Looking for fun and Feelin' Groovy . . .

Doot-in' doo-doo,
Feelin' Groovy.

Got no deeds to do,

No promises to keep.
I'm dappled and drowsy and ready to sleep.
Let the morning time drop all its petals on me.
Life, I love you,
All is groovy.

II.

Dahab, Spring 1978, seven years earlier

Evening at this main sedentarized oasis along the ʿAqaba Gulf, a community of eighty-nine nuclear households live here permanently. Dinner smells, still in the air, mingle with the salty sea breeze softly blowing among the fronds of the date trees scattered in clusters on the coastline. A mother's undulating melancholy voice, singing a lullaby, tenderly echoes the cry of the muezzin calling for the *ʿasha* after-dinner prayer. Answering the call, fourteen men from the northern neighborhood's magʿad enter the newly built nearby mosque. After about ten minutes, some of them begin to go back to the magʿad, where they sit in a circle around the embers of a small fire. The older men stay a few minutes longer for pious individual prayer. Moonlight glows on the faces of people tranquil because they have fulfilled another duty of their religious routine. The youngest of the men serves small glasses of sweet dark tea that was heated on the embers. A quiet conversation emerges from the silence.

The conversation focuses on the hippies in al-Billij, called by the Mzeinis "Batānka," a *nisba* (group name) for "Beatniks." Since the Mzeinis considered the hippies to be sort of an international clan, they gave them a group name ending in "-a," like their own clan names. They were sure that the word "Beatnik" was derived from the Arabic *nīk*, meaning, "to fuck." This made sense to them because the Mzeinis, both women and men clad in their traditional attire, observed the Batānka from close range, doing it on the beach daily.

ʿĪD: By Allah, today there was such a fat, healthy girl on the beach. Did you see her? The one with that dark, skinny guy.

KHḌEIR: Yes, I think I know who you are talking about. They are in Ḥammūda's hut, under the palms he shares with Freij.

ʿĪD: Too bad she sunbathes. Her beautiful milky skin has turned red like a roasted lobster.

JUMᶜA: Yeah, she came to me asking for tobacco. I told her I smoke only *banjo*, and asked her if she would like to buy some.

The listeners grin with amusement, knowing that Jumᶜa was offering the woman cheap homegrown green tobacco, which smells very much like marijuana but of course lacks its active ingredient.

When the first Batānka arrived in the South Sinai, they asked the Bedouin for marijuana. When it became clear that the Bedouin did not know that word, the hippies resorted to the exotic term "ganja," which the Bedouin misheard and then mispronounced as "banjo." The local folk wisdom has it that one day a naked beatnik sniffed the smoke from an ordinary rolled green tobacco cigarette a Bedouin was smoking, and instead of shouting "Eureka!" he pointed and gleefully exclaimed, "Ganja! Ganja!" Whereupon the Bedouin realized they had a common product with extraordinary commercial possibilities.

JUMᶜA: I sold her three cigarettes at four American bucks a shot.

The circle is sprinkled with wry smiles.

RĀSHED: I saw her too. I think she dyes her hair. Her pubic hair is black and her hair is kind of red.

ABU-MŪSA [*muttering in dismay*]: Oh evil of disaster!

Everyone but Abu-Mūsa is snickering as if at a dirty joke, but also with embarrassment, because not only have they all seen the young woman naked, but she didn't at least follow the proper custom of removing her body hair, which the Mzeinis considered religious pollution.

ᶜĪD: I swear by my life, I can't figure out what she sees in that guy, he's so dark and skinny.

People laugh again. For the Mzeinis, being dark meant a person had to work hard in the sun, and being skinny meant that the person did not get enough to eat—so he was poor and ugly.

SWĒLEM: This summer the Batānka increased like the amount of rubbish they throw on the beach. They throw themselves on the sand, too—dirty.

The atmosphere sobers at this distressing reality.

A MAN SIFTING HOME-GROWN GREEN TOBACCO ▶

JUMᶜA [*raising his voice*]: What do you want? It's their vacation. This is how they enjoy themselves. Tell me, isn't it fun to take your girlfriend, or even come by yourself—everybody's naked, and you—just pick the one you like? And with their exchange rate, a vacation like that is pretty cheap.

ABU-MŪSA [*loud*]: Pray to the Prophet! You two have turned into Beatniks. Aren't you fed up with staring at the genitals of heretic girls? Do we have to discuss it every evening here in our magᶜad by the holy mosque?

ᶜAWAYED [*louder*]: All of us are gradually joining the Batānka. Today when I was praying the noon prayer to myself near the hut I rent out in al-Billij, two guys with their uncircumcised penises dangling—tphooo [*he spits on the ground in disgust*]—and wearing only their cameras—they took pictures of me, just like that, without asking and without paying me. [*very upset, beating his hands on the air*] Who do they think we are? Their free picture show? It's bad enough they put on *their* free picture show for us all over our beach.

KHḌEIR [*just as loud, with gestures that punctuate the air*]: Other places don't have this mess that we do. People still follow the old ways. The hell with money—what kind of a life are we living?

ABU-MŪSA [*firmly*]: Have you ever seen or heard of an Arab praying right in the middle of a bunch of naked ladies and their lovers?

The anthropologist, in spite of hearing the pain in Abu-Mūsa's voice, barely manages to suppress a grin at the incongruity of this image.

ᶜAWAYED: Allah the Great! The Bedouin live in the desert, in Egypt, in Saudi Arabia, everywhere, without being touched by this pollution. Why do we have the bad luck to have to do this for a living?

ᶜĪD [*with deliberate calmness, to tone down the argument in tempo and volume*]: You think you got problems? Just try raising goats in this desert and see how far you get. Within a week all your money will have gone for their food. Our desert has lots of the wrong kind of grass.

ᶜĪd meant to end the argument with a funny pun: both pasture grass and dope were referred to by the word "hashish." But by now, the men are so demoralized by the subject that the joke musters only a few weak smiles.

JUMᶜA [*flares up*]: We are all Batānka now. Living on as little money as they, spending no more than they do. What property do we own? Our land is all bare rugged mountains and jagged corals, good for nothing except attracting crazy tourists to dive and climb and risk their necks for the fun of it. Real Bedouin have fields and flocks. Every once in a while they go to the market and exchange some goats for [consumer] goods. But these dollars are killing us.

ᶜAWAYED [*with conviction*]: The Bedouin are people of honor. They believe in God and His Disciple. They disdain money-grubbing!

ᶜĪD [*with a voice of sugarcoated poison*]: Oh yes, we all saw you yesterday haggling with those scumbags over exchange rates of Israeli and German money down to the last penny, nervously counting your sheaf of bills. Oh Great Lord, we're not like the rest of 'em, the Bedouin.

RĀSHED [*furiously jumps into the conversation*]: Who needs money anyway? The Bedouin need freedom. Let them roam around in the desert like they used to, riding their camels, singing *hejēni*s (caravan songs), courting the veiled goatherds.

SWĒLEM [*with authority*]: The Bedouin don't put their heart in money. One helps the other: the father his sons, the sons their old father, everyone their uncles and cousins. They are organized better than the Eged Corporation.

The anthropologist is startled to hear this comparison made between the classic agnatic-corporate tribe and Eged, the powerful transportation monopoly that owns and runs almost every bus in Israel and the Occupied Territories.

ABU-MŪSA [*with finality*]: For the Bedouin, *al-damm dhamm, ma fi khramm!* (The blood is protected—there are no holes).

"Al-damm dhamm, ma fi khramm" was a legal statement taken from the codex of Blood Vengeance Law. It meant that, in a social network based on blood relationship, there could not be any gaps. When such a statement was uttered in everyday discourse, it meant that the conversation had reached a moment of crisis and could no longer proceed.

All of a sudden, out of the silence following this weighty declaration, a very short, skinny, sharp-boned and sloppily dressed figure rises, waving his hands.

"Ho!" exclaims this Shgēṭef, the local Fool.

The others, realizing he has not spoken yet and has something to say, turn their heads in his direction.

With all solemnity he declares, "The Bedouin pee in a squat and so do we."

After initial puzzlement, the group bursts into hearty laughter. The Mzeinis believed that squatting was the proper way Muslims should urinate in order not to become polluted with drops of urine. The Fool's remark drew a sharp line between the magʿad and al-Billij. In that absurd context, peeing while squatting meant existing in the world qua Bedouin.

After the last peals of laughter fade away, the Fool starts speaking in the calm and measured voice that signifies a shift into a storytelling mode.

*

"Yesterday a couple came to me. They wanted to rent one of my huts. I think they were from a kibbutz because they wore those plaid flannel shirts. But the guy looked Swedish."

"You mean, he had those devil-colored eyes?" asks ʿĪd, to show he is listening attentively.

"Yes, his eyes were as green as the eyes of those accursed cats. And believe it or not, *she* was driving the car and *he* unloaded it."

The Fool stops to give his audience a chance to laugh at the ridiculous gender-role reversal of the Batānka tribe. When the Mzeinis migrated, or even just went away with the family for a couple of days to visit friends and relatives, it was the husband who loaded and drove the pickup truck, and the wife who unloaded it.

"That devilish guy shut up, and *she* haggled with me over the price of the hut and then tried to cheat and pay less."

The Fool again pauses to let his audience savor yet another role reversal that delineates the boundaries between the Batānka and themselves.

"So finally, after all that, they took all their clothes off and went for a walk on the beach, like Adam and Eve in the Garden."

And then the Fool stands up, violating the convention of the magʿad and starts miming an imitation of a Batānka woman delicately prancing on the beach.

"Wait a second," he suddenly says, still jogging around the amused circle. "I forgot my tits!" He holds his open hands under the places where his size D breasts would have been, and with huge motions moves them up and down. The men crack up. The Fool stops to catch his breath and again violates convention by wiping the sweat off his brow with the hem of his long caftan, deliberately raising it to an immodest height and revealing his undergarment.

ʿĪd, the youngest among the men, whistles with his fingers, but immediately stops because of Abu-Mūsa's piercing look.

"And that Swede, he had the biggest foreskin I've ever seen in my life." And the fool jabs his elbow into his navel and dangles his arm from side to side, using his whole forearm to represent the tourist's penis, with the hand being the huge foreskin. The men roar with laughter.

"There really is some difference between the Batānka tribe and the Mzeina tribe," chokes Jumʿa through his guffaws.

"There is indeed a difference," agree ʿAwayed and Khḍeir.

"In the afternoon she pulled the guy by his hand from the water and shoved him into the hut. There they did all sorts of things that people never do." And the Fool mimes hugging the air, kissing it, and mounting around it.

These gestures were all varieties of sexual foreplay foreign to the Mzeinis, though they had seen them many times on their own beach. Nevertheless they now cheerfully volunteer lots of free advice to the Fool, just as they had gotten into the habit of doing when they walked on the beach among the bodies of the Batānka.

"Hey, give her another kiss there."

"No, no, above, on her neck."

"Don't forget her navel . . ."

"And believe it or not, by the end of it all, she was on top," Shgēṭef proclaims.

Everyone is weeping with laughter at this final proof of the topsy-turvy world of Batānka.

"And that's the way it is," the Fool concludes, using this formulaic statement typical of codas for solo performances.

"And that's the way it is," all the men repeat in unison.

After several moments of awkward silence, which the anthropologist is careful to record, the conversation begins to flow again. Now the topic is the prices, and amount of stock on hand, of the tourists' favorite designs for Bedouin caftans and so on, as if the bitter argument had never happened.

I look around for the Fool, but it seems he has already left the circle. "Where is Shgēṭef?" I ask Jumʿa, sitting on my right.

"He's already gone back to his Billij huts, to make some more money off the tourists just arriving on the evening bus."

So the Fool has walked right back into the source of all the tension

A MZEINI BEDOUIN VOLUNTEERS HIS FREE ADVICE TO A TOURIST COUPLE. RIDING ON HIS CAMEL'S BACK IS ANOTHER TOURIST.

played out just now on the stage of the magᶜad. But where did it go? This quirky tension-dissolver has taken it with him until his next performance.

III.

In the summer of 1979, the same dispute kept arising in Dahab's northern magᶜad. The Mzeinis juxtaposed their Muslim, Bedouin identity with that of their drifting Batānka neighbors, and the Fool had to keep reassuring them in his farcical, convoluted way, that there were clear boundaries between them and their neighbors. A couple of days after one of these performances, I was sitting on the beach, leaning my back against a date-palm trunk. These were the smudgy hours of dusk, when the sharp red-granite cliffs seemed to glide into the Red Sea and be mirrored in its reddish-blue water. These were also the soon-to-be sacred moments when men washed in the tidal zone, purifying themselves for the *maghreb* prayer, while smells of poached fish, black pepper, and cumin drifted in the air. Jumʿa and Rāshed completed their ritual purification and seated themselves near me beneath the palms, silently waiting for the muezzin cry.

The anthropologist dropped a casual remark, as if to herself: "This Shgēṭef is an incredibly funny guy. I have notebooks and rolls of film full of his antics."

There were almost sixty seconds of silence—a very long pause in a regular Mzeini conversation. Then Jumʿa said, somehow baffled: "You came all the way here just to write and picture some fool?"

After another very long pause, Rāshed slowly and carefully chose his words. "No, ya Jumʿa," he said frankly, "Shgēṭef is no fool. His mind is sharp as a sword. This summer he earned more than any of the rest of us off the tourists. And if it had not been for Shgēṭef's generosity, we would not have our mosque. But let me tell you, ya Smadar," Rāshed went on, turning his head towards me, "at times, this Fool's mind goes with the *tarāwa* (early evening breeze). His mind and his tongue then go separate routes, and he thinks of himself as if he's one of those Batānka."

"Poor Shgēṭef," added ʿAwayed, who had just joined our little group after finishing his ritual washing while half-listening to the conversation. With matter-of-fact finality he declared, "The Fool is a *fool*."

"Is *he* a fool?" Rāshed immediately responded, "*All* of us have become fools!"

"All of you? Fools?" The anthropologist perked up. "What do you mean?"

"The tourists have made us into fools," Rāshed replied at once. "They photograph us, they even make movies of us. There's no mountain left they didn't climb, no wadi they didn't hike, no coral reef they didn't scuba. They want to drink our tea and eat our bread and then complain of constipation and *we* are to blame." Then he stopped his diatribe. His deeply lined face grimaced, and he continued: "Our children, our own children, they don't know this desert, their own land, as well as some of these Batānka tourists do. They just want to hang around Eilat, and eat white bread soaked in factory milk. And all they dream of is owning Mercedes taxis and screwing in the foreign style."

There were five whole minutes of silence. In that moody limbo of the waning day, I mourned how so many romantic pasts are dissolving into the transnational future, and the anthropologist wanted me to stop being sentimental and try to rescue this disappearing culture by getting it into text.

"The Fool is a *fool*," Jumᶜa, Rāshed, and ᶜAwayed said in quiet unison, and then ᶜAwayed proceeded with a slow, monotonous recitation of a traditional *gaṣīda* (poem) about the Fool, careful to note that I had turned on my cassette recorder while the men repeated the rhymed syllables.

Al-Ahabal la shāf al-ḍeif ma yewanni,
Ya ḥasrati minno la leginā.
Damm al-ḍabāyeḥ jamb beit'ho yejanni—
Mabsūṭ ill ᶜind'ho we-illi ḥawelā.

Ya karwato tishbaᶜ al-ḍeif watethanni!
Wasamn al-mebahhar minho ganā.
Wenghāb ᶜanna gheibto ma temanni!
Kul ḥayii yugᶜud ᶜala darbo yetaḥarrā.

Wanwagef ᶜindok tegūl ghazāl mit'ḥanni,
Waṭarrad al-fagr ᶜannok— weyaglaᶜ mada'ā.
Wankheito lel-molma yeẓarret ma yewanni,
Mithel al-beᶜīr illi khabrīn ma ᶜashā.

Walā lo ma al-ḥayii min al-maḥalīg ḥanni,
Middat ḥayāti—wana māshi warrā.

The fool jumps up to greet his guest,
But each time we meet, it's the end of rest.
Such lavish sacrifices—too much blood to clean—
He thinks he makes everyone glad and free of sin.

So many guests his hospitality stuffs!
Spiced ghee rivers from him gush.
How we'll miss him when he leaves!
But waiting on his path is all that lives.

He tries to visit like a delicate gazelle,

Wishing poverty away from you—he throws it to hell.
But he gives communal feasts only fearless farts
Like those of a camel before his dinner starts.

All God's creatures can live without his strife
But me—I'll follow his footsteps the rest of my life.

IV.

al-Billij, Christmas Night, 1985

ṢUBḤI [*still in Hebrew*]: Remember Manṣūr? He is in Switzerland. His girlfriend, Ursula, took him there. He can't leave because he still doesn't have a Swiss passport. So Ursula, who's now his wife, came here with a big pack of money to give to his father. But his father would not touch it. "Give me back my son," he yelled.
And remember Ḥamd? He married his Dutch girlfriend, Lizzy. She has converted to Islam. She even veils. They live in Nuwēbᶜa and have a business where they take tourists on camelback all over the place. But they don't live with the Bedouin. They don't live with the Egyptians either. They live in the middle of the road between the two.
And Rubḥi? Remember him? Last week he and Ruth left for Florida. Her father bought plane tickets for them and their three children. She couldn't take it any more. The Egyptians treat all these foreign women who fall in love with us and marry us as prostitutes, and the policemen gave her a lot of grief.
And you wouldn't believe it! Mūsa, who used to call himself Mike, and started all this Beat-meets-Bedouin brouhaha—he shaved off his long hair and beard, traded his jeans for some beautiful Saudi caftans, sold his cafe to Shgēṭef, and married his own cousin, the Fool's daughter. Next year, they plan to ḥajj to Mecca together. When the Israelis ran the show, we tried hard to be Egyptian-style Muslims. But now, under the Egyptians, the old folks are into Saudi-style Islam,[3] and me and my buddies are goofing around with Christmas. But Mike and Shgēṭef are on their way to Mecca—who would have believed that?

8
THE SYMBOLIC BATTLE COORDINATOR

Al-Galīd

The struggle of man against [oppressive] rule is the struggle of memory against forgetting . . . And these days the memory has become irreal, as if a caricature . . . In times when history still moved slowly, events were few and far between and easily committed to memory. They framed a commonly accepted *backdrop* for thrilling scenes of adventure in private life. Nowadays, history moves at a brisk clip. A historical event, though soon forgotten, sparkles the morning after with the dew of novelty. No longer a backdrop, it is now the *adventure* itself, an adventure enacted before the backdrop of the commonly accepted banality of private life.[1]

MILAN KUNDERA
The Book of Laughter and Forgetting

"Every tribe has to have a father. This father is succeeded by (*ʿagab*) two sons. These two sons are followed by their two sons, and these four grandsons who succeed the first father make the four *rbāʿ* of the tribe (*rubʿ*, singular—quarter). The sons of these four grandsons are the ones after whom the *frūʿ* are named (*faraʿ*, singular—stream, tributary). Then there are the sons of these sons, who form the *nbāz* (*nabaz*, singular—nickname). And each nabaz is divided into *khamsāt* (*khamsa*, singular—five). And most importantly, no one can be a Bedouin without having a khamsa."

So said the late Mūsa abu-ʿAteish, the founder of the short-lived Smuggling Court, who in his old age was an oral thesaurus of sorts for genealogies not only of the Mzeina, but of the rest of the Ṭawara tribes. This was also a typical answer many men gave me when I asked if they could explain how tribes were built. When I asked women the same question, many said that tribes and other abstractions of chains of succession were men's business.

I was very pleased with this abstract though indigenously narrated model of the tribe. I could directly compare it to Evans-Pritchard's model of the Nuer (1940)—the Nilotic progenitor of all anthropological tribes. An enthusiastic diary entry from my first year in the field (1976) reads:

> The parallels between what the Mzeina conceive of as a tribe and the classic tribal structure are striking. Two moieties stem from the ancestor. (It is interesting to note, though, that the Mzeina do not have an indigenous term for "moiety.") These two moieties divide into four equal phratries which the Mzeina call "quarters." The phratries divide into clans that the Mzeina term "streams." It is unclear, though, whether or not these stream-like clans divide symmetrically from the phratries. It is interesting to note that the

◄ A TRIBAL ELDER.

"nbāz" units are often named not after the unit's progenitor but after his nickname, like for example, the Date Frond Stumps (*al-Karānfa*) or the Baldheads (*al-Garʿān*). One might be able to compare these with the Nuer maximal lineages. The "khamsāt" seem to parallel the Nuer's minimal lineages. But in this case, unlike the Nuer, the dual symmetry of division is somehow lost from the clans on. As for the "khamsa," it is similar to the typical five-generations-deep blood feud unit mentioned in all the literature discussing the Arab tribe.

But alas, the Mzeina didn't last long in my notes as a Nuer facsimile. If the Nuer's tribal structure was "ordered anarchy," and other Bedouin tribes resembled them,[2] from my painstakingly collected genealogies I gradually discovered that the Mzeina tribal structure was an anarchy without any order. A diary entry from my second year in the field (1977) reads:

Time to draw a big chart of the genealogical relationships of the whole tribe. I have enough individual genealogies to construct it. For the last three nights, I combed my fieldnotes to extract all the relevant data. Somehow I can't put it all together. I write and erase and frown and write and erase. Even the Ghawānma, which everyone seems to agree is the purest of the phratries, is a total mess. Take for example the Ṭabāṭba nabaz or maximal lineage group. Some say it descended from the Wlād abu-Ṣabḥā. Others say that the Ṭabāṭba descended from the Neḥeirāt. Three men said that the Ṭabāṭba's original name should have been the Ramaḍiyyīn, because they descended from someone named Ramaḍān. Several elders from the Ghseināt phratry argue that the Ṭabāṭba are not direct descendants of the tribal ancestor Faraj, but joined the tribe along with the Safāiḥa when these two groups were seeking refuge with the Mzeina because of a blood feud they escaped in Saudi Arabia. On the larger scale, there isn't even agreement on whether Faraj was the only progenitor of the tribe, or whether he was joined by someone named Shadhdhān. There is a big argument whether Shadhdhān was Faraj's best childhood friend, his uncle, his servant, perhaps even a slave. This is a total chaos, and I am desperate. I've got to have this chart, say my professors, and I've got to have it right. Otherwise, my colleagues might invalidate my fieldwork.[3] Tomorrow I should look for a jeep going in the direction of Mūsa abu-ʿAteish's encampment.

Ten days later I arrived at Mūsa's encampment. We spent four whole days trying to regroup the genealogical data, but no luck. Finally, Mūsa had a hearty laugh and said, "Well, ya Smadar, when you write about the Mzeina, forget what I told you last year about the typical Bedouin tribe. We are not like the rest of them, the Bedouin. We are a big mess. We are scattered all over, and our khamsāt are all scrambled (*makhalūṭa*)."

Indeed, in the sphere of the tribe as a whole, it was very difficult to create a successive order of descent and arrange the lineages in some sort of historical order. But all the while, each Mzeini adult, man or woman, was definitely able to clearly recite his or her version of personal descent line for at least five generations deep. And this struck me as paradoxical and odd.

Though the Mzeinis conceived of tribes as separate and independent entities, the Mzeina was a member of the Ṭawara—an alliance uniting all the South Sinai tribes. This alliance was divided into two major factions (*ḥizb*): one consisted of the Mzeina, ʿAleigāt, and Ḥamāda tribes, the other, the Ṣawālḥa, Garārsha, and Wlād Saʿīd tribes. Three other tribes were nonallied. These were the Jebaliyya, a small fraction of the Ḥeweiṭāt, and the Bani Wāṣel.[4]

Just as the Mzeina differed from the classic Bedouin tribe, there were further paradoxical relationships between the Ṭawara alliance, of which the Mzeina was a member, and the classic Bedouin intertribal alliance. The classic Bedouin alliance was termed *ʿashīra*—a concept that implied that members of such a large group were to be associated by blood relationship or by marriage.[5] The ancestors of the tribes that formed the ʿashīra were also blood- or marriage-related, and this, in turn, was reflected in the ʿashīra myth of origin (cf. Marx 1967, 1977*b*). The ancestors of the tribes that formed the Ṭawara, however, had no kinship or marriage relations. The Ṭawara mythology, though, was woven around a series of battles that marked the arrival of the Mzeina to the South Sinai around the seventeenth century. Perhaps this lack of common ancestry accounted for the fact that the South Sinai alliance was named after the topography of the area, Ṭawara, from *ṭūr* (mountain), whereas other alliances in the region, such as the Rawala, the Shammar, or the ʿAnazah were named after their founders.

Throughout their histories, the region's largest tribes were always engaged in intertribal warfare. The heroic deeds of these tribes' warriors were memorized and passed from one generation to the next through epic poetry that could be dated as far back as pre-Islamic times.[6] Ṭawara members, in contrast, though able to recite such poems, candidly admitted that they picked them up from the radio or from poets of the Ṭarabīn, Aḥeiwāt, or Tiyāha (the neighboring tribes, members of the Negev-North Sinai alliance). Aside from a continual border dispute with the Ṭarabīn, the oldest living members of the Ṭawara in the 1970s, whose personal memory dated back to the 1880s, could not recall any intertribal raid or conflict in which they personally engaged. I assumed that the lack of large-scale pastoralism in the South Sinai diminished their interest in controlling vast pasturelands through intertribal warfare. The very few incidents of violence the Ṭawara elders remembered concerned individual British and German gentry who explored and mapped the peninsula while it was still under Ottoman rule, and therefore were suspected as spies. Among the Mzeina, poetry about war mainly protested foreign occupation of the Sinai, rather than celebrating heroic deeds in battle against other Bedouin tribes.

"So what's the point in dividing the alliance into two rival factions?" I asked.

"Each tribe in each faction should act as a legal guarantor for the other two tribes in its faction in case intertribal war breaks out someday," explained many Mzeini men, young or old. "Our history started here with an intertribal war. Although we do not have wars now, we can never tell about the future."

Another paradox existed between what the Mzeinis perceived as the typical structure of a Bedouin tribe and their own structure. Huwēshel, the middle-aged son of one of the Mzeina's three supreme court judges, expressed it eloquently: "If we really believed in our khamsāt, and didn't turn to them only when disputes broke out and tribal holidays were celebrated, we wouldn't have had very rich people and very poor people and people in between. But because so many of us choose to ignore their own kin when they smell a little money, some of us are very rich, and some are very poor" (cf. Hart 1970). Perhaps if he were an anthropologist, he would have phrased the same idea differently, arguing that because the fission and fusion model surfaced into the social reality only at moments of crisis or communal ritual, the Mzeinis could not, in their everyday life, live up to the ideal of an egalitarian, pastoral democracy (cf. Lewis 1961).

And perhaps all these paradoxes were of the sort that interest only anthropologists. In the flow of everyday life, Mzeinis rarely reflected about the problematics of a society that had an egalitarian ideology, but actually was not egalitarian. Nor were they bothered by the striking incongruity between their personal descent lines and their communal genealogies. And aside from an occasional recitation of a warfare poem (usually into some scholar's tape recorder), they never prepared for intertribal battles. Both in everyday life and during holidays, they were struggling to maintain some sort of human dignity through allegorical enactments of their tradition while their land kept oscillating between Egypt and Israel in accordance with the superpowers' whims. They perceived both the Egyptians and the Israelis as occupiers who took away from them their pride, freedom, and independence. And in their struggle to preserve their tradition, they felt they had to present a united front.

But this was difficult. While trying to act out their tradition, particularly during communal ancestral pilgrimages, the acuteness of the structural paradoxes immanent in both the Ṭawara and the Mzeina existence qua classic Bedouin emerged. Communal rituals were awkward reminders for the Mzeinis that, despite the ways their lives had modernized and changed, they still formed a distinct set of nomadic cultural categories with its own idiosyncratic history. They were wage-labor Bedouin who resembled yet differed from those pastoralists whom they cherished and made into their archetype.

Ironically, the Israeli and later the Egyptian governors of the South Sinai encouraged communal tribal rituals. Because of the Bedouin tradition of hospitality, they knew they were always to be invited. They used this invitation to make their presence felt. The Mzeinis then felt even more pressed to orchestrate a show of unity almost impossible to achieve due to the three structural paradoxes in their tribal existence.

Only one Mzeini, the Galīd, was able to help both his tribe and the tribal alliance reconstruct their traditional unity in keeping with these paradoxes. People explained to me that he was traditionally a tribal warrior of sorts—a man who, in case tribal warfare broke out, would be the one to coach and coordinate the various troops, and afterwards to negotiate for peace. But since there were no intertribal wars, and a rebellion against the occupying government was impossible to organize, his role was merely symbolic. A Symbolic Battle Coordinator.

The Galīd was able to assume symbolic ritual leadership because he was almost one of a kind—a traditional Bedouin. He was one of those rare Mzeinis or Ṭwairis who lived mainly from pastoralism, still conducting some form of the traditional *riḥla* (annual migration cycle).

He traced a relatively pure descent to Faraj, the ancestor of the Mzeina, and he was the only Mzeini whose personal descent and communal genealogy did not conflict. Amazingly, only a handful of tribesmen argued over his version of his genealogy (though almost everyone definitely disagreed with his version of their genealogies). Most importantly, in both the spheres of tribal and of intertribal affairs, the Galīd was the only person capable of a solo summation of a decision made through a process of consensus either between the phratries of the Mzeina or between the factions of the Ṭawara.[7]

Like the Pueblo Indian ritual pair of kachina and clown (Handelman 1981), the Galīd often appeared with the Fool. But while the Indian clowns reaffirmed for the audience the moral authority of the kachinas, the Mzeini Fool was careful to humorously remind the audience that the Galīd's authority was fleeting and temporary, limited to the communal ritual frame, and that the structural center of the tribe was always empty. Only in moments of situational crisis, when tribal or intertribal consensus was needed but could not be achieved, did the Fool pave the way for the Galīd's stage entrance. The Galīd would then rise up and unfold an allegory on the theme of the egalitarian, divided yet united, segmentary tribal society. Being a living remnant of traditional nomadism long gone (if ever even practiced), and therefore standing as a complete reification of what being a Mzeini or a Ṭwairi qua Bedouin meant, the Galīd was able to temporarily unite the reality of the here-and-now of wage-labor, poverty-ridden Sinai with the Bedouin aspirations for a proud and noble life, independent of any centralized government.

I.

Thursday morning, a day pilgrimages often begin, October 1976

Zuārat Faranje.[8] The Mzeina annual pilgrimage to their ancestral tomb, Faraj, literally, "the savior." From this name, the place name is conjugated into Faranje, "estrangement"—perhaps an unconscious slip, perhaps not.

Early dawn in Wadi Saʿāl. The night before, I didn't sleep a wink, rolling from side to side in my light summer sleeping bag. This is the first zuāra I will participate in. I feel as I did when I was a little girl and didn't sleep the night before the Seder, awake due to stage fright before my first time to ask the four questions. Fieldwork makes one a child of sorts anyway, having to learn new rules all over again.

Early dawn. The morning tea fires send up curling plumes of gray smoke, drifting slowly into the purple gray of the sky. It's cold. X the Ex-Smuggler hurriedly loads me into the bed of his pickup truck, together with the flour-sack tent, his third wife, and their four children. We share the small space with two large sheep that will be (as I learn later) two of the four that X's phratry will sacrifice in the late afternoon. We bump our way up the dirt road enveloped in dust, to the watershed plateau where the shrine is. X collects three more beautifully groomed mustaches dressed in pastel holiday clothes, the drape of their shiny white headdresses falling to their waist. The four men are jammed into the cab. Women, children, livestock, and other stuff in the back.

Journey to estrangement. To the "center out there" (Turner 1973). A bumpy ride in a jet black canyon fissured with striations of reddish brown. The pickup bumps along and suddenly the black wadi opens, like a mouth asking "When do we get there?" into the plateau of Faranje, into the barren heartland of the South Sinai—a windswept highland surrounded to the south by magnificent red granite mountains, towering at three thousand meters, and bounded to the north by sandstone cliffs striped purple, yellow, and beige. We enter the plateau. Jutting from its center, a white domed structure looms up with the crescent moon on its top. South of the white shrine the sun reflects on a rectangular sheet metal roof, supported by eight large square stone pillars, a wall at each end. This is the shrine's *ʿarīsha* or ritual men's club.

The ʿarīsha's rectangle is enclosed by a larger rectangle of dirt roads (some accessible only by front-wheel-drive vehicles) leading eastward to the Gulf of ʿAqaba, westward to the Gulf of Suez, north to the Tih Plateau, and south to the Santa Katarina monastery. Seemingly a strategic crossroad. But on ordinary days, Mzeinis focus their strategic interest on the steep mountain passes zigzagging down into this plateau, just stuck there. Large stone storage depots stand nearby, northwest of the shrine. The place is almost deserted. Only one extended family lives here year round. In the center of their garden is a well with a small mechanized pump. Its gas tank is open. Something doesn't work.

Six-thirty in the morning. We are the first pilgrims here, small colored dots swamped by the huge landscape. X parks his pickup to the right of the depots. We quickly unload the cargo, and X's wife starts erecting the tent that will protect her privacy and modesty during the zuāra.

"It's better for your work if you hang out with the men today," says X. "Come sit in the front."

The four mustaches move to the back of the truck. Do I read anger on their faces, or is this the anthropologist's projection? We drive a very short distance across the plateau. X's brakes squeal as he stops dangerously near the east wall of the ʿarīsha. "Now it's kind of permitted," he explains his motorized intrusion into sacred space. The goats peacefully chewing their cud in the shade of the ʿarīsha are startled when the humans reclaim their ritual space, and scatter in every direction.

"Lazy scumbags! Can't trust them!" X seethes, pacing furiously inside the ʿarīsha, up to his ankles in heaps of dried goat shit, his hand swatting the flies from his face. "They haven't even gotten rid of the bones from last year's sacrifice!"

From the direction of the orchard three men in well-worn caftans walk hesitantly into the ʿarīsha. The anthropologist is relieved that she recognizes them and won't have to go through the embarrassment of asking their names and their kinship and descent lines for her notes. They are old Ḍaifallah and his two sons, Morḍi and Darwīsh—the caretakers of the shrine. X, his fine mustachioed friends, and I shake hands with them while kissing the air.

Shabby old Ḍaifallah greets us, "Welcome! Welcome! The blessings of our father Faraj be upon you."

X and his friends do not reply. The anthropologist is stunned. This is the first time she has witnessed a greeting exchange that is not reciprocated.

"You, the shrine-caretakers, what the hell have you been doing all year? Why is this place as dirty as you are?" X bursts out in his cigarette-raspy voice, sailing on with a long string of insults. These insults, which in normal life would have brought him to court, perhaps signal that we have left the linear progression of everyday time.[9]

"And where is the firewood [for cooking the sacrificial meal]?" In his anger, X reaches his hand into his caftan pocket and throws the keys of the pickup in the direction of Darwīsh.

"Fill up the truck with firewood and be back here in an hour," he snaps. "Take some of the youngsters to help you. Get moving! Go!"

Darwīsh starts the pickup and disappears in a cloud of thin dust. His brother Morḍi walks back toward the orchard as old Ḍaifallah moans and seats himself, carefully placing his back against one of the pillars. X and his friends stand silent, faces frozen.

I am at a loss. Later, after I have attended the zuāra three consecutive years, the anthropologist will realize that this sequence is repeated exactly every year. But now I am shocked at the violent scene, and the anthropologist wonders, if this is the beginning of the ritual, what kind of data, if any, will she get?

Morḍi returns from the garden with a large rake and starts to vigorously rake the goat shit and the butchered bones out of the ʿarīsha. Since the four elegant mustaches and I are still planted where we stand, he rakes around us. X looks at the small pile of shit we are standing in, surrounded by the now-clear ground, and gingerly shakes out the hem of his immaculate caftan where the dust has settled. He makes a small gesture with his head and we leave the ʿarīsha.

Seven-thirty in the morning. The whole Faranje area looks as if it has had a face-lift. Stacks of firewood are piled northwest of the ʿarīsha. Ḍaifallah brings from one of the depots a huge, thick, and heavy traditional copper cooking pot, blackened from countless fires for cooking the sacrificial meal. He returns for three large factory-made aluminum pots with side-handles (which had to be purchased to replace the three old copper ones stolen earlier by tourists hunting for personal museum pieces).

Family after family arrives in pickup trucks and erects their flour-sack tents in two crescents, one north of the shrine, the other, south of the ʿarīsha. Groups of men arrive in pickups sagging from the excessive load. I help old Ḍaifallah to dig out long narrow handwoven rugs. Even faded, their colors are striking oranges, greens, reds, blacks, whites, and blues. We spread them on the inner rectangle of the ʿarīsha and Ḍaifallah chooses the best rug for the northwestern wall. He places reclining pillows along it at regular intervals.

"He who leans against this wall will be facing Mecca," the old man smiles at me toothlessly. "Here will sit *al-kbār*." The big ones who are the old ones. "This is the wall of our leaders."

Meanwhile, as if following a script, one that will be repeated in years to come, the men flow into the soothing shadow of the clean ʿarīsha. The Mzeinis carry small bundles wrapped in cloth. Neatly wrapped inside are smaller bundles of green coffee beans, tea, sugar, and flour. Ḍaifallah has already changed his clothes and has been promoted to head of the kitchen crew. Festive but restrained, he collects the bundles and opens them, pouring the contents onto one of the four separate piles, and supervises the serving of tea and coffee.

"You are a guest upon us," he declares to every man who enters the ʿarīsha empty-handed. The anthropologist knows these men and she knows they are not Mzeini tribesmembers.

In her fieldnotes of the 1978 zuāra she will find the following entry:

Transformation. Perhaps this is the meaning of the throwing of the keys. X the Ex-Smuggler brings with him his everyday power of economic and social resources from the margins of the territory into its center. By throwing the keys he initiates the process of transforming Faranje from an empty forsaken plateau, just stuck in the middle of Mzeini territory, into the sanctified center out there. Or perhaps I just look for symbolic meanings, and the throwing of the keys is just the throwing of the keys.

Eight-fifteen on an October morning, 1976. The rugs begin to fill up in straight lines. X and the mustaches, in contrast, are the center of an amorphous group, ebbing and flowing like musical chairs, squatting in a semicircle in the southeast corner of the ʿarīsha, opposite to the Wall of Honor. All are dressed in elegant terylene caftans in soft colors, some with matching jackets, their headdresses secured to their heads with two black hoops. And many have well-groomed mustaches. They offer each other expensive American or less-expensive Israeli cigarettes. Above them rises a cloud of pleasing scent, a mixture of fancy after shaves and colognes. The semicircle is moving constantly. Every so often, two or three men leave the ʿarīsha together and confer privately, squatting on their hamstrings in the shadow of a pickup truck. When they return they push to a new place in the shifting semicircle.

X returns from a private conference with a mustache. They look toward the empty wall facing Mecca. X glances at his automatic gold watch. Eight-thirty-five. He glances back at the inviting cushions and beautiful rug by the Wall of Honor. Does the wall look back? X whips out his money roll and peels off a one hundred lira bill bearing the face of Theodore Hertzel[10] and gives orders to Mnēfi, one of the young hangers-on of the ex-smugglers' corner: "The Galīd and the rest of 'em, al-kbār. Your pickup. Don't forget the change."

Mnēfi disappears into a thick cloud of dust pointing towards ʿEin al-Akhaḍar, the summer residence of the Galīd, or "our heart" as the Mzeinis refer to this oasis.

Nine-thirty. The pickup, jouncing on its worn springs, returns. It circles the ʿarīsha and stops with a groan in the middle of the dirt road that separates the ᶜarīsha from the shrine. To my surprise, four resplendent old nobles leap gracefully to the ground. One of them immediately straightens up, and with a dignified stance walks to the passenger side of the cab, grandly opening the door. As a short, bony old man steps stiffly out, a hush falls and people talk in whispers. The four tall men struggle to shorten their stride to match the halting pace of the short old man, who uses his walking stick to support his dignity, not to increase his speed. As the five nobles pass, the anthropologist writes in her fieldnotes that unlike the ex-smugglers, these nobles are wearing the traditional Sinai headdresses, as though they came out of the pages of a nineteenth-century British travelogue. Their white caftans, faded from too many launderings, are topped by faded black vests, their many small cloth buttons unbuttoned. Washed-out brown or black woolen wraps, threaded vertically with gold, hang cloak-like from their shoulders. Secured with a woolen scarf, their faded white headdresses are simply wrapped around their heads. The thin white stubble of their beards, only a centimeter wide, traces their jawlines. With their air of another century, they radiate traditional authority.

As if on cue, all the men rise when the elders enter the ᶜarīsha. They dutifully deliver their bundles of coffee, tea, sugar, and flour to Ḍaifallah, who pours these final contributions on the neat communal piles. These piles seem to me to be the physical evidence of the ties reestablished this morning, defining the tribe's membership. After the delivery is finished, the nobles pass quickly from one person to another, guest or Mzeini, shaking the hand, kissing the air three times, moving on, two hundred and seven times.

After I, the only woman in the ᶜarīsha, have shaken all the dignitaries' hands, my adoptive uncle ᶜAṭṭallah whispers in my ear, "The short man is Shaᶜabān abu-Srayaᶜ, the Symbolic Battle Coordinator of the Mzeina. The tall one who's blind in his right eye is his brother. And the other three are the [traditional] supreme court of the tribe." After years of reading British travel literature on the Bedouin, I realize with shock that this is a moment when the tribal nobles pictured in nineteenth-century drawings and photographs appear in a contemporary colonial context. The Galīd of the Mzeina, the Symbolic Battle Coordinator in the flesh, not in a tribal myth.

As though performing for an audience, the elders simultaneously remove their cloaks, haughtily seating themselves upon the rug of honor, the Galīd in the middle, two elders on either hand.

The anthropologist is so excited. Immediately, dozens of questions she would like to ask, and dozens of topics she would like to discuss, and masses of information she would like to verify, mushroom in her brain. But I restrain her. The ritual flows in its tempo, and I tell her that she cannot impose on it her own anthropological caprice. So she makes do, leafing in her notebook, reading past entries about the Galīd.

January 1976. The crossroad of Wadi Mukattab and Wadi Firān. Winter encampment, under the lee of a rock bearing Nabatian rock art. Manṣūr's family and I whiled away the evening talking about the impact of migrant labor on nomadism. His wife says that in the whole Mzeina tribe there is only one poor man who makes his living solely from pastoralism. Someone named Shaᶜabān abu-Srayaᶜ. He has around sixty goats, exactly nine camels, eight male and one female. I am impressed. The average Mzeini has seven goats and one camel, if any. That Shaᶜabān, so says Manṣūr, is the only Mzeini who carries out a full migratory cycle, like the one Mzeinis like to tell stories about and to perform only parts of, if they do it at all. I'll have to meet him. The man sounds like a remnant of the Bedouin traditional past.

The anthropologist looks up from her notebook at the Galīd, thinking to herself how hard it is to survive by pastoralism alone under the precarious conditions of the Sinai. The Galīd stands to greet Sheikh ᶜAlwān, who brought with him his entourage of military officers and their miniskirted secretaries. These non-Bedouins have come to experience the ritual and to make their presence felt. She goes back to her notes.

Beginning of March, 1976. Bir al-Bāgha. Centimeters from the temporary borderline of the recent Kissinger disengagement agreement. I spend the day at the home of Farrūja, a powerful Old Woman of the ᶜAleigāt tribe. Her brother is one of the tribe's judges. Her father was also a judge. Her sister, so I learn, is married to one of the most important men of the Mzeina, Shaᶜabān al-Galīd, someone who is to coordinate intertribal raids in case, God forbid, there should be any. But in the life outside of stories these never occur—so says Farrūja. Farrūja explained to me that the ᶜAleigāt, the Mzeina, and the Ḥamāda tribes constitute a moiety of the Ṭawara. This is why her sister's marriage is good, she says. The second wife of that Mzeina Battle Coordinator is his cousin. And this is why that marriage is good, she says. And the two wives churn yogurt together [i.e., they live in separate households but in the same encampment] and get along fine, which is also good, she summarizes.

The noise level in the ʿarīsha increases. Many discussions focus on the likelihood of Israel giving up the Sinai as a result of the 1973 war. The anthropologist glances over at the Wall of Honor, and in the midst of political arguments, thinks about the Symbolic Battle Coordinator's fulfillment of traditional Bedouin leadership values. The Galīd probably married his parallel cousin to keep the title in the family, and Farrūja's sister to strengthen the alliance between the Mzeina and the ʿAleigāt. She continues to leaf through her notebook.

End of March, 1976. Sil Themmān, at the edge of the desolate Gaʿ. This is the only encampment of a remnant of the Bani Wāṣel tribe, a tribe that began to decline both in territory and numbers when the Mzeina settled in the South Sinai in the seventeenth century (cf. Levi 1988). I sit with the eldest of the Bani Wāṣel, who validates the assumption that many Mzeinis hold, that their lineages are all scrambled, as they say. Parts of the Ghawānma phratry remained relatively pure, being more concentrated, living mainly in the center of the tribe's territory—the ring of mountains and wadis surrounding Faranje. Among the whole tribe, there is only one extended family that can trace its descent directly from Faraj, the father of the tribe, the eldest of the Bani Wāṣel adds. This is the family of Shaʿabān abu-Srayaʿ. And so he is the Galīd.

"Galīd," the anthropologist thinks as she looks around for a pilgrim familiar with classical Arabic. What does it mean? Could it be a conjugation of the classical *taqalīd*, an uncritical faith in tradition or custom, emanating from an authoritative source, the qalīd?[11] The fact that his descent from Faraj is said to be almost pure gives him traditional authority. She warns me that if I cross the ʿarīsha to ask one of the Mzeini teachers, I'll draw attention to myself. I decide to stay where I am.

May 1976. Ghānma's hut. The daily midmorning gathering of married women, babies, and toddlers. They talk about authentic Bedouin cuisine, *jarīsha* with *ʿafīg*, the cracked wheat porridge mixed with grated dried goat cheese. How monotonous it is. How boring. Dull. "If there are no fish, my mom complains when we eat those cans of bully-beef, peppered up with tomato paste and cumin, and she reminisces about the days when she ate only jarīsha with ᶜafīg and was never constipated," says one, rolling with laughter. "She and the wives of the Galīd," says her friend with a gesture of dismissal, and they all laugh contemptuously.

Once more the anthropologist looks across the ᶜarīsha at the Galīd. He returns her gaze with curiosity. She looks down and thinks about the entry she has just read. Unlike other Bedouin, the Galīd lives off his pastoralism alone, and so he stays away from the well-grazed vicinity of the main dirt roads, where many Bedouin families have moved because the merchants from al-ᶜArīsh came with their trucks regularly once a week to make money by selling not only fresh produce, but canned food, beads, fabrics, batteries, radios, car parts, refilled propane tanks, dried corn, and whatnot. Away from the dirt roads, the Galīd cannot easily supplement his traditional diet.

July 1976. An evening chéz Mnēfi's Cafe, Abu-Zneima. Sheikh Ṣāleḥ of the Wlād Saᶜīd: "And then, can you imagine, the new military governor asked, no less, if Shaᶜabān abu-Srayaᶜ can be replaced. Can you believe it?! Shaᶜabān abu-Srayaᶜ and not anyone else! He said that the Galīd is a really nice man, who understands honor, but he has no power. He [the governor] is looking for someone whom he can find when he needs him, not someone poor like this, who wanders around just with his goats. He wants someone who will agree to work with him. Sheikh ᶜAlwān explained to the governor that the Galīd doesn't work with the government. Never. Absolutely never. The Galīd is a noble Bedouin. There is no one more noble than he is. The government has to let him be. And that's that."

The anthropologist looks around her at the flow of men and the still center of the nobles sitting before the Wall of Honor. The power of the Galīd is evident as an expression of the consensus of the tribe as an autonomous whole, not a power that the Israeli governor can coopt or use for his own needs. She leafs through her notebook back to where she is writing today's description of the pilgrimage.

"What are they talking about?" I can't stop her from probing X, catching him between an entrance and an exit from the amorphous mass milling about the wall opposite the Wall of Honor. "Probably important things," X says seriously. "There in the middle sits our 'Number One.'"

Just before the circumambulation of the shrine is about to start, I return to my seat near ʿAṭṭallah. "What do they talk about?" I ask him. "The history of the tribe. They always talk about the history of the tribe," he answers with a bored look. "Every one of them is like the Sinai mountains—good for naught; can't be used, can't be bought." The anthropologist notes how ʿAṭṭallah molds this proverb about the Sinai mountains to comment on the irrelevance of the Mzeini nobles to daily life, even as he acknowledges their mountainous place in the tribal eternity.

ZUĀRAT FARANJE, A YEAR LATER, OCTOBER 1977: THE HOLY OF HOLIES OR THE CLIMAX OF THE RITUAL— THREE SLIDES

Slide I: The Circumambulation of the Shrine. A row of Mzeini men climbing from the ʿarīsha to the hill where Faraj is buried patiently wait in a straight line, in order for each man to individually circle the shrine. The non-Mzeinis are in the ʿarīsha.[12] Deep blue sky. Reddish brown mountains encircling the horizon. The still men's faces and the stance of their bodies reveal a reverent quietude. Only Shgēṭef the Fool waves a hand, perhaps brushing away a fly, perhaps joking with the camera lens. The anthropologist tries to find patterns: who stands where and why. Here is X, but he is not surrounded by his coterie from the ʿarīsha. And here you are, Galīd. But your entourage is scattered in the line with no apparent order. And here is Sheikh ʿAlwān, in front of him Ḥajj Ḥamdān, the old fisherman, and behind him, Rāḍi from Umm-Baʿatheirān. This is the literature's acephalous, egalitarian society at its best. No hierarchy and no flashes of charisma.

Slide II: The Argument. After the circumambulation, protected by the precarious noon shadow of the depot, the straight line of the previous slide transforms itself into a mass of people standing and arguing heatedly. The topic (according to anthropological interpretations): an attempt to negotiate a way to force the classic Bedouin tribal structure of four phratries onto the Mzeina, a nondually organized tribe (cf. Lavie 1980). They are arguing for this so that the number of sheep slaughtered can be divided equally among the phratries of the not-so-classic Mzeina. There is a staged, phony quality to this argument. Although hands rise in emphatic gestures or clamp on the arm or wrist of the listener, on many of the faces there is the hint of a smile. In the middle, amidst the standing squabblers, you squat with your entourage, Galīd, leaning on the walking stick planted in the ground before you. With your outmoded dress you look like an island of stability in the midst of this seething crowd. Pity about the film, you'll say to me tomorrow, in your end-of-summer encampment, ʿEin al-Akhaḍar, the Mzeina's heart. Every year, it's just the same argument, you'll say.

Slide III: The Sacrifice. The harsh sun beats down upon the plaza beneath the shrine. The non-Mzeinis and the officers with their mini-skirted secretaries join the crowd. But this time the anthropologist notices that within the human crescent there are definable groups.

The carcasses of nineteen dead sheep are lying in front of everyone. Standing between the crowd and the sheep, X and another ex-smuggler hold the last, twentieth sheep. A thin jet of blood arcs and stains X's peach caftan. (I've seen a change of clothes in his pickup.) Standing astride, the hem of his caftan tucked up in his belt, Huwēshel, the son of a judge, holds his scimitar in his right hand, drops of blood falling to the ground. He dedicates the sheep to God and to the Mzeina.

In the second row, to the right of the empty center, stands Sheikh ʿAlwān in his jaunty turquoise caftan, smoking a cigarette. Sticking close to him, the officers and their female entourage. Captain Yoram takes a picture. Captain Doubi covers his nose and mouth with a checkered handkerchief. In spite of the crowd, one can see a space between the turquoise caftan and the pastel caftans of X's coterie, who stand in a group together to the right of Sheikh ʿAlwān, defining another social category. You and your entourage, and the elders who came and sat with you in the ʿarīsha, also keep some distance from the sheikh and his entourage. Despite the crowd, you spaciously place yourselves to the left of the empty center.

In the third row, a hodgepodge of Mzeinis and their non-Mzeini guests. Here is Shgēṭef the Fool, poking his head out of the empty center space, sticking out his tongue and making a face for my camera.

Returning to the foreground of the slide, to the sheep's carcasses. They lie in four piles. In the first, second, and third piles there are four carcasses. In the fourth pile, three. The sheep X holds will probably join the fourth pile.

Tomorrow you'll explain: the four piles represent the four tributaries of the Mzeina.

Four tributaries? I'll question, but Faraj had two sons, ʿAli and Ghānem. He also had an uncle, or a servant, or a slave (depending on who recites the mythical genealogy) whose name was Sadhdhān. ʿAli, Ghānem, and Sadhdān, three, I'll argue.

No, you'll say dogmatically. Ghawānma—one, you'll fold your thumb over; Ghseināt and Meḥāsna—two, folding your index finger; Darārma—three, folding your middle finger; Shadhādhna—four, folding your ring finger.[13] Period.

But Ghsein, Meḥeisen, and Darrūm are ʿAli's sons, I will continue to argue. They are one generation above the generation of Ghānem and ʿAli. Sadhdhān, as a matter of fact, belongs to the generation of Faraj, I'll say, and it will suddenly dawn on the anthropologist that this is a moment of cross-cultural insight while she will reflect on the relevance of the proliferation of segments among the Libyan Bedouin (cf. Peter 1960).

Every Bedouin tribe must have four tributaries, you'll conclude with finality.

Immediately afterwards, Shgēṭef the Fool will wink from behind you. And I will write, not knowing whether to put, in the parentheses at the end, a question mark or an exclamation mark.

II.

Wadi Firān, August 1977, 2 months before the zuāra

A clear hot night, moonless, still. The air, entangled in the branches of the date palms, refuses to move up the wadi from the Suez Gulf. The sudden clap of the wings of a bat, having peacefully finished his nocturnal meal of ripe dates. Tomorrow, at the harvest, someone will curse it. The Firān oasis, ten kilometers of densely planted date palms, looks like one big slumber party. Group after group arrives here from all corners of the South Sinai for the annual date harvest and they all camp on the ground, tentless, even without the temporary flour-sack tents. Just like that, without any kind of privacy, even for the women. The only hiding place is between the trees, and when more privacy is needed, the corners where the clay of the wadi kisses the huge reddish whitish grayish walls of the canyon.

Night in the Firān. The cloud of smoke from many campfires chases the mosquitoes away. The whole time the constant roar of pickups and jeeps racing up and down the oasis interrupts the constant monotonous hubbub of nonstop talking through the night. Despite the motorized roar, snatches of conversation float from one circle to another.

Muscles loosen at night, groaning the pain of a hard day's work. My demanding, dangerous climb to the date tree top, a rope securing my waist to the trunk like a fetus with its umbilical cord, the stumps of the newly cut fronds piercing my bare feet; the knife drumming rhythmically on the base of the bunch of dates, and the rising anxiety (despite the banality of gravity) that the bunch will not fall exactly where the plastic tarp is spread; the fast descent from the tree to the mirthfulness of children and the bent backs of the childless widows and widowers gathering the few dates that miss the tarp—the children to prepare for the responsibilities of the future, and the childless elders because of the poverty of the present; the tying of the corners of the tarp, the dates inside, and its communal loading on the backs of my adoptive family and me; the slicing lower back pain that immediately follows, when I bend over, arranging the dates for drying on another tarp; the fist stuffing, compressing, crushing the dates into the *shanna*, the goatskin that gradually starts to be reshaped into a goat, the same goat that was slaughtered a week ago by our hosts in our honor. But when I see how our shannas pile up and up, I smile contentedly, saying to myself, "*kheir wājed*," "a bounty of good," that lush coinage reserved especially for the date harvest in the Firān.

A date harvest night in the Firān. We encamp in the garden of Mismaḥ al-Dgheishi, the old man of the Dgheishāt clan of the Garārsha, who lives here all year round and who is in charge of the peace of the date trees of many Dahabians, including the pollination of the female flowers by the male flowers in the spring, for which he gets two bunches (*ginu*) from each tree pollinated by his sons. Every date tree contains twenty-four *geirāt*s (karats), which are ownership shares. Mismaḥ is in charge of our karats. His wife serves us a large platter of rice and a little dried fish from the ten dried parrot fish we have given him as a gift for his dedication in protecting of our karats.

As we eat, I listen to Abu-Mūsa, the oldest fisherman of Dahab, who, with Mismaḥ, conjures up memories of years gone by, of bountiful and poor crops, of disputes, some settled, some unresolved, concerning ownership of land and trees.

A jeep squeals nearby as we drink the sweet dessert tea. Swēlem jumps out. Trained in Israel, this Jebaliyya tribesman is the Firān's first-aid medic and ambulance driver. Since his return from Tel Aviv to Wadi Firān, he has been very eager to be the cultural broker for all sorts of strangers of the academic persuasion. Sure enough, he chooses our circle and seats himself at my side.

"If you want to, I can take you to the *barlimān* (parliament) of the Ṭawara," he whispers in my ear. "It happens only in Wadi Firān and only during the date harvest. And even then, not every year, only in years when there are good crops so many people come, like this year."

We leave the circle abruptly, without good-byes or apologies, as everyone does to move to the next circle. Everyone knows that this is prime time for networking, and it is a pity to waste time on etiquette and all that sort of thing.

Swēlem and I bounce our way for a short time in his jeep, heading to the tribal alliance's "parliament." The moon is yet to rise, but to preserve what little privacy the people camping between the trees have, Swēlem doesn't use his lights. "People your age drive with full lights," I tease him. "*Ganazīḥ* (dandies)," he mutters.

Swēlem talks nonstop to cram in all the details before we arrive at our destination. After his long stay in Israel he has become an insider-outsider of sorts, an anthropologist perhaps, analyzing for me the composition of the relationships about who's who and who's here.

"Write, it's important," he encourages me, as I struggle to write in the galloping jeep. "When you read it afterwards, it might help you to understand what's going on."

"Everyone who's anyone is here this year," he reels on, as he pulls over to give himself more time to talk. The anthropologist writes blindly, by the light of the dim stars coming through the date tree tops, scribbling hurriedly as Swēlem tries to shove in the last bit of cultural explanation before we get out of the jeep.

"Pay attention to three kinds of people especially," he says. "First of all, this year, many of the old fishermen, whose fathers and grandfathers and great-grandfathers were fishermen, have shown up. They don't own many karats, but they always used to exchange dried fish for dates. Many of them have not been here since they [the Israelis] opened the new asphalt road, because they started marketing fresh fish to Eilat. But this year they came with dried fish. They are losing money, I want you to know, but they came. As a matter of fact some of them were here two years ago, because we had bountiful crops then too. That was the year of the big flash flood, two years after the last war [1973], the year when . . . visited in Israel and Egypt . . . what's his name, that guy . . . Kissinger."

The anthropologist writes with enthusiasm, blessing both Swēlem's fine-tuned observations and the Bedouin custom of linking meaningful events to natural disasters.

"This year there are many ex-smugglers here too," Swēlem goes on. "When the ex-smugglers were big, they bought many karats here. Not only do they have their own dates, but many people give them gifts of whole trees [date crops]. Yesterday, my father did it. The ex told him, 'Allah will bless you and the rest of those generous people, rich with dates, who gave me the crops of twelve trees as gifts.' But he is so proud he didn't even bother to harvest my father's dates."

"Why?" the anthropologist asks in wonder.

"Not only does he pay money to the pickup driver to bring him here and back home, you think he wants to throw more money away on extra baggage that no one needs? Since they opened the road," Swēlem continues, "every year only three or four came, but this year, more have come."

Interesting, the anthropologist thinks, the 1972 opening of the road was the last straw on the smugglers' back. "And in the year of the last big flash flood, two years ago?" she asks, while actually meaning the 1975 Kissinger shuttle diplomacy.

"Well, that year many of them came, and also the year before [1974]. But in that year we didn't have a large harvest."

"Yes, I heard the harvest was small." The anthropologist signals her active listening while noting to herself that the summer of 1974 was the first Firān summer after October 1973. The 1973 war caused the Mzeini insecurity index to rise and consequently the serious guessing game to resume as to when Israel would leave the Sinai as part of an overall political settlement for the region. There is a direct connection between traditional tribal gatherings and regional political events, she theorizes. The greater the insecurity about the political future of the Sinai, the larger the gathering (cf. Marx 1977*a*).

"And guess who else has arrived here?" Swēlem asks rhetorically. "Musa *al-Garᶜān* (the Baldhead). He hasn't been here since they opened the road. He was busy making money off the Jews. You know, he was the first one to build huts for tourists, and he organized workers for the development authorities. He was the first one to drive tourists in his pickup from Nuwēbᶜa to the Monastery. He's losing now at least IL 1,500 a week just because his truck is here with him.[14] When I was a young boy, ten years ago or so, he used to come here and behave like a regular guy. Now he runs around in his pickup truck up and down the wadi doing favors for everyone."

The nouveaux riches, the anthropologist categorizes, are those who amassed capital and social influence since 1972. These people started their career as simple laborers with the Israeli developers. Due to the mutual trust created between these Bedouin and their employers, and due to their organizational and entrepreneurial skills, they became labor contractors for Israeli employers and wove a thick net of relationships with the Israeli civil and military authorities. They came to be the local and regional leaders in the everyday life of the communities gradually sedentarizing near the Israeli settlements.

"Mūsa al-Garʿan bought thirty-seven karats this year in different places [in the Firān]. He has money. And believe me, I don't know who needs date trees now. Times have changed."

"Yes, times have changed," the anthropologist repeats, while thinking to herself that she has met several nouveaux riches this week. Are they coming to cash in on their new rich power with the traditional Bedouin leadership?

"Even the Galīd of the Mzeina is here," Swēlem adds matter-of-factly, "because he has many, many karats here, from long ago. And every year, this old man harvests all of them. While everyone else tries to take the minimum they can in their pickups, he loads everything he has harvested and stuffed in shannas on his eight camels."

Thank you, Swēlem, I muse with deep gratitude. Here you have categorized for the anthropologist in me the four groups that represent traditional political-economic power: the ideological leadership of the tribe, the Symbolic Battle Coordinator and his entourage, who inherited their power through genealogical purity; the fishermen, who also inherited power, due to their clan's control of beachfront territories, enabling them to monopolize fishing and therefore have great access to dates; the ex-smugglers, who bought traditional political-economic power with money during the Egyptian occupation prior to 1967; and the nouveaux riches, who also bought this kind of power with money, but during the Israeli occupation that lasted until 1982.

Swēlem stops near a huge conversation circle of about fifty people. The human circle is enclosed by a circle of seven pickups, four jeeps, and three camels parked among the motor vehicles. We seat ourselves without the ritual greetings. Immediately, the youngest in the crowd serves us bitter coffee and then sweet tea. I question Swēlem with my eyes. "You can write what they say," he whispers. "Every parliament in every country is open to the public."

Wow! All the bigwigs are here! the anthropologist thinks. Great data! She happily writes the names of all the people present, pleased that she knows them from memory along with their tribal affiliations and social classifications. Shaᶜabān abu-Srayaᶜ, the Symbolic Battle Coordinator of the Mzeina, she writes, turning on him an objectifying gaze. He sits there like everyone else, perhaps less noticeable than others because of his faded traditional attire. He acknowledges her gaze with a gaze of his own. She feels as if she has stumbled into the theatre of politics, a play already well advanced toward the last stages of the crisis that will lead, Allah willing, to the catharsis.

*

ZĀYED [*a judge of the Ṣawālḥa tribe, his finger pointed towards Freij, a head of a very powerful family of the Jebaliyya tribe*]: And I tell you, ya Freij, we both live here all year round. This place is becoming as crowded as a city. It's impossible! More and more people who used to wander around this area are coming all the time to live here year round, without moving even a centi(meter). They come here on their goats and sheep and donkeys and camels, and the animals mill about here among the trees all year round, and they graze on the new offshoots and the young trees. It ruins the place. It becomes impossible.

FREIJ: I know. But what can we do? The Firān belongs to everyone. Almost every Ṭwairi has at least one karat here, and that makes it his right to choose to live here. We can*not* tell him no.

SHEIKH ᶜALWĀN [*of the Mzeina*]: And even if you sit here until the end of night and scream at each other, will it help? The government wants people to stop moving from one place to another. Like that [with migration], it's hard for them to know what everyone does, especially since the *faṣal* (Kissinger's disengagement agreement) after the last war [1973]. Till then it was easy to control us because the border was clear—the Bar-Lev Line and the Suez Canal. Now the new border cuts through our land here, and they are afraid. These Israelis, they are smart. They dig for us wells and give us motorized pumps on the main roads of our land. They know that people will move where there is lots of water and where the al-ᶜArishian trucks pass.

MŪSA AL-GARᶜĀN [*a Mzeini nouveau riche*]: Everything that you say, ya sheikh, it's all right and good. But they [the Israelis] help us. They also build centers for us, with clinics and schools, and for example here, in the Firān, that center they started to build, they say that in the fall there will be an Israeli guy here with his family and his jeep.

ZĀYED: An Israeli boss with his family and jeep! Allah ruin their house! They don't help us. They help themselves, even though they taught you how to make money.

Mūsa the baldhead, perhaps unsure of his newly acquired traditional power, doesn't respond to this jibe, and sulks.

ZĀYED: By God! They are really making the Firān into a city! This place is heading for ruin. We have to do something!

SHEIKH ṢĀLEḤ [*of the Wlād Saʿīd*]: What can be done? We are under the government, and the government wants us to sit in one place. No government these days wants Bedouin moving around. Not even the Saudis, who are themselves Bedouin. The Arab governments want the Bedouin only as soldiers or for the taxes they take from the money we make off tourists.

ḤAJ ʿĀYED [*an ex-smuggler of the Garārsha*]: Wait and see how the Egyptians are going to make us into urbanites everywhere we are. My sister who came for a family visit with the help of the Red Cross said that now that the Egyptians have gotten the city of Suez, they will put all the Bedouin in apartment buildings. In every apartment there will be a guest room, a bedroom for the people, a bedroom for the goats, and the balcony for the pigeons. And they promise that every house will have a telephone and a TV connection. *Khalās* (finished—that's the way it's going to be). We will have to urbanize.

MŪSA AL-GARʿĀN: The Egyptians, gentlemen, are not returning anytime soon. Their army is not good enough. Give them three, four more wars.

X [*a Mzeini ex-smuggler*]: You! Just sit tight on that money you made off the Jews. You're going to miss it. And listen to me: the Egyptians—not only will they return, but they will return and do more than Israel did. They've taken the canal away from Israel [1973], and they will eventually get here. And because Israel built and paved and brought people, they will want to show us that they are better. This is their character. They will do more.

MŪSA AL-GARʿĀN: By the life of the Prophet! The Egyptians will not return soon. They have enough troubles in Egypt, they don't need more troubles here.

ABU-MŪSA [*an elderly Mzeini fisherman*]: They *will* return, and *soon*. Because they have problems in Egypt, they will bring people here. Just like Israel, which had its own problems inside it, so it brought its people here. All of Israel is around two million, but Egypt is forty.

SHEIKH ʿALWĀN: Wait and see. Israel is always in the hands of America, and that guy came in a special plane from America to take Egypt from the hands of the Soviets and give it to America. And the Egyptians are a hungry people. They will not go with America for nothing, so America will give them back the Sinai.

Pause.

FREIJ: Ya Zāyed, my friend the judge—if you want people to do something in the Firān, this is the right time. The Americans will want the Israelis to return the Sinai to Egypt one piece after another, like they have started doing. Two or three years from now, maybe the border will cut us in the middle, between al-ʿArīsh and Ras-Muḥammad, half of us in Egypt, half of us in Israel.

When I transcribe this dialogue now in 1988, I am stunned by this exact political prophecy. The Bedouin of the South Sinai relied on cheap transistor radios and were always restlessly scanning Arabic radio stations. Not all of the news was understandable because, aside from the static, it was read in Modern Standard Arabic, which they didn't fully understand. Yet they accurately predicted the political future of the Sinai. In early 1977 they already recognized that the 1975 borderline created by the Kissinger disengagement agreement was only temporary, and that the United States would apply pressure on Israel to return the Sinai to Egypt as part of some sort of a regional settlement, perhaps to consolidate Egypt's role as a U.S. client state. Despite the fact that Anwar Sadat did not consult with the Ṭawara Bedouin before his historic late 1977 visit to Jerusalem, the borderline Freij speculated about in the above conversation (summer 1977) would be the very one to slice the peninsula by the end of 1979.

FARRŪJA [*apart from me, the only woman present, a powerful Old Woman of the ʿAleigāt, sitting slightly removed from the circle of men*]: All of what you say here is useless. The Firān belongs to all of us Ṭawara, and we cannot tell anyone not to come here. Perhaps we should make an *ʿanwa* (intertribal legislation)[15] so that we can all live here in peace.

There is an uncomfortable silence after the short and poignant comment by Farrūja. It's a good example of the brief but effective style of an Old Woman participating in male political discourse, shifting it from the conceptual level to the operational, the anthropologist writes in her fieldnotes. She wants to expand on the point, but she has to leave several empty lines, because someone breaks the silence.

X: Why all of a sudden another ʿanwa? All of us Ṭawara have only two *ʿanawāt* (plural of ʿanwa): the ʿanwa that regulates wood cutting for charcoal and the ʿanwa about camels who wander off into territories of other tribes. Everyone is fully permitted to graze his animals any place he wants.

ABU-MŪSA: But this is for as long as he builds a tent to live in, not a stone house. He can build a stone house only on lands that belong to his tribe and are written as such in the books of the Monastery. On that land his ancestors dug wells and bought karats of date trees and took the pilgrims through on camels. And Wadi Firān is for all. Every tribe has houses here and wells and date trees.

Abu-Mūsa here summarizes the traditional principles of tribal dominance of lands in the South Sinai. By presenting them in this context he gives public acknowledgment to customary values at a time when tradition is endangered by impinging superpower concerns.

MŪSA AL-GARʿĀN: With all honor, ya abu-Mūsa, you tend to forget that gone are the days when we obeyed only our own laws.

ZĀYED: But it's better if we have our own ʿanwa about the Firān than having the government come and make theirs [laws].

The anthropologist notices that the conversation gradually shifts from speculating about the impingements of superpower concerns that might threaten the Bedouin stability to public acknowledgment of the traditional Bedouin values such as dominance over territory. Ironically, even these are somehow regulated by a foreign agency—the Santa Katarina Monastery (cf. Rabinowitz 1985).

X: Let the government come with its own laws. Let it come. Laws of the government, we can ignore about half of them. But our laws—we can't ignore them. One must be responsible. One must go to court and pay in camels and money and one's honor. And one's honor might be lost for good. [*He stops and reflects, then taunting*] Let the government come, it's better.

FARRŪJA: But our laws are tougher than the government laws. So we must have our own laws for the Firān.

RAḌWĀN [*a Garārsha judge, who until now had sat quietly, bursts out*]: By God! This Old Woman is right! If we don't have laws here, there will be wars. The Mzeini will come and say, this is my land! Here my goats will graze. So the Ṣālḥi will tell him, no, this is my land! Here are my dates, and here my goats will graze! And the Wlād Saʿīdi will say, no! This is my land! You two get out of here! Leave it to my goats, here is the ownership paper of my karats. And the Ḥamādi will say, all of you get out of here! We arrived in the Sinai before all of you! And the Jebāli will come saying, this is not true! We were in the Sinai even before Islam! We built the Monastery! So the ʿAlēgi will tell him, this is all true, but you don't deserve anything! You are the slave of the Monastery! We are the strongest tribe! and so, where will we Ṭawara go?

SHEIKH ṢĀLEḤ: I'll tell you where we'll go. Every time the tribes fight among themselves, the government is happy, because they don't give the government trouble.

RAḌWĀN: Forget about the government now. We're talking about the Ṭawara. I swear by the Prophet, we're trustworthy people. Since the day the Turks left, we've had only one blood feud. And with the other tribes, [members of the neighboring North Sinai-Negev alliance], I myself disentangled *(fakētu)* at least five blood feuds of the Ṭarabīn. Allah helped us live in peace.

ZĀYED: Allah and our ʿurfi (customary Bedouin law). Let me tell you, gentlemen. We are the poorest Bedouin in the area— laborers, not Bedouin. If someone breaks the law, how could he pay with forty camels or with forty gold coins?

SHGĒṬEF [*Mzeini fool*]: You could always borrow camels from Shaʿabān al-Galīd, he has eight too many. Really, gentlemen, bring your goats under my date trees, give me your gold and I'll buy another pickup.

Shgēṭef, to my surprise, an official member of the Ṭawara parliament, breaks the intensity of the disagreements with his relevant but slightly skewed comment. People are laughing, and I sense a change toward a funny interlude.

X [*mockingly*]: How will you buy yourself a second pickup if there is no law against the animals grazing on your trees?

Another round of laughter.

SHGĒṬEF: Shaʿabān abu-Srayaʿ will give us a law and the people of the Ṭawara will give me gold.

People are laughing really hard now.

SHGĒṬEF [*whining*]: By God, you holy man, on the life of your grandfather, the great legislator, give us a law! Give us a law! I've got to get my second pickup from the law. Give us a law!

The fool joins in riotously with the laughter of the rest. The laughter is so loud it covers the sound of the pickups roaming now and then in the wadi.

FREIJ: Shut up, you fool! Enough! We've heard you!

The laughter subsides as people respond to the anger in Freij's voice. The fool says nothing more, knowing that everyone has already gotten his point: if he will get rich from the fines, there is obviously a serious problem of too many animals devouring the ecologically fragile oasis.

FREIJ [*turning his entire torso to look at Shaᶜabān, and addressing him directly in violation of the egalitarian etiquette of this context*]: By the life of the Prophet, your honor, Shaᶜabān, let's do something before it's too late.

ZĀYED [*also turning his entire torso towards Shaᶜabān*]: Only you, ya Shaᶜabān, are able to disentangle this.

SHEIKH ṢĀLEḤ [*looking at Shaᶜabān straight in the eye*]: Indeed, ya Shaᶜabān, I have nothing to do with this. This is an issue for the Bedouin government. It's not an issue between the Bedouin and the [occupying] government.

X: And by your life, ya Shaᶜabān, make it really light. We have enough tough laws.

Between the roars of the pickups as they come and go, the silence, pierced only by the sudden flap of a bat's wings. We all gaze expectantly at the shriveled, plain little man who sits as just one of the circle. There are echoes from a tourist group camping at the oasis tonight, probably sitting around the fire I hear crackling. In this hot night, what a waste of wood. But the campers have unwittingly joined the annual Bedouin slumber party. A guitar's major chords, along with young voices in a heavy New York accent, waft over to us: "The answer, my friend, is blowin' in the wind . . ."

The little old man in his embarrassment starts fingering the nubby long gold threads, faded from age and use, that decorate the edge of his woolen cloak. He rubs them between his thumb and forefinger as he would gently crush fragrant desert herbs.

"Wait and see," whispers Swēlem the medic, who also observes the

Ṭawara parliament as if it were an action film. "Until he decides what to do, he will stretch everyone here out like chewing gum. He looks like a plain guy, but he's tough and noble."

"The answer, my friend, is blowin' in the wind, the answer is blowin' in the wind." The tourists sound like a broken record, stuck on the same patch of the song.

Shaʿabān straightens up and clears his throat, but then whines in his countertenor voice, "I'm supposed to make you a law? Why me? Why not you?" He points at Sheikh Ṣāleḥ. "Or you?" He points at X the Ex. "Or even you?" He points at Shgēṭef the Fool.

The anthropologist suspects that this is all an act, but she might be wrong because even though the Symbolic Battle Coordinator points at the Fool, no one laughs. A grave silence. Sanctity, perhaps?

"We all can make a law," the Galīd continues. "All of us, everyone who belongs to the Ṭawara tribes, starting with the Bani Wāṣel, the oldest and smallest tribe, and ending with the Mzeina, the youngest and largest. And even the Jebaliyya, even though they were once Christians. All of us. I am only one among many."

"One among many," some murmur in agreement.

"And the date trees of the Firān belong to everyone," he states firmly.

"The dates of the Firān belong to everyone," we all repeat in a chorus.

"And because there are so many of us in the Firān, we have to make an ʿanwa," he announces with authority.

"We have to make an ʿanwa," we chorus.

"With legal guarantors," he emphasizes.

"With guarantors," we repeat dutifully.

And then silence prevails again. Shaʿabān draws his faded black cloak about him and looks out upon the assembly. His brow furrows. Then his hand slowly emerges from the folds of the cloak and he thoughtfully strokes the white stubble at his jawline. Sheikh Ṣāleḥ says to X, almost in a whisper, "Go get the teacher. We need someone to write the law so it is official, like in the barlimān."

X approaches Swēlem, who is sitting by me. "Go get the teacher. If he is already asleep, go wake him up. Fast."

Swēlem pounces to his jeep, and the roar of the motor echoes between the wadi walls.

From the silence, Shʿabān's voice emerges. "What is the date today?" he asks somewhat hesitantly of Sheikh ʿAlwān. Sheikh ʿAlwān looks at his automatic Seiko watch with the English/Arabic day/time. "Today is 16-IX-77 *milādi* (the Georgian calendar), corresponding with Shawwāl, 1397 (the Muslim calendar)," answers the Sheikh.

"Today is 16-IX-1977 milādi, corresponding to Shawwāl, 1397," Shaʿabān announces. "Does everyone agree?"

"Agreed," we chorus.

"All right, agreed," Shaʿabān summarizes. He clears his throat, closes his eyes, and cradles his temples between the thumb and middle finger of his right hand, thinking deeply.

"*Bismallah al-raḥmān wal-raḥīn.*" He is slow, emphasizing each word, and as he lifts his head he drops his right hand to his lap.

"Please, just a moment, your honor the Galīd, Swēlem went to get the teacher so he'll write," X requests, knowing that what will follow will be the intertribal law.

"Isn't it enough that this one will write?" the Galīd asks, gesturing his chin in my direction, and I feel how everyone is looking at the anthropologist.

"She writes in her own language, but we want something official written in Arabic that we will put tomorrow inside the tomb of Sheikh Ibn-Shabīb," says Sheikh Ṣāleḥ.[16]

"All right. Let us wait. Let it be written," agrees the Galīd.

So everyone in the circle waits patiently. Outside it, the revelers at this annual slumber party are mercifully asleep. No more roaring pickups. No more constant hubbub. No answers in the wind. Just the sudden whip of a bat's wings. It is also enjoying the bounty of dates. Kheir wājed.

Swēlem returns with the teacher, threads of sleep still clinging to his face, which looks as if he feels he has entered a bastion of power where he is an outsider.

"Give him some pages of your notebook, we forgot to bring his," Swēlem requests. "And also your pen."

"Bismallah al-raḥmān wal-raḥīm," the Galīd intones.

"Bismallah al-raḥmān wal-raḥīm," the people echo, as they do each of the Galīd's legislative utterances that follow. It is their ratification of the law.

*

"On this day the Bedouin agreed *(tawāfaga)* that there will be from this day forth an ʿanwa on Wadi Firān among all the tribes of the Ṭawara: the Garārsha tribe, the Ṣawālḥa tribe, the Mzeina tribe, the Wlād Saʿīd tribe, the Jebaliyya tribe, the Ḥamāda tribe, the ʿAleigāt tribe, and the Ḥeweiṭāt tribe. And this is the content of the ʿanwa, which concerns the goats and sheep *(ghanam)* and camels and donkeys.

And for unauthorized grazing on date tree offshoots or young transplants, the fine on the goats and sheep will be—how much shall it be?"

"Five hundred lira," shouts Zāyed.

That's too much," X counters. "One hundred lira."

"Two hundred," haggles Shgēṭef the Fool. "If everyone pays that, I can still get my second pickup."

"Two hundred lira on every head [sheep or goat]," agrees the Galīd. "And it will be considered as if sacrificed or dead after three days of unauthorized grazing without its owner reclaiming it and paying the fine. And the fine on camels will be—how much shall it be?"

"Don't let the Fool decide this time—you decide," requests Sheikh ᶜAlwān, half-kidding.

"What does a poor man like me understand about money?" says the Galīd. "I know how much I could sell my young kidgoats and lambs for, and that's it. You have to figure out how much the fines should be."

"Five hundred for the camels," bids Mūsa the Baldhead.

"And the fine on camels will be five hundred lira on each camel head," agrees the Galīd. "And the fine on donkeys will be—how much shall it be?"

"A big fine for a big dick," Shgēṭef proposes.

"Then you should pay an even bigger fine," Raḍwān teases back.

"It's late, folks, let's just get it over with," Farrūja complains, "Donkeys usually don't wander around by themselves as often as camels or goats. People keep them nearby so that they can carry their water. The fine should be small."

"And each donkey's fine will be one hundred lira," Shaᶜabān decides on this matter himself. "And in this agreement every man will be responsible for his whole tribe in this ᶜanwa. And the ᶜanwa's lower border will be Sil ᶜAlayān and its upper border will be Tarīg omm-ᶜAjram."[17]

"Your honor, ya Galīd, Sil ᶜAlayān is fine as a lower border, because the date trees start there, but Tarīg omm-ᶜAjram is quite a distance from the upper end of the oasis," Freij gently comments.

"I think it's all right," counters Mūsa al-Garᶜān. "You yourself said that this place is expanding, and will continue to expand. It's good to leave some extra space."

But the Galīd ignores these remarks. "And the fines for the offshoots and the young transplants on which the Bedouin agree will be two for one *(dafaᶜa bidafᶜein)* on each guarantor [i.e., a guarantor in each of the Ṭawara alliance tribes will be the authority a man goes to for compensation when his date offshoots or transplants have been destroyed by animals; this guarantor demands from the guarantor of the violator's tribe a payment double the value of the damage]. And everyone who pollinates a date tree of absent owners will be only from the Garārsha tribe or the Ṣawālḥa tribe, unless the trees belong to the Monastery and are pollinated by the Jebaliyya tribe. And he who pollinates will get in exchange two bunches *(ginwēn)* of dates, as it was. And he who does not receive his due from the pollination will have to get it in accordance with the Feud Law."

"The words of our Galīd are like the toughest of *ḥadīd* (iron)," Haj ʿĀyed rhymes, and we echo him, despite his interruption of the Galīd.

"The agreement on the ʿanwa is declared. And the guarantor for the Ṣawālḥa tribe will be the judge Zāyed, and all the other tribes—for each of the four guarantors required, there will be two [instead of only one] *(wayakūn kiflo bekiflēn ʿala aṣḥāb arbāʿ)*."

The anthropologist digs out her spare pen from her bag, and records the very rare event that, once again, just as during the sacrifice at the pilgrimage to Faranje, the double-dual structure of the Bedouin tribe has surfaced. Every tribe will have four pairs of guarantors, each pair to represent one phratry. The Ṣawālḥa, however, will have only one guarantor because only one of its four phratries, and a small one, lives largely in the South Sinai. The majority of members in the other three phratries of the tribe are in Egypt. She also notes that this shows that the Symbolic Battle Coordinator, though bounded by the traditional tribal structure, is flexible enough to adapt it to the current situation.

"And who will be the guarantors of each tribe?" X asks.

"You can argue over it tomorrow, in the pilgrimage to Sheikh Ibn-Shabīb," says the Galīd with a wave of his hand.

"What's important is that we now have an ʿanwa," says Sheikh Ṣāleḥ, without giving credit to the one who has just declared it. "Tomorrow will be hot."

"It will be hot," we all repeat, and the anthropologist struggles to accept the incredible amount of work that will be involved in recording all the arguments and their subsequent analysis. But the data will be great.

Silence. It is almost 2 A.M. The hot air stands still. The clapping wings of bats, and their constant gnawing on dates. The weird crescent moon of the end of the month collapses on the tree tops, but rising, instead of setting, in the dark.

"Enough. Let's go to sleep." Farrūja stretches and leaves the circle.

"It's just that I don't know which of my grandchildren's families I will join for sleep tonight," she grouches.

"Look who's still here, Smadar, the One Who Writes Us. Go tuck yourself into your sleeping bag. If you're tired tomorrow, you'll fall out of the tree," says X in a fatherly voice.

"She's the only one here who really came to work," Mūsa the Baldhead jokes, tapping on his little belly.

When I pack my notebook and my pen and spare pen, preparing to walk in the hot darkness to the date garden of Mismaḥ al-Dgheishi, I look around, trying to identify the source of the sound of light snoring. It's little old Shaᶜabān abu-Srayaᶜ, already asleep, curled like a fetus, enveloped in his black woolen cloak, his bony elbow his pillow. Planted. He has not even left his spot in the now scattered circle of the parliament.

"Why didn't he go to sleep near his wives?" I ask Swēlem, my culture broker.

"He's just married to two old women," Swēlem answers curtly.

And when I walk alone, the end of the month crescent, low in the eastern sky, focuses its spotlight along the wadi. Only the steps of my thongs squeak in the arcosis. And the anthropologist feels that tonight she has discovered how the consensus works in this strange variation of segmentary lineage, acephalous, egalitarian society.

III.

Zuārat Faranje, 21 September 1978, a year later

Dusk. In the news they said that maybe tomorrow or the day after Menachem Begin, Anwar Sadat, and Jimmy Carter will sign the draft of the peace treaty between Israel and Egypt someplace in big America named Camp David. This year—a record number of pilgrims. Until the ᶜ*asr* prayer in the late afternoon, all the men were in the ᶜarīsha. Surprisingly, the ex-smugglers' corner was fairly quiet. No ebbing and flowing. But one would have needed only a plain, dull kitchen knife, not a scimitar, to cut the thick tension in the air. The semicircle of men opposite the Wall of Honor was glued to three transistor radios simultaneously broadcasting nonstop news and analysis. One voice was from Cairo, the second was the Israeli Arabic broadcasts from Jerusalem, and the third was the BBC in Arabic ("The British were the first to actually bring their government people into the Sinai, and this is why their news is the most reliable," X will explain). And beginning in the spring of 1979 and ending in the early winter, Israel will gradually return the western part of the peninsula piecemeal, so that in December 1979 the borderline will slice the Sinai and the Ṭawara into two equal halves, stretching from al-ʿArīsh in the north to Ras-Muḥammad in the south, just as the Ṭawara parliament predicted over a year ago.

The anthropologist has noticed that this year, the semicircle of the ex-smugglers and their groupies had an interesting addition—the nouveaux riches and their groupies.

But at the Wall of Honor, facing Mecca, there was no change: on the same faded but still bright handwoven rugs, each man reclining on a colorful pillow, where Shaʿabān abu-Srayaʿ in the center; on his right, his brother, who is blind in one eye, and one of the entourage of three judges who are the supreme court of the tribe; on his left, the other two judges. Near them were other elders, who also look as if they had emerged from the pages of a travelogue of the previous century.

Dusk. The sharp mountain horizon lines that encase this windswept plateau of estrangement have become blurred. The red of the mountains to the south, the black of the mountains to the east, and the cognac-brown of the mountains to the west, smudged as if by a soft brush stroke into grayish-purple, merging with the lavender of the sky orphaned by the burning ball of sunset. These are the hours when it is no longer too hot to lie on the open ground, when a person can rest there, welcoming the last waves of heat radiating into the cold night falling from the skies.

Curls of gray smoke climb to the sky north and south of the shrine. The women in their tents blow on the evening tea fires. After the ʿasr prayer earlier this afternoon, the military governor and his entourage left, and the web of men in the ʿarisha unraveled. They all went for a round of visits in the women's tents—temporary tents with only one section, for the women and children, where, due to modesty in the usual mundane days, it is taboo for men to visit.[18] But today, not only did groups of men appear at the women's tents, but the men and women also exchanged verbal erotic teasing, telling each other embarrassing compliments, and gossiping about the love life of their friends—on ordinary days this kind of talk would have no place in mixed-gender company. And with no deep canyon nearby, the peals of laughter that rose from the flour-sack tents went straight to the sky, without the usual polyphony of echoes.

COOKING THE SACRIFICIAL MEAL AT THE PILGRIMAGE TO FARANJE

Everyone was having a great time except shabby old Ḍaifallah and his two sons, Morḍi and Darwīsh, who had been miserable ever since X had hurled his pickup keys at them. All day in the blazing sun they sweated in front of the fires under the four huge pots, from which the steamy fragrance of the sacrificial meat rose. Near them, a group of young unmarried men Ḍaifallah had rounded up labored kneading dough and baking thin flatbread—a labor reserved for women in everyday life.

But the gleeful laughter did not disturb the sleep of Shaᶜabān abu-Srayaᶜ and the other resplendent nobles, curled in their woolen cloaks and snoring lightly under the soothing shadow of the ᶜarīsha.

And when the red sun disappeared, so that it could rise in Camp David, somewhere in America, the men arranged themselves facing Mecca in three long rows in the area between the ᶜarīsha and the hill of the shrine, and prayed the *maghreb* prayer. Even Ḍaifallah left his pots and boys, wiping heavy drops of sweat from his forehead, but because he noticed the sleeping Galīd and his entourage and felt he had to wake them up, they all arrived a split-second late. The anthropologist searched for her favorite social categories among the rows and could not find them. The three rows reminded her of the long line waiting to circumambulate the shrine. But this time, the guests from the other tribes had joined the Mzeinis in the rows.

After the maghreb prayer, at dusk, the men seat themselves in a very large circle west of the ʿarīsha. The circle is constituted from smaller circles of men—Mzeinis and non-Mzeinis—sitting and talking with each other. The radios have been squelched, and most of the conversations now focus on the price the Ṭawara people will pay for the caprices of three megalomaniac politicians—the new borderline will divide families and friends until 1982, when Egypt will get back the rest of the Sinai. And Allah save us from the devils, next year, there might not be a zuāra, for the first time since all these men remember themselves. The Faranje plateau is just stuck there, in the middle of the South Sinai. It will be sliced in half.

"Stack all the flatbreads in one big pile," Ḍaifallah orders the kitchen boys. "Get the pots from the fire and bring them after me. The sacrifice is ready!"

While the anthropologist writes how the political secular penetrates the tribal sacred, Ḍaifallah brings some embers and wood scraps and starts a fire exactly in the center of the large circle. His boys put the four pots on the fire, and beside it, the stack of flatbreads. Ḍaifallah draws the meat from the pots and puts the slices on four huge platters. A cloud of savory steam rises to the skies, which have covered themselves with a black cloak dotted with silvery stars, still moonless.

From the great circle of everyone present, Shaʿabān al-Galīd and his entourage emerge all at once, as though performing for an audience, and grandly seat themselves in a smaller, perfectly shaped circle around the pots. X and eight other mustaches from the ebbing and flowing ʿarīsha corner opposite the Wall of Honor also rise and form a line that stretches from the inner circle of the sacrifice pots and their old nobles to the outer circle. X is nearest the outer circle and starts to walk counterclockwise. As he stops at each man in turn (the line adjusts after him), he shouts abruptly, "*Ḍeif*" (guest) if the man is not a Mzeina tribesmember, or "*meḥalli*" (native) if the man is of the Mzeina. In immediate response to each shout, Shaʿabān efficiently reaches his hand to one of the platters and chooses a piece of meat—bigger and better for the guest, smaller and less succulent for the

Mzeini. His brother or one of the judges hastily wraps it inside a flatbread, and then it starts its journey from one quick ex-smuggler hand to the next until X hands it to the man whose title he had announced.

And so it goes, time after time—the anthropologist stops counting after the one-hundredth serving. Interesting, she would write in her notebook, the Symbolic Battle Coordinator controls the tribal resources. He is the one who sits by the cooked sacrifice and decides who eats what. But the ex-smugglers are the ones who actually distribute the tribal resources. Her turn arrives, and she chokes when X announces, "*Meḥallīya*," native, rather than guest, as in the previous years. He was even willing to adjust the language to take account of her gender, by adding the feminine suffix "-a" to "meḥalli"—making a word that exists in the classical Arabic dictionary, but whose use, to the best of her knowledge, was unprecedented in this male-oriented context. And despite the loneliness of fieldwork and the cold of the desert night, she feels enveloped by a warm wave of belonging. She decides that this year, she will eat the sacrificial meat despite being a vegetarian.

Talking and chewing. Talking with each other and chewing into the night. In the outer circle they talk and chew future Middle Eastern politics, and in the inner circle they talk and chew old stories from the rich reservoir of tribal histories.

Around nine o'clock the outer circle starts to unravel. To the southwest I spot X, his four mustaches, Sheikh ʿAlwān, Sheikh Ṣāleḥ (of the Wlād Saʿīd), Mūsa the Baldhead, and four others who participated in the barlimān meeting last summer. In the faint starlight, they form a straight row, clap their hands, stamp their feet, and sing rhythmically: "*Daḥiyya erdaḥiyya! Daḥiyya erdaḥiyya!*" "Clap your hands, oh clap your hands! Clap your hands, oh clap your hands!"

Those who sat in the outside circle during the sacrificial meal now have moved to form an audience on three sides of the rectangle, completed by the line of the dancing men. And here, disguised by the lack of moonlight, I see black tunics and shawls glittering with the sequins of married women, who have slipped from their tents and glided to the dance plaza. One after another they dance solo, facing the line of men. As the line stomps forward, the woman gracefully backs away, clasping her sequined shawl in modesty about her and waving the end of it in soft, sleek gestures at the men. Then the glittering sequins dance assertively toward the line of men, who cautiously retreat.

Back to the four big pots. Shaʿabān the Galīd and his friends guard them faithfully, even though they have been empty for a while. They huddle in their cloaks near the warmth of the ashes and embers.

"It's late. We're tired. Time to sleep," says one of the judges.

"The zuāra this year was even bigger than the zuāra after the last war [1973]," moans another.

"The zuāra this year was so beautiful, though, and what a pity . . . The dance is *ḥarām* (taboo) to the Muslims," the Galīd responds, with a yawn of five teeth.

"The dance is ḥarām for the Muslims," his one-eyed brother echoes.

"Ḥarām or not—they dance every year," mutters the third judge, putting his head on the angle of his sharp, bony elbow. Digging his feet into his sprawled woolen cloak, he falls asleep immediately.

In the background, the improvised rhymed verses of X the Ex, Sheikh ʿAlwān, and their friends drift around the huge plateau:

Galbi nāro shaʿalāb,
Ma tagdar tōgaf ʿala sanāha.

Daḥīyya,
Rayḥīni,
Gul, "Arid'ha, rid'ha."

Bint al-sabʿa nagīyyeh,
Wallah ma taʿaṭi karāha.

Daḥīyya,
Rayḥīni,
Gul, "Arid'ha, rid'ha."

I'm a hearthfire burning so hot,
You can't even touch the blackened pot.

O ye people, clap,
O spangled dancer, come,
O fellows, say "I want her, I want her."

The Daughter of the Lion is so noble and pure,
Your best hospitality cannot her lure.

O ye people, clap,
O spangled dancer, come,
O fellows, say "I want her, I want her."

It's eleven at night. I sit among the audience, rocking to the rhythm of the clapping and stamping. From afar, I see four pots and five curled cloaks, the heads peeking out and resting on their elbows. The sacred part of the ritual is over. The Galīd and his entourage have finished their performance. Good-night.

The groaning of a command car indicates that the military governor and his entourage have returned. I am surprised that they respect the privacy of the dancers and drive without lights despite the moonless night. All of a sudden, over me loom shadows—the governor, his Druze translator, and his everchanging secretary, now wearing pants because of the cold night.

"You know what's going on here, where's the food?" he asks me in Hebrew, in an authoritative baritone.

"The people ate the sacrifice around seven," I answer in Arabic, so that the Bedouin near me can understand.

The Druze translator translates and then asks me, to my surprise also in Hebrew, "Did they leave us anything?"

"I don't think so," I answer in cold politeness, again in Arabic. "This year there were so many people that there was barely enough meat."

"I told you that the Arabs eat right after sunset," the secretary kvetches in Hebrew, "but you were in the middle of your umpteenth backgammon game and now we're all hungry."

"If you want, we can return now to our base, and you will make us sandwiches," the governor remarks.

And the singing and dancing pick up new energy from the dancers' awareness of the governor's presence. Taking turns, they improvise two lines each in a Bedouin dialect that they assume, correctly, the Druze translator won't understand.

Gāᶜed fi dhraᶜ gheiro
Gheir illi shāreb shagāha.

Daḥīyya,
Rayḥīni,
Gul, "Arid'ha, rid'ha."

Irᶜi al-dunya al-malᶜūna,
Ghathāna waṭawwal ghathāha.

Daḥīyya,
Rayḥīni,
Gul, "Arid'ha, rid'ha."

Kud teʿud al-ḥuriyya,
Rud al-amāna lil-ma-jarālha.

Daḥīyya,
Rayḥīni,
Gul, "Arid'ha, rid'ha."

The man to others' warm arms always drawn
Is not the one who drinks the bitter dregs alone.

O ye people, clap,
O spangled dancer, come,
O fellows, say "I want her, I want her."

Look at this universe—so evil and cruel,
The silence it forced on us, now deep in our soul.

O ye people, clap,
O spangled dancer, come,
O fellows, say "I want her, I want her."

If we should ever get our freedom again,
The old trust and faith will return among men.

O ye people, clap,
O spangled dancer, come,
O fellows, say "I want her, I want her."

"This music can drive even elephants crazy," the governor complains. "It's so monotonous. Hey, let's get back to our base." The command car disappears into the night.

The dancing and singing goes on and on. Beads of sweat drop from the forehead of Sheikh ʿAlwān, pooling in his thick brows and mustache. X's pastel coat is also soaked with sweat. (I know this is his change, and no more changes of clothes lurk in his pickup.) But the earth sends cool waves that fuse with the cool night air.

Ya maḥala sidfet ḥabībok
Fi balad—wablādok ḥaliyya.

Daḥīyya,
Rayḥīni,
Gul, "Arid'ha, rid'ha."

Min illi yadri bewujʿāti?
Illi fi galbi ghabīyya.

Daḥīyya,
Rayḥīni,
Gul, "Arid'ha, rid'ha."

How wonderful to meet your dear old friend at last
In a strange new land—and the old one, so vast.

O ye people, clap
O spangled dancer, come,
O fellows, say "I want her, I want her."

Who on earth would know my pain in any way?
What's in my heart is hidden from the light of day.

O ye people, clap,
O spangled dancer, come,
O fellows, say "I want her, I want her."

Eyes struggle against sleep, burning from sun, dust, dry air, and weariness, but refuse to close. We all shift to the rhythm of the Daḥīyya, as if in a trance.

The sad thin crescent of the end-of-month moon suddenly appears at 3 A.M., as if afraid to lose its night. The startled women scatter in panic toward their tents, covering with their shawls the exposed rectangle between their veils and head-covers, fearing that, God forbid, someone from the audience, especially their husbands, might identify them.

The line of dancing men dissolves into a circle. X offers the dancers the heavily taxed Marlboro cigarettes. While I try to fall asleep in my sleeping bag, I hear the intermingling scratches of the BBC, the Egyptian station, and the Israeli Arabic station. The Camp David Treaty will be signed tomorrow.

Lying in my sleeping bag, I keep drifting off and then suddenly waking up. The picture show of the zuāra reels in my head, and I am excited but worried about the big news. What shall I do tomorrow? I ask myself, while massaging one of my feet with the other against the cold. ʿEin al-Akhaḍar, I think. Tomorrow I will look for a ride to ʿEin al-Akhaḍar, the Mzeina's heart and the seasonal encampment of Shaʿabān the Galīd. I hope someone going down in the direction of the Firān will be kind enough to make this detour to the remote little oasis ʿEin and drop me off.

"There's not much to do there, and as a matter of fact, it's quite boring," warned the Galīd when he gave me the invitation. He promised that, so I wouldn't get bored, he would teach me *shīza*, the complicated cross between "checkers" and "go." Usually he whiles away his days playing games with one of the judges, he said. This is how he passes his time to make space for more time, he joked about himself. Until next year's date season and the zuāra, I said, wanting to hint at his once-a-year glory. But he did not get it. An equal among equals.

9
THE ONE WHO WRITES US

Dī Illi Tuktubna

If he were the narrator, he would have ended it like this: "He opened a drawer and took out a pencil and wrote on the file: My Story. He frowned at this a moment, then he used an eraser, leaving only a single word: Story. That seemed to satisfy him."

But maybe, out of polite arrogance, he might have finished with a paraphrase of Borges: "Which of the two of us has written this book I do not know."

ANTON SHAMMAS
Arabesques

THE AUTHOR READS DRAFT OF THIS BOOK'S MANUSCRIPT TO AN OLD MZEINI BEDOUIN TO ELICIT HIS CRITIQUE

On 24 September 1978 Anwar Sadat, Menachem Begin, and Jimmy Carter signed an almost final draft of a peace accord at the Camp David retreat that was to give the accord its name. At that moment, thousands of miles away, in the very Sinai desert on which all the diplomatic hullabaloo had been focused, I labored in ʿEin al-Akhaḍar, a Mzeina oasis. An Israeli anthropologist of half Yemenite, half Lithuanian heritage, I listened to the Arabic version of the radio news as it wafted in a scratchy voice across the hot, lugubrious atmosphere of the magʿad. Two days later I was to be the victim of the local Fool, who sent me to a deserted well in the middle of nowhere. There I spent a memorable night alone on an empty stomach. That day's tragedy was compensated for the following day by a remarkable stroke of good luck: here, in the middle of nowhere, I met with a Mzeini woman. In a display of typical Bedouin hospitality and generosity, she shared with me what little food she had and took me to her encampment.

A month later, my pride still smarting, I related my humiliation to several Mzeinis. I was surprised at myself in that, despite my embarrassment I mustered—without really trying to—the calm, distanced style that typifies Bedouin storytelling. Had my audience been professional anthropologists, I no doubt would have delivered a disquisition on "The Impact of Global Politics on the Tribal Structure of the Mzeina." But as my story represents not so much distancing, objective observations by a detached scholar, but deeply felt experiences shared with the Mzeinis, it is best told as an allegory. After all, at those points where my identity and that of the Mzeinis meet and converge, the global politics observed and analyzed by scientists becomes the local poetics experienced and lived by the participants.

*

The mundane dialogues of the Mzeinis reflected their inconsistent and insecure living conditions. These were consequences of the occupation of the Sinai, a political football tossed back and forth between Egypt and Israel. When the Mzeinis pondered how they ought to relate to the Israeli or Egyptian soldiers, the military governors, the civil administrators, the assorted settlers, and the international tourists, they were faced by the dilemma of adapting traditional hospitality to quite untraditional "visitors."

Karwat al-Ḍeif or the code of hospitality was a pillar of Bedouin tradition (cf. Sowayan 1985). Mzeinis viewed it as a sacred commitment on the part of each tribal member to the honor of his or her community and tribe and to the honor of the Ṭawara alliance. Hospitality also embraced spheres beyond the tribe. Hospitality toward any member of the community of Muslim believers *(al-umma al-Islāmiyya)*, or to anyone in the whole world *(ahl al-dunya)* visiting the South Sinai, was to bring honor to the Mzeini displaying it.

The duty of hospitality involved both the tribal structure and its many organizational modes. Any stranger who came to the Sinai was traditionally considered a guest and was expected to introduce him- or herself according to a rigid etiquette reflecting tribal and regional affiliation. If a guest was not known to the host from previous meetings, he or she was to introduce him- or herself by name and give a three- to five-generation genealogy of his or her *khamsa* (feud group), clan and phratry affiliations, and the tribe of which he or she was a member. Since among the Mzeina descent and territoriality did not exactly correspond, the guest also mentioned the name of the regional alliance to which he or she belonged. Then, before turning to talk of other matters, the host and guest gossiped about the overlapping areas of their kinship and friendship networks.

Many Mzeini dialogues on the nature of hospitality degenerated into bitter arguments in which the participants' value of honor, derived from being Bedouin hosts, was confronted by the indeterminacy characterizing their life as voiceless pawns of their uninvited guests.

Once, during a liminal moment (Turner 1967) when the tradition of hospitality was called into question, I found myself acting as an "allegorical type"—the same objectified analytical construct that is the focus of this book. Allegorizing my memorable night experience, I was able to bridge the gap between the Mzeina's tradition of hospitality and the inconsistencies of their current lives. As guest and yet as the most marginal tribesperson, as a Jew of both European and Arab descent, someone conjoining Self and Other in herself (Mead 1962),[1] I spontaneously staged an allegory enabling my audience and myself to reconstruct the tradition of hospitality in both reality and structure. I was thus able to resolve momentarily the ambiguities associated with Mzeina hospitality and the paradoxes faced by the Mzeina (and myself) in relating to Western culture and politics.

1.

I will begin decoding the contradiction and mystery of being sent to the wilderness by a Fool, and of being saved the next day by a woman, both members of the same tribe, by referring to portions of my field diary. All references to "days before" refer to the number of days before my encounter with the oasis Fool.

---

26 September 1978, Bir al-Sarādga

Dear Diary,

I thought my war scars from the Sinai healed since I treated them with anthropological hopes for mutual understanding. To hell with it! Here I sit, in the middle of nowhere, and instead of writing my regular evening fieldnotes I stupidly write "Dear Diary."

After almost three years of fieldwork, years when I imagined myself crossing the emotional wilderness of mutual distrust, years when I assumed that I, an Israeli anthropologist, had exposed the essence of my Self to that Bedouin Other, and years in which that Other, in exchange, seemed to absorb me into itself. After all, we are but trivial beings who disintegrate into small particles in the shadow of the Arab-Israeli conflict.

The dark sky awaits the late moonrise. Smadar, how did you ever get into this?

21 September 1978, Faranje

Five days before.

The Pilgrimage to Faranje . . . The ambitious and vague hopes of Camp David have shrunken here to penetrating questions: about the temporary borderlines that will separate families during the gradual return of the Sinai from Israel to Egypt between 1979 and 1982; about how to obtain licenses to visit relatives on both sides of these borders; about the shrinking possibilities of migrant work with the Egyptians and Israelis; about speculations that further development projects will be imposed on the locals . . .

22 September 1978, Faranje, still

Four days before.

Ashes of the pilgrimage. Bedouin cynicism about the real importance of the Sinai in future peace treaties. And their nice rhyme. The Sinai mountains—good for naught. Can't be used, can't be bought . . .

Noon prayer. Afterwards I join the Galīd, who has just completed his annual show as the Symbolic Battle Coordinator of the tribe, his one-eyed brother, and the entourage made up of three ancient customary judges. We bump along for about half an hour—five nobles resplendent in formal robes and one anthropologist in baggy jeans and T-shirt, six people in a dilapidated pickup going to ʿEin al-Akhaḍar.

ʿEin al-Akhaḍar. The Green Spring. The whistling wind in the wide wadi. Rounded black hills of metamorphic rock flowing forth from the windswept plateaus of the peninsula's watersheds. A few small fruit orchards and date trees embrace the wadi wall. Often the fruit does not ripen because of the cold. A well, buckets, a sweep. The Mzeina call this oasis, which sits on the fringes of their territorial center, "our heart."

24 September 1978, ʿEin al-Akhaḍar

Two days before.

It is said, rather cynically, that the customary summer residence of the Symbolic Battle Coordinator is here, in the heart of Mzeina. But alas, nothing stirs in this heart but two young goatherds, some twenty goats, and a donkey burdened with six empty water jerrycans. Every other morning the girls emerge from the yellow dunes, wash their long hair near the well, fill up the jerrycans, and disappear again into the dunes in the direction of their summer encampment.

Like Mzeina elders everywhere, the Galīd, his brother, one of the three judges, and their entourage spend most of their days and nights sitting or reclining in the magʿad. But the magʿad in ʿEin al-Akhaḍar is the only sign of community life in this forsaken tribal heart.

A transistor radio barks out news in Modern Standard Arabic (and thus it is only partially understood by these nomads, because they speak a dialect). Someone painstakingly scans the dial in an almost desperate search for the elusive stations. Our ears strain to discern meanings amidst the scratches, while our eyes focus on a square drawn in the sand. Finger-made crosshatchings transform the sand into a checker board. The Judge and the Coordinator while away their days in a sequence of slow and calculated *shīza* games. One player moves small pieces of dry, pale camel manure; the other player uses small pebbles of red granite. Some of the entourage bless the players with their unsolicited advice, while others advise the advisors, until one can no longer tell players from advisors, or advisors from advisors of advisors.

"Shgēṭef, could you pour more tea?" the Galīd nonchalantly requests the local Fool. Shgēṭef enters the magʿad and for the umpteenth time pours us yet more cups of hot sweet tea.

"So what did the news say?" the Galīd asks the man with his ear glued to the transistor radio, but doesn't wait for an answer. "I'll tell you," he says with a half-bemused, half-serious expression, "No one will solve the problems between Russia and America. Only the Chinese will ever figure a way out. And when the day comes that they conquer the Sinai, that will be the end of that."

It's a good pun—the Arabic for "Sinai" is *Sīna*, for "Chinese" is *Sīni*—and we laugh heartily. But Shgēṭef, perhaps betraying his deep Fool's wisdom, stares at us with eyes wide open.

The Galīd continues, "The Greeks were here and left behind the Monastery [Santa Katarina], the Turks were here and left behind the Castle [in Nuwēbʿat Ṭarabīn], and the British drew up maps, and the Egyptians brought the Russian army (and a few oil wells), and the Israelis brought the Americans who made the mountains into movies, and tourists from France and Japan, and scuba divers from Sweden and Australia, and, trust Allah to save you from the devil, we Mzeina are nothing but pawns in the hands of them all. We are like the pebbles and the droppings of the shīza."

Everyone but Shgēṭef again roars with laughter. The Coordinator points to me with his long index finger, saying in a commanding voice, "Write it all down, The One Who Writes Us!" (*Dī Illi Tuktubna*—one of my two Mzeini nicknames).

26 September 1978, ʿEin al-Akhaḍar, still

Noon. Enough. I am shīza-ed out. Between shīza moves, the men exhaust most of the possible scenarios for the near and distant future of the Middle East. The Egyptian-Israel peace treaty may

TRIBAL ELDERS, WHILING AWAY THEIR DAYS, PLAYING *SHĪZA* ▶

loom large on the global horizon, but locally it has been torn to shreds.

I recall a nearby well, Bir al-Sarādga, six kilometers down the wadi. Several families encamped there during winter. I wonder how Sadat's peace initiative echoes in the walls of this well. The negotiated temporary border will pass right through it.

I ask Shgēṭef the Fool if there are any camels grazing in the surrounding hills and if it might be possible to rent one, to load it with cameras, cassette recorder, a huge and clumsy backpack (only thirty kilograms!) and travel to Bir al-Sarādga. Shgēṭef raises one eyebrow, a Bedouin gesture indicating a dubious "why not?" I join him in the search for fresh camel footprints. We search in vain. He stares at me, pretending to be amazed, and says, "Ya Smadar, owner of big hips (*omm al-jaᶜāb*—my other nickname), a tough and skillful Israeli like you, who lives with us in this desert, can't you even load yourself up and go down the wadi as far as Bir al-Sarādga? The Bedouin encamp right there, winter and summer."

26 September 1978, Bir al-Sarādga

Here, again, at tonight's page.

. . . And I carried myself and my heavy load down the wadi. When I saw the well from afar—I felt relief. The place hadn't changed since winter. For a moment I thought I heard a dog bark in the distance, suggesting the existence of an encampment. But alas, arriving at the well I found only leftovers from the previous winter encampment. I dropped my stuff near the well and started walking quickly, almost hysterically, in one direction after the other, hoping to find someone, anyone, before nightfall. Within the radius of a kilometer not a living thing was to be found. Around the well were many fresh footprints of women and children, but still I dared not hope.

I am afraid. I had trusted Shgēṭef, a channel for the region's gossip. But while the tribe's resplendent leadership verbally expressed their anger at the Camp David Accord, the fool, as a Fool, acted out his anger by dispatching the most available Israeli to the middle of nowhere. Now I know what the Mzeina mean when they say, "The Fool's mind is sharp as a sword."

As the day recedes into dusk, I gather some dry twigs and light a small fire. I have no food, but at least I have enough cigarettes and matches to get me through the night. OK, so I'll try to fall asleep. Tonight, even the habitual sadness of sunset does not move me.

Maybe I deserve it?

27 September 1978, Bir al-Sarādga

A new day. During the night I jolt awake several times, shivering with fear, unable to decide whether to be angry at myself or at Shgēṭef. Finally I wake up at 7 A.M. and decide that, if no one arrives at the well by eight, I will leave my stuff, fill my three canteens, and continue down the wadi for 25 kilometers to the settlement where Wadi al-Akhaḍar meets Wadi Firān. People live there year round, and this *I* know without having to count on any clever fool.

I am starved, and the sun beats down on everything. My back hurts from yesterday, but I've got to go on. After a hasty hike down the wadi I suddenly see a Bedouin woman, two toddlers, and a donkey loaded with empty jerrycans. Are these the owners of the footprints I found yesterday near the well? My eyes fill with tears of relief. The woman notices me and veils herself. From afar we exchange the customary greeting sentences said between a guest and a host. Hoping that she does not notice, I wipe my tears away with my Mickey Mouse T-shirt. Bedouin are not supposed to cry.

II.

After a month I returned to my "base camp" in Dahab. But rumors of the misdeeds of Shgēṭef the Fool, and of my rescue by the woman with her two toddlers, arrived in Dahab even before I did.

28 October 1978, Dahab

Wintry Dahab. The north wind has already swept away the scents of dinner and the last whispers of the ʿ*asha* prayer. The tales of the fearful Abu-Zāyed, accompanied by the sad sound of a *rabāba* (one-string fiddle) ooze out of the transistor radios, whose antennas are trained towards Egypt, and pour into the night.

Flattened cartons and wooden boxes, supported by dry palm branches, are the materials out of which Ghānma and Mūsa's hut has been fashioned. In the inner yard Ghānma, Abu-Mūsa (Mūsa's old father), who makes his living from fishing, and Omm-Mūsa (Mūsa's mother) sit in a circle around the radio. The scene is faintly illuminated by glowing embers. A tea kettle bubbles above red hot coals. Next to Ghānma sit Mabsūṭa and Farḥāna—two neighbors whose husbands are now employed as unskilled, underpaid, but tenured workers at the Israeli army camp at Sharm al-Sheikh. ʿĪd and Salīm, their elbows resting on their woolen body wraps, recline near Abu-Mūsa. ʿĪd is a neighbor temporarily hired several times by the local Israeli ranger to clean up the heaps of trash left by tourists. Salīm is married to Omm-Mūsa's brother's daughter and lives in the western peninsula, to be returned to Egypt next summer. He is about to go job hunting in Eilat. Smadar huddles in the corner, trying to write down every detail.

When the legendary feats of Abu-Zāyed are all recited, Salīm nonchalantly turns the radio dial in search of the evening news. We gallop between Cairo, Monte Carlo, Damascus, Jerusalem, Amman, the Voice of America, and London, straining to catch elusive stations amidst serious Standard Arabic voices relating bits of news.

MABSŪṬA [*puzzled*]: The people in the radios—they always say the same things. But each station and every state says it in its own way. It's something I don't understand. Never.

OMM-MŪSA [*with an air of indifference*]: Every one and his rabāba.

ʿĪD [*sarcastically*]: Ah-ha . . . What's the distance between Abu-Zāyed's rabāba and the rabāba of the news . . . [*laughs to himself and lowers the transistor's volume*]

GHĀNMA [*briskly, switching the radio off*]: Enough! I'm fed up with the news. One and all, they're all the same! Tea?

Pause. Ghānma once again fills the empty tea cups handed to her. Some, attempting to cool the boiling tea, whistle air through their lips.

ABU-MŪSA: Ya Salīm, soon we'll need a passport and some licenses to visit you and your family, and your family is our family. [Salīm is a member in Mūsa's lineage in addition to his marriage to Omm-Mūsa's brother's daughter.] What do you think [*a mischievous look in his eyes*], will the Egyptians photograph my bald head in color, or black and white? [*He laughs and the rest join in*]

SALĪM [*with a raised voice*]: Folks, this is no time for jokes! When the Egyptians find out that I drive a Russian jeep [left behind in 1967], you will probably need to apply for a license to visit the jail.

MABSŪṬA: Drop it. A lot of time has passed since then. They've forgotten all about it.

SALĪM [*louder*]: I swear to God, they haven't forgotten. [*Slowly, emphasizing each word*] When they got Ras-Sadr back [in 1976, due to Kissinger's shuttle-diplomacy], they fined everyone who drove Russian vehicles. Those who couldn't afford to pay went to jail. I heard it from those who came from [the Egyptian-controlled] Ras-Sadr area for visits to relatives through the Red Cross.

OMM-MŪSA [*awakening*]: *Aii-wah!* (yeah!), this is the time for us to start thinking about where to hide what we took from the Egyptians, and to start "collecting" things from the Jews.

The term "Jews" was often used to describe the generic anyone who was not Bedouin and who came to the Sinai during the Israeli occupation, including tourists from all over the world, and even Palestinians.

ʿĪD [*to Salīm*]: I heard that somebody from your encampment has "taken" a Mercedes taxi from Eilat with the help of friends, took it apart, hid it in the wadis, and the Israeli police couldn't find a thing.[2]

ABU-MŪSA [*playing with the prayer-beads between his fingers, mutters to himself*]: Ḥarām! (taboo!)

SALĪM [*chuckling*]: They said that some guys got arrested in Eilat, but were freed. Lack of evidence, they said.

ABU-MŪSA [*to himself*]: Thank God! [*Thoughtful for a moment*] Still, it's ḥarām!

Another silent pause.

MABSŪṬA: My husband says he doesn't know what to do: to leave his work and start "collecting," or wait till the Israelis are about to leave and get his severance pay—he worked for them since 1972.

OMM-MŪSA: If they'll give him his severance pay in dollars, let him wait. If in Israeli pounds, he should "collect" other things, since the Israeli money is nothing but worthless paper, buying us nothing from the Egyptians. But if you ask me, I think he should both "collect" *and* take his severance pay. This time, it doesn't look like these people [the Israelis] will return again for several years.

ABU-MŪSA [*stops playing with his prayer-beads, firmly*]: Ya wife, the Bedouin don't work for and steal from the hand greeting them with peace, be it Egyptian, Israeli, or Greek. Our God is one, and all of us wish to live in honor and peace. Enough of this ugly talk!

Israelis, Egyptians, and all the rest of them are now our guests in the Sinai, and our Mzeina code of hospitality is well known and respected!

ʿĪD: You mean, every *ʿīd, ṭīt,* and *ʿafrīt* ("holiday," "twitter," and "demon") who arrives here must be received as if he were a Bedouin? I will go bankrupt if I have to host those strangers!

GHĀNMA [*very angry*]: Ya Abu-Mūsa, guests don't give you ID cards and licenses and tell you where to go and where not to! Guests don't employ you or give you severance pay! Guests don't prescribe you medications or take your blood samples to Tel Aviv! Guests don't govern and punish you! What sort of guests are you talking about?

We are all quiet for several hesitant moments.

FARḤANA: And what about the huts in al-Billij? We have four huts. Now we have there a couple from near Tel Aviv, a German couple, three girls from some *moshāv*, and a strange American guy with a long beard—yuukk!—who doesn't haggle with my son over the price, and doesn't lie naked on the beach. Always, when the tourists come, they buy clothes like ours. And my son, he prepares for them *farashīḥ* (flatbread) and tea. Sometimes some suckers give him some of their food, because they think he's hungry. Afterwards [*bemused, chuckling*] they also pay for what he prepares for them. And this sort, they want to be like us. Sometimes, when I see them from afar, dressed in our men's robes, believe me, I am not sure who they are.

OMM-MŪSA [*angrily*]: We also have to "take" from them: sleeping bags, watches, dollars. Half of the day, when not dressed in our clothes, they go around naked and screw each other in front of all. Disgusting! [*She spits on the ground*] These are no Bedouin!

ʿĪD [*shouts*]: So tell me, you, Omm-Mūsa! Tell me, you [*pointing with his long index finger at each person sitting in the circle*], and you, all of you! Who are the Bedouin and who are the guests?! Our kids—they run around in Eilat and Sharm al-Sheikh with pants and shirts, and not only during worktime. [*Lowering his voice*] Do you remember the film that they shot about the life of—what's his name—Brian, in the Castle of Nuwēbʿa? That short *Inglīzi* (Englishman) wanted forty Bedouin to work with him [as extras]. When they came, they dressed up for work [i.e., with pants], and *he* was wearing a caftan *and* a headdress. His translator yelled at them: "You, Bedouins, should come to work as *Bedouin*, because you have to be Bedouin in the film," [*raising his voice*] See how? Soon the day will come when men start showing up to the magᶜad in pants!

There is a short, though disquieting, silence.

ABU-MŪSA [*shaking his head, to himself*]: And we, where shall we go? These days, even the tradition of hospitality is not with us any more. We don't know who is Bedouin and who is a guest. We don't know whether our guests respect us nor how we should respect them. And Honor has left us. Disappeared.

A long silence prevails. When honor is mentioned, silence always descends: honor is holy. The stormy wind, still beating the date trees, now brings us the sounds of a faraway cassette recorder.

The anthropologist finishes writing Abu-Mūsa's question and I tell her to try to immerse herself in the dim and distant sounds of the field night. But instead, she embarrassedly points to the fact that my fresh memories of that scary Bir al-Sarādga experience are now emerging from the silence.

When I finally arrived at Dahab after the Shgēṭef-the-Fool episode, Abu-Mūsa and several other elders insisted that I take Shgēṭef and his khamsa to the tribal customary court for having sent me off into the wilderness. But as an Israeli I felt I had hardly any right to stay with the Mzeina, let alone sue them.

But this evening Abu-Mūsa's penetrating question shakes me. The anthropologist wants to tell the people present that, despite the intrusions of the many foreign agencies into their daily life, ideas like tribal structure, social organization, and rituals of tradition remain alive and well. As a matter of fact, every day she fills her notebook with them.

"I swear to God, ya Abu-Mūsa," she can't hold me from bursting out. "Among the Mzeina, a guest is still a guest, and hospitality *is* hospitality. If one has a khamsa or is a ṭanīb of a khamsa, if that person or the ones who have offered him protection have only, really, only one karat of dates, then it becomes as clear as the morning's sun when one is a guest and when one is a host." In this way I repeat to Abu-Mūsa and ᶜĪd what they once told me about tribal membership and hospitality.

All eyes are focused on me. I feel the urge to continue, and tell the happy ending to my ᶜEin al-Akhaḍar experience.

"You might have heard how Shgēṭef the Fool fooled me when I wanted to visit the people of Bir al-Sarādga," I ask rhetorically.

"A deed that should *not* be done among us," some murmur to themselves.

I take a long breath. As I start narrating, the anthropologist reminds me: Smadar, now narrate your personal experience in Bedouin storytelling style. Don't be emotional. It is not allowed!

*

"After I spent the night alone, I woke up the next morning and decided to go down to where Wadi al-Akhaḍar meets Wadi Firān. I knew that people were there. I walked for a bit down the wadi. Suddenly I saw a woman, two toddlers, and a donkey climbing towards the well. When the woman noticed me, she veiled herself, grabbed her kids, left the donkey, and fled to the surrounding hills. I think she thought I was from some tourist group because of the way I dressed. Since my 'father' told me that one can never simultaneously have one's Self and also be an Other (*ma fi wāḥad illi yākhodh zamāno wazamān gheiro*—a Mzeini proverb), I wear long pants and a shirt. Yet I cover my head with a Bedouin white headdress *(ʿamāma)* because it helps against sun and dust."

"Yes, it helps," affirms Farḥāna, smiling and winking.

"It helps indeed," echoes Salīm with a serious voice.

"'Good morning, a morning of roses and jasmines to you, the mother of children,' I shouted to the woman while she was running away. 'God will bring good to your children,' I continued with a dry throat. Suddenly, the sound of rolling pebbles stopped. The woman had stopped running. She was trying to listen carefully.

"'I'm from the people of Dahab, the ṭanība of Khnēbish abu-ʿŌda abu-Ṣabbāḥ, from [the agnatic blood group of] the Wlād Salīm, of the [clan] Ghseināt, from [the phratry named] Wlād ʿAli,' I said in the way you taught me to introduce myself."

"Exactly in the way we taught her to introduce herself," Ghānma repeats my words to the rest, whose attention moves from my corner to her center spot near the bubbling tea kettle, and then immediately back to my corner.

"'Are you the one people call The One Who Writes Us? Her color is like yours, and your hips, like hers,' the woman shouted, removing her veil so that I could hear her more clearly [and also to connote that I was no longer a stranger].

"'Yes, it's I. I cut down the wadi [Mzeini's vernacular] from ʿEin al-Akhaḍar,' I said. She returned to her donkey, which stood calmly at the wadi's center and brushed its tail back and forth trying to shoo the flies from its back. And I approached her. The moment her children noticed my clothes, they started crying. We greeted each other, hugging the back of each other's neck and rapidly uttering, 'Salamāt, Salamāt, Salamāt,' kissing the air three times, swaying back and forth to the rhythm of the greetings. This is exactly how you taught me to greet women."

"And this is exactly how we taught her to greet us," echoes Mabsūṭa, swaying her head back and forth.

"'Shut up, kids! This is a woman from the people of Dahab, on the coast. That's the way our people there learned from strangers how to dress, so don't be afraid,' she soothed her kids, while winking at me.

"Then she said quite formally, 'I am Fṭaima omm-ʿAbdallh abu-Maḥmūd,[3] from the Rawāḥla [clan]. Our people encamp in Umm-Baʿatheirān, near here.'

"'You must be the sister of Faṭṭum abu-ʿAbdallh abu-Maḥmūd. I met him with the rest of the Shadhādhna [the phratry to which the Rawāḥla clan belongs] last week, during the pilgrimage to Faranje,' I said, trying to find mutual friends and relatives *(nas waʿeila).*"

"Friends and relatives," Abu-Mūsa mutters to himself while rolling his prayer-beads between his right hand fingers.

"'Yeah, my brother told me that you even donated money for repairs to the shrine, like all the rest. Allah's blessing be upon you.'"

"Suddenly we established eye contact. Fṭaima held my arms and said, 'You, what's wrong with you?! Your eyes are red and yellow! Last night—where were you?' I told Fṭaima the events of that night.

"'No one believes Shgēṭef. Three wives have left him. The Fool is a *fool*,' she said angrily. Immediately she searched the pocket sewn to the bottom of her head-cover *(wugā)* and took out a mash of sweet large dates. 'Eat, my child,' she said. I ate the dates as if they were manna from heaven and said, 'God will bring peace to the mother of children.' She smiled, and we started walking towards the well while gossiping about who's doing what in Dahab, and in Umm-Baʿatheirān and vicinity.

"Arriving back at the well, Fṭaima seated me and her kids in the shade and then went to gather dried twigs. She soon returned and started kneading dough, from which she baked *gurs bil-nār* (a type of bread served to guests). She served it with hot, sweet tea."

"So Fṭaima served her little guest gurs bil-nār soaked in tea," adds Salīm.

"We spent a whole day near the well. Goatherds arrived, a man on his camel passed by, a sheikh and his family on their personal pilgrimage to the shrine of Ḥbūs, there to ask for health, joined our lunch.

Fṭaima told my story to everyone. 'The Fool can't tell who's a guest and who is an outsider,' they said."

"The Fool is a *fool*," some of the audience murmur to themselves.

"Just before dusk we slowly carried ourselves back to Umm-Baᶜath-eirān. Fṭaima brought me to the magᶜad. She introduced me and my Bedouin *aṣal* (descent line) to the men and told them my story. One went aside and took from a box a long narrow rug, reserved for guests. He spread the rug and told me to sit on his right. Soon we found out that we had all joined in on the last pilgrimage to Faranje.

"'The duty of hospitality is with us tonight,' said Fṭaima's husband, who sat down to my left, between me and the other man. He took green coffee beans out of one of the boxes and roasted them in a pan on the glowing embers. Then we heard the blessed sound of a pestle pounding the mortar, and echoes answered from the surrounding hills. We started to drink cycles of bitter coffee followed by sweet tea, as hosts and guests do."

"As hosts and guests always *must* do," Abu-Mūsa slowly and firmly repeats the end of my sentence, while the rest nod their heads in agreement.

"'Tonight is a night of meat,' Fṭaima's husband declared solemnly. 'I am *not* so important that you need to waste your *ḥalāl* in my honor,' I protested."

While I'm telling this detail to my audience, the anthropologist notes that I used the Bedouin vernacular, where "ḥalāl" refers to livestock. Interestingly, she muses, in Classical Arabic, as well as in the Mzeina vernacular, "ḥalāl" is what is permitted to Muslims, as opposed to "ḥarām," the taboos. I cut short her scholarly meditations, reminding her that I'm in the middle of telling a *Bedouin* story to a Bedouin audience.

"'I swear to God, I have no hunger for meat!' I said firmly, as you taught me to say in such situations."

"As we taught her," echoes Omm-Mūsa.

"So Fṭaima's husband didn't press any more. After the *maghreb* prayer, Fṭaima's eldest son brought a round platter packed with rice and those precious dried fish. We blessed, ate, blessed again and washed our hands. After dinner, the men prayed the ᶜasha. Then, we talked about things, the situation, and the world."

"Things, situations, and the world," Salīm parrots. "*Ya rab* (oh, God), how she has learned to talk like a Mzeini," he continues with astonishment.

"Then Fṭaima returned, her hands loaded with blankets, and asked if I wanted to be hosted as a woman [i.e., to sleep in the corner of her family tent], or as a man, [i.e., to sleep alone in the magʿad]. After a short argument, I convinced her that my sleeping bag was quite adequate, the same way you taught me to say things in such a situation, and I slept in the magʿad—as you instructed me when I asked you what I should do when I am invited to stay in a woman's tent while her husband is home."

"Right!" Omm-Mūsa approves of my action.

"Aa-ha!" agree some of the rest.

"Three evenings I spent with the men, and wrote about summer migrations, and date tree ownerships, and conflicts, and trials, and the Israeli and Egyptian governments, and the Camp David agreement, and on war and on peace. Three days I spent with the women, and wrote about marriages, and divorces, and births, and illness, and amulets, and herds, and on the Camp David agreement, and on war and on peace.

"Afterwards I rented a camel and joined riders who came from ʿEin al-Akhaḍar, and we went down to the orchards of Ṭarfat al-Gdeirain. And here I have told you about Mzeina's tradition of hospitality, and this is the end of my story, and this is your peace." The anthropologist instructs me here to end with this common closure of stories or rhymed epics.

"And this is your peace," everyone responds in unison.

Once again Salīm turns on the transistor radio and hunts for late night news.

III.

During the following winter I related my ʿEin al-Akhaḍar story five more times to groups of Mzeinis. The context leading to it was always some unresolvable argument about the Mzeina tradition of hospitality. Among the "guests" who arrived in the Sinai that winter were high ranking army officers of Egypt, Israel, the United States and the United Nations, various developers of large-scale international tourism making preliminary surveys for the Egyptian government, and thousands of tourists, who felt that this would be their last chance to catch a glimpse of the "real" wilderness of the South Sinai peninsula before it lost its pristine charm forever.

I spent that spring in Jerusalem, completing my bachelor's degree and classifying piles of fieldnotes in preparation for graduate school in Berkeley. I puzzled over whether my story reconstructed the Mzeinis' image of themselves, or their image of me, or perhaps even of my professional image of myself. I was also unsure as to whether my role as an anthropologist included telling the people I studied stories about themselves.

In May 1979, I returned to the Sinai but felt embarrassed asking why Shgēṭef and Fṭaima had treated me in contradictory fashions, what the meanings behind their actions were, and what meanings my story had generated.

Ramaḍān in August 1979 was the last month of my fieldwork. Arriving at Dahab, I told myself that this was my last chance to decode the mystery of the contradictions. Was I just another Israeli to the Mzeina? And if so, why was I assigned a fictive genealogy and adopted into the tribe?

During the long, hot days of the daytime fast, everyone but the children napped between the daily prayers. In the shade of date trees on the outskirts of the settlement, men lay on the beach. The women rested in the huts. During the short nights men gathered in their magᶜad while women gathered in one of the huts, each group spending its time eating slowly, reciting long traditional poems, or discussing human relations.

12 August 1979, Dahab, 11:00 A.M.

Since I didn't wake up and thus missed the late night meal, I go down to the coastline to gather some sea snails which I'll boil for lunch. I notice Abu-Mūsa and ᶜĪd stretching after post-morning-prayer naps. In preparation for the noon prayer they go down to the tidal zone and wash their arms, legs, and faces in the sea. I finish gathering sea snails and sit nearby, under the shade of a date tree. On this dry, hot day the three of us are captivated by the moist caress of the breeze as we wait for the muezzin's cry. I am reluctant to interrupt the flow of silence, but I have only three weeks left.

As if talking to myself I hesitantly say, "Ever since last summer, I have been perplexed as to why Shgēṭef the Fool sent me, with all my equipment, to the deserted Bir al-Sarādga."

A long moment passes till ᶜĪd says, "You are an Israeli. Very soon, all sorts of Jews will go away from here, and then the Egyptians will come. Now we don't owe you anything any more. Not that we want the Egyptians over here, but your peace has left us no choice. Shgēṭef knows that like the rest of us."

More long moments pass, during which I count over and over again the sea snails in my lap.

"If so, why did Fṭaima respect me with all the tradition of hospitality?" I ask with less hesitation.

Abu-Mūsa shifts his back, negotiating a new leaning position on the date tree trunk and says, "Because you are one of us. You are The One Who Writes Us. Write that we have a proverb which says: O, flee from the friend who abandons you, in his hands lie your family's graves. But breastfeed him who breastfeeds you—tell your children to serve him like slaves *(Min ʿadāk ʿadī, ʿomrok ma hu fi īdo. Wa-min dadāk dadī—wakhalli wlādoc ʿabīdo)*. Now, we breastfeed you with our lives and with the stories about our lives, and your children are the notebooks you fill. That's why you're almost twenty-five and still unmarried. And the stories in your notebooks on our lives and our words serve us too, and one day they'll also serve our children."

At this moment I suddenly perceive the paradox and say, "Once you taught me that one can *never* simultaneously have one's Self and be an Other."

Abu-Mūsa and ʿĪd spontaneously rhyme their answer, "But The One Who Writes Us has taken both selves."

And then we laugh.

22 August 1979, Dahab, 5 P.M.

The last day of the Ramaḍān fast. Ghānma's hut. Ghānma, Omm-Mūsa, and I have just finished cooking the meal that will break the fast. We try to keep talking in order to forget our hunger and the creeping time. I sneak in a tough question. "By the way, why did Shgēṭef the Fool fool me last summer?"

"Don't worry," says Omm-Mūsa. "Next year he'll do the same thing to every Egyptian who sniffs around ʿEin al-Akhaḍar. He didn't know that you're also from here."

My feeling that the politically alert "Fool" knew exactly what he was doing is strengthened. I guess that that "memorable night" was part of the price I pay for being an Israeli who studies a Muslim Arab culture. I am very sad and silent for a while, but still . . .

"And Fṭaima, God bless her, does she think differently?" I continue. Ghānma laughs and says, "The women of Umm-Baʿatheirān saw the tourists only a few times in their lives. For them, everyone who knows how to say, 'I am a Bedouin,' is a Bedouin. Ah . . . the people of the Highlands!" And she laughs contemptuously.

I take a deep breath and dare to ask it: "So, what do I mean to you?"

Omm-Mūsa answers decisively: "You are The One Who Writes Us. Once we had a silly argument about what kind of Bedouin we are, and you had your notebook opened, and read us one of the stories about our roots."

"OK, but other Israelis also write about your lives," I argue.

Omm-Mūsa thinks for a moment and says, "True, but all those people do not physically stay *only* with us when they come to the Sinai. They live in the settlements of the Jews."

Ghānma continues and compliments me on how well I fish and graze and churn yogurt and climb on date trees and ride camels and play the goatherd flute, and whatnot, after four years of living with the Mzeina. Why does she try to make me feel so good about myself now, when I am about to leave? She has always been so honest with me. I stop listening attentively and become immersed in my own thoughts. I perk up when I hear her say:

"And your eyes are as dark as ours, and you don't become a roasted lobster after long days in the sun." Noticing my response, she pauses.

It's my turn to talk now, but I can only search for the words. At this silent moment we once again become aware of the smell of the taboo food and of the animal coiled in our souls, ready to pounce the moment the muezzin cries for the last time, "Eat now, you who are fasting!"

"My roots are jumbled." Thankfully, in the shade no one can easily tell that I am blushing. It never occurred to me that my split Israeli ethnic identity would be of any interest to the Bedouin, aside from the fact that the many Mzeinis who went to the Al-Aqsa mosque in Jerusalem for the Friday prayer visited the nearby house of my grandmother. She speaks a Yemenite dialect of Arabic, one very close to the Eastern Bedouin dialect,[4] and she felt she had to reciprocate the hospitality her granddaughter received in the South Sinai.

"One of my halves is from Yemen. In Israel we are called Arab Jews." I immediately stop without finishing what I had intended to say. Suddenly I connect my Israeli label with Mzeina vernacular. In the South Sinai dialect of Arabic only Bedouin are referred to as Arabs. The rest are labeled peasants or city dwellers, who are Egyptians, Syrians, Lebanese, or natives of other Middle Eastern countries. For them, an Arab Jew is a Bedouin Jew.

Aii-wah! the eyes of the two women light up. "We know you, ya Smadar," says Ghānma. "Only you and Mister Marri, the English

TWO MZEINIS PEERING IN G. F. MURRAY'S TRAVELOGUE, *SONS OF ISHMAEL* (1935). ONE IS AMAZED TO FIND THERE HIS FATHER'S PICTURE.

Bedouin, lived with us," continues Omm-Mūsa. And the anthropologist immediately connects Mister Marri with George F. Murray, the only one to actually live with the Mzeina for a couple of years during the 1920s, and with his travelogue, *Sons of Ishmael* (1935). "You came here to update and correct his book . . . Both of you always told us how beautiful it is to climb to the top of the mountains just for looking at the rest of the mountains. Besides, my great-uncle taught Mister Marri to fish, and my husband taught you to fish. Old people like me know how to connect the past with the present (*illi kān lilmakān*),"[5] says Omm-Mūsa, and I wonder whether we are still in the same story or if perhaps we have started narrating another one.

IV.

Writing about the process of authorship in allegorical narration, Paul De Man has argued that "The moment when th[e] difference" between the persona of the author and the persona of the fictional narrator "is asserted is precisely the moment when the author does not return to the world. He asserts instead the ironic necessity of not becoming the dupe of his own irony and discovers that there is no way back from his fictional self to his actual self" (1969:200). And interestingly, both De Man and Arthur Koestler (1964:73) have viewed allegory and irony as the two poles of a similar genre.

I think it would be somewhat easier for someone who feels like an equal member of Western Culture to agree with De Man's assertion. Nonetheless, I feel that my allegorical Other (The One Who Writes Us) and my personal Self (consisting of both The Anthropologist and Smadar the woman) are fused. Searching for my identity, as the Bedouin do, I find that it is not at all an essence, but entirely conjunctural, arising out of the circumstances of my being born into a certain family in Israel, and my choice of profession.

Part of my identity is that of a Western-trained professional anthropologist. Moreover, my father was a Northern European. From my mother I have my Arab culture, color, and temperament. In spite of the fact that ethnic identity is determined by the Israeli government according to the father's origin, and thus I appear as a European piece of data in bureaucratic statistics, it is my Arab half that counts socially. Since I am of dark complexion, Israelis always assume that I am a full Yemenite and treat me accordingly. Unlike my European descent, my Arab heritage qualifies me (at least in Israel) as a genuine, semicivilized Other. During my graduate studies, as I went back to classifying and analyzing my fieldnotes, I noticed that a theme of two exotic and voiceless Others emerged: my life experience in Israel was somehow mirrored in the life experience of the Mzeinis—and theirs in mine.

As a woman anthropologist, I was fully dependent on the Mzeina's hospitality once I reached the South Sinai. When the tradition of hospitality was called into question, despite my embarrassment I felt an urge to rise up and allegorize my Shgēṭef-the-Fool and Fṭaima-and-her-two-toddlers experience. In spite of being a stranger dressed in baggy jeans and a Mickey Mouse T-shirt, I had been taught how to introduce myself to my hosts. Whenever I introduced myself to my Bedouin hosts, I momentarily became a living representation of their traditional tribal structure and organization. I was adopted by the tribe, and as such was shown the path of Mister Marri. I was breastfed on stories about the life of the Mzeina, and now, by telling you my anthropological interpretations, I am enacting once again The One Who Writes Us.

Insofar as my Self is composed of two quite distinct identities, I am myself a composite of two Others. Each half of me is the Other of my other Self. I am able to be an Other both to European Israelis and to the Bedouin Mzeinis. In an ever more complicated relationship, I could spontaneously satisfy the Mzeinis' need to have someone play the part of an Other who, simultaneously, is not an Other. As neither identity may be reduced to the other, like those other quirky Mzeini tension dissolvers, I am in myself a metaphor of bifurcation, of unity in division, of a paradox without resolution.

INTERLUDE

HAJJ X: But you, why did you finish this part of the story with so much *khantarīsh* (bullshit) that sounds just like the lessons in Islam that come from the transistor radio?

ANTHROPOLOGIST: We have agreed that I should write some general remarks . . . Well, this is how we tell stories in my work.

HAJJ X: You and your work . . . And the university . . . Since Israel occupied these lands I've seen so many people from universities—collecting stones, plants, mice, rain, even hyena dung . . . God! you make me laugh!

◂ A LEADER OF A FISHERMEN GROUP

10
WHEN IDENTITY BECOMES ALLEGORY

The Poetic Reconstruction of Military Occupation

When . . . history becomes a part of the setting, it does so as script. The word "history" stands written on the countenance of nature in the characters of transience. The allegorical physiognomy of nature-history, which is put on stage . . . is present in reality in the form of the ruin. In the ruin history has physically merged into the setting. And in this guise history does not assume the form of the process of an eternal life so much as that of irresistible decay. Allegory thereby declares itself to be beyond beauty. Allegories are, in the realms of thoughts, what ruins are in the realm of things.

WALTER BENJAMIN
The Origin of German Tragic Drama

A BEDOUIN TOUR GUIDE AND "HIS" TOURIST

FRAGMENTATION

"But we know damn well how to play our stories!" So said Sheikh ʿAlwān, and any of the other six characters to whom this book has been devoted—the Madwoman, the Ex-Smuggler, the Old Woman, the Fool, the Symbolic Battle Coordinator, and The One Who Writes Us—could have said the same. Indeed, the collective lived experience of the Mzeina as a tribe, under perpetual military occupations generating an atmosphere of continual crisis, is mirrored in the personal narratives of this cast of characters. From the polyphonies of the many voices conversing, arguing, teasing, laughing, telling stories, and reciting or improvising poetry, it is clear that the Mzeinis as individuals and as members of their tribe—a social construct having no "pure essence" (Husserl 1962:50), but rather, requiring continual re-creation—are torn between economic and cultural survival (cf. Lavie and Young 1984; Marx 1977*a*, 1980; Rabinowitz 1985). Mzeini women and men struggle to preserve their tribal identity by trying to sort out their lived experience under foreign occupation, in order to reconstitute, at least temporarily, their own tradition as tribesmembers (cf. Shils 1981:256-261; Wagner 1981:51). This reconstitution of tradition salvages Bedouin identity from the cultural infringement of Israeli and Egyptian political and economic forces, which Mzeinis can confront directly only at great risk to their lives.

Fredric Jameson (1986:68) has argued that due to the hegemonic relationship between West and East (cf. Said 1978), one of the few kinds of resistance tribal societies can mount to Western economic and political encroachment is cultural (cf. JanMohamed, 1983, 1985). Joel Fineman (1981:28) has noted that "allegory seems regularly to surface in critical or polemical atmospheres, when for political or metaphysical reasons there is something that cannot be said." Both these statements find support in the ways Mzeinis generate meanings that they attribute to the symbol of the tribe, and translate these meanings into cultural action, repeatedly transmuting their everyday experience of life under occupation into allegorical stories they tell only among themselves. The history of the present, what happened just yesterday or a week ago, often conceived as the impingement of an alien nation-state upon the Mzeinis' idyllic image of the classic Bedouin tribe, is called upon to salvage the tribe's nostalgic history of its past.

The Mzeini allegories embody current personal stories improvised as a variant on a particular traditional genre of legends, the *Kān Ya Makān*. The literal meaning of "Kān Ya Makān" is both "once upon a time there was a place," and "it has or has not happened that . . ." It is a genre of fantastic tales that are didactic in showing shining examples of noble Bedouin behavior occurring in the "pure," ideal setting of free-spirited nomadism, outside the context of any colonial power or its nation-state replacement. The Kān Ya Makān legends are believable as stories. But since the fate of the protagonists might not have been in fact what the legends tell, these stories are unbelievable if claimed to be factual. The Mzeini improvised allegories of everyday life, in contrast, are full of incongruities so extreme that they are hardly believable as seamless, artificed stories, but since they are performed with artistic persuasion and unity, any Mzeini of the audience can accept them as perfectly true representations of his or her fragmented daily life.

Extemporaneously reversing the conventions of the Kān Ya Makān genre, the Mzeinis create their allegories by telling each other their own stories about the fantastic components of their everyday lives, laced with absurdities like an Israeli minister who comes down from the skies in a helicopter, in search of a puppy. He requests it not from the tribal dignitaries but from a crumpled little old woman, who cleverly takes advantage of this fortuitous event to bargain for some urgently needed water storage barrels for her community.

Other such incidents abound. A young, muscular Israeli ranger forces a reluctant old sheikh to drag his bones up a mountain, just to hear yet another restriction announced on the Bedouin way of life. But the sheikh outsmarts him twice. First he talks him out of the new law by revealing the amazing fact that the Bedouin have longstanding intertribal agreements to protect the fragile desert ecology. Then the ranger asks him the name of the sunset-glorified mountaintop they are on. Though from time immemorial it has had no name, the sheikh, aware of the Western obsession with exerting control over uncivilized nature by moving from one named point to another on a topographic map, spontaneously announces that it is called "Peak of the Sunset." In due course this name starts appearing on official maps.

An Ex-Smuggler, to avoid admitting he had been in error in an argument about validating the social structure of the traditional Bedouin tribe, appeals for authority to the work of a Canadian anthropologist, and quotes a proverb that must be a traditional Bedouin one, he says, because it has been published in America.

The annual pilgrimage of the Mzeina to their ancestral shrine has to be held in the presence of the Israeli military governor, accompanied by his miniskirt-clad secretary. He speaks no Arabic, and his translator is not fluent in the Mzeini dialect and therefore cannot understand the Mzeinis' improvised verses of resistance, sung right under his and his boss's noses.

At the Dahab beach, young Mzeinis, who are of course Muslim, toy around with celebrating Christmas, even sacrificing a lamb for a holiday feast, while their pious fathers have learned to give free unsolicited advice about coitus to the naked hippies frolicking on the sand.

Traditional gender roles become severely stressed and dislocated in a society that believes passionate wives have to be subordinate to rational husbands, even when the husbands are absent for up to a month at a time due to economic and political pressures. The women find they have to develop their female capacity for endurance into what they were brought up to recognize as an active male rationality, in spite of the fact that Islam does not attribute this to women.

A Mzeini woman from the remote inland highlands has never been to the coast but has heard rumors about how Western tourists have affected Bedouin life there. When she first encounters a bedraggled female anthropologist wearing not only jeans and a Mickey Mouse T-shirt, but also a traditional male headdress, she assumes the apparition must be one of those tourists. When the strange woman speaks to her in the coastal Mzeini dialect and introduces herself with all the proper personages, the Mzeini woman accepts her as a true Bedouin deserving the best she can muster in the way of hospitality.

Making events such as these into stories, the narrators reify to both the audience and themselves that in the here-and-now of occupied Sinai, the absurdly impossible is not only possible but commonplace, whereas what ought to be within the realm of Bedouin everyday possibilities has become impossible to attain by common-sense courses of action. The absurd and the quotidian therefore merge to generate not only a hybrid Bedouin lifestyle far outside the conventions of what has been depicted in the anthropological literature, but also to generate the Mzeinis' own spontaneous stories they tell about this "culture shock of daily experience" (Wagner 1981:35), nestling them intuitively in the archaic "once upon a time" genre.

Mzeina allegories, like all allegories, have a dialectical nature. They elevate, yet devalue, the immoral profane world of global politics by memorializing ordinary events as grotesque didactic tales emphasizing indigenous ethics and morality (Benjamin 1985:168–175). They sustain the Mzeina belief in the immortality of their collective tribal past, yet all the while, they repeatedly make the Mzeinis confront and mourn the extent to which they are entrapped within the global fluctuations of the present (Benjamin 1985:209). They attempt to represent the image of the tribe as being a noble whole (Fernandez 1986:206–211), but this is impossible, in fact, because in recent history the Mzeina as a tribe has never had a political and economic existence independent of the colonial powers or an occupying nation-state. Therefore, "in the field of allegorical intuition, the image is a fragment, a rune. Its beauty as a symbol evaporates . . . The false appearance of totality is extinguished" (Benjamin 1985:176)—the image of the tribe becomes fragmented.

PARADOX

Unlike many other literary forms, an allegory is deliberately self-critical, a cultural text already containing literary criticism of itself (Frye 1976:89–90; Quilligan 1979:25–26).[1] The narrator who tells the allegory, and the narrative that constitutes his or her story, artistically construct a portrait of a given reality, while at the same time culturally criticizing that reality as well as him- or herself. These allegories are therefore not only tropological constructions of a given reality (White 1983:96), but are also the "tropes of tropes," or "representative of critical activity *per se*" (Fineman 1981:27). Jameson has argued that "the story of the private individual destiny is always an allegory of the embattled situation of the public . . . culture and society" (1986:69). In this manner allegories simultaneously voice both subjective and objectified representations (Berger and Luckman 1967:19–23, 34–37) of both the logico-meaningful texts and their many causal-functional meanings (Parsons 1951).

Northrop Frye considered allegorical literary forms to be the most explicit, in contrast to paradoxical ones, which he described as anti-explicit and elusive (1973:92,103). Stephen Greenblatt (1981), however, has suggested that allegory, being a text that contains its own criticism, is itself paradoxical: it arises from the loss of an authoritative tradition that it aims to recover. For the Mzeina, their identity as Bedouin is what is at stake, and it may indeed never have existed as they yearn for it to be.

The Mzeini allegories told by the characters are saturated with both personal and tribal paradoxes, reflecting and revealing each other. The allegories per se, as literary artifacts, serve at least temporarily to solve the paradoxes that constitute them. Paradoxical themselves, they clarify for their listeners some of the conundrums in the crisis in Mzeini Bedouin identity. The ambiguities of Mzeini daily life implicitly provide the materials for everyday conversation (cf. Jackson 1982). As soon as these ambiguities surface and are verbalized explicitly by any one of the characters, a temporary coherence seems to have been achieved by both the teller of the allegory and the audience, even though they all realize that the paradoxes of life under occupation remain to be faced, as before. These allegories, in fact, could not have emerged *unless* there were paradoxes outside the allegorical frame, in real life. When that was the case, allegory might emerge from the interstices of everyday life because it provided the audience with an "iconographic" way (cf. Daniel 1984:1–57; Firth 1973:61, 202–203) of integrating these paradoxes into their lives.

In each chapter the set of paradoxes—those of the tribe as reflected in the character, and those of the individual character as reflected in the tribe—were unfolded, re-unfolded and further unfolded in three or four interrelated vignettes. Sheikh ʿAlwān's vignettes exposed the difficulties he encountered while trying to represent the tribe to the external occupying power. The paradoxes that frustrated him included the fact that the Mzeina conceived of themselves as the people of the land, but had no say in who occupied it. Also, the Mzeina did not respect their Sheikh but were still dependent on him for most communication with the occupier. Thus the Sheikh embodied not only the Mzeina in the eyes of the occupier, but also the occupier in the eyes of the Mzeina. All these equivocalities were first revealed to me in the emotional outburst of the sheikh's wife, elaborated upon in the conversation in the magʿad, clarified by Sheikh ʿAlwān's story about how he prevented yet another law from being imposed on the Bedouin, and then explained to me in my conversation with the three sheikhs several months later, where they admitted the irony that their power was limited to telling stories of defiance against the government they had to serve.

While Sheikh ʿAlwān's conundrums emanate strictly from the juncture of the state and the tribe, Ḥajj Khantarīsh, the fictional Ex-Smuggler, had to juggle the impacts of the occupiers on two conflicting sets of relationships among the Mzeinis themselves: kinship and wage-labor. As we have seen, the Mzeinis draw their idealized identity from the image of the nomad, all the while being forced to subsist on wage-labor. The tribe also declares that it bases itself on the tradition of segmentary agnation, but people's everyday relations (such as wage-labor) are spun from individually based networks. According to the creative imagination of X the Ex, Ḥajj Khantarīsh had made the best of both worlds by using the traditional strategies of free-spirited nomadic pastoralism to underpin his 1950s wage-labor smuggling fiefdom. The kinship/wage-labor incongruities surfaced when X the Ex and I told Ḥajj Khantarīsh to ask his anthropologist to take his genealogy, as he knew anthropologists usually wanted to do, but then to immediately contradict this generous offer by declaring that genealogies were meaningless. These antinomies arose again in Khantarīsh's conversation with his guests, followed by his awkward unexpected silence that served to acknowledge the importance of segmentarity as a tribal ideology, even though he avoided admitting this outright. When X the Ex and I discussed the strategies we should use to textualize the tribe as an abstract model capable of cross-cultural comparison, I took notes in conventional anthropological jargon. When I read these notes back to X, he remarked that this kind of rhetoric had nothing to do with the life it claimed to describe. And both X the Ex's conversation with me, and our fictional Ḥajj Khantarīsh's conversation with his anthropologist were punctuated by long silences, pointing to the fact that the paradoxes of both the tribe and its ethnographic textualization have no solutions—the meaning of the ethnographic construct of tribe is determined contextually.

The Symbolic Battle Coordinator pushes the paradoxes emanating from the tribe-state juncture—conundrums resulting in the kinship/wage-labor discrepancies—further into the inner topoi of inter- and intratribal discourse. The Mzeinis routinely described their agnatic units as "scrambled," despite the fact that they yearned to be like "the rest of 'em," the classical Bedouin, with dual opposition segmentarity of communal genealogies that agree with personal descent lines. And unlike other tribal alliances, the Ṭawara lacked any mythical kinship or marriage relationship between the ancestors of the tribes comprising it and did not wage intertribal battles, not even poetic ones. As members of the Ṭawara, the Mzeinis conceived of themselves as egalitarian pastoral nomads, whereas they were in fact quite stratified and not so pastoral. The Symbolic Battle Coordinator, however, was a representational disposition of these equivocations. As one of the very few remaining shining examples of the classical nomad, he held to the full traditional migratory cycle, lived almost solely by pastoralism, and had a relatively pure line of descent he could trace from the tribal ancestor—a personal descent congruent with the communal genealogy. He was therefore one of the few Bedouin capable of leading the Ṭawara in internal political decision making by using the traditional process of negotiated consensus. These South Sinai intra- and intertribal incongruities with the classical model of the Bedouin alliance first appeared in the ʿarīsha during the pilgrimage of the Mzeinis to their ancestral tomb, and were further reinforced in the Wadi Firan intertribal *barlimān*. The Symbolic Battle Coordinator's legislation, protecting the traditional Ṭawara assets from rapid state-initiated sedentarization, was a forceful reification of the consensual pastoral democracy. But this action was not solely within the topos of internal Bedouin discourse. Because he insisted that his legalistic formulations be ratified by acclamation of the people, the Symbolic Battle Coordinator's lawmaking was the polar opposite of the decrees issued by the occupiers.

The occupation not only made the genuine and venerable conductors of segmentary concensus somehow irrelevant except on strictly ritual occasions, but had also penetrated the locus of gender relations. In the absence of many Mzeini men due to labor migration, Ḥajja Ḥmēda, the Old Woman, found that the prohibition against interaction with male strangers now had to oddly coexist with nosy military officials, developers, and even with naked tourists. Worse was the economic reality of skimpy wages that forced the women to assume income-generating roles that contradicted purdah restrictions. One of the results of such heresies was a gender role reversal: an old woman grammatically referred to by the name "old man," a woman unofficially filling the role of settlement headman, a woman allowed to shed the visual symbols of controlled womanhood. The paradoxicality of forced redefinitions of gender roles first appeared in Ḥajja Ḥmēda's enterprise of marketing the generic Bedouin woman's cloistered image for money from tourists. It then gradually surfaced in the conversation in the inner yard of her son and daughter-in-law, then was made explicit in her performed story about how she traded a puppy to some Israeli Minister for really valuable storage barrels that had been military property. Her assertive behavior in Tel Aviv, insisting on her rights at the dolphin show, reinforced the portrayal of her ambiguous womanhood and the symbolic and practical ways it had come to serve the tribe.

The lives of other Mzeini women, who were still confined to the code of shame, suffered the effects of the breakdown of the tribe's traditional constructions of gender and sexuality. An extreme example of the way in which geopolitical forces can shake out of balance the innermost sexual feelings of an individual is the tragic fate of ʿAlyii, whose madness erupted out of two paradoxes: men were expected to be orthodox, rational Muslim fathers but they had to depend on forming far-flung marriage networks as economic insurance against shifting geopolitical circumstances—rather than forming marriage networks for religious or familial reasons. They felt forced to keep remarrying their daughters off to young men those daughters did not love—men the daughters even blamed for being "lusty." Concurrently, women were expected to be orthodox, passionate wives, yet they found that they had to develop a rationality that was believed to be exclusively male just to endure their fathers' and husbands' frequently shifting strategies of coping with the vicissitudes of the hinterland's daily life. Those conundrums first surfaced in the wish of young Kāmla, on the eve of her first marriage, to have the Madwoman's freedom from reconciling herself with her husband, though Kāmla was unable to admit ʿAlyii's entrapment in her madness. The incongruous notions of rational/lusty men and passionate/enduring women were further revealed during the conversation in Ghānma's inner yard and then artistically expressed in the Madwoman's melodramatic performance, where she revealed to her exclusively female audience how her desperate efforts to reconcile these two paradoxes had driven her mad—far away from the norms of women's behavior. Later, after reflecting about the different *jinn*s that possess men and women, the Madwoman once again reenacted these unsolvable conundrums in her riotous march into the hightide sea.

Paul De Man (1969:191–209) and Arthur Koestler (1964:73) have viewed allegory and irony or satire as the two poles of a similar genre. Many paradoxicalities discussed above received their most trenchant expression in the buffoonery of Shgēṭef the Fool, which combined the two poles. Shgēṭef, a fully dressed pious Bedouin, nevertheless catered to shockingly naked hippies on the spectacular Sinai beaches, where a hybridized oxymoron had sprung up between Western tourism and its romantic image of outlandish Bedouin life. This silly klutz, a savvy entrepreneur, was selling sins but donating his profits to support a local religious revival. In the Dahab fake tourist village during the

Christmas night celebration, to the music of Madonna and Simon and Garfunkel, he cryptically expressed this oxymoron, muttering that he was wage-working at playing the image of the noble nomad. It reappeared in the evening conversation of the Dahab men who tried unsuccessfully to reconcile themselves to the distasteful idea that "selling sins" was a better way to make a living than doing menial labor for the occupier. The oxymoron was brilliantly and hilariously dramatized in the Fool's farce about the topsy-turvy world of the hippies—a performance that reaffirmed Mzeini tribal identity by way of negation. And due to the Fool's eloquent and whimsical expression of the not-so-laughable Mzeini oxymoronic existence, the men in his audience were willing, as their old poem about the Fool phrased it, to follow in his footsteps.

The anthropologist conducting fieldwork in this enigmatic context came to a fresh realization that she herself embodied paradoxes of identity. The Mzeinis considered her to be an Arab almost like themselves, not only because she had inherited from her mother Yemenite physical features, but also because her Jewish Yemenite grandmother had invited a dozen or so Mzeinis as overnight guests to her traditional Jerusalem home, and they had discovered that her native tongue was an Arabic dialect quite close to their own. So to the Mzeinis, the anthropologist was both an Arab and an Israeli like those who occupied the Sinai during the first four years of her research (1975–1979). And although the Israeli bureaucracy recorded her statistically in her father's line as a European Jew, she was denied the social benefits from this higher status in Israel because she looked Arab (cf. Shohat 1988). She had been sent to the middle of nowhere by one Fool who was taking out on her his resentment at the occupying Israelis; but she was rescued by another Bedouin, a woman, who treated her as a tribesperson, reenacting the almost defunct tradition of hospitality. As the guest of the Mzeina tribe, yet adopted into it—adopted, yet the most marginal member of the tribe—the anthropologist was able to clarify the Bedouin tradition of hospitality by sharing her unique perspective on the problem of unwanted guests. Her conversation with Mzeina men and women regarding the "we relationship" (Schutz 1962:316–318) that developed in the course of her fieldwork helped both her and the Mzeina to recognize their relationships to each other as simulacrums of Westernized Selves who were their own non-Western Others (cf. Baudrillard 1983; Koptiuch 1988).

Several anthropologists have pointed out the connection between liminality and paradox,[2] arguing that the surfacing of existential paradoxes brings about a transformation from the linear mundane flow to cyclical ritual discourse (cf. Leach 1961). Unlike ritual, however, which purposely functions to solve paradoxes, the Mzeini allegories serve only to explicate the paradoxes through performance. But these explicative declarations of the allegorical personae are so powerful that, although they do not have any effect on the policies of the occupier, they still provide some form of restoration of tribal dignity and identity.

INCARNATION

At what Peter McHugh termed moments of "emergence" (McHugh 1968:24), moments where the past, present, and future are analytically distinct and yet inextricable, allegories of Mzeina Bedouin identity arise. In such moments, feelings of social order dissolve into feelings of "anomie" (Durkheim 1933:192). And out of that anomie some attempts to reorder the social order might emerge. These moments occur when Mzeinis' everyday conversations about life in the here-and-now of occupied Sinai—life in contradiction to both the invented nonsectarianism of the Egyptian nation-state, and the exclusively Jewish Zionism of Israel (Lavie and Rouse 1988)—disintegrate into bitter arguments about what Bedouin identity under occupation should be. Feelings about the present precarious political situation are juxtaposed with feelings of eternity and fatalism associated with the Mzeinis' longstanding belief in the pure essence of the classical Bedouin tribe.

Historical scrutiny, however, demonstrates this essence to be an artifact. This model of "the tribe" Mzeinis held might have been an accurate reflection of the historical reality of other Bedouin tribes, who were relatively free from state control until the British central government was established in 1922.[3] Even as early as the eighteenth century, gentry who traveled to the South Sinai to observe and document free-spirited nomads like those they have seen in the Arabian peninsula wrote in their travelogues that the South Sinai Bedouin were not the classic nomadic pastoralists, but rather, skimping along in wage-labor poverty and therefore not free economically or politically (Rabinowitz 1985). This essence of the tribe is nothing but something to yearn for and argue about in allegories, which are therefore not practices of tribal "archaic survival, but . . . an ongoing process, politically contested and historically unfinished . . . [where] identity is conjunctural, not essential" (J. Clifford 1988:9,11).

The seven characters recounted personal experiences that conjoined the fragmented image of the tribe with the reality of their lives under the rule of the state—experiences of frustration, pain, physical discomfort, and spiritual humiliation. They fashioned these experiences into distanced, at times even funny, stories of the present, and thus molded current events into the stylized oral literary form of allegory. Therefore, despite the volatile subjects, both these characters and their audiences were able to grasp that their accounts were authentic legends of contemporary reality, reviving from personal and collective memory indigenous traditions long gone or about to disappear. These newly invented stories, cast in the "once-upon-a-time" genre, ceaselessly delineated for the Mzeina the boundaries between their own culture and the cultures of their occupiers. Individual trauma became a metonymy for the geopolitical trap, because "the telling of the individual story and the individual experience cannot but ultimately involve the whole laborious telling of the experience of the collectivity itself" (Jameson 1986:85–86; cf. Fletcher 1964:13). Moreover, the characters' experiences, molded into stories, succeeded in bringing to the surface other already familiar and easily recognized Bedouin stories, poems, and proverbs from the reservoir of collective memory—about past intertribal agreements, legal disputes, migration cycles, folk remedies, hospitality protocols, kinship and marriage patterns, issues of life and death, and the history of resistance to colonialism.

Each chapter's vignettes are stories within stories about stories. The Old Woman, for example, starts her performance by narrating to her audience the fact that, as much as the Bedouin are dependent on their occupier, the occupier also has some dependency on them. But later she begins another story, within the story about the occupier, by using the formulaic expression "Once." Then comes the fantastic tale of reality, about how the Israeli minister came down from the sky to look for a puppy. Within this tale she casually weaves in other stories about the customs of wheat grinding, bread making, and hospitality, all the while aware that she might be one of the last of her kind who is still able to practice the old ways and talk about them from personal experience. The anthropologist relates two additional vignettes that further illuminate the Old Woman's point that the occupiers are also dependent on the occupied. We meet the Israeli male tour guide who supports himself by showcasing the harems of those mysterious Muslim women to Israeli and American tourists. In the second vignette, the ethnographer tells how she took the Old Woman and her husband and daughter to the Sea-World-style dolphin show in Tel Aviv. When the police asked to see their IDs, and later when the group learned that the show was sold out, the Old Woman stood up to both the police and the cashier by asserting that their imperialist enterprises could not exist without resources that had been taken from her ancestral land. She insisted on being treated as an honored guest when she came for one day to visit the dolphins and fish that had belonged to her tribe for generations.

The most multilayered example of stories within stories about stories is that of X the Ex-Smuggler. First the reader encounters the dialogue of Smadar and X the Ex-Smuggler in the geographically remote but strategically central oasis. Encased in this first layer of narrative is the story that X and Smadar make up about Ḥajj Khantarīsh and his anthropologist. These fictional characters, however, are composites of several real people from real time. But the fictional characters proceed to narrate yet other stories that also occurred in real time: the story of Khantarīsh's worthless brothers, the story of Ṣabbāḥa, the woman married for five years yet still a virgin, and also a brief historical overview of the 1952–1972 smuggling period. Throughout the chapter, all the layers are laced with interruptions, when X the Ex and Smadar ponder how to construct the fictional characters based on the previously collected field data from which the fictive elements are being taken. In addition, all the story layers are ruptured with critiques of both the story that has just been constructed, and the actual process of composition.

Such layers of reflexivity evoke the feeling of being in a hall of mirrors. Like a hall of mirrors, an allegory captures the inclusiveness of timespans and the completeness of spaces (cf. Wimsatt, 1970:215–221) by providing so many partial fragments of reality so close together that the whole can be perceived from the fragments (cf. Fernandez 1986:188–191). Standing on the ruins of their culture, the Mzeinis mourn as they glimpse from the carefully arranged stones that used to delineate their fireplaces and tentsites, how beautiful the traditional way of life, in any of its incarnations, must have been.

VOCALITY

This book has been an attempt at contrapuntal narration, with the narrating voices being those of all the Mzeinis portrayed throughout (J. Clifford 1983). I have transcribed the flow of Mzeini lived experience even as the people were transforming it into their own cultural text. In addition, I have tried to capture the flow of ethnographic knowledge as it condenses from the field experience into finished ethnographic texts liked this one.

The paradoxes that surface in each character's dialogical vignettes (Bakhtin 1981), each vignette reflecting on the others, reveal that the culture of the Mzeina qua text, as well as this ethnographic text about the Mzeina culture, are both "orchestrations of multivocal exchanges occurring in politically charged situations" (J. Clifford 1988:10). But unlike conventional, seamless, classical symphonic texts, based on the principle of creating and resolving dissonances back into consonance, these orchestrations erupt spontaneously and are full of the unresolved dissonances that forced the eruptions.

During my first four years of fieldwork (1975–1979), I recorded many mundane after-prayer conversations that disintegrated into loud and hurtful arguments. Some were open-ended, abruptly discontinued, and never resolved. Others ended in communal agreement accompanied by the elevated feeling of *communitas* (Turner, 1969:96–7). A contemplative entry in my field diary reads:

Three years of fieldwork. What I miss the most is classical music. . . . I sometimes wonder what it is about these after-prayer conversations-turned-debates that reminds me so much of the first movement of a Beethoven piano sonata. This form begins, just like these arguments, with an exposition of two basic themes, a harsh and grandiose one—maybe the military occupation?—and an undulating, comforting one—perhaps Bedouin tradition? As the conversation develops into an argument, in various major and minor keys, it explores and exhausts all possible variations of the themes. In the finale the themes return. But something here is different from Beethoven! There is a reversal! The sumptuous theme becomes fleetingly evasive—it is the undulating theme that returns with grandeur. Indigenous tradition prevailing over foreign occupation? Also, something awkward happens in these arguments, something that differs from sonata rules of vocality. Here, while the exposition and development phases are multivocal, the recapitulation of the two themes is performed by a solo voice. Listening to it, I am amazed by its persuasive power to bring the argument to a harmonious conclusion.

The powerful soloists of these conversations-cum-debates were the seven characters who are the focus of the data chapters. I earlier argued that Mzeini men and women, in the era of colonialism followed by regional nationalism, tried to develop their economic and political talents to fine-tune their daily and ritual life to the discordant instruments of tribe and state. From the several vignettes that present each character in his or her fullness, I hope to have conveyed the fantastic idiosyncrasies of the South Sinai geopolitical situation. Perhaps in this era of superpower dominance over the local states of Egypt and Israel, and the concurrent state dominance over tribes, tribal identity can develop little further than allegory (Jameson 1981:34; 1986:78). Only the occult, the grotesque, or the fantastic multivocalities of allegory (cf. Benjamin 1985:171; Todorov, 1975:32) can transcend the cacophony of tribe and state.

The whole cast of characters demonstrated theatrical skills enabling them to play on the fact that, though Mzeina tradition is marginal to the tribe's everyday life, it still serves to define the identity of every tribesperson. Like the *allos* or otherness of allegories, each character conjoined in him- or herself the Mzeini Self and the occupier's Other. When each of them chose, on the spur of an angry moment, to rise up and take over the discussion, even by contributing an intimidating uninterrupted silence, as Ḥajj Khantarīsh did, they changed the abrasive open-ended argument by recapitulating its major themes. The characters first formulated the Mzeina paradoxes arising from the political situation, and then reformulated them. Acting these conundrums out while being their living embodiments, demonstrating how they were embodied in and acted out in themselves, these characters thus redefined the identity issues from a new, artistic perspective. Gifted with persuasive dramatic power, each summated the argument by improvising on traditional tribal themes, poetically "adjusting" them to present circumstances (cf. Lavie 1984, 1986, 1989).

In the course of thirteen years of fieldwork (1975–1988), I recorded many traditional stories, poems, and proverbs about Sheikhs, Ex-Smugglers, Fools, Madwomen, Symbolic Battle Coordinators, Old Women, and about George W. Murray, one of the few foreigners who came and lived for a couple of years with the Mzeina to write about their lives. This repository of folkloric texts led me to realize that the lives of my chosen characters, as storytellers caught up in the present, extended beyond their lifespans as real people in real time: they were both persons and allegorical personae. The allegories of present experience they told would have been meaningless if each character had not been able to act as an interlocutor by transforming him- or herself from a mere person to a dramatic persona, reenacting past exemplars of his or her type (Benjamin 1969; 1985:184). I wanted to explore what in the social context allowed these characters-as-persons first to transform themselves into their allegorical personae; then to communicate not only a message about themselves as particular types, but a further message about the historical context of the discrepancies between the tribe and the dominant state, and also between Mzeina tribal structure, social organization, and cultural action; and then to leave their allegorical personae and return to being plain persons until they chose once again to come upon the societal stage as personae.

PROCESS

Decomposition.[4] Caught in the midst of "familiar scenes" (Garfinkel 1967:35–36)—the ᶜId al Faṭr holiday activities; women gossiping while churning yogurt or casually chatting with guests; after-dinner mixed-gender conversations, or conversations in the magᶜad; the date harvest in Wadi Firān—Mzeini conversations sometimes gradually drifted from quotidian matters, under the rule of "The People of Politics," into argument. An anthropologist could theorize that the factious Mzeinis, regarding themselves as "The People of the Land," were intuitively trying to find both the structural essence (Lévi-Strauss 1967:271) and the experiential essence (Husserl 1962:48) of their being-in-the-world qua members of a Bedouin tribe.[5] As theoretically awkward as it may seem, it is conceivable that the Mzeinis were trying to reduce their cultural texts to what they thought was the essence of being "like the rest of 'em, the Bedouin." They were frustrated in their repeated attempts to do this, however, because they somehow could not admit to themselves that late twentieth-century Bedouin identity cannot be experienced as a genuine essence, but only, realistically, as a conjunction.

In Richard Grathoff's language (1970:58–61), while the Mzeinis were reflecting about themselves in these reductionist, bracketed terms, their routine typifications of reality became temporarily inconsistent, anomalous, and contradictory. From this "profoundly discontinuous spirit, a matter of breaks and heterogeneities, of the multiple polysemia of the dream rather than the homogeneous representation of the symbol" (Jameson 1986:73), paradoxes gradually surfaced. These paradoxes were imbued with liminal qualities, and immanent both in the position of the Mzeina vis-à-vis the homogenizing world, and in the position of each of the characters vis-à-vis the Mzeina. The paradoxes then penetrated *both* the context *and* the text of the quotidian dialogue, until all the participants were struck by their powerlessness to define their own situation. Therefore their definition of the social situation temporarily unraveled into anomie (McHugh 1968).

Transformation. Precisely at that moment of decomposition, the moment of recomposition through emergence became possible. Each character, while still just a plain person, rose up and, by temporarily fusing him- or herself with his or her folkloric persona, became the interlocutor, in the folk genre, between the tribal collective memory of the past and its present circumstances. When these characters transformed themselves from ordinary persons into dramatic personae, they conjoined their living selves with the tribal pantheon of Sheikhs, Symbolic Battle Coordinators, Madwomen, Fools, Old Women, Ex-Smugglers, and Anthropologists as allegorical types belonging to tribal folkloric genres that differentiate the history of the tribe from the histories of its occupiers.

Each character abruptly intruded into the anomic social situation by violating conversational protocol. The following examples will show how this act transformed the character-as-person into an embodiment of his or her past persona. Being a person-cum-persona, he or she was able to transform the ordinary group of people present, who until then had been each other's performers and audience (Goffman 1959), into the spectators for the allegorical spectacle about to come.

Merging himself with the persona of the Leader Sheikh, ʿAlwān angrily stubbed out his cigarette, snarled a self-critical proverb, and demanded (against all rules of proper politeness) that all the men shut up.

ʿAlyii enabled her transformation into the Madwoman's interlocutor by violating conventional etiquette, rudely bursting into Ghānma's inner yard dressed in an incongruous mixture of styles and accompanied by her three sickly goats. Such a dramatic entry allowed her to further act out her madness and to monologue melodramatically about the tabooed topic of the "wounds of the heart." Aware of the ripped taboo, the women made available the societal stage for the ʿAlyii-cum-Madwoman performance.

X insisted that the fictional Ḥajj Khantarīsh make his three guests wait for him to speak, until the silence of the waiting pressed on them like the early autumn heat. When Khantarīsh finally spoke, it was in the cunning persona of the Ex-Smuggler, who was acted out, conjoining itself with both Ḥajj Khantarīsh the person, and his narrator, X the Ex.

Ḥajja Ḥmēda kept her dignified silence until provoked by a particularly obnoxious attack by young Sallām, whom she did not even have to bother answering. Responding to him by addressing the issue of clitoridectomy—a taboo subject for discussion in mixed-gender company—and proceeding with a tautological statement about the Mzeini/Israeli interdependence, she fused herself with the fantastic character of the Old Woman, telling her legend of reality to the amazed family and friends who had no choice but to become her willing audience.

Silence during the interactional decomposition also brought about Shgēṭef's emergence. He only listened to his friends' serious argument about their religious conflict, having to sell sins to make a living. Finally he suddenly interrupted them with a surprisingly foolish interjection: "Ho!"—an utterly unexpected contribution to the grim context. This violation of etiquette facilitated the further conflation of himself-as-person with the Fool persona. His speech act, so stunning, transformed not only himself, but all the men in the magʿad, when he chose to act out his Fool role.

The Fool was also the quirky tension dissolver in another allegorical transformation. When the discussion at the Ṭawara barlimān got "stuck," only the Fool, by way of humorous reversal, was able to allow Shaʿabān abu-Srayaʿ to transform himself from the mundane old man who did not keep up with the times to the grandiose Symbolic Battle Coordinator. Genuinely reluctant to play the role of intertribal legislator without the full consensus of the entire barlimān, Shaʿabān used negotiation as an entry into his Galīd persona. Contemporaneously enacting himself, as the little old man, and the Symbolic Battle Coordinator, he transformed the members of the barlimān into partial participants in his solo act.

And Smadar, the most marginal member of the tribe, merged herself with The One Who writes Us, thus transforming not only herself, but also her listeners. As the most marginal Mzeini person-cum-persona, but paradoxically the only one able to define the characteristics of a "real" Bedouin, she temporarily sorted out the enmeshed web of East–West relationships for both her audience and herself.

Recomposition. Having marked the transformation into the status of "persona" by violating convention, each character allegorized his or her own lived experience, thereby reconstructing the thematic meaning of the social context, and reordering the anomie (cf. Grathoff 1970:122–130; Handelman 1981, 1986; Handelman and Kapferer 1980). Each was able to eliminate the previously open-ended argument, caused by discontinuities in the culture, by transmuting the paradoxes intrinsic in the taken-for-granted, precarious realities of both the Mzeina tribe's and his or her own societal position. Each character transcended the paradoxes (cf. also Jackson 1982:250) by creating an interplay of concrete images that he or she linked to the immortality of tradition.

Out of the banality of everyday life, the personal/collective transformative allegories emerged (Benjamin 1985:185). The characters' nonquotidian acts marked a point of entry from the casual flow of everyday life into the numinous cyclical framework of ritual time and space. Each character can be seen as imposing his or her own "ritual process" (Turner 1969) on the flow of everyday life, bringing about liminality by transcending collective paradoxes through enacting the paradoxes immanent in him- or herself as person-cum-persona. Each spectator listening could see his or her own experience embodied in the one being acted out.

Perhaps each character was able to bring about spontaneous liminality, transcending the collective paradoxes all by him- or herself, because of his or her charisma, that "inner determination . . . demand[ing] obedience and following by virtue of his [or her] mission" (Weber 1946:246) and leading the audience at least temporarily to recognize him or her as "their master—so long as he [or she] knows how to maintain recognition through 'proving' himself [or herself]" (ibid.; cf. Handelman 1986). Max Weber further argued that charismatic individuals act only where commonsense rationality or intellect fail. Their action, which he termed "charismatic justice," is not only a critique of formality and tradition. In order to lead the society in times of anomie, these individuals' charisma further liberates the culture from "formal and traditional bonds, and . . . is just as free in the face of the sanctity of tradition as it is in the face of any rationalist deductions from abstract concepts" (Weber 1946:250).

In the Mzeina case, many of their common-sense attempts to analyze their situation by conversational dialogue did fail, because of the absurdities inherent in their lived reality, so there was indeed opportunity for charismatic individuals to act. The Mzeini charismatic action, however, elevated rather than devalued the tradition of tribal authority and identity that was threatened with effacement. Therefore the "charismatic justice" sanctified the tradition, reconstituting a conjunctural essence of pure Bedouin rationality while liberating the Mzeinis from the rationale of their occupier. The allegorical outbursts always happened during the "everyday routine structures" (Weber 1980:234)—thus preventing the charisma itself from becoming routinized—because it was precisely these fantastic structures of reality that were so susceptible to cracking apart.

The sheer force of the character's charisma in his or her performance overpowered the audience's fragmented representations of the collective tribal selves, as expressed in the abruptly and outrageously transformed inconclusive dialogues that now formed the setting for this liminal event. The liminality of the performance depended on a playful "code switching" (K. Basso 1979:8) that replaced the ruptured logic of the quotidian-qua-experience with the logic of fantastic legends told about the quotidian-qua-text. And the audience was now able to accept its absurd lived-reality as normal within the framework of the reenacted current events, because it made such a good story. The story itself, embodying familiar images and persons remolded into narrative, and thus emphasizing the transcendent significance of Bedouin identity, had such powerful artistic unity that it was utterly persuasive. It therefore succeeded in convincing the audience to agree with the character's didactic assertions, even though the experiences narrated were hardly believable, as a typical "once upon a time" seamless artificial legend would be. Being so persuasive, performed allegory served as a shining example of how to live and even exploit the Mzeini existential paradoxes—a mission repeatedly impossible in the jumbled bickering preceding the transformation. Further, the performing persons-personae could get away with pithy phrasings of hard truths that their audiences could not otherwise acknowledge—to say, or even to hear.

These truths, though partial due to their being bound to the performance's time and space, recomposed the situation outside the performance framework. Because the didactic conclusions of the fantastic allegory delineated definite boundaries, separating what was Bedouin from what was not, the "seams" in the everyday enactment of Bedouinness seemed to be mended, at least for the moment. The artistic recomposition of everyday life as allegory reified and therefore reaffirmed the Mzeini identity as Bedouin even though the hegemonic relations of the Mzeinis with their occupiers remained unchanged.

Closure. From the grandeur of the collectivity reached in the story, a collectivity reflected in each of the listeners, the narrator brought back the collective experience to the banality of everyday life by using one or more of several means of reaching closure—repetition, simple declarative statements, conventional formula endings, and traditional proverbs or poems—signaling that the end of the story had come.

The Madwoman, for example, ended her melodramatic performance by repeating the very cry she used upon entering: "Have you seen my goat? Have you seen my goat?!" The Fool, having used his societal stage to reconjure the hippies as a farce, ended by uttering his formulaic statement, "And that's the way it is." And after bringing his audience to the traditional mode of consensus, the Symbolic Battle Coordinator declared that the agreement was made. Ḥajj Khantarīsh ended his performed silence with the ancient proverb that captured the essence of the segmentary lineage system: "I against my brother; I and my brother against my cousin; I and my brother and my cousin against the world." Ḥajja Ḥmēda al-ʿAjūz ended her story with the formulaic statement "Your peace." She used another closure device, reciting a brief verse that also retransformed her from the majestic Old Woman to the crumpled old woman: "What pain it is to enter the market of old age; Colors all are changed, things blur around the edge."

Reflexivity. I have already pointed out that the shift in the style of interaction following the allegorical emergence transformed the people routinely living their familiar scenes into a somewhat passive audience. This is a shift typical of liminal performance by individuals capable of symbolizing the collective community (Handelman and Kapferer 1980). During the allegorical performance, due to the collective/personal mirroring (cf. Babcock 1980), "The social selves of the participants become irrelevant and epiphenomenal—but the [persons-cum-personae] retain the identities which they embody and which they communicate, directly and unequivocally, to others" (Handelman 1979:186).

But since allegories are dialogical monologues, where "the reader is a participant in the fiction . . . [and whose] activity is a translation of action into commentary" (Quilligan 1979:226–227), members of the audience did get involved in the telling and interpreting of the characters' mundane experiences as these events were transformed into didactic moral narratives. After each subepisode of the story was recited, members of the audience would repeat the last sentence, and express their approval, surprise, bafflement, anger, or other response to the ongoing drama. They were the "what-sayers . . . , signaling that the images created [were] not simply understood, but [were] enhancing the listener's appreciation of the story" (E. Basso 1984). Thus did the members of this nonliterate culture not only acknowledge, but also reinforce and preserve, their traditional knowledge.

Retransformation. Applauded by the audience, the persona completed his or her literary and didactic mission. At that time, when someone in the audience recapitulated the story's main point, careful to emphasize that it was just a story, the audience gracefully retransformed the persona back into being a person. For example, when someone in Sheikh ᶜAlwān's audience questioned the accuracy of his story's details, another listener remarked that it was just a story. The listener proceeded to offer ᶜAlwān coffee, thinking he might be thirsty after his long monologue. And while magnificent Leader-Sheikhs might never be thirsty, sheikhs of flesh and bone might suffer from a dry throat after a long speech.

Use of the character's ordinary name or actual kinship relationship was another common means of accomplishing the retransformation. After the Madwoman had accomplished her dramatic exit from Ghānma's yard, one of the women listeners murmured, "Poor ᶜAlyii, how men ruined her." Because the woman used the character's first name rather than her appelation "The Madwoman," it was clear to the other women that this sympathy was for the woman ᶜAlyii herself, not for the dramatic persona she had just been enacting.

When the Old Woman finished her tale, her son Ṣāleḥ said, "My mother is a lioness. My mother." Referring to their actual kinship relationship rather than to the generic persona of the feisty Old Woman she had just completed enacting, he transformed her from that persona back to her ordinary Ḥajja Ḥmēda personhood. The Old Woman further retransformed herself, by reciting the poem expressing her fears of old age and death—human fears that seem so uncharacteristic of her warrior persona.

The Fool did not wait to be retransformed. He simply left the group—a departure understood by the remaining group as his retransformation into the Clever Merchant, rushing to make money off the tourists who had just arrived on the evening bus. Interestingly, only the anthropologist did not grasp the retransformative meaning of his rushed absence. "Where is Shgēṭef?" she asked, unaware that she too had retransformed him, calling him by his personal name instead of his persona title.

As for the Symbolic Battle Coordinator, he completed his allegory and fell asleep—once when he finished delivering the intertribal agreement in the barlimān of Firān, and again, at the end of the sacrificial meal, completing his temporary control over both the pots and the division of tribal resources. And as soon as the news came on the radio, The One Who Writes Us was transformed back to Smadar. As an Israeli and also the most marginal of tribesmembers, she was simply ignored.

When the audience completed the retransformation of the persona-cum-person back to a plain person, there was always a short pause, perhaps to mark a return from the fantastic to the banal. The "ritual process" was over (Turner 1969). After this short pause, a fresh, low-key conversation developed, leaving only the anthropologist baffled by its lack of connectedness to the previous spectacular discourse.

RITUAL/PLAY

The cycle of entry, establishing performance space, the performance itself, and the exit from the stage by literary closure devices, could be viewed through the optics of both ritual and play, since both are framed, liminal, and reorder the social reality so that the social selves of the participants become superfluous (Handelman 1977:190). But unlike the typical ritual or play, these individual-cum-collective performances are not interactions where all the participants in the staged event are equally each other's actors and audiences. Even ritual solo performers such as clowns or demons, who impose their nonnegotiable frame on the rest of the ritual participants, occur in designated time slots that are written into the text of the ritual, which, in itself, is a time/space-bound frame (Handelman 1981; Handelman and Kapferer 1980; Werbner 1986). But the transformations into and out of these allegorical performance frames are not elaborate and calendar-bound, but rather, spontaneous, fluid, and improvisational (Bateson 1956, 1972; Ehrmann 1968; Handelman 1977), occurring only at the whim of the performing character.

In his insightful work comparing play and ritual, Don Handelman (1977) has argued that ritual defines the moral community, and that play accentuates the plasticity of ideation of the community—and these allegorical performances do both. Handelman writes that ritual generates meta-messages of sanctity, morality, and truth, while play generates meta-messages of doubt, amorality, and fallacy—but each of these characters' meta-messages conflates the genres of ritual and play. Handelman further argues that ritual, well-bounded by time and space, comments on the totality of societal structures, while the loosely framed play comments on the immediate, ongoing fragments of social reality—but Mzeini allegories comment on both. According to Handelman, then, ritual reaffirms the core values of the society, while play criticizes them. Since allegory is a literary genre that contains, in addition to its affirmations, criticism of both the society and itself, I consider the Mzeini allegories to be conjunctures—ritual/play.

ALLEGORICAL POLITICS AND OCCUPATIONAL POETICS

In retrospect, one can see that the characters created redemptive allegories out of their frustrating experiences under occupation—experiences of lack of leadership, struggle for dignity in old age, expressing one's wisdom through foolishness to avoid offending the rulers, madness as the only solution to insoluble female gender conflicts caused by political forces beyond any tribesmember's control, and the perpetual struggle to maintain a balance between the meager cash economy and the traditional inadequate subsistence economy.

These allegories are redemptive, however, not in any traditional sanctimonious and preachy manner (Fletcher 1964:21–22) but by using humor, satire, and comedy to mock the silly and irrational Western ways some Bedouin have adopted, so that the tribesmembers have a negative example, a clear image of what behavior to avoid, in order to maintain their Bedouin identity (cf. K. Basso 1984). And only then and there, when the everyday experience was processually transformed into stylized allegories, were these characters able to exert the charismatic authority emanating from their position as *traditional* personae-types. Each character as a *person*, on the other hand, palpably expressed *the* identity-as-paradox of his or her fellow tribesmembers, one they abstrusely sensed in themselves even before the character artistically intruded into their familiar scene as a *persona*.

Northrop Frye has argued that allegory *is* interpretation, "an attaching of ideas to the structure of poetic imagery" (1967:89–90; cf. G. Clifford 1974:53). Jameson has sharpened this definition by discussing "the capacity of allegory to generate a range of distinct meanings simultaneously" (1986:74). I would add that, in the Mzeina case, the interplay of allegorical images affects both poetic and political interpretations. It thus produces allegories in which new experiences attached to the traditional structure of tribal poetics are conjoined with encroaching Western cultural influences that reconstruct and reshape the old yet liminal political structure of the classic tribe. Mzeini allegories are therefore "successful as allegory only to the extent that [they] can suggest the authenticity with which the two coordinating poles," the poetic and political, "bespeak each other" (Fineman 1981:83). While First-World cultures differentiate between the private and public, and between the poetic and the political, the Mzeina culture, being under the continual threat of effacement, tells itself in an allegorical way that it exists, metonymizing private experience for the history of the collectivity, and conjoining the local poetics of storytelling with the global political realities of neocolonialism (cf. Jameson 1986:69).[6]

The Mzeina are able to construct their identity as a conjunctural "ideal type" (Weber 1949) of a Bedouin tribe through allegorical transcendence, exploring tribal reality by means of literary illusion, and testing tribal illusion against the transitional, homogenizing reality that claims tribes should not exist. The allegorical transcendence contains embedded within its ironies and paradoxes fearless criticism not only of the occupiers, but of the Mzeina themselves. Thus the allegories contain their own indigenous poetics of the military occupation that has so shaped the Mzeina tribal identity. In their stories, ordinary persons temporarily fuse themselves with their heroic personae from the communal reservoir of the tribal past, to authentically perform allegories of mundane experience. During these performances, they are at once living persons and traditional personae—residing in that peculiar limbo where the fantastic and the real coincide.

*

We were sitting somewhere in the white-gold sand dunes around ʿEin Khuḍra in the shade of a large sandstone purple boulder—fourteen Mzeini men in many layers of heavy brown and black cotton robes typical of the Sahara Desert Touareg tribe, three Mzeini women in their heavy holiday clothes and coined veils, and one anthropologist in her customary baggy jeans, Mickey Mouse T-shirt, and white Mzeini headdress. To our right, some Hollywood stars had locked themselves in an air-conditioned four-wheel-drive van to renew their melting makeup. Contentedly chewing their cuds were two dozen

WAITING IN LINE TO BUY ICE CREAM AND COLD DRINKS AT THE CAFE OF MOSHĀV DI-ZAHĀV ▶

SEA FISH

festively decorated camels, including mine, Zreigān. My two co-owners had rented him to the Club Med Desert Safari Tour Company of Nuwēbʿa, who in turn had sublet him to the film crew.

This was late winter of 1978. Michael Caine, Peter Ustinov, and the beautiful black American model/actress Beverly Johnson were in the South Sinai with their Swiss producer, American director, and supporting actors from France, India, Israel, and Africa to shoot the Sahara Desert scenes for the move *Ashanti.* Caine and Johnson were playing doctor, as a married pair of World Health Organization medics inoculating some generic drumming and dancing African "savages" (filmed in Kenya). Peter Ustinov, playing the stereotypical Western description of the fat, greedy, Arab villain, a pious slave trader constantly rolling his prayer-beads, captured Johnson and chained her to his captive African tribespeople for the long trek across all of Africa to be sold on the Red Sea coast to Omar Sharif (filmed in Sicily), who played a slimy caricature of the Harvard-educated Saudi prince.[7]

"Look what they've made us into now," complained the thin bony Mzeini fellow who, a year later, would play the Fool and have his Mzeini audience in stitches from his miming of the Passover 1979 Rock Festival, described as this book opened. He wiped his sweaty brow with the rolled sleeve of his costume. "Just so our kids can eat, we have to play slave traders. But it is *we* who are the real slaves! When those Westerners hired us on our camels, they were so surprised and angry that we didn't dress like the Bedouin they had in mind, that they decided to ship these Touareg clothes all the way from somewhere called France. We can hardly move in them and they make our tongues hang out likes dogs in summer heat, even though it's still winter. And just because they couldn't let us be Bedouin in our own clothes, they docked our wages."

"So why do you do it?" I asked.

"If my only other choice is to wash dishes and clean toilets and streets for these people, I'd rather be in their movies. At least I get to be *some* kind of a Bedouin."

NOTES

CHAPTER ONE

1. *Magᶜad rejjāl*, hereafter, simply *magᶜad*. In a summer encampment of flour-sack tents, it consisted of a stretched sheet of woven goat hair, providing protection from the sun and wind, and was located on the outskirts of the encampment so that the men and their guests did not invade the privacy of the women and children. In semipermanent settlements of palm-frond, plywood, and cardboard huts, the club was a structure of one or two parallel stone walls, supported by wooden pillars, and roofed with sheet metal. A semipermanent or permanent settlement's magᶜad was situated in the settlement's spacious center. Both types of magᶜad shared several features. In the center a circle of stones marked the stove area, containing burning coals. In the corner were storage boxes for coffee beans, tea, sugar, and flour, a mortar and pestle, a roasting pan for the beans, a copper coffee pot and an aluminum teakettle, special cups for tea and coffee, and sometimes a round piece of sheet metal for baking flatbread. Long, narrow handwoven rugs were used for sitting or reclining in a circle around the embers. The best rug was reserved for guests.

2. The sumsumīyya was a traditional stringed musical instrument played by Bedouin fishermen. During my fieldwork in 1975–1979, a typical sumsumīyya found on the South Sinai coasts was made from a goatskin and a few recycled industrial materials. The musician would usually remove one of the larger sides from a rectangular, thin-walled steel gasoline can. He covered the open side with a stretched goatskin to get better resonance. Sometimes he cut a circular hole into the skin and rimmed it by hammering onto the cut edge some metal from the discarded face of the can. Under the skin he cut holes into two sides of the can and inserted sticks, often pieces of broomsticks he found in Israeli or Egyptian trash, or ones he decided to take home from his janitorial work, to supplement his meager pay. The two sticks, about fifty centimeters long, formed a forty-five-degree angle, made into a triangle by another stick tied on with shoelaces across the top. On this frame were five metal strings, usually telephone wires or thin electrical

wires from which he had stripped the plastic insulation. If the musician could not find suitable wires in the local Israeli or Egyptian dumpsters, he might cut into a working telephone line to get his raw materials. The strings were tuned by means of wooden pegs made from chips from the broomstick. The instrument was tuned as five notes in sequence, either whole steps or half steps, with the highest and lowest notes forming the musical interval of a fifth. The starting position for playing was to cover all strings with fingers of the left hand. The player sounded notes and chords by lifting fingers of the left hand and striking the strings with the fingernails of his right hand, or with a pick made from the tip of a goat-horn held between the right forefinger and thumb.

3. Incidentally, in the Mzeina dialect of Arabic *zub mar* means "a bitter penis."

4. Although the word "ṭanība" can exist grammatically, as the feminine form of "ṭanīb," I have not heard of Mzeini women who actively participated in blood feuds and therefore had to run away on their own to seek protection with another Bedouin tribe.

5. Amal Rassam [Vinogradov], who studied the Ait Ndhir tribe of Morocco, also mentions that the men "graciously put up with [her] female presence in their *jamʿas*," or official gathering places (1974:v). This despite the fact that the tribe she studied did not live in the somehow surreal context forced on the Mzeina, on which I elaborate in subsequent pages.

6. Handelman further pursues the analytical construct of "symbolic type" in Handelman and Kapferer (1980). Interestingly, in theater studies the same construct appears even earlier in Burns (1972:122–143).

7. In the context of this book I have chosen not to discuss Aijaz Ahmad's (1987) eloquent critique of Jameson. This is because here I focus on one particular Fourth World culture, and therefore I do not use the Jamesonean "Third World" as a generic category (cf. also Jameson 1987).

CHAPTER TWO

1. Most of this chapter's data was previously analyzed and published in collaboration with William C. Young (Lavie and Young 1984; see also acknowledgments).

2. Shoukair (1916), however, argued that during his research period, the South Sinai Bedouin population was about 11,000. Nir's excellent historical demographic essay on the South Sinai Bedouin disagrees with his findings (1988:816).

3. CARE is the Cooperative for American Relief Everywhere, Inc.

4. After the 1967 war, Yigal Allon designed a so-called peace plan for developing the territories Israel had occupied in the war, to use them later as bargaining chips in peace negotiations. According to this plan, the narrow waist of the central part of Israel was to be eliminated by annexing more territory around the city of Qalquilyeh. Several areas were to be annexed to Israel and settled by Jews who would farm land expropriated from indigenous owners: the Palestinian part of Jerusalem and its surrounding mountains, the Jordan Valley lands, the Golan Heights, the ʿAqaba Gulf coast and mountains, and all the Egyptian lands surrounding the Gaza/Rafaḥ refugee camps. The densely populated Palestinian areas of the West Bank were to be returned to Jordanian jurisdiction, with unlimited Israeli access rights to its annexed territory along the Jordan River. A corridor was to connect the West Bank with Gaza, which would be under some sort of rule yet to be determined. What was left of the Sinai was to be returned to the Arab Republic of Egypt. The plan was presented to Premier Golda Meir on 15 September 1970.

5. In 1977, the year Anwar Sadat visited Israel, the unemployment rate in Egypt was 8 percent. In 1981, the year he was assassinated, unemployment rose to 10 percent. In 1986 the unemployment rate was 29 percent. In absolute figures, the number of unemployed people (age twelve and up) in Egypt in 1988 was estimated at around 2.8 million. Twelve million Egyptians are employed in Egypt, and around 1.4 million work outside Egypt, particularly in Iraq, Saudi Arabia, and the United Arab Emirates (Mansour 1988).

NOTES

CHAPTER THREE

1. *Ahl al-dageʿa* means literally "the people of the land." *Shughlīn al-siyāsa'* means "the people of politics," or "the ones who work in politics." *Tabaʿ al-siyāsa*, a term also used to describe the occupiers, means "of politics."

2. The inland residents of Bīr Njeima and other encampments around the Wadi Firān Oasis considered dried parrot fish a delicacy to be eaten with rice on very special occasions such as thanksgiving meals, holidays, and meals cooked for guests from afar.

3. A *ṭarḥa* was a piece of thin black cotton fabric that married women wrapped around their face and head as part of everyday dress. During holidays and on other special occasions, married women wore a heavy coined veil, *burguʿ*, which hung from their foreheads.

4. Since cotton was a cheaper fabric, terylene caftans were worn during holidays and celebrations, while cotton caftans were everyday dress.

5. The Mzeinis referred to the Federal Agency for Nature Reserves, in Hebrew, *Rashūt Shmurōt Hatēvaʿ*, in a Bedouinized shorthand version of the Hebrew: *Shmurā*, here translated as Reserve.

6. All Jewish-owned food establishments in Israel, the vast majority of Israeli food establishments, must have a kosher license and are subject to routine kosher inspections. Gourmet restaurants, however, do serve non-kosher dishes made with seafood or pork. Some of these are referred to euphemistically. He who orders "white steak" dines on pork chops.

7. *Ḥawāja* was a respectful title by which Bedouin addressed non-Bedouin men.

8. Jebaliyya tribesmen were often employed by the Santa Katarina monks in remodeling the few isolated chapels in the mountains near the monastery. Greek Orthodox monks have been building and remodeling these chapels since the fourth century (see chap. 2).

9. As with the Federal Agency for Nature Reserves, the Mzeinis referred to the Society for the Protection of Nature, in Hebrew, *Haḥevrā Lehaganāt Hatēvaʿ*, with a Bedouinized shorthand version of the Hebrew: *Tēbaʿ*, which means Nature. A detailed discussion of the activities of the Israeli Society for the Protection of Nature is provided in chapter 2.

10. After cleaning them thoroughly, Ṭawara Bedouin used empty fuel barrels to store water. I discuss in greater detail the friction between the Israeli army and the Bedouin concerning fuel barrels in chapter 6.

11. A detailed discussion of the Israeli punishment of Bedouin who sold "nature souvenirs" to tourists is provided in chapter 2.

12. This brings to mind more recent visits to the Sinai, when I encountered Bedouin who now referred laughingly to the mountain by this same name. I assume this is because the sheikh's story was told more than once since I finished my first period of fieldwork. There is another South Sinai Peak, "*Jabal Zubb al-Baḥar*," The Peak of the Penis-of-the-Sea (the latter being the local name for a sea cucumber). Transliterated, this name has become standardized to the point that it appears on old British topographic maps, as well as on their updated Egyptian and Israeli versions. Old Mzeinis told me that when the British mapped the Sinai, they wanted to know the name of that mountain. Standing on its peak, their Bedouin guide told them that the peak is called "The Penis of the Sea" because its shape resembles an erect penis and from this peak one can see the Gulf of Suez.

13. The words of poems that were usually recited without an accompanying melody were sometimes set to the melodies of hejēnis, or caravan songs.

14. The sheikh is referring to a wooden structure built by King Farouq as a summer retreat in the late 1940s. During the Israeli period it became the home and office of the Santa Katarina area ranger.

15. This reference is to Ḥammām Mūsa, or Mūsa's hot spring, a natural hot spring, on top of which a waist-deep pool has been constructed, encased in a stone structure. It stands in the midst of a date grove on the property of the Santa Katarina Monastery. Two men from the Wlād Saᶜīd tribe used to pollinate the trees and harvest the dates for the monastery. The monks visited the place three or four times a year, supervising the date harvest. During the Israeli occupation the place became popular with both organized tours and the many soldiers who swam there in various degrees of undress.

16. The Arabic for authentic, *aṣli,* is also used in Hebrew slang.

CHAPTER FOUR

1. Among the scholarly works discussing honor and shame are Abou-Zeid (1966), Abu-Lughod (1985, 1986), Abu-Zahara (1974), Antoun (1968), Beck and Keddie (1978), Bourdieu (1966), Crapanzano (1973, 1980), D. Dwyer (1978), E. Fernea (1965), Kressel (1981), Levy (1957), Meeker (1979), Mernissi (1975), Rosen (1978), Sowayan (1985), and Wikan (1984).

2. Many works discuss parallel cousin marriage in the Middle East. Among these are Barth (1954), Cunnison (1966), Kressel (1986), Marx (1967), Murphy and Kasdan (1959), Patai (1955), Peters (1965, 1980), and Robertson-Smith (1903).

3. Unlike the usual patterns of virilocality or uxorilocality, in Mzeina virilocal or uxorilocal residence, the newlywed couple often ended up living with nonimmediate kin of the groom's patrilineage or of the bride's patrilineage. This enabled them and their respective kin to further maximize alliance options.

4. During my second year of fieldwork in the Sinai, people pointed out to me three girls in three different encampments whose names were Zᶜeila (Anger). I was told that their social fathers and their genitors differed. The genitors were the first loves of their mothers, and these mothers were daring enough to name their daughters Zᶜeila. These were rare cases wherein the platonic relationship of a woman to her first love developed into a sexual relationship. Later, when these girls became adolescents, their name was changed to Jamīla (Pretty). Frank Stewart, who has done extensive fieldwork among the Aḥeiwāt Bedouin of Central Sinai told me that he encountered several cases of legal feud between women's husbands and their first loves.

5. Mzeinis, as well as other South Sinai Bedouin, save the male foreskin, which they dry, add to water, and give to a barren woman. By washing herself with this solution she may enhance her fertility (cf. Levi 1978). On the other hand, clitoris tips of girls have no medicinal value.

6. Of their later years of marriage, men said they were never sure when their wives would send them to the female donkey. "The female donkey" is literally that. I assume that Mzeini men engaged in bestiality instead of masturbation. During the Israeli soldiers' long stay without leave in the South Sinai in the first months of the 1973 war, some Mzeinis described to me with great amazement scenes of groups of

Israeli soldiers showering outdoors and masturbating with soap. For the Mzeini men, masturbation was an undesirable option and was considered sexually abnormal. One man explained to me, "The sperm of these guys [the Israeli soldiers] will eventually become thin if they continue doing this [masturbating]. If I want to have a strong sperm, when I ejaculate, my 'stick' must be tightly surrounded and warm."

7. In "Insanity in Byzantine and Islamic Medicine," Michael Dols (1983) discusses the conscientious attitudes of medieval Muslim scholars toward mad and deviant people. For centuries Muslim cultures have had a special sensitivity to insanity, resulting in counseling rather than imprisonment as the preferable method for dealing with the insane. Scholars and doctors such as eleventh and twelfth century A.D. Ibn-Sina and Saᶜid Bakhtishu argued that the psychic causation of mental illness was epitomized in passionate love.

8. In Mzeina vernacular, *sil* is a geographic term for either the juncture where a smaller wadi drains into a larger one, or as in this case, the juncture where a dry delta of a main wadi drains into the sea.

9. A *ḥirga* was a black shawl, about 1 by 1.5 meters, worn by all Mzeini women from early adolescence on. The shawl draped from the head to the back part of the woman's body. Married women made a special point of showing off the elaborate, colorful patterns of embroidery and silver sequins of their holiday ḥirgas. Due to the strict codes of modesty that virgins were subject to, unmarried girls were not allowed to have colorful, elaborate patterns of embroidery on their ḥirgas.

10. A *nugba* was a veil worn by newlywed women or recent young divorcees who had not yet conceived.

11. Families who did not have daughters of goatherding age or of marriageable status requested the goatherd daughter of their neighbors to herd their flocks. As payment for this service they gave the girl a female kidgoat twice a year during the parturition season.

12. While in many dialects of colloquial Arabic *ṭīz* refers to the buttocks and *kūs* is the vaginal area, in the South Sinai vernacular, the buttocks is termed *mabᶜar*, and the vagina, *ṭīz*.

13. Abu-Zāyed al-Helāli is a folkloric figure, the hero of sung or recited epics throughout the Middle East (cf. Ayoub 1982, Slymovics 1988).

14. *Marbūᶜa* and *redēḥi* are line-dances. In both dances the men form a line, linking their elbows and clapping their hands. The women take

turns, each dancing alone in front of the men. The movement of the dance is as follows: while the men brazenly step eight steps forward, the woman retreats gracefully; then she moves gently forward eight steps while the men march in measured steps back. This is repeated several times, then another woman replaces her. Hence it is not clear who is chasing whom in the dance. The melodies of the dances are the following:

The rhyming texts matched to these repetitious melodies may be poetry improvised by the male dancers, who take turns improvising. If the dancers are young, it is more likely they will match sultry proverbs to the melodies such as the one hummed by Salwa. See also chapter 6.

15. The literal meaning of *ṣāḥib* (masculine) and *ṣāḥiba* (feminine) is "friend." But when a Mzeini man said "friend" in the feminine form, he meant his first love. Conversely, when a Mzeini woman said "friend" in the masculine, she meant her first love. For the purpose of translation, I employed "sweetheart" to convey a first love.

16. The Mzeina term for hell is *nār*, which literally means fire. Hell is associated with images of burning heat.

17. It is interesting to note that in classical Arabic, the verb *k.w.n.* in its tenth form, *istikana*, means, to surrender, to become miserable, to be submissive or oppressed.

18. *Gibleh* was the hairstyle of adolescent, unmarried young women. The hair was parted from one ear to the other. The top half was gathered with a rubber-band at the center of the forehead at the hairline, then divided into two parts which were braided. The top two braids were looped gracefully along the temples and around the ears. The lower braids were then brought forward and woven at the jawline with the top braids to form two thick braids which drop over the woman's breasts. When men talked among themselves and wanted to refer to a virgin, they said "omm-gibleh," or one having a gibleh hairstyle.

19. *Masāyeḥ* was the more fashionable current hairstyle of a married woman. The hair was parted from one ear to the other. The top half was gathered with a rubber-band in the center of the forehead at the hairline. The rubber-band was disguised by rolling hair around it. The

hair was then parted into two equal pieces that were combed and gently looped along the temples and around the ears. The parted top hair was traditionally stiffened with camel's urine, and nowadays with unrinsed shampoo, if available. Then a symmetrical collection of about a dozen colored hairpins decorated and held the hair. The hair was left smooth until the ears, where the two halves were braided. The bottom half of the hair was simply braided, brought forward, and woven with the top braids at jaw-length.

Guṣṣa was the more traditional hairstyle of married women, losing popularity very fast with younger Mzeini women, but still popular with tribes like the Jebaliyya or Wlād Saᶜīd. In this style, the hair was also parted from one ear to another. The top part was gathered in the center of the forehead at the hairline, braided in one thick braid, and then rolled around a bone, a wood piece, or a smooth narrow stone each about eight centimeters long. The bottom part of the hair was simply braided in two braids that were dropped forward over the women's breasts.

Men laughed at the guṣṣa, and said that it made the women look like they had goat horns growing from their foreheads. After recent pilgrimages to Mecca from 1975 on, one of the arguments men expressed against the guṣṣa was that the guṣṣa's horn made women look as if they tried to elevate themselves up to God. Interestingly, old women who also went to the ḥajj told me that this explanation was total nonsense and said that the move from guṣṣa to masāyeḥ was only a change of fashion, because with a masāyeḥ hairstyle women could show more of their hair.

20. Once, when I was on a demographic survey in the area of the cleft slopes of the southwestern mountains of the peninsula, a man was introduced to me by my two Bedouin guides as "The Sheikh of the Female Donkeys" of the area. The three men laughed after the introduction. Their laughter increased when I innocently asked for the meaning of the title. The "Sheikh of the Donkeys" blushed and said he had been divorced for four years and could not find a suitable bride-to-be, and hence, he had to resort to bestiality. When I suggested masturbation, it offended all three men. One said, "No! This may be good for your own people! Your men are busy only with themselves. We have to do it with someone, even a donkey." Another said, half-joking, that he had heard, probably from the radio, of a *ḥadīth* (a tradition of the Prophet) concerning the matter of whether having sex with a female donkey was *ḥarām* (taboo for Muslims) or *ḥalāl* (rec-

ommended for Muslims). The ḥadīth argued, that if the female donkey is white, she is ḥalāl for Muslims, and if she's black, she is ḥarām. Then he said, that since most donkeys are gray, the answer is somewhere in the middle. The color classification of female donkeys was a topic I heard joked about elsewhere in the South Sinai. My sense is that the matter is in fact an issue, and hence, the jokes.

21. Lust poetry, or *gaṣīd al-ghayii* was a genre of "porno" poetry. Unlike the metaphors men used in love poetry, there was in these poems direct reference to the actual sexual organs and acts. While love poetry was recited by men among themselves in the encampment, lust poetry was considered shameful and was therefore recited only when men were alone in work situations.

22. Interestingly, the verb *kh.r.b.* is used here in the second form, meaning, "to ruin." Among the Wlad ʿAli Bedouin of the Egyptian western desert, it is also used in the second form to express the same concern. The question "*man kharabha*?" or "who ruined her?" is asked among women when they want to find out which man hurt the emotions of a particular woman (Abu-Lughod 1985:247).

CHAPTER FIVE

1. Among the classics are Evans-Pritchard (1940, 1949), Meyer Fortes (1945, 1953), Max Gluckman (1959), Frederik Barth (1959), Emrys Peter (1960, 1967, 1975), I. M. Lewis (1961), and Emanuel Marx (1967, 1977b).

2. The Saudi Arabian radio stations broadcast several folklore and news programs about traditional Bedouin lifestyle. These programs are very popular with the South Sinai tribes. Throughout my fieldwork (1975–1988) I noticed that for the Mzeina, these programs served as a model for authentic Bedouin life.

3. After Egypt regained the Sinai between 1979 and 1982, the Egyptian officials outlawed the consumption of alcohol by Bedouin. Tourists were exempt. European alcoholic products, consumed by both the tourists and a small number of Egyptians, were and still are available at tourist-oriented bars in the newly established Egyptian towns in the Sinai. The few indigenous Sinai Bedouin who drink alcohol therefore resorted to Israeli alcoholic products. These were brought into the Sinai by Israeli tourists with whom the Bedouin had established friendships during the period of the Israeli occupation.

4. Fteiḥ and his friends quote here a line from the following refrain of a *gaṣida* (poem):

> *Yōm benashrab ʿasal, wayōm benashrab khāl,*
> *Yōm ʿala ḥarīr, wayom fal-tall*
>
> One day we drink honey, vinegar the other,
> One day (sleep) on silk, on sand the other.

5. For further explanation of the intricate web of Mzeini gender and sexual relationships, see chapters 4 and 6.

6. The inner workings of Bedouin courts of customary law, including the role of the *kafīl*, are discussed in ʿAref (1934a), Levi (1988), Mohsen (1975), Perevolotsky (1979), and Stewart (1987a,b).

7. Ṣbayyel here addresses a single person but uses the plural form of *rājel*, "man"—*rejjāl*, "men." Addressing a single person in the plural connotes an emphasis on the point that will follow.

8. Because smuggling in the South Sinai started in the 1950s, smuggling laws were not included in the traditional ʿurfi codex. Bedouin laws concerning smuggling have emerged through process, each case fleshing out a growing and disputed set of precedents.

CHAPTER SIX

1. An elaborated discussion of the codes of conduct emanating from the concepts of honor and shame may be found in chapter 4.

2. Gender segregation stemming from the strict code of honor and shame is discussed by Abou-Zeid (1966), Abu-Lughod (1985, 1986), Abu-Zahara (1974), Antoun (1968), Beck and Keddie (1978), Bourdieu (1966), E. Fernea (1965), Herzfeld (1980), Mernissi (1975), Rosaldo and Lamphere (1974), and Wikan (1984); see also Elshtain (1981).

3. In "Reclaimed Powers: Towards a New Psychology of Men and Women in Later Life," David Gutmann (1987) provides a thorough cross-cultural analysis of the gender and sexual role reversal that takes place in old age. Ethnographic descriptions of this phenomenon can be found in Amoss (1981), Brown (1985), Chagnon (1968), Colson and Scudder (1981), Goody (1962), Levy (1967), and Morsy (1978).

4. "Kessef" is Hebrew for "money."

5. The Hebrew for "are there any explanations?" is *yēsh hesberīm.* The ʿAjuz mispronounces "yēsh hesberīm" as "yesh zberīm."

6. In 1979, two Israeli shekels were worth around fifty cents U.S.

7. I discuss in detail the relevance of the concept of *ṣabr* (patience) to gender relations in chapter 4.

8. In 1979, an ʿomda received from the Israeli civil administration around 100 Israeli Shekels a month, which was around $25 U.S.

9. This in spite of continual pressure from ex-smugglers who, during their heyday, wanted Ḥajj Ḥamdān al-Shēba to let them marry his daughter so they could get access to his beachfront territory.

10. Mzeina Bedouin stored their personal belongings in used wooden artillery ammunition boxes they would collect from the dumps of military bases, or in suitcase-like wood boxes that they built from scraps of plywood they picked up from the municipal garbage dump of Eilat.

11. For a detailed description of the redēḥi dance, see footnote 12 in chapter 4.

12. South Sinai Bedouin referred to the Federal Agency for Nature Reserves, in Hebrew, "Rashūt Shmurōt Hatēvaʿ," in a Bedouinized shorthand version of the Hebrew: "Shmurā."

13. *Jarīsha* was a porridge made from ground wheat which retained the husk, cooked with water and salt to the consistency of a coarse cream of wheat. Caper fruit, churned goat yogurt, or spices were sometimes added as flavoring.

14. In her book, "Talking Straight: *Dugri* Speech in Israeli Sabra Culture," Tamar Katriel (1986) dwells on the cultural reasons for this typical Israeli form of address, considered rude by non-Israelis.

15. The Tel Aviv municipality bulldozed an entire Palestinian neighborhood of Jaffa to plant this strip of grass—Charles Klor Park.

CHAPTER SEVEN

1. Generally I describe the hippies as naked, as distinguished from nude, since "nude" connotes asexuality; the tourists' shedding of clothes on the South Sinai beaches had definite sexual overtones.

2. The unresolved contradictions built into the composition of fools or tricksters are discussed in Charles (1945), Cox (1970), Crumrine

(1969), Fellini (1976), Handelman (1981, 1987), Klapp (1949), Makarius (1970), Parsons and Beals (1934), Radin (1956), Stevens (1980), Willeford (1969), and Zucker (1969).

3. Official Islam, both in Egypt (see chap. 2) and in Saudi Arabia, is influenced by government concerns. During the last years of the Israeli occupation (1975–1982), many old Mzeinis listened to radio programs broadcast by the al-Azhar Academy in Cairo, perhaps as a quiet protest against their scantily clad Jewish occupiers. When it became clear to the Mzeinis that Egypt was going to be just another occupier, they switched stations and listened to Saudi religious radio broadcasts by Sheikh Bin Baz.

CHAPTER EIGHT

1. In consultation with Ruth Bondy, Kundera's translator from Czech into Hebrew, I have rendered five words slightly differently from the translation of Michael H. Heim (Kundera 1981).

2. Among the works discussing Arab tribal structure are ʿAref (1934*a*,*b*), Black-Michaud (1975), Cole (1975), Cunnison (1966), Dresch (1986), Marx (1967), Meeker (1979), Peters (1960, 1967), and Salzman (1978*a*,*b*).

3. An 8 September 1987 letter to me from William Lancaster (1981) reads: "Both my wife and I found your material fascinating and full of insights, however there are a few caveats which we would like to record. In the first place it must be admitted that neither of us are fully competent to judge your approach. We find allegory and symbolism rather beyond us as we were both trained in the English structural/functional school. Whatever may be its inadequacies (and they are many) such a training does lay a very firm foundation of straight observation and logical analysis which we find is often at variance with more modern approaches . . . If it were possible we are sure that you would find it of enormous value if you continued your field research with the Mzeina but concentrated on gathering a complete family tree with all the marriages. While this is tedious in the extreme (and is never publishable as such) it provides a solid base upon which to found theoretical issues. We have found it of inestimable value and provides many of the answers even before one has asked the questions! Another reason for it is that it provides a jumping off point for comparative research. It is virtually impossible to compare and con-

trast two tribes if you only have literary allusions for one and only an ethnography for the other."

4. For detailed discussion of the Ṭawara structure, see chapter 2.

5. In Classical Arabic, the verb *ʿa.sh.r.* connotes conception, reproduction, and intimate association.

6. Some of the classics discussing the epic poetry of Bedouin warfare are Bailey (1972), Meeker (1979), Musil (1928), and Sowayan (1985).

7. It is interesting to note that the gentry who explored Bedouin life during the nineteenth and early twentieth century did not mention the Galīd in their detailed descriptions of Bedouin life. "The noblemen of the desert, [those] of ripe moderation, peacemakers of a certain erudite and subtle judgment" (Doughty 1921) were the sheikhs (cf. also Bartlett 1849; Burckhardt 1822, 1831; Conder, 1878; Henniker 1823; Jarvis 1931, 1937; Laborde 1836; Lepsius 1853; Murray 1935; Musil 1928; Palmer 1871; Ritter 1866; Stanley 1856; Tristram 1865). Perhaps the position of the Galīd was idiosyncratic only to the South Sinai. Although all tribes needed "men of ripe moderation" to negotiate the outcome of intertribal wars, historically in the South Sinai (even prior to the establishment of the central government by the British in the 1920s), sheikhs were always perceived as serving the interests of the occupying government (see chap. 3). Someone else therefore had to have the role of keeping the peace in the feud.

8. "Zuāra" literally means "pilgrimage." "Zuārat" is "the pilgrimage of."

9. Zijderveld (1968) discusses the role of humor as a transformative device, leading the jokers from the flow of everyday life into more structured frames of social knowledge. Labov (1972) and Reifler-Bricker (1973) discuss the humorous role of insults in ritual.

10. In 1976, IL 100 were equal to around $20. The Bedouin referred to the IL 100 bill as "the man with the beard," not realizing that this man, Theodore Hertzel, was a key thinker and founder of the Zionist political movement.

11. The Bedouin pronounce the classical "q" as "g." See also note on transliteration.

12. Unlike Zuārat Faranje, in some South Sinai zuāras both tribesmembers and nontribesmembers circumambulate the ancestral shrine of the tribe that celebrates the zuāra.

13. The name of a genealogical group is conjugated from the name

of the group's ancestor. Therefore, the Ghawānma are the people whose progenitor was Ghānem; the Ghseināt are the people whose progenitor was Ghsein; the Meḥāsna, the people whose progenitor was Mḥeisen; the Darārma, the people whose progenitor was Darrūm; the Shadhādhna are those whose progenitor was Shadhdhān.

14. In 1977, IL 1,500 were around $80, but only during the heavily toured summer months did the Mzeini pickup owners make this much.

15. For a detailed discussion of South Sinai ʿanwas or intertribal legislation, see chapter 3.

16. Sheikh Ibn-Shabīb was the ancestor of the Shabaiba phratry of the Garārsha tribe. He was also the guardian saint of the date trees of the Firān.

17. Sil ʿAlayān is where Wadi ʿAlayān meets Wadi Firān, in the lower part of the oasis. Tarig omm-ʿAjram is a dirt road that crosses Wadi Firān a kilometer above the 1977 upper end of the oasis.

18. The black wool winter tents had two sections—one for the man and his guests, with a door that opened in the direction of the sun; the other a closed section, with a small opening, for the women and the young children, to protect their modesty. Summer flour-sack tents had only one section, the private section, and therefore the man could not invite his guests from the magʿad to visit his home.

CHAPTER NINE

1. I would like to thank Don Handelman here for pointing out to me this crucial issue.

2. This phenomenon even made it to the American media. A short item in the *San Francisco Chronicle* (24 January 1980) describes the recovery of 127 disassembled and partially buried stolen Israeli vehicles in the South Sinai.

3. Among the Mzeina, the prefix "omm" can mean either "the mother of," such as in the case of Omm Mūsa, or "the daughter of," such as in the case of Fṭaima omm-ʿAbdallah.

4. The consonant "q" is pronounced "g" in many Bedouin dialects and in the Yemenite dialect of Arabic my grandmother speaks.

5. It is interesting to point here at the linguistic similarity between *illi kān lilmakān*, or the connection of the past to the present, and the

Kān Ya Makān or "once upon a time" genre of fantastic legends discussed in chapter 10.

CHAPTER TEN

1. Although I recognize the insightfulness of Quilligan's (1979) comprehensive analysis of allegory, as a scholar of nonliterate cultures I cannot agree with her assessment that "unlike epics, which can be oral, allegories are always written" (1979: 25).

2. Among the anthropologists who discuss the connections between liminality and paradox are Babcock (1980), Crocker (1973), Handelman (1979), Handelman and Kapferer (1980), and Shore (1983); see also Colie (1966).

3. The pre-1922 relative freedom of Arab tribes from state control is described in Antoun (1972:157), R. Fernea (1970:116), and Lancaster (1981:84). See also Meeker (1979), and Sowayan (1985).

4. I find Buelow's analysis of "verbal decomposition" (1989:47) in written allegorical poetics relevant to my discussion even though the focus of my research is orally performed allegories.

5. In this context, a *noesis-noema* relation (Husserl 1962) may be viewed as some kind of intersubjective signifier-signified relation (Lévi-Strauss 1967).

6. It seems to me that this Mzeini genre of allegory, interestingly, emanating from the experience of the colonized, might be the opposite of the colonialist manichean allegory discussed by Abdul JanMohamed (1985). Here it is the occupier, rather than the occupied, who is "fed into the manichean allegory," while in the genre of colonialist allegories discussed by JanMohamed, it is the occupier who "commodifies the native subject into a stereotyped object and uses him as a resource for colonialist fiction" (1985:64, See also 1983).

7. Not surprisingly, the filmmakers gave no credit to the Mzeini extras, nor did they mention that the film was partly shot in the Sinai. Instead, they credit Israel, even though the Sinai has never been part of Israel proper.

GLOSSARY OF ARABIC TERMS

afranj (pl.), ***faranji*** (sing.) Westerners.

ᶜagl rationality, a male quality.

ahabal a fool.

ahl al-dageᶜa the people of the land, the Bedouin.

ᶜajram glasswort bush (*ochradenus*, Lat.).

ᶜajūz an old woman.

amāna trust.

ᶜanwa (sing.), ***ᶜanawāt*** (pl.) intertribal legislation.

arāk mangrove bush (*salvadora*, Lat.).

ᶜarīsha a men's club adjacent to a saint's tomb.

aṣal roots, genealogical descent line, tribal affiliation.

ᶜashīra intertribal alliance.

bedu Bedouin

bint ᶜam parallel cousin, father's brother's daughter.

dākhel seeking sheltered refuge with another family.

ᶜeib shame.

fallaḥīn peasants.

faraᶜ (sing.), ***fruᶜ*** (pl.) stream; tribal clan.

faranji (sing.), ***afranj*** (pl.) Westerner.

fāreᶜ the highlands.

gaḍiyya a court case; the law.

galīd the symbolic battle coordinator of a tribe.

gaṣīda a long epic poem.

ghayii sexual lust, a male quality.

ḥakūma government.

ḥalāl all the religiously permissible thoughts and deeds; livestock.

ḥamsīn a hot and dry eastern storm.

ḥarām taboo, all the religious sins.

ḥaṭab firewood.

ḥawāja mister, a respectful title for addressing a non-Bedouin man.

hejēni a caravan song.

ᶜilu the watershed plateau.

jinn demon.

junūn madness.

kafīl (sing.), ***kufalā*** (pl.) a man who acts as a legal guarantor in a customary court.

kalām rejjāl a man's word, on a man's honor.

kān ya makān "once upon a time there was a place;" a genre of fantastic, didactic tales.

karwat al-ḍeif the code of hospitality.

kbār the tribal elders.

khamsa (sing.), ***kahmsāt*** (pl.) five-generation-depth lineage that constitutes the blood vengeance group.

khantarīsh the worst quality hashish; a nickname given to someone or somebody whose worth is negligible.

kheir wējed "a bounty of good," an expression reserved for festive occasions.

magᶜad rejjāl or ***magᶜad*** a fenced area where men get together and talk, a men's club of sorts.

majnūna a madwoman.

miḥrāb the small protruding semicircle in a mosque, before which the prayer leader stands.

moshāv (sing.), ***moshavīm*** (pl., Hebrew) Israeli agricultural cooperative.

mudunnīyya urbanities, city dwellers.

mukhabarāt the secret police.

nabaz (sing.), ***nbāz*** (pl.) nickname; a tribal maximal lineage.

nafs soul, a female quality.

ᶜomda a headman of a sedentarized community, appointed by the government.

Prayers:

- ***fajr*** dawn prayer, around half an hour before sunrise.
- ***ẓuhur*** noon prayer, at 12:00 noon.
- ***ᶜasr*** afternoon prayer, around 2:30–3:30 P.M.
- ***maghreb*** early evening prayer, at dusk.
- ***ᶜasha*** after-dinner prayer, around 8:00–8:30 P.M.

purdah an Indian term generally referring to the seclusion of women.

rabāba one-string fiddle.

raḥḥāla or ***raḥlīn*** nomads.

raᶜi a shepherd; a male non-blood-relative who is given permission to act in the customary court as if he were a member of a *khamsa*.

ratam broom-bush (*retama roetam*, Lat.).

riḥla the complete classic annual migration cycle.

rubᶜ (sing.), ***rbāᶜ*** (pl.) a quarter; phratry, the largest tribal segment.

ṣabr patience, endurance, tolerance, equanimity, a female quality.

sayyāl acacia tree (*acacia rediana*, Lat.).

shaghalīn laborers.

shaiṭān satanic spirits.

shanna a goatskin stuffed with ripe dates.

shayyalīn couriers.

shēba an old man.

sheikh an administrative leader of a tribe.

shīḥ wormwood (*artemisia herba alba*, Lat.).

shīza a game, a complicated cross between checkers and "go."

shughlīn al-siyāsa the people of politics, the occupiers.

ṭahawa a thanksgiving meal.
ṭanīb a man, nonmember of a tribe, who is given fictive tribal kinship for the purpose of protecting him.
ṭāref the flatlands.
ṭuhūr circumcision (both male and female).
ʿ***urfi*** Bedouin customary law.
wadi a dry riverbed.
yahūd Jews.
zuāra a visit; a pilgrimage to a holy shrine.

REFERENCES

ABRAHAMS, ROGER D.

1986. Ordinary and Extraordinary Experience. In *The Anthropology of Experience*. Ed. Victor W. Turner and Edward M. Bruner, 45–72. Urbana: University of Illinois Press.

ABOU-ZEID, AHMED M.

1966. Honour and Shame among the Bedouin of Egypt. In *Honour and Shame*. Ed. J. P. Peristiany, 243–259. Chicago: The University of Chicago Press.

ABU-LUGHOD, LILA

1985. Honor and the Sentiment of Loss in a Bedouin Society. *American Ethnologist* 12(2):245–261.

1986. *Veiled Sentiments: Honor and Poetry in a Bedouin Society*. Berkeley, Los Angeles, London: University of California Press.

ABU-ZAHARA, NADIA

1974. Material Power, Honour, Friendship, and the Etiquette of Visiting. *Anthropological Quarterly* 47:120–138.

AHMAD, AIJAZ

1987. Jameson's Rhetoric of Otherness and the "National Allegory." *Social Text* 17:3–25.

Ahrām, al- (Cairo, in Arabic)

11 June 1975. Aid for the Natives of Sinai to be Continued. Page 6, Column 2.

9 December 1975. Petitions are Welcome. Page 9, Column 2.

8 July 1979. A Dam for Storing Water in Sinai. Page 8, Column 5.

15 July 1979. A Comprehensive Plan for Developing Health Services in [Sinai] Province and for Ration Cards for the Inhabitants of the Liberated Region. Page 8, Column 2.

16 July 1979. The Agricultural Land Tenure System is Applied in Sinai—Seven Thousand Acres to be Reclaimed. Page 11, Column 1.

31 March 1980. The Difficulties Facing the Minister of Repopulation—The Bedouin Prefer to Live in Metal Shacks and Refuse to Live in the New Housing! Page 11, Column 6.

25 January 1982. A Comprehensive Plan for Developing the Cities and Villages of the South Sinai. Page 11, Column 1.

24 April 1982. 88 Million Pounds for Emergency Services for the Bedouin of Sinai. Page 1, Column 1.

27 April 1982. The Bedouin Turn Out in Sharm al-Sheikh to See the City that They were Forbidden to Enter for 15 Years. Page 5, Column 5.

29 April 1982. A Standing Commission for Repopulating Sinai. Page 1, Column 4.

Akhbār, al- (Cairo, in Arabic)

17 January 1981. The Short Path to Industrialization. Page 3, Column 1.

AMIḤAI, YEHOUDA

1976. Lamentation for Those Who Die in War. In *Behind All This Hides One Great Happiness*, 87–92. Tel Aviv: Schocken [in Hebrew].

AMOSS, PAMELA T.

1981. Coast Salish Elders. In *Other Ways of Growing Old: An Anthropological Perspective*. Ed. P. T. Amoss and S. Harrell, 227–247. Stanford: Stanford University Press.

ANDERSON, JON

1982. Social Structure and the Veil: Comportment and the Composition of Interaction in Afghanistan. *Anthropos* 77:397–420.

ANTOUN, RICHARD T.

1968. On the Modesty of Women in Arab Muslim Villages: A Study in the Accommodation of Traditions. *American Anthropologist* 70:671–697.

1972. *Arab Village: A Social Structural Study of a Trans-Jordanian Peasant Community*. Bloomington: Indiana University Press.

ʿAREF, ʿAREF AL-

1934*a*. *The Law among the Bedouin*. Jerusalem: Beit al-Maqdas [in Arabic].

1934*b*. *The History of Beer Sheba and its Tribes*. Jerusalem: Beit al-Maqdas [in Arabic].

ASAD, TALAL
1973. *Anthropology and the Colonial Encounter*. London: Ithaca Press.

AYOUB, ABDERRAHMAN.
1982. The Hilali Epic: Material and Memory. Unpublished Manuscript.

BABCOCK, BARBARA A.
1980. Reflexivity: Definitions and Discriminations. *Semiotica* 30(1/2):1–14.

BAILEY, CLINTON
1972. The Narrative Context of the Bedouin Qasidah-Poem. The Hebrew University of Jerusalem, *Folklore Research Studies* 3:67–105.

BAKHTIN, MIKHAIL
1981. Discourse in the Novel. In *The Dialogic Imagination*. Ed. M. Holquist, 259–442. Austin: University of Texas Press.

BARTH, FREDRIC
1954. Father's Brother's Daughter Marriage in Kurdistan. *Southwestern Journal of Anthropology* 10(2):164–171.
1959. *Political Leadership among Swat Pathans*. London: Athlone Press.

BARTLETT, WILLIAM H.
1849. *Forty Days in the Desert, on the Track of the Israelites; or, A Journey from Cairo, by Wady Feiran, to Mount Sinai and Petra*. London: A. Hall and Co.

BASSO, ELLEN B.
1984. Monological Understanding in Dialogic Discourse. Presented at the Annual Meeting of the American Anthropological Association.

BASSO, KEITH H.
1979. *Portraits of "The Whiteman:" Linguistic Play and Cultural Symbols among the Western Apache*. New York: Cambridge University Press.
1984. "Stalking with Stories": Names, Places, and Moral Narratives among the Western Apache. In *Text, Play, and Story: The Construction and Reconstruction of Self and*

Society. Ed. E. M. Bruner, 19–54. Washington, DC: The American Ethnological Society.

BATESON, GREGORY
1956. The Message "This is Play." In *Second Conference on Group Processes*. Ed. B. Schaffner, 145–241. New York: Josiah Macy Foundation.
1972*a*. Double Bind, 1969. In *Steps to an Ecology of Mind*, 271–278. New York: Ballantine.
1972*b*. A Theory of Play and Fantasy. In *Steps to an Ecology of Mind*, 177–193. New York: Ballantine.

BAUDRILLARD, JEAN
1983. *Simulations*. Trans. P. Foss, P. Patton, and P. Beitchman. New York: Semiotext(e).

BECK, LOIS, AND NIKKI KEDDIE, EDS.
1978. *Women in the Muslim World*. Cambridge, Mass.: Harvard University Press.

BEN DAVID, YOSSEF
1981. *Jebaliyya: A Bedouin Tribe in the Shadow of the Monastery*. Jerusalem: Kana [in Hebrew].

BENJAMIN, WALTER
1969. The Storyteller: Reflections on the Works of Nikolai Leskov. In *Illuminations*. Ed. H. Arendt. Trans. H. Zohn, 83–110. New York: Schocken Books.
1985 [1963]. Allegory and Trauerspiel. In *The Origin of German Tragic Drama*, 159–235. Trans. J. Osborne. London: Verso.

BERGER, PETER L., AND THOMAS LUCKMAN
1967. *The Social Construction of Reality: A Treatise in the Sociology of Knowledge*. Garden City, N.Y.: Doubleday.

BERREMAN, GERALD D.
1981. *The Politics of Truth: Essays in Critical Anthropology*. New Delhi: South Asian Publishers PVT LTD.

BLACK-MICHAUD, JACOB
1975. *Cohesive Force: Feud in the Mediterranean and the Middle East*. Oxford: Basil Blackwell.

BOURDIEU, PIERRE

1966. The Sentiment of Honour in Kabyle Society. In *Honour and Shame*. Ed. J. G. Peristiany, 191–241. Chicago: The University of Chicago Press.

BROWN, JUDITH K.

1985. *In Her Prime: A New View of Middle-Aged Women*. South Hadley, MA: Bergin and Gravey Publishers, Inc.

BRUNER, EDWARD M.

1986. Experience and Its Expressions. In *The Anthropology of Experience*. Ed. V. W. Turner and E. Bruner, 3–30. Urbana: University of Illinois Press.

BUELOW, CHRISTIN VON

1989. Vallejo's *Venus de Milo* and the Ruins of Language. *PMLA* 104(1):41–52.

BURCKHARDT, JOHN L.

1822. *Travels in Syria and the Holy Land*. London: J. Murray.

1831. *Notes on the Bedouins and the Wahabys*. 2 vols. London: H. Colburn and R. Bentley.

BURNS, ELIZABETH

1972. *Theatricality: A Study of Convention in the Theatre and in Social Life*. London: Longman.

CALVINO, ITALO

1974. *Invisible Cities*. Trans. W. Weaver. New York: Harcourt Brace Jovanovich.

CHAGNON, NAPOLEON A.

1968. *Yanomamo: The Fierce People*. New York: Holt, Rinehart and Winston.

CHARLES, LUCILLE HOERR

1945. The Clown's Function. *Journal of American Folklore* 58:25–34.

CHESLER, PHYLLIS

1972. *Women and Madness*. New York: Avon Books.

CHOMSKY, NOAM

1974. *Peace in the Middle East?* New York: Vintage Books.

CLIFFORD, GAY

1974. *The Transformation of Allegory*. London: Routledge & Kegan Paul.

CLIFFORD, JAMES

1983. On Ethnographic Authority. *Representation* 1(2):118–146.

1986. On Ethnographic Allegory. In *Writing Culture: The Poetics and Politics of Ethnography*. Ed. J. Clifford and G. Marcus, 98–121. Berkeley, Los Angeles, London: University of California Press.

1988. *The Predicament of Culture: Twentieth-Century Ethnography, Literature, and Art*. Cambridge, Mass.: Harvard University Press.

COETZEE, J. M.

1982. *Waiting for the Barbarians*. New York: Penguin Books.

COLE, DONALD P.

1975. *Nomads of the Nomads: The Al-Murrah Bedouin of the Empty Quarter*. Chicago: Aldine.

COLIE, ROSALIE

1966. *Paradoxia Epidemica: The Renaissance Tradition of Paradox*. Princeton: Princeton University Press.

COLSON, ELIZABETH, AND THAYER SCUDDER.

1981. Old Age in Gwembe District, Zambia. In *Other Ways of Growing Old: Anthropological Perspectives*. Ed. P. T. Amoss and S. Harrell, 125–153. Stanford: Stanford University Press.

CONDER, CLAUDE R.

1878. *Tent Work in Palestine: A Record of Discovery and Adventure*. London: R. Bentley and Son.

COX, HARVEY

1970. *The Feast of Fools: A Theological Essay on Festivity and Fantasy*. New York: Harper and Row.

CRAPANZANO, VINCENT

1973. *The Hamadsha: A Study in Moroccan Ethnopsychiatry*. Berkeley, Los Angeles, London: University of California Press.

1980. *Tuhami: Portrait of A Moroccan*. Chicago: University of Chicago Press.

CROCKER, CHRISTOPHER

1973. Ritual and the Development of Social Structure: Liminality and Inversion. In *The Roots of Ritual*. Ed. J. D. Shaughneasy, 47–86. Grand Rapids, Mich.: Eerdmans.

CRUMRINE, N. ROSS

1969. Capakoba, the Mayo Easter Ceremonial Impersonator: Explanations of Ritual Clowning. *Journal of Scientific Study of Religion* 8:1–22.

CUNNISON, IAN

1966. *The Baggara Arabs*. Oxford: Clarendon Press.

DAFNI, YA^cAKOV

1969. The Fauna in the Gulf of Eilat and in the Eastern Shore of the Sinai. *Teva^c va-Aretz* 11(4):173–176 [in Hebrew].

DANIEL, E. VALENTINE

1984. *Fluid Signs: Being a Person the Tamil Way*. Berkeley, London, Los Angeles: University of California Press.

DANIN, AVINO^cAM

1978. Plant Species Diversity and Ecological Districts of the Sinai Desert. *Vegetatio* 36(2):83–93.

DE MAN, PAUL

1969. The Rhetoric of Temporality. In *Interpretation: Theory and Practice*. Ed. C. C. Singleton, 173–210. Baltimore: Johns Hopkins University Press.

1979. *Allegories of Reading: Figural Language in Rousseau, Nietzsche, Rilke, and Proust*. New Haven: Yale University Press.

1981. Pascal's Allegory of Persuasion. In *Allegory and Representation*. Ed. S. J. Greenblatt, 1–25. Baltimore: Johns Hopkins University Press.

DOLS, MICHAEL

1983. Insanity in Byzantine and Islamic Medicine. Unpublished Manuscript.

DOUGHTY, CHARLES M.

1921. [1888] *Travels in Arabia Deserta*. 2 vols. London: Jonathan Cape.

DRESCH, PAUL
1984. The Position of Shaykhs among the Northern Tribes of Yemen. *Man* (N.S.) 19(1):31–49.
1986. The Significance of the Course Events Take in Segmentary Systems. *American Ethnologist* 13(2):309–324.

DURKHEIM, EMILE
1933. *On the Division of Labor in Society*. Trans. G. Simpson. New York: The Macmillan Company.

DWYER, DAISY H.
1978. *Images and Self-Images: Male and Female in Morocco*. New York: Columbia University Press.

DWYER, KEVIN
1982. *Moroccan Dialogues: Anthropology in Question*. Baltimore: The Johns Hopkins University Press.

EHRMANN, JACQUES
1968. Homo Ludens Revisited. *Yale French Studies* 41:31–57.

ELSHTAIN, JEAN B.
1981. *Public Man, Private Woman: Women in Social and Political Thought*. Princeton: Princeton University Press.

EVANS-PRITCHARD, E. E.
1940. *The Nuer*. Oxford: Oxford University Press.
1949. *The Sasnusi of Cyrenaica*. Oxford: Clarendon Press.

FABIAN, JOHANNES
1983. *Time and the Other: How Anthropology Makes its Object*. New York: Columbia University Press.

FELLINI, FEDERICO
1976. Why Clowns? In *Fellini on Fellini,* 115–139. New York: Delacorte Press.

FERNANDEZ, JAMES W.
1974. The Mission of Metaphor in Expressive Culture. *Current Anthropology* 15(2):119–145.
1986. *Persuasions and Performances: The Play of Tropes in Culture*. Bloomington: Indiana University Press.

FERNEA, ELIZABETH W.
1965. *Guests of the Sheik: An Ethnography of an Iraqi Village*. Garden City, N.Y.: Doubleday.

FERNEA, ROBERT A.
1970. *Shaykh and Effendi: Changing Patterns of Authority among the El-Shabana of Southern Iraq.* Cambridge, Mass.: Harvard University Press.

FIELD, HENRY
1948. Sinai Sheds New Light on the Bible. *National Geographic Magazine* 94(6):795–815

FINEMAN, JOEL
1981. The Structure of Allegorical Desire. In *Allegory and Representation.* Ed. S. J. Greenblatt, 26–60. Baltimore: Johns Hopkins University Press.

FIRTH, RAYMOND
1973. *Symbols: Public and Private.* Ithaca: Cornell University Press.

FISCHER, MICHAEL M. J.
1988. Scientific Dialogue and Critical Hermeneutics. *Cultural Anthropology* 3(1):3–15.

FISHELSON, LEV, AND DAVID PHILOSOPH
1981. *The Secrets of the Red Sea.* Tel Aviv: Massada [in Hebrew].

FLETCHER, ANGUS
1964. *Allegory: The Theory of a Symbolic Mode.* Ithaca: Cornell University Press.

FORSYTH, GEORGE N., AND ROBERT F. SISSON
1964. Island of Faith in the Sinai Wilderness. *National Geographic Magazine* 125(1):82–106.

FORTES, MEYER
1945. *The Dynamic of Clanship among the Tallensi.* London: Oxford University Press.
1949. *The Web of Kinship Among the Tallensi.* London: Oxford University Press.
1953. The Structure of Unilineal Descent Groups. *American Anthropologist* 55:17–51.

FOUCAULT, MICHEL
1965. *Madness and Civilization: A History of Insanity in the Age of Reason.* Trans. R. Howard. New York: Pantheon Books.

FRYE, NORTHROP
1967. *Anatomy of Criticism: Four Essays.* New York: Atheneum.

GARFINKEL, HAROLD
1967. *Studies in Ethnomethodology*. Englewood Cliffs, N.J.: Prentice-Hall.

GLASSNER, MARTIN I.
1974. The Bedouin of Southern Sinai under Israeli Administration. *The Geographical Review* 64(1):31–60.

GLUCKMAN, MAX
1959. *Custom and Conflict in Africa*. Glencoe, Ill.: Free Press.

GOFFMAN, ERVING
1959. *The Presentation of Self in Everyday Life*. New York: Doubleday.

GOODY, JACK
1962. *Death, Property and the Ancestors: A Study of Mortuary Customs of the LoDagaa of West Africa*. Stanford: Stanford University Press.

GRATHOFF, RICHARD
1970. *The Structure of Social Inconsistencies; A Contribution to a Unified Theory of Play, Game, and Social Action*. The Hague: Martinus Nijhoff.

GREENBLATT, STEPHEN J., ED.
1981. Preface. In *Allegory and Representation*, vii–xiii. Baltimore: Johns Hopkins University Press.

GUINDI, FADWA EL-
1981. Veiling *infitah* with Muslim Ethics: Egypt's Contemporary Islamic Movement. *Social Problems* 28(4):465–485.

GUTMANN, DAVID
1987. *Reclaimed Powers: Toward a New Psychology of Men and Women in Later Life*. New York: Basic Books.

HANDELMAN, DON
1977. Play and Ritual: Complementary Frames of Metacommunication. In *It's a Funny Thing, Humor*. Ed. A. J. Chapman and H. Foot, 185–192. Oxford: Pergamon Press.
1979. Is Naven Ludic?: Paradox and the Communication of Identity. *Social Analysis* 1:177–191.

1981. The Ritual Clown: Attributes and Affinities. *Anthropos* 76(1/2):321–370.

1986. Charisma, Liminality, and Symbolic Types. In *Comparative Social Dynamics: Essays in Honor of S. N. Eisenstadt*. Ed. E. Cohen, M. Lissak and U. Almagor, 346–359. Boulder: Westview Press.

1987. Clowns. In *The Encyclopedia of Religion*. Vol. 3. Ed. M. Eliade, 547–551. New York: The Macmillan Company.

HANDELMAN, DON, AND BRUCE KAPFERER

1980. Symbolic Types, Mediation, and the Transformation of Ritual Context: Sinhalese Demons and Tewa Clowns. *Semiotica* 30(1/2):41–71.

HART, DAVID M.

1970. Conflicting Models of a Berber Tribal Structure in the Moroccan Rif: The Segmentary and Alliance Systems of the Aith Warayachar. *Revue De L'Occident Musulman et de La Méditerrenée* 7:93–100.

HENNIKER, FREDERICK

1823. *Notes, During a Visit to Egypt, Nubia, the Oasis, Mount Sinai, and Jerusalem*. London: J. Murray.

HERZFELD, MICHAEL

1980. Honour and Shame: Problems in the Comparative Analysis of Moral Systems. *Man* 15:339–351.

HILL, JANE

1986. The Refiguration of the Anthropology of Language. *Cultural Anthropology* 1(1):89–102.

HOWELL, RICHARD W.

1973. *Teasing Relationships*. Reading, Mass.: Addison-Wesley Publishing Company Inc.

HUSSERL, EDMUND

1962 [1931]. *Ideas: General Introduction to Pure Phenomenology*. Trans. W. C. Boyce Gibson. New York: Collier Books.

ISSAR, ARIYE

1980. Water Resources in the Sinai. *Madaʿ* 15(4):202 [in Hebrew].

JABARTY, ʿABD AL-RAḤMAN AL-
1879. Marvelous Legacies of Biographies and Events. 4 vols. Cairo: Matbaʿat Bulaq [in Arabic].

JACKSON, MICHAEL
1982. *Allegories of the Wilderness: Ethics and Ambiguity in Kuranko Narratives.* Bloomington: Indiana University Press.

JAMESON, FREDRIC
1981. *The Political Unconscious: Narrative as a Socially Symbolic Act.* Ithaca: Cornell University Press.
1986. Third-World Literature in the Era of Multinational Capitalism. *Social Text* 15:65–88.
1987. A Brief Response. *Social Text* 17:26–27.

JANMOHAMED, ABDUL M.
1983. *Manichean Aesthetics: The Politics of Literature in Colonial Africa.* Amherst: University of Massachusetts Press.
1985. The Economy of Manichean Allegory: The Function of Racial Difference in Colonialist Literature. *Critical Inquiry* 12(1):59–87.

JARVIS, CLAUDE S.
1931. *Yesterday and To-Day in Sinai.* Edinburgh: W. Blackwood and Sons.
1937. *Three Deserts.* New York: E. P. Dutton and Co.

JOSEPH, SUAD
1988. Feminization, Familism, Self, and Politics. In *Arab Women in the Field.* Ed. S. Altorki and C. Fawzi El-Solh, 25–48. Syracuse, N.Y.: Syracuse University Press.

Kashshāf al-Ahrām (Cairo, in Arabic)
May 1982. 1.5 Million Pounds Set Aside for Compensating the Sinai Bedouin. Page 5, Column 6.

KATRIEL, TAMAR
1986. *Talking Straight:* Dugri *Speech in Israeli Sabra Culture.* Cambridge: Cambridge University Press.

KLAPP, ORRIN E.
1949. The Fool as a Social Type. *American Journal of Sociology* 55(2):157–162.

KOESTLER, ARTHUR
1964. *The Act of Creation*. New York: The Macmillan Company.

KOLTON, Y.
1980. Hydrology of Alluvial Fans on the Shores of the Gulf of Eilat. *Abstracts of the Israeli Geological Society Annual Meetings*, p. 22.

KOPTIUCH, KRISTIN
1988. Egypt's Informal Sector in the Postmodern Economy: Historical Continuity or Simulacrum? Presented at the Annual Meeting of the Society for Economic Anthropology.

KRESSEL, GIDEON
1977. Bride Price Reconsidered. *Current Anthropology* 18(3):441–458.
1981. Sororicide-Filiacide Homicide for Family Honor. *Current Anthropology* 22(2):141–158.
1986. Prescriptive Patrilineal Parallel Cousin Marriage: The Perspective of the Bride's Father and Brothers. *Ethnology* 25(3):163–180.

KUNDERA, MILAN
1980. *The Book of Laughter and Forgetting*. Translated by M. H. Heim. New York: Penguin Books.

LABORDE, LEON E. S. J.
1836. *Journey Through Arabia Petraera, to Mount Sinai, and the Excavated City of Petra*. London: J. Murray.

LABOV, WILLIAM
1972. Rules for Ritual Insults. In *Studies in Social Interaction*. Ed. D. Sudnow, 120–169. New York: The Free Press.

LANCASTER, WILLIAM
1981. *The Rwala Bedouin Today*. Cambridge: Cambridge University Press.

LAVIE, SMADAR
1980. Are the Mzeina Bedouin?—The Annual Pilgrimage to the Mzeina Ancestral Tomb: Scenario and Analysis. Unpublished Manuscript.
1984. The Fool and The Hippies: Ritual/Play and Social Inconsistencies Among the Mzeina Bedouin of the Sinai. In

The Masks of Play. Ed. B. Sutton-Smith and D. Kelly-Byrne, 63–70. New York: Leisure Press.

1986. The Poetics of Politics: An Allegory of Bedouin Identity. In *Political Anthropology*, vol 5: *The Frailty of Authority*. Ed. M. J. Aronoff, 131–146. New Brunswick, N.J.: Transaction Books.

1988. Sinai for the Coffee Table: Birds, Bedouins and Desert Wanderlust. *Middle East Report* [MERIP] 150:40–44.

1989. When Leadership Becomes Allegory: Mzeina Sheikhs and the Experience of Military Occupation. *Cultural Anthropology* 4(2):99–135.

LAVIE, SMADAR, AND FOREST ROUSE

1988. Notes on the Fantastic Journey of the Ḥajj, His Anthropologist, and Her American Passport. Presented at the Annual Meeting of the American Anthropological Association.

LAVIE, SMADAR, AND WILLIAM C. YOUNG

1984. Bedouin in Limbo: Egyptian and Israeli Development Policies in the Southern Sinai. *Antipode* 16(2):33–44.

LEACH, EDMUND L.

1961. Two Essays Concerning the Symbolic Representation of Time. In *Rethinking Anthropology*, 124–136. London: Athlone Press.

LEPSIUS, RICHARD

1853. *Letters from Egypt, Ethiopia, and the Peninsula of Sinai.* Trans. L. and J. B. Horner. London: H. G. Bohn.

LEVI, SHABETAI (SHABBO)

1978*a*. *Medicine, Hygiene and Health among the Bedouin of the South Sinai.* Tel Aviv: The Society for the Protection of Nature [in Hebrew].

1978*b*. "Riḥle"—The Migration after Pasture Resources. *Teva*ᶜ *va-Aretz* 20(2):65–67 [in Hebrew].

1982. The Process of Settlement of the Tribes of South Sinai. In *South Sinai Researches*. Ed. I. Lachish and Z. Meshel, 177–188. Tel Aviv: Society for the Protection of Nature in Israel [in Hebrew].

1988. *The Bedouins in Sinai Desert: A Pattern of Desert Society.* Jerusalem: Schocken Books [in Hebrew].

LÉVI-STRAUSS, CLAUDE

1967. *Structural Anthropology*. Garden City, N.Y.: Anchor Books.

LEVY, JERROLD E.

1967. The Older American Indian. In *The Older Rural Americans: A Sociological Perspective*. Ed. E. Youmans, 231–238. Lexington: University of Kentucky Press.

LEVY, REUBEN

1957. *The Social Structure of Islam*. Cambridge: Cambridge University Press.

LEWIS, IOAN M.

1961. *A Pastoral Democracy: A Study of Pastoralism and Politics among the Northern Somali of the Horn of Africa*. London: Oxford University Press.

MCHUGH, PETER

1968. *Defining the Situation: The Organization of Meaning in Social Interaction*. New York: Bobbs-Merrill.

MAKARIUS, LAURA

1970. Ritual Clowns and Symbolical Behavior. *Diogenes* 69:44–73.

MANṢOUR, ʿATTALLAH

1988. They Can't Finish the Month. *Ha'aretz* (Tel Aviv), 11 September, Page B6 [in Hebrew].

MARCUS, GEORGE E.

1986. Contemporary Problems of Ethnography in the Modern World System. In *Writing Culture: The Poetics and Politics of Ethnography*. Ed. J. Clifford and G. E. Marcus, 165–193. Berkeley, Los Angeles, London: University of California Press.

MARCUS, GEORGE E., AND MICHAEL M. J. FISCHER

1986. *Anthropology as Cultural Critique: An Experimental Moment in the Human Sciences*. Chicago: The University of Chicago Press.

MARX, EMANUEL

1967. *Bedouin of the Negev*. Manchester: Manchester University Press.

1977*a*. Communal and Individual Pilgrimage: The Region of Saints' Tombs in the South Sinai. In *Regional Cults*. Ed. R. P. Werbner, 29–51. London: Academic Press.

1977*b*. The Tribe as a Unit of Subsistence: Nomadic Pastoralism in the Middle East. *American Anthropologist* 79:343–363.

1980. Wage Labor and Tribal Economy of the Bedouin in South Sinai. In *When Nomads Settle: Processes of Sedentarization as Adaptation and Response*. Ed. P. C. Salzman, 111–123. New York: Praeger.

MEAD, GEORGE H.

1962. *Mind, Self, and Society*. Chicago: Chicago University Press.

MEEKER, MICHAEL E.

1979. *Literature and Violence in North Arabia*. Cambridge, England: Cambridge University Press.

MERNISSI, FATIMA

1975. *Beyond the Veil: Male–Female Dynamics in a Modern Muslim Society*. Cambridge, Mass.: Schenkman.

MILLS, C. WRIGHT

1959. *The Sociological Imagination*. London: Oxford University Press.

MOHSEN, SAFIA K.

1975. *Conflict and Law among the Awlad ʿAli of the Western Desert*. Cairo: National Center for Social and Criminological Research.

MORSY, SOHEIR A.

1978. Gender, Power, and Illness in an Egyptian Village. Unpublished Doctoral Dissertation. Michigan State University at Lansing.

MURPHY, ROBERT, AND LEONARD KASDAN

1959. The Structure of Parallel Cousin Marriage. *American Anthropologist* 61:17–29.

MURRAY, GEORGE W.

1935. *Sons of Ishmael: A Study of the Egyptian Bedouin*. London: George Routledge and Sons, LTD.

Musawwar, al- (Cairo)

7 March 1980. Sinai Tribal Sheikhs Urge February 26 as a National Holiday. In *Transdex Index to the United States Joint Publications Research* (JPRS), pp. 30–32. Wooster, Ohio: Micro Photo Division, Bell and Howell Co.

MUSIL, ALOIS
1928. The Manners and Customs of the Rwala Bedouins. American Geographical Society: Oriental Explorations and Studies, no. 6. New York: Crane.

MYERS, FRED R.
1986. The Politics of Representation: Anthropological Discourse and Australian Aborigines. *American Ethnologist* 13(1):138–153.

NIR, YAᶜAKOV
1988. The Bedouin Tribes of the South Sinai—Their Socio-Familial Structure. In *Sinai.* 2 vols. Ed. G. Gvirtzman, A. Shmueli, Y. Gardos, Y. Beit-Ariyeh, 807–817. Tel Aviv: Eretz—Researches and Publications in Geography. Ministry of Defense Publishing House [in Hebrew].

OREN, URI
1968. The Revelation at Mt. Sinai by the Twelve Tribes. *Yediᶜōt Aḥaronōt* (Tel Aviv), 14 August. Page 11 [in Hebrew].

PALMER, EDWARD H.
1871. *The Desert of the Exodus: Journeys on Foot in the Wilderness of the Forty Year's Wanderings.* 2 vol. Cambridge: Deighton and Bell.

PARSONS, ELSIE CLEWS, AND RALPH L. BEALS
1934. The Sacred Clowns of the Pueblo and Mayo-Yaqui Indians. *American Anthropologist* 36:491–514.

PARSONS, TALCOTT
1951. *The Social System.* New York: Free Press.

PATAI, RAPHAEL
1955. Cousin-Right in Middle Eastern Marriage. *Southwestern Journal of Anthropology* 11(4):371–390.

PEREVOLOTSKY, AVI
1979. *Aspects of Bedouin Judicial Practice in Southern Sinai.* Tel Aviv: Society for the Protection of Nature [in Hebrew].
1981. Orchard Agriculture in the High Mountain Region of Southern Sinai. *Human Ecology* 9(3):331-357.

PEREVOLOTSKY, AVI AND AYELET
1979. *Subsistence Patterns of the Jebaliyya Bedouin in the High Mountain Region of the South Sinai.* Tel Aviv: Society for the Protection of Nature [in Hebrew].

PETERS, EMRYS L.
1960. The Proliferation of Segments in the Lineage of the Bedouin of Cyrenaica. *Journal of the Royal Anthropological Institute of Great Britain* 90:29–53.
1965. Aspects of the Family among the Bedouin of Cyrenaica. In *Comparative Family Systems.* Ed. M. F. Nimkoff, 121–146. Boston: Houghton Mifflin.
1967. Some Structural Aspects of the Feud among the Camel-Herding Bedouin of Cyrenaica. *Africa* 37:261–282.
1975. Forward. In *Cohesive Force.* J. Black-Michaud, ix-xxvii. Oxford: Basil Blackwell.
1980. Aspects of Bedouin Bridewealth among Camel Herders in Cyrenaica. In *The Meaning of Marriage Payments.* Ed. J. L. Comaroff, 125–160. London: Academic Press.

PRICE, RICHARD
1983. *First Time: The Historical Vision of an Afro-American People.* Baltimore: The Johns Hopkins University Press.

QUILLIGAN, MAUREEN
1979. *The Language of Allegory: Defining the Genre.* Ithaca: Cornell University Press.

RABINOWITZ, DAN
1985. Themes in the Economy of the Bedouin of South Sinai in the Nineteenth and Twentieth Centuries. *International Journal of Middle East Studies* 17(1):211–228.

RADIN, PAUL
1956. *The Trickster: A Study in American Indian Mythology.* London: Routledge & Kegan Paul.

RASSAM [VINOGRADOV], AMAL
1974. The Ait Ndhir of Morocco: A Study of the Social Transformation of a Berber Tribe. Anthropological Papers. Museum of Anthropology, University of Michigan, no. 55. Ann Arbor: University of Michigan Press.

REIFLER-BRICKER, VICTORIA
1973. *Ritual Humor in Highland Chiapas.* Austin: University of Texas Press.

RITTER, CARL
1866. *The Comparative Geography of Palestine and the Sinaitic Peninsula.* Trans. W. L. Gage. New York: D. Appleton and Co. [printed in Edinburgh].

ROBERTSON-SMITH, WILLIAM
1903. *Kinship and Marriage in Early Arabia.* Ed. Stanley A. Cook. Boston: Beacon Press.

ROSALDO, MICHELLE Z., AND LOUISE LAMPHERE, EDS.
1974. *Women, Culture, and Society.* Stanford: Stanford University Press.

ROSALDO, RENATO
1988. Ideology, Place, and People Without Culture. *Cultural Anthropology* 3(1):77–87.

ROSE, DAN
1986. Transformations of Disciplines Through their Texts: An Edited Transcription of a Talk to the Seminar on the Diversity of Language and the Structure of Power and an Ensuing Discussion at the University of Pennsylvania. *Cultural Anthropology* 1(3):317–327.
1987. *Black American Street Life: South Philadelphia, 1969–1971.* Philadelphia: University of Pennsylvania Press.

ROSEN, LAWRENCE
1978. The Negotiation of Reality: Male-Female Relations in Sefrou, Morocco. In *Women in the Muslim World.* Ed. L. Beck and N. Keddie, 561–584. Cambridge, Mass.: Harvard University Press.

RUSHDIE, SALMAN
1983. *Shame.* New York: Alfred A. Knopf, Inc.

SAID, EDWARD
1978. *Orientalism.* New York: Random House.
1983. Opponents, Audiences, Constituencies, and Community. In *The Politics of Interpretation.* Ed. W. J. T. Mitchell, 7–32. Chicago: The University of Chicago Press.

1989. Representing the Colonized: Anthropology's Interlocutors. *Critical Inquiry* 15(2):205–225.

SALZMAN, PHILIP C.
1978*a*. Does Complementary Opposition Exist? *American Anthropologist* 80:53–70.
1978*b*. Ideology and Change in Middle Eastern Tribal Societies. *Man* 13:618–637.

San Francisco Chronicle
24 January 1980. Sinai Diggers Find 127 Cars. Page 22.

SCHUTZ, ALFRED
1962. *Collected Papers, I: The Problem of Social Reality*. The Hague: Martinus Nijhoff.

SHAKESPEARE, WILLIAM
1958. *King Lear*. Baltimore: Penguin Books.

SHAMMAS, ANTON
1988. *Arabesques*. Trans. V. Eden. New York: Harper and Row.

SHILS, EDWARD
1981. *Tradition*. Chicago: The University of Chicago Press.

SHOHAT, ELLA
1988. Sepharadim in Israel: Zionism from the Standpoint of its Jewish Victims. *Social Text* 19/20:1–35.

SHORE, BRADD
1983. Meno's Paradox and the Ritualization of Knowledge. Presented at the Annual Meeting of the American Ethnological Society. Baton Rouge, LA.

SHOUKAIR, NAᶜUM BEY
1916. *The History of Sinai and the Arabs*. Cairo: Matbaᶜat al-Maᶜaref [in Arabic].

SLYMOVICS, SUSAN
1988. *The Merchant of Art: An Egyptian Hilali Oral Epic Poet in Performance*. Berkeley, Los Angeles, London: University of California Press.

SOWAYAN, SAAD A.
1985. *Nabati Poetry: The Oral Poetry of Arabia*. Berkeley, Los Angeles, London: University of California Press.

STANLEY, ARTHUR P.
1856. *Sinai and Palestine in Connection with their History.* London: J. Murray.

STEVENS, PHILLIP JR.
1980. The Bachama Trickster as Model for Clowning Behavior. *Rice University Studies* 66(1):137–150.

STEWART, FRANK H.
1987a. A Bedouin Narrative from Central Sinai. *Zietschrift für Arabische Linguistik* 16:44–92.
1987b. Tribal Law in the Arab World: A Review of the Literature. *International Journal of Middle Eastern Studies* 19(4):473–490.

STRATHERN, MARILYN
1987. Out of Context: The Persuasive Fictions of Anthropology. *Current Anthropology* 28(3):251–281.

SWEDENBURG, TED
1989. Occupational Hazards: Palestine Ethnography. *Cultural Anthropology* 4(3):265–272.

TODOROV, TZVETAN
1975. *The Fantastic: A Structural Approach to a Literary Genre.* Ithaca: Cornell University Press.

TRISTRAM, HENRY B.
1865. *The Land of Israel: A Journal of Travels in Palestine.* London: Society for Promoting Christian Knowledge.

TSAFRIR, YORAM
1970. Monks and Monasteries in the South Sinai. *Kadmoniyout* 3:2–18 [in Hebrew].

TURNER, VICTOR W.
1967. *The Forest of Symbols: Aspects of Ndembu Ritual.* Ithaca: Cornell University Press.
1969. *The Ritual Process: Structure and Anti-Structure.* Chicago: Aldine.
1973. The Center Out There: Pilgrim's Goal. *History of Religions* 12:191–230.

TYLER, STEPHEN A.
1986. Post-Modern Ethnography: From Document of the Occult to Occult Document. In *Writing Culture: The Poetics and Politics of Ethnography*. Ed. J. Clifford and G. E. Marcus, 122–140. Berkeley, Los Angeles, London: University of California Press.

WAGNER, ROY
1981. *The Invention of Culture*. Chicago: University of Chicago Press.

WEBER, MAX
1946. The Sociology of Charismatic Authority. In *From Max Weber: Essays in Sociology*. Ed. and Trans. H. H. Gerth and C. Wright Mills, 245–252. New York: Oxford University Press.
1949. The Ideal Type and Generalized Analytical Theory. In *The Structure of Social Action*. Ed. T. Parsons, 601–610. Glencoe, Ill.: Free Press.
1980. Charismatic Authority. In *Max Weber: The Interpretation of Social Reality*. Ed. J. E. T. Eldridge, 229–234. New York: Schocken Books.

WERBNER, PNINA
1986. The Virgin and the Clown: Ritual Elaboration in Pakistani Migrant's Weddings. *Man* 21(2):227–250.

WHITE, HAYDEN
1983. *Tropics of Discourse: Essays in Cultural Criticism*. Baltimore: The Johns Hopkins University Press.

WIKAN, UNNI
1984. Shame and Honour: A Contestable Pair. *Man* 19:635–652.

WILLEFORD, WILLIAM
1969. *The Fool and His Sceptre*. London: Edward Arnold.

WIMSATT, JAMES I.
1970. *Allegory and Mirror: Tradition and Structure in Middle English Literature*. New York: Pegasus.

ZIJDERVELD, ANTON C.
1968. Jokes and Their Relation to Social Reality. *Social Research* 35(2):286–311.

ZUCKER, WOLFGANG M.
1969. The Clown as the Lord of Disorder. In *Holy Laughter*. Ed. M. C. Hyers, 75–88. New York: Seabury Press.

ACKNOWLEDGMENTS

Omar Khayyam's position as a poet is curious. He was never very popular in his native Persia; and he exists in the West in a translation . . . I, too, am a translated man. I have been *borne* across.

SALMAN RUSHDIE
Shame

This book is based on thirty months of fieldwork carried out between October 1975 and August 1979 in the South Sinai peninsula and four additional shorter trips made in 1981, 1985, 1987, and 1988. The research was sponsored by a grant from the Ford Foundation, given to me through the Desert Research Institute in Sde Bokker, Israel (principal investigator Emanuel Marx), and by the Lowie Fund and the Humanities Fellowship of the University of California, Berkeley. I would also like to acknowledge the Mabel McLeod Lewis Fund and the Hebrew Free Loan Association for their support during the writing stage.

The list of friends and colleagues who have helped me appreciate the poetics and politics of Mzeini allegorical narratives steadily grew. If I had not met Frank Stewart on the ʿAqaba Gulf coast in the hot late spring of 1976, I perhaps would not have embarked on the professional study of anthropology. Frank informed me that my careful scribbles, written out of pure curiosity about the Bedouin, were uninitiated anthropological fieldnotes. He was very interested in what he called my fieldwork and introduced me to Emanuel Marx, who provided me with guidance for years to come and supervised my fieldwork from 1976 to 1979. Emanuel introduced me to the vast scholarly literature on tribalism, Bedouin and other, and to the many early travelogues about the Sinai. Throughout my undergraduate and graduate studies, he offered good advice and detailed comments and critiques. I am very grateful to him and his wife Dalia for their hospitality on so many evenings between my bouts of Sinai research and whenever I returned to Israel from Berkeley. Many of my ideas developed as we sat in their living room discussing anthropology and Bedouin issues.

Many thanks to my professors at the Hebrew University of Jerusalem, particularly Erik Cohen, Gideon Kressel, and Henry Rosenfeld, for allowing me to spend most of my undergraduate years in the field in the South Sinai, instead of in the classroom (as long as I kept doing all the recommended as well as the required reading, and kept my grades high). They were very generous with their time in office hours and were always encouraging.

I am deeply indebted to Don Handelman, with whom I studied in my final year at the Hebrew University. He introduced me to the fields of symbolism, phenomenology, ritual, and play. The honors paper I wrote for him helped me focus what I wanted to do in graduate school and was the first of many versions of what is now chapter 8 of this book. Don encouraged me to start the arduous journey of pursuing a Ph.D. in the United States and spent many hours helping me refine my theoretical ideas. Even after I was in Berkeley, we vividly corresponded, and during each of my visits home we spent long hours discussing the theatre of Mzeini daily life. Don offered me valuable feedback on almost every term paper I wrote, suggested books to read, and gave me close readings of the early drafts of the theoretical sections of this book.

I am profoundly grateful to the staff of the Eilat Field School of the Israeli Society for the Protection of Nature for providing a refuge for my monthly short escapes into the unaccustomed luxuries of speaking Hebrew over a hot meal with knives and forks and indulging in a hot shower and a toilet bowl. Together with Amnon Tzvieli, the Israeli physician dedicated to serving Bedouin medical needs, the members of this staff were among the first to let me bounce my ideas off them, and they gave me valuable feedback.

Irit Averbuch, Chico (Avi) Gripel, Salmān Maṣālḥa, Nimrod Ran, and Jan Ziff comforted me on my occasional visits to the Hebrew

University, and sometimes came to see me in the field. They also helped me a great deal in hosting Mzeinis who visited me in Jerusalem.

I would not have survived the transition to American academic culture, and to the rigors of writing in a foreign language, without the guidance and encouragement of Elizabeth Colson. In my first years of graduate school, she taught me how to pursue the direction I wanted my research to go. Under her skilled and caring tutelage, I was first able to crystalize my amorphous mass of data into a workable proposal.

As a foreign student in the United States, I was totally at the mercy of the capricious United States Information Agency, which, amazingly, wanted to deport me from this country as soon as I married an American citizen. This book is the best tribute I can offer to Marvin Baron and the staff of the Office of Advisors to Foreign Students and Scholars at the University of California, Berkeley, and to Larry DiCostanzo, who went far beyond the call of duty to enable me to stay here and complete my doctorate.

Grace Buzaljko first pointed me to allegory and helped me define the difference between allegory and symbol. James Clifford and Stephen Greenblatt were most helpful in suggesting readings in the field of Literary Criticism, thus enabling me to embark on a fruitful journey into unfamiliar territory. My conversations with Ḥannan Ḥever and Abdul JanMohamed about political allegory helped me understand more deeply the subtleties of the stories Mzeinis tell about their military occupiers.

In 1982, William C. Young contacted me and suggested that we coauthor an article comparing the Egyptian and Israeli development policies for the Sinai (Lavie and Young 1984). I contributed my relevant field data, and he thoroughly combed the Egyptian press for data, since the Egyptian government does not permit primary field research on the topic. With his kind permission, our joint effort appears here as chapter 2, the second half of which has benefited from many of his ideas and phrasings.

Writer Marco Fong and playwright Fred Kennamer helped me establish consistent rules for writing all the script-like vignettes. Sarah al-Fadl, Saᶜad Sowayan, and ᶜAli al-Faraiḥy ably assisted me in translating from Bedouin Arabic into English some of the poems appearing in this text. Helene Knox, with her poetic gifts, worked side by side with me to hone all the raw poetry and proverb translations into aesthetic phrasings of image, metaphor, connotation, tone, voice, meter, and rhyme, and thus restored to the English some of the music inevitably lost in accurate literary translation. I am grateful for her expert professional assistance in the editing and word-processing of the final book manuscript.

Many of my ideas were rehearsed on Anjali Bagwe, Joel Beinin, Eytan Berkovitz, Ken Brown, Kevin Dwyer, Jim Fernandez, Orna Goren, Benjamin Gregg, Richard Gringeri, Fred Huxley, Larry Michalak, Kirin Narayan, Judd Ne'eman, Tony Robben, Renato Rosaldo, Dan Rose, Ella Shohat, and Pnina and Dick Werbner. I thank them for their time and many good suggestions. Richard Grathoff, Shabbo Levi, and Yaʿakov Nir sent me several long letters with systematic and detailed thoughtful comments.

Special thanks to Paul Stoller, whose enthusiastic support for this book from its beginnings has so helped it come to fruition. His many long letters and phone calls full of detailed constructive comments, and his insistence that I write about real people rather than theoretical constructs of them, greatly influenced the final shape of this book.

The enthusiastic, efficient advocacy of Stanley Holwitz of the University of California Press was crucial to the birth of this manuscript in book form. I also wish to thank Paula Cizmar for her caring, meticulous editing and the rest of the staff at the University of California Press for their professional efforts on behalf of this book. Randall Goodall is the one who deserves credit for the delightfully aesthetic presentation of the distressing political realities depicted in this text. And a big hand to Shirley Warren, the managing editor, who made things happen to get this book through production.

Gershon Goldhaber, George Trilling, and the rest of the Mark II collaborators of Lawrence Berkeley Laboratory and the Physics Department of the University of California, Berkeley, were very generous and kind to permit me to share the office space of my spouse, Forest Rouse. Many ideas were born as I was gazing from its window toward the Golden Gate Bridge and the tiny sailboats bobbing on San Francisco Bay.

I wish to express my most profound gratitude to my doctoral dissertation committee, William Shack (Chair), Gerald Berreman, Stanley Brandes, and Ira Lapidus, especially for their fine examples of socially responsible scholarship. Gerald Berreman taught me much about problems of phenomenology, symbolic interactionism, and ethics. Stanley Brandes introduced me to the vast field of humor. Ira Lapidus was a great resource for my study of Muslim theology and history. Throughout my graduate school years, all the members of my committee consistently provided me with valuable support, encouragement, feedback, and academic breadth.

I wish to express very special thanks to my dissertation advisor, William Shack, for being demanding of me even while he left me free to explore all paths where my research was leading. He allowed me what felt like a vast creative space always enlarged by his meticulous constructive criticism. His commitment to his role as my teacher went beyond helping me master the vast field of Symbolic Anthropology—he was always there for me, even at my hardest moments.

And last but not least is Forest Rouse, my spouse, who was wonderful! He was persistently involved in my work and gave me not only encouragement, pushes, and comfort, but incredible practical help and support. He went with me into the arduous field environment in 1985 and 1988 and intensely read and responded to each of the seemingly endless drafts of chapters. In the manuscript's last stages, he freed me from my equal half of the household duties so I could pour my undivided energy into the writing.

In Israel, where the Zionist master narrative of education, the media, and the politics of self-righteous rationalization teaches one from childhood to be suspicious of goyim and to fear the Arab enemy, I could hardly have developed a humanistic perspective toward the Arab World without the unprejudiced home created by my late father, Salman Lavie, and my mother, Shoshana Gamlielit-Lavie, who provided me with alternative modes of discourse about culture and politics. I remember how, after lighting the Sabbath candles, blessing the wine, eating the festive meal, and often singing Sabbath songs, we would sit and carry on intense discussions that socialized me to view the world through the humanistic optics of cultural difference. This book is dedicated to my parents. It is also dedicated to my Mzeini adoptive parents, who graciously shared with me their life and discourses, and showed me the same open-hearted human spirit by accepting an Israeli Other into their family.

INDEX

DESIGNER
Seventeenth Street Studios

COMPOSITOR
Another Point, Inc.

TEXT TYPE
Sabon

DISPLAY TYPE
Neuland

PRINTER
Haddon Craftsmen

BINDER
Haddon Craftsmen